*U*sing the term "melodrama" as an abstract category to describe almost any literary mode—from nineteenth-century novels to twentieth-century films—modern critics have obscured the genre's historical and cultural functions as well as the nature of its specific appeal to working-class audiences. To rectify this situation, the essays in this volume redirect attention to the historical, social, and cultural milieu in which melodrama emerged.

This collection of essays addresses the following important questions: What were the social, cultural, and ideological conditions under which this genre became popular among nineteenth-century theatre audiences? How do ideological and social issues such as nationalism, colonialism, ethnicity, race, gender, and class surface in melodrama? What was the social and cultural profile of its audiences? How do individual playwrights, such as Holcroft and Boucicault, represent changes in the features of melodrama throughout the nineteenth century? Responses to these and other questions will emerge in the essays of this innovative and international collection.

MELODRAMA

MELODRAMA
The Cultural Emergence of a Genre

Edited by

~~334~~

MICHAEL HAYS
AND ANASTASIA NIKOLOPOULOU

ST. MARTIN'S PRESS
NEW YORK

MELODRAMA: THE CULTURAL EMERGENCE OF A GENRE
Copyright © 1996 by Michael Hays and Anastasia Nikolopoulou
All rights reserved. Printed in the United States of America. No part of
this book may be used or reproduced in any manner whatsoever without
written permission except in the case of brief quotations embodied in
critical articles or reviews. For information, address St. Martin's Press,
Scholarly and Reference Division, 175 Fifth Avenue, New York, N.Y. 10010

ISBN 0-312-12692-1

Library of Congress Cataloging-in-Publication Data

Melodrama : The Cultural Emergence of a Genre
  Michael Hays and Anastasia Nikolopoulou
      p.   cm.
  Includes bibliographical references and index.
  ISBN 0-312-12692-1
  1. Melodrama. 2. Drama—19th century—history and criticism.
I. Hays, Michael. II. Nikolopoulou, Anastasia.
  PN1912.M46   1996
  809.2'52—dc20   95-51255
                                                           CIP

Interior book design by Harry Katz

First Edition: October 1996
10 9 8 7 6 5 4 3 2 1

C·O·N·T·E·N·T·S

I·N·T·R·O·D·U·C·T·I·O·N

Michael Hays and Anastasia Nikolopoulou

In the past fifteen years or so the terms "melodrama" and "melodramatic" have appeared in ever more disparate venues. Indeed, their critical relevance for film studies and for the examination of genres as different as the novel and soap opera seems to be a given. Altogether then, it would seem that the theoretical status of these terms and their availability for contemporary usage are settled matters, despite the fact that there has been little systematic effort to demonstrate that there are firm historical, cultural, and ideological continuities linking, for example, the melodramas performed in nineteenth-century working-class theatres with recent bestsellers or the series that dominate daytime television. Indeed, the theories that do make such linkages remain quite problematic insofar as they tend to move away from the concrete situation of the melodrama as it was initially conceived and staged toward propositions about an emotional content usually circumscribed by the term "melodramatic." It appears to us, however, that this move does much to obscure the historical situation, the ideological dynamics, and the function of the melodrama in the nineteenth century in favor of overarching generalizations about affect. Such generalizations have frequently depended on claiming for the melodrama a subversive essence, a "melodramatic" core that dehistoricizes the melodrama and allows it to be transformed into something more contemporary: the transhistorical marker of a disruptive, modern mode of consciousness and representation.

Certainly the most influential assertion of this idea is to be found in Peter Brooks's groundbreaking work, *The Melodramatic Imagination*.[1] For Brooks, the melodrama is no longer to be considered (as it was in earlier criticism) a form rooted in questionable tastes and a desire for cheap thrills. Neither is it a genre belonging merely to the vulgar masses. It is, rather, to be understood as a peculiarly modern form, "a mode of high emotionalism and stark ethical conflict that is neither comic nor tragic" (12). For Brooks and those who follow in his wake, the melodrama is a drama of "excess" in which life choices seem finally to have little to do with the surface realities of a situation and much more to do with an intense inner drama of consciousness, and a "manichaestic struggle of good and evil" (5, 12). Although Brooks admits that the melodrama did not maintain this high calling throughout the nineteenth century, he insists that its melodramatic core always remained intact and that if we turn to its earliest theatrical manifestations we will discover the beginnings of an aesthetic mode and enterprise that not only continues to function in the present day but serves to define it.

We certainly would agree with the first of these assumptions. Indeed, one aim of this book is to further substantiate the fact that the melodrama played an important role in the cultural dynamics of the nineteenth century, a role that was downplayed or outright denied by most earlier critics. Yet any attempt to define (or redefine) melodrama by turning away from a historical understanding of the genre and its uses and reinscribing it under an aesthetic category named after the adjective derived from it is bound to move critical discussion into a subjective arena that must inevitably disregard the cultural dynamics underlying the actual production and reception of the melodrama. In order to get at the historical significance of melodrama it remains important to ask, for example, about the implications of its "illegitimate" status in the nineteenth century. Why did contemporaries attack it as a monstrous aesthetic configuration or, more interestingly, as Coleridge put it, a "modern Jacobinical drama," and why were large segments of its audiences regarded as criminal elements?[2] Why were these "senseless, illiterate savages . . . [this] capricious ungrateful rabble" juxtaposed to Charles Lamb's "man of genius" in some of these critiques?[3] One aim of this book is to inquire after some of the motivation for such attacks, but only insofar as these questions contribute to the goal of uncovering the ways in which the melodrama served as a crucial space in which the cultural, political, and economic exigencies of the century were played out and transformed into public discourses about issues ranging from the gender-specific dimensions of individual station and behavior to the role and status of the "nation" in local as well as imperial politics.

In terms of the early melodrama in England, the claim for a linkage between the melodrama and the political and social conditions of the world in which it emerged seems quite unproblematic. Most critics would agree, for example, that the work of Thomas Holcroft, who is often credited with launching the genre in England, is grounded in the populist radical rhetoric that erupted in England in the aftermath of the French Revolution. He was specifically accused of Jacobin activities, it must be remembered.[4] Furthermore, there is no doubt that early artisan spectators of melodrama, the same folks who also took part in the "making of the English working class," were the readers and, on occasion, the creators of the radical literature of the time.[5] And, as the Old Price riots of 1809 demonstrate, the artisan public saw clear connections between its theatrical and political rights and had few reservations about asserting these rights inside as well as outside the theatre.[6]

Neither is there any doubt that the melodrama continued to send out radical messages against the government and in favor of revolution. Fifteen years after the Old Price riots, George Colman, the censor of plays, noted that even though such revolutionary messages were now concealed behind the pretense of displaying "gallant heroes" and "hapless lovers," the plays in which these "tender disrespects . . . of the heart" appeared also managed to "preach up the doctrine that government is Tyranny, that Revolt is Virtue, and that Rebels are Righteous."[7] If the critical record of melodrama's early radical traces seems incomplete, that fact is but part of a larger critical and discursive problem that has also remained relatively unexamined, perhaps because the study of the melodrama calls for a historical method that aims more at something like Walter Benjamin's patchwork history than a seamless narrative, a method that, ultimately, would also have to turn to the evidence that can be found in little-read material such as police records as well as memoirs and journals. The present volume can only suggest the range of materials that might be examined, but we think it will, nonetheless, provide numerous points of departure for further discussion.

The essays collected here investigate precisely those areas that have remained largely unexamined, or buried by a literary history and theory that have themselves been deeply embedded in the cultural affairs of their age (whether of this century or the last). These essays address the specificity of the dramaturgic practice and the sociocultural context of the melodrama at various moments in the nineteenth century and, as a whole, indicate that although melodrama underwent multiple transformations—moving from "outlaw" to domestic and then imperialist modes, for example—these metamorphoses carried with them the unmistakable traces of the socioeconomic and political transformations that were played out at the same time in the home, the academy, and the political sphere, and even in the theatres where the melodrama was staged.[8]

If, as Thomas Postlewait suggests, it was only after the liberal humanism of the nineteenth-century academy blocked melodrama's access to the canon that it was given the role of bit player in literary and cultural history, it is important that our exploration of nineteenth-century melodrama also include a look at some of the academic practices that were operative in the creation of the academic canon as well as at the melodrama itself. As Postlewait shows, American theatre histories downplay the melodrama in order to announce the success of a realism that is the prelude to our own triumphant modernism. This leads to further questions about the institutional and academic establishments that authorize such categories, and about the ideological function of the critics and writers who expounded on the supremacy of modern art and culture—thereby eliding both earlier "truths" and the complex realities of actual cultural practice. Michael Booth's essay demonstrates that a historical analysis of melodrama can, by contrast, unmask these dynamics by exposing the differences and contradictions that emerge at various moments of its development. There are, for example, clear ideological distinctions between early melodramas promoting nationalism and later imperialist melodramas. Booth suggests that the primary audience addressed by the later melodramas was "the middle of the middle class," that is, people seeking a form of national identity by identifying with the state through a show of "patriotic sentiment and heroic characters" (much in the same way the early modernist supporters of realism formed grand narratives about the cultural supremacy of this new literary mode). The needs and desires of this audience were quite different than those of the public that had supported the populist nationalism represented in the pre-1850 melodrama. There the British flag was flown as a symbol of national rather than imperial glory, and the renown of the British military was not measured by its success in subjugating and colonizing other peoples. Yet, Booth suggests, even in its stages of "apotheosis," the melodrama's imperial displays were no more than a smoke screen concealing cultural tensions and "fear of the future" rather than demonstrations of an "overwhelming confidence in the present."

In the colonies themselves, on the other hand, a different historical tale may well be told by the evolution of the melodrama. From Jim Davis's essay we learn that even when colonial melodrama seems to succumb to and repeat the master narratives sustaining the imperialist adventure, it remains caught in a web of ambiguity in which the differences between the metropolitan center and the colonial periphery emerge as antagonistic impulses that erode the discourse of British dominance. As Davis points out, although the Australian melodrama at the end of the last century was indeed complicitous in the elaboration of the grand narrative of British imperial power and cultural identity, representations of Australia's spontaneous commitment to the Boer War on the side of the British also engendered a countercurrent of local, nationalist sentiment that contributed to the rite of passage experienced by the Australian public as it began to confront its colonial legacy and search for a separate cultural identity.

The capacity of melodrama to simultaneously incorporate the discourses of imperialism, nationalism, and class and gender conflict points not only to the genre's structural malleability but to the role it played in approaching and "resolving" the historical complexities that lie behind its intersecting horizons. Melodrama seems to correspond to what Hans Robert Jauss has called a process-like genre, that is, a genre that does not come to rest in fulfillment but, rather, presents a continually renewed realization.[9] Such an interplay of intersecting cultural and ideological horizons is also clearly present in some of the melodramas staged in Bulgaria during the period prior to independence, but in this case the melodrama plays out the complexities of revolution rather than empire. As Kornelia Tancheva shows, the melodrama became a locus for the development of Bulgarian nationalism and a triumphant narrative about the final revolutionary overthrow of the Ottoman Empire. But rather than contributing to a monochrome history of national triumph, this melodrama also parses the intricacies of class difference and weaves in the larger history of a Pan-Slavic spiritual awakening.

Melodrama's process-like characteristics and generic adaptability are also evident in its capacity to appropriate prior discourses, such as the story of the sixteenth-century French peasant Martin Guerre, whose melodramatic narrative is the subject of Barbara Cooper's essay. Her description of the melodramatic adaptation of the documents and traditions relating to Martin Guerre in early-nineteenth-century France shows the specific cultural usefulness of such popular juridical cases *(cause célèbres)* and their wide appeal precisely at a time when "popular illegalities" were on the rise and the dominant classes were in need of cultural images that could counter the political dangers of such behavior. The ideological complexities underlying melodrama's appropriation of historical material as well as other genres can also be seen in its convoluted and often antagonistic relation to the novel. As Anastasia Nikolopoulou indicates, the early melodramatic adaptations of *The Bride of Lammermoor* and *Guy Mannering* emphasize the material obstacles faced by the characters (hunger, poverty, rising prices) — issues relevant to the artisan public — whereas Scott's novels tend to suppress such conditions in a narrative overloaded with historical detail. Here, the fragmented structure of the melodrama seems to help raise questions about current cultural and political "difficulties" while the novel elides such issues by offering a closed historical narrative that overwhelms the present.

If the melodrama can open issues of nation and class, it can, of course, also function as a means of revising notions of value and behavior. In his essay on the origins of the English melodrama, Lothar Fietz suggests that the sentimentalism in early melodrama introduces an ideology of defeat that actually inverts the bourgeois ethos of moral superiority and altruism that we find in eighteenth-century sentimental dramas such as Lillo's *The London Merchant*. The transformation of the political economy that unfolded in the early nineteenth century brought with it a mutation in cultural models that emerges in these melodramas as a refashioning of the terms that define interpersonal relations. In lieu of public benevolence, individualistic self-assertion and a competitive mentality began to prevail. Altruistic feelings and acts gradually began to signify weakness and the former sentimental hero is recast as a victim. Thus, in Sheridan's *Pizarro*, which stands at the threshold of the nineteenth century and the emergence of the melodrama as a significant genre, humane and generous behavior signals the quasi inevitability of the hero being sacrificed to the "vultures" of the play—a shift in the representation of cultural value that again shows the underlying historical impetus behind the mutability of the melodrama in comparison with its tragic and comic counterparts.

The scope of the ethic of victimization that unfolds in the melodrama is fully apparent by the middle part of the century, especially in the context of the domestic melodramas that opened a niche for themselves by offering disciplinary lessons for and about women. As Léon Metayer points out, representations of women in the Paris theatres connected with this generic subtype—the Ambigu, Gaîté, and Porte-Saint-Martin—served a function that was also directly tied to the changing socioeconomic situation in France. They provided highly overdetermined images of gender relations that responded to real social dislocations with ideological paradigms that enabled both sexes to grasp and operate within the newly gendered stratification and hierarchization of society inaugurated by the capitalist matrimonial market. Of course, the main lesson was enacted on, if not by, the heroine. If she proved unable to protect and uphold the newly inscribed "values" of fidelity, chastity, motherhood, loyalty, and obedience she could, nonetheless, demonstrate their validity by experiencing the humiliation, degradation, and even death that are the inevitable lot of the fallen woman. Metayer suggests that by applauding these images of terrorized woman, male and female spectators alike signal their submission to a disciplinary ideology that insists that such social as well as judicial punishment is the necessary upshot of individual moral error. This is a theme that reemerges in the drama of empire, but in a form that substitutes race for gender.

Portrayals of domestic space also served as a means of defusing representations of social and economic hardship and rebellion among the working classes. John Walker's *The Factory La∂* (1832) takes up the question of machine breaking and points toward Owenite and pro-Chartist understandings of the relation between laborers and employers, which it juxtaposes to a bourgeois discourse founded on competition and exploitation. But, as Hartmut Ilsemann points out, although the audience is initially invited to sympathize with the factory workers in the play, a shift in focus to the terrifying helplessness of the wife and children of one of the workers introduces a sentimental turn that mutes political and economic conflicts while at the same time encouraging the lower-class members of the audience in particular to withdraw into a state of "psychological regression" in the face of the "harsh external world."

The function of the ideological discourse on class and personal experience in the melodrama is equally evident in the nautical works explored by Marvin Carlson and Jeffrey Cox. Unlike earlier nautical works such as Arnold's opera *The Shipwreck* (1796) and J. C. Cross's *Benevolent Tar* (1794), whose appearance was concurrent with the emergence of radicalism among British sailors, the nautical melodramas of the 1820s, Cox argues, attempted to "consolidate the pacified image of the loyal British sailor," often by first limning and then displacing the historical causes of rebellion—questions of class and disciplinary measures, for example—with issues such as personal and sexual rivalry that allow the dominant system of control to remain innocent of the abuses that foment the mutinies in many of these plays. As metaphors for order, these nautical melodramas become vehicles for representing the necessity of submitting to the (military) rule of the traditional authority structure. In Jerrold's *Mutiny at the Nore*, the rebellious tars may protest about short rations and poor pay and comment on the customs of the disciplinary culture of the early nineteenth century, such as lashing and flogging, but, as Carlson notes, these are ultimately portrayed as military practices "necessary for the maintenance of a strong and disciplined force to protect the nation." The realm of the personal is again submerged, this time in the narrative of national destiny.

In the second half of the century then there seems to be a substantial shift in the context as well as the substance of the melodrama. In works representing the Irish Famine (a topic that was not often represented on the stage), for example, the lower-class public is not drawn into the material problems of the protagonists in the ways it was earlier, thus marking a shift in the political consciousness of this segment of the audience. As Julia Williams and Stephen Watt show, melodramas representing the Famine might have provoked some gender and class "sympathies" among British artisan and working-class audiences, but such sympathies were not strong enough to engender a broader understanding of the social and political forces behind the Famine, since the suffering of the Irish peasants was construed as the byproduct of a corrupt Irish bourgeoisie rather than British imperialism.

Should one, therefore, assume that private readings or performances of melodrama would give the genre an equally private tone that would deprive it of the combustive themes earlier available to the public? David Mayer demonstrates that while the private performances of narrative melodramas in the late nineteenth century managed to bridge the gap between low and high culture and "elevate" melodrama into a more refined genre (preferably called "drama"), the culture of parlour melodrama also evinced some of the internal contradictions in middle-class and artisan aesthetics. And if the vogue for private entertainments and parlour melodrama contributed to further detaching melodrama from issues of class, privilege, and money, it also created an alternative space in which the representation of controversial themes — poverty, vice, deceit, and despair — remained distantly possible.

Indeed, one of the most striking characteristics of many of the melodramas discussed in these essays is the tension they generate by juxtaposing two different "horizons" of understanding and desire. Representations of imperialist culture or bourgeois economic morality, for example, are accompanied by moments that question the dominant horizon, usually without displacing it, however. Speaking of Bertolazzi's *El Nost Milan,* a play that depicts the existence of a Milanese subproletariat in the 1890s, Louis Althusser has suggested that such horizons may represent two different "temporalities" or modes of consciousness, one of which exists as a potential that is held in check by the other, which has been more actively realized.[10]

This may be a useful starting point for inquiring after the cultural dynamics that produce the need for intersecting spaces in which ideology (nationalism, imperialism, and class), institutions (prison, family, court, military), and even other genres are brought into play and interrogated. Clearly, the generic mutability of melodrama is a sign that it responds more to historical than to aesthetic demands, no doubt because it occupied a space that, unlike tragedy and comedy, had no canonical history or status to limit it. And because this space had not yet been fully codified, it could be put to use either to imagine alternatives or to enforce the cultural paradigms that dominate its thematic conflicts. Individual claims made on behalf of revolution, freedom, and justice in the melodramas discussed here are intercepted by a discursive consciousness that often, though not always (that is, Tancheva, Davis) voids these claims, but these plays still trace the dramaturgic and historical outlines of the (mainly) failed efforts to realize these alternative modes of theatrical and social representation.

Although the dramatic conflicts in much melodrama, especially the post-1820 melodrama, seem to be enacted within the bounds of a morality authorized by the cultural discourse of the bourgeoisie — what Althusser calls the "sublimations and lies of bourgeois morality," or the "law of the heart"[11] — we need to avoid a purely psychological reinterpretation of this law and language of the heart as unarticulated desire. Instead it may be worthwhile to posit a dissociated consciousness consisting of a dimension referring to the

potentialities that were present, though unactualized, in the real world
betokened by and interpreted through the poverty, rebellion, and popular
illegalities adumbrated by the hero or heroine, and another, a "false" consciousness, that imposes itself on the first. In this case, the melodrama is not
a prisoner of the "law of the heart" because the dissociated temporalities of
the genre enabled the audience to perceive the tensions between the two
modes of consciousness even though it may have not been able to translate
them into active alternatives: the mutineer, the Luddite, and the woman who
transgresses in these melodramas bear the traces of intersecting temporalities. They are the sites where the ideological and historical complexities of
the genre emerge for the audience. "Here we can truly say that consciousness is delayed, for even if it is still blind, it is a consciousness aiming at last
at a real world."[12]

Notes

1. Peter Brooks, *The Melodramatic Imagination: Balzac, Henry James, Melodrama, and the Mode of Excess* (New York: Columbia University Press, 1984). All other in-text page references in this chapter refer to this work.
2. See Samuel Taylor Coleridge, *Biographia Literaria*, in *The Collected Works of Samuel Taylor Coleridge*, ed. James Engelle and W. Jackson Bate, vol. 7, part 2 (Princeton: Princeton University Press, 1983), 233.
3. Charles Lamb, "On the Custom of Hissing at the theatres, with some accounts of a club of damned authors," in *The Works of Charles and Mary Lamb*, ed. E. V. Lucas (New York: Methuen, 1968), 1:91.
4. William Hazlitt, *Memoirs of Thomas Holcroft* (London, 1816), 2:144-50.
5. See, for example, Jon P. Klancher, *The Making of English Reading Audiences, 1790-1832* (Madison, WI: University of Wisconsin Press, 1987), esp. 76-135.
6. For the Old Price riots see Marc Baer, *Theatre and Disorder in Late Georgian London*, (New York: Oxford University Press, 1992) and Anastasia Nikolopoulou, "Artisan Culture and the English Gothic Melodrama" (Ph.D. diss., Cornell University, 1990).
7. George Colman to Covent Garden Theatre, 9 February, 1824, in *Letters and Documents written as Theatre Censor, 1824-1834*, Mss Huntington Library, San Marino.
8. See, for example, Michael Hays, "From Public Space to Private Space: Stag-ing the Discourse of the Academy," *boundary 2* (winter-spring 1985): 173-188.
9. Hans Robert Jauss, *Toward an Aesthetic of Reception* (Minneapolis: University of Minnesota Press, 1982), 94.
10. Louis Althusser, *For Marx* (London, New York: Verso, 1969), 135.
11. Ibid., 140, 133.
12. Ibid., 142.

Part I

Grand Narrative(s): Variations on a Theme

FIGURE 1. *At Duty's Call:* A touring poster from the late 1890s. FROM THE COLLECTION OF THE AUTHOR.

1

SOLDIERS OF THE QUEEN: DRURY LANE IMPERIALISM

MICHAEL BOOTH

In the night the savage foemen
Crept around us as we lay;
To our arms we leap'd and faced them,
Back to back we stood at bay.
As I fought, a savage at me
Aimed his spear like lightning's dart,
But my comrade sprang to save me,
And receiv'd it in his heart.

IN "COMRADES," A MUSIC-HALL SONG OF 1890, the narrator and his friend since boyhood, Jack, have been ordered into battle because "England's Flag had been insulted." In a poster for the touring company of *At Duty's Call* (1898), the prototypical imperial hero stands at bay, guarding his fallen comrade, knocking down his savage opponents with his bare fists. *At Duty's Call* was not performed at Drury Lane, but its heroic sentiments, its treatment of patriotic themes, and its ennobling of the brave soldier mark it as falling into that category of late-Victorian drama that glorified military prowess in the service of the imperial cause and formed a distinctly identifiable branch of melodrama: spectacular, patriotic as a matter of course, exultantly jingoistic in its emotional excesses. In the hierarchy of this dramatic category, which flourished especially in the 1880s and 1890s, Drury Lane autumn drama was supreme.

The manager at Drury Lane during most of these years was Augustus Harris, who took over the empty theatre in 1879 after the bankruptcy of the previous lessee. Harris soon instituted a commercially successful policy of dividing his season into three segments: a spectacular melodrama opening in the late summer or early autumn, an equally spectacular Christmas pantomime that succeeded the melodrama and ran until April the following year, and a short spring season of the Carl Rosa opera company. Unlike other West End theatres, Drury Lane did not close for the whole summer, when the fashionable, leisured, and professional classes left town for the country.[1] The potential audience remaining in London, the audience that attended the first few weeks of the annual melodrama, was for this one reason—without taking other factors into account—a distinct social cut below the audience for Irving's Lyceum or Hare and Kendal's St. James's in the regular theatre season. Another aspect of audience composition, beside seasonal factors and seat prices, was repertory policy. This had to be carefully calculated by late-Victorian managements, the successful ones establishing a distinct repertory and character of their own: a so-called legitimate repertory consisting of Shakespeare and modern romantic drama at Irving's Lyceum; upper-middle-class adaptations from the French and modern plays with "social" themes at the St. James's; Pinero's farces at the Court; English comic opera at the Savoy; popular middle-class melodrama at the Princess's, and so forth. Harris elected to offer spectacle in pantomime and melodrama, and a short opera season at prices lower than Covent Garden's to satisfy the arguments of those who claimed that because of its history and traditions Drury Lane should be offering serious and respectable art.

In 1882, three years after Harris inaugurated his management, the official seating capacity of Drury Lane was about 2,700, but a really full house crowded in perhaps 1,000 more. Whatever the precise numbers, Drury Lane had the largest capacity in the West End, a big stage, and a lot of space to fill. To a considerable extent Harris's choice of repertory was dictated by the physical character of his house as well as by the social composition and theatrical taste of his audience. Both his melodramas and his pantomimes were elaborately spectacular in the late-Victorian manner of mass, color, and scenic effect: huge crowds of supers thronged the stage; horses galloped across it; panoramas unrolled; land battles and naval engagements were fought with gusto; avalanches and earthquakes shook the theatre; colored limelights bathed leisurely transformation scenes with the richest effulgence of hues, gleamed from the silver and gold armor of pantomime supers, and twinkled from jewels and spangles sewn into costumes and scenery alike.

Out of this material there evolved a distinctive Drury Lane house style that characterized this theatre until the First World War. Reviewing the sporting drama *A Run of Luck* in 1886, the *Illustrated London News* (4 September) commented, "The drama that might pass muster at another theatre would seem weak, trivial, and insignificant on this monster stage. The dramatists who write for Drury Lane must be bold and sweeping in their treatment. They must paint with a big brush. Each curtain must fall on an effect: each act must contain a special example of scenic excitement." Harris said of the Drury Lane audience that "they demand a performance which must be, above all things, dramatic, full of life, novelty, and movement; treating, as a rule, of the age in which we live, dealing with characters they can sympathise with, and written in a language they can understand. It . . . should appeal rather to the feelings of the public at large than the prejudice of a class."[2]

Such a style had its detractors; indeed, Harris was continually under attack from the more intellectual critics for the subordination of actor to spectacle, for the alleged tedium of so much accumulated spectacle in one evening, and for the popular content of his melodramas. Of *The Armada* in 1888—in which the climactic scene was of course the attack of the English fireships and the ensuing sea battle, leaving the house "choked with gunpowder"[3]—the *Illustrated London News* (29 September) declared that acting at Drury Lane was of no account compared to pageantry and scenic elaboration: "All of its subtlety and refinement are lost on a stage peopled with an army of supernumeraries and dedicated to din. It would require lungs of leather to shout louder than the din of carpenters and scene-shifters." One of London's leading dramatic critics, Joseph Knight, was nevertheless willing, if grudgingly, to accept the facts. Of *Pluck* in 1882, a melodrama with a snowstorm, a mob storming a bank, and two train wrecks in one scene, he said that the play's laborious progress "is not to be interrupted while any actor, no matter who, gesticulates or makes faces. . . . A series of tableaux having to be exhibited, the object of all concerned was to make way for them. . . . Upon the well-drilled stage of Drury Lane, no actor is so ill-advised as to seek to interfere with the scenery."[4]

Such a repertory policy and production style ideally fitted Drury Lane for the role of theatrical purveyor of the patriotic and the jingoistic, the presenter of huge and colorful images of popular social and political taste, the illustrator of the new imperialism. This is not to say that theatrical expression of patriotic feeling and imperialist sentiment began with August Harris's tenure of Drury Lane. Patriotism and the glorification of British feats of arms and the heroism of the British soldier and sailor had marked the spectacle entertainment of the early years of the nineteenth century, such as *The Siege of Gibraltar* (1804) and *The Battle of Trafalgar* (1806), fought by fully rigged model ships in the forty-by-one-hundred-feet water tank installed on the stage of Sadler's Wells. The sailor-hero of nautical melodrama is a direct creation of this patriotic spirit. Battles on land, as in *The Battle of Waterloo* (1824) and *The Invasion of Russia* (1825), were the specialty of the stage and attached circus ring of Astley's Theatre. Such spectacle melodramas continued at Astley's until its demise in 1882, but, managed by the redoubtable "Lord" George Sanger and renamed Sanger's, the theatre maintained for another decade its policy of presenting in realistic and impressive spectacles the military engagements of the Empire. Before this, the Crimean War spawned several melodramas, immediately dramatized from newspaper accounts, on the London stage.[5]

In all these plays, which were by no means politically sophisticated, British aims are not questioned; indeed, they hardly arise. The Englishman and the Union Jack are exalted wherever they occur. In *The White Slave; or, The Flag of Freedom* (1849), the heroine calls out to the villain, "Touch us at your peril now England's flag of freedom waves proudly over us!" In *British Born* (1872), like *The White Slave* a melodrama written for a working-class audience, the hero is about to be executed by a firing squad when the heroine intervenes:

> HOPE. Then upon this [*wrapping the flag around* SEYMOUR],
> the British flag, fire if you dare! [DON ANDRE *waves
> his hand. Soldiers drop their muskets. Curtain descends to
> "Rule Britannia."*]

Foreign countries seemed to bring out extremes of national feeling in melodramatic characters. An audience of unfortunate Mexicans is the recipient of this contemptuous speech by the English hero of *The Sin and the Sorrow* (1866), another East End drama:

> The Englishman set you to work, *created* this village, and *made* the
> port. There is the school the Englishman built—there the chapel he
> founded, that you might worship heaven in your own form. Why,
> you and such as you should bless the Englishman's energy and the
> Englishman's wealth, which to fertile fields converts your barren
> lands, and transforms a useless body to a prosperous people.

This is imperialism with a vengeance—except that it is imperialism without colonization, which distinguishes a play like *The Sin and the Sorrow* from late-century Drury Lane imperialist drama, largely concerned as it is with rebellion in the colonies, and with asserting Britain's power and fitness to rule subject peoples. In this respect it is different from pre-1850 melodrama that apotheosizes the British flag. There the emphasis is on national, rather than imperial glory; the Briton—the Englishman in particular—is superior to anybody else because he is a Briton, not because he is involved in subjugating and colonizing. Similarly, British soldiers and sailors will triumph because they are British and per se braver and more heroic than their foreign equivalents, not because they are engaged in conquest or elevated above inferior races, lesser breeds without the law. That came later, and found its fullest expression upon the huge stage of Drury Lane because it was by the 1880s and 1890s technically so well equipped to enact the pomp, spectacle, and pageantry of military conflict that nourished the imperialist faith and distinguished the conduct of imperialist policies. Earlier in the century, except for the battle spectacles in Astley's circus ring, theatres were not equipped to do that kind of thing, the ideology of production did not yet encompass such a large scale, and the social and political climate was not yet appropriate. The full-blown theatrical expression of imperialism had to wait for "the feelings of the public at large" as well as for grander notions of production and a suitable technology.

Historians have noted an increase in the tempo of British imperialism in the last quarter of the nineteenth century, a proliferation of popular rhetoric, a greater willingness on the part of the government to take preemptive military action and increasing pressure from the public to do so, a new arrogance toward colonial, native peoples, and a determination to thwart the expansionist efforts of other European counties in Africa. By the 1890s the popular press, the public schools, and the governing class were fervent and zealous supporters of the fact and virtue of Empire, although it by no means commanded universal support. In part this new imperialism was a reaction arising out of fear and apprehension of the future rather than an overwhelming confidence in the present, but one would not know that from the *Daily Mail,* the music hall, or the pages of *Chums* and the *Boy's Own Paper,* founded in 1879, the year Augustus Harris came to Drury Lane. Nor would one know it from the anti-Russian "War Song," sung in the halls by the Great Macdermott in 1879, remarkable not only for its "by jingo" chorus but also for its sentiment, as in the lines:

> *Let them be warned, Old England is brave Old England still.*
> *We've proved our might, we've claimed our right, and ever ever will,*
> *Should we have to draw the sword our way to victory we'll forge*
> *With the battle cry of Britons, "Old England and Saint George."*

It is doubtful if that was the particular battle cry of British regiments fighting the multifarious battles of Empire, but ever since the campaigns in

China in 1837 and Afghanistan in 1838 those regiments had been almost unceasingly occupied on the military business of the Queen. Since 1879 they had been especially busy: the first Boer war and Afghanistan again in that year, the invasion of Egypt in 1882, the Sudan and Burma in 1885, guerilla warfare in Burma for several years after that, Rhodesia in the 1890s, the Sudan once more in 1896 — not to mention sundry minor affrays and skirmishes. The number of these encounters is a direct reflection of the acquisition and maintenance of a vast collection of heterogeneous colonies, protectorates, trading markets, spheres of influence, naval bases, and coaling stations scattered over the entire globe. It was true that by the Diamond Jubilee the sun never set upon the British Empire.

The expression of Empire upon the stage of Drury Lane is sometimes significant, sometimes subordinate to other elements of plot and setting in six autumn dramas produced between 1881 and 1902: *Youth, Freedom, Human Nature, A Life of Pleasure, Cheer, Boys, Cheer,* and *The Best of Friends.* Harris and Paul Meritt wrote *Youth; Freedom* was by Harris and G. F. Rowe; *Human Nature* and *A Life of Pleasure* by Harris and a prolific author for East End theatres in the seventies, Henry Pettitt. *Cheer, Boys, Cheer* was a tripartite collaboration between Harris, Cecil Raleigh, and Henry Hamilton; Raleigh was the sole author of *The Best of Friends.* In addition to the content of the melodrama, the affairs of Empire — especially the glorious deeds of British soldiery — were sometimes glanced at in the Christmas pantomimes; the *Jack and the Beanstalk* of 1899 is the most striking of these in an imperial sense.

The question of the composition of the autumn drama audience is a vexed one, since there has been no research on the subject and no evidence is readily available. Drury Lane had a huge following that cut across class lines for its Christmas pantomimes. It also had a very large gallery, and contemporary illustrations show that it was inhabited by the lower classes. No doubt there was a crossover from the pantomime audience to the autumn drama audience, since Drury Lane was, as a time when most of the East End popular theatres were in decline, London's popular theatre par excellence. One supposes that its substantial audience supported both elements of Harris's production policy: spectacular melodrama and spectacular pantomime. It is doubtful whether the fashionable class or the upper middle class was much in attendance; they occupied boxes, stalls, and the front of the dress circle at their own theatres of resort and their own kind of drama: Shakespeare, adaptations of French society plays, the "new" drama of Pinero and Henry Arthur Jones, the elegant comedy dramas of Oscar Wilde. Old-fashioned melodrama in the West End was pretty much confined to the Adelphi, the Princess's, and Drury Lane, and it is tempting to suggest that Harris's overall support for his patriotic spectacle plays was drawn from the segment of society no higher than the middle of the middle class. The mass audience at that level had always enjoyed a combination of spectacle and melodrama wherever it could be found in the theatre; English audiences, indeed, have always loved a big show—and in this case, at this time in history, a big show combined with patriotic sentiment and heroic characters of a familiar stage stamp was irresistible.

The head of this list of autumn dramas, *Youth* (1881), followed by a year *The World*, the first of the elaborate and sensational autumn dramas and Harris's first great box-office hit. In *Youth* the hero is Frank Darlington, a clergyman's son, an example of downward social mobility in the melodramatic hero and in the treatment of the characters of military melodrama— although, indeed, the soldier-heroes of Drury Lane imperialist drama are mostly an aristocratic lot. Darlington is entrapped by an adventuress who, manipulated by the villain, leads him into an undesirable marriage. We know that she is evil since early in the play she is discovered reading Zola. Villain and adventuress frame Darlington, who is convicted of a crime he never committed and sent to Dartmoor; he escapes, avoids discovery, and enlists as a private soldier. In tableau 6 he participates, as the program tells us, in a "Realistic Scene of Embarkation of Troops." On stage, the troopship moved slowly away from the Portsmouth dock while a brass band played and crowds waved, wept, and threw streamers. The big scene of the drama was tableau 7, "The Entrenchment," near the Khyber Pass. When *Youth* was revived in 1883, the setting was changed from Afghanistan to Egypt, a reference to the campaign of the previous year.

In either setting, the entrenched soldiers are in dire straits after an enemy attack. Darlington volunteers to break through the besiegers and ride for help, and immediately gallops off on his impossibly dangerous mission. The colonel addresses the survivors:

> Remember, no surrender. Bring the colours. Wrap them round me. Tie them tight in knots. Where I go follow me. If I fall surround me. Back to back, and let them cut you to pieces before they have a shred, a stitch of this flag. Remember Great England is looking at you. Show how her sons can fight and die. [*The fight commences. Just as the English are at the mercy of the enemy,* FRANK *returns with troops, and the tide of victory is turned. GRAND AND ELABORATE TABLEAU. RULE BRITANNIA.*][6]

Real Gatling guns and rifles had been supplied by Armstrong and Company and Martini-Henry rifles by the Birmingham Small Arms Company.

Evidently the realism of the Afghan attack was striking; the *Illustrated London News* (13 August 1881) believed that "the grouping and stage management are more than worthy of the skilfullest tableau of the Meiningers." The Meininger Company had visited Drury Lane a few months earlier and impressed everybody with their stage management and handling of crowds. Another reviewer describes the scene vividly:

> The besiegers are met with a withering fire from Martini-Henry rifles, whilst the murderous Gatlings bellow forth ever and anon. Eventually the combatants are completely enveloped in smoke amidst which are discerned the spurts of fire from the weapons of the assailed, and the huge sheets of flame which belch forth repeatedly from the mitrailleuses. Then the Afghans with their broad, heavy swords, rush in, and a hand to hand *melée* occurs, in which scimitars and bayonets clash together, the din of the strife being added to by the sharp detonations of the officers' revolvers and the deep bass voices of the troops as they cheer each other on to the fray.[7]

The critic Dutton Cook commented, not quite so enthusiastically, that the use of blank cartridges by the British soldiers "so filled the house with noises, fumes, and odours, that by the more sedate spectators the victory of our arms was strongly felt to be dearly purchased."[8] Needless to say, Frank Darlington is awarded the Victoria Cross and returns to England to discard the adventuress, who turns out to be a bigamist, and marry the heroine after all.

While only one scene of *Youth* is set overseas, the whole of *Freedom* (1883) takes place in Egypt. Of all the Drury Lane autumn dramas to be concerned with Britain's imperial role, if only (like all of them) in a largely military sense, *Freedom* is the most aggressive, the most jingoistic, the nastiest toward a foreign people. In September 1882, eleven months before *Freedom* opened at Drury Lane, the British sent an expeditionary force to Egypt to suppress a nationalist revolt. Alexandria was bombarded and Cairo occupied the next day. The Khedive of Egypt, nominally a satrap of the Ottoman Sultan of Turkey, became a political bystander and mere observer of British rule.

In the play, a rich and villainous Arab named Araf Bey (clearly a reference, understood by the reviewers, to the nationalist leader Ahmad Arabi) says to the British consul of an unnamed town, "The eyes of every hungry power in Europe gloat upon the fertile valleys of the Nile, and each thirsts to make our river its pathway to the great East." The consul disagrees, and advances a standard Victorian economic justification for imperialist expansion: "I repudiate such motives for England. We come to your cities, as to a market, and with our inventions we bring you progress." Araf Bey's denunciation of "the interference of foreigners" and his cry of "Egypt for the Egyptians" naturally do not impress the British.

The plot of *Freedom* is about the heroism, suffering, and final triumph of Ernest Gascoigne, captain of the gunboat HMS *Arrow*. Gascoigne has seized a shipload of slaves at sea, and frees them with a patriotic flourish, hurling defiance at the Egyptians as he does so. The Egyptians revolt and attack the consulate, killing the consul. The villainous Araf Bey abducts Gascoigne's fiancée, Constance, and imprisons her in his palace. Gascoigne comes to the rescue; Araf Bey is killed by his jealous wife. Gascoigne escapes with Constance but is wounded and taken captive by the even more villainous slave trader, Sadyk. Constance is taken to safety by the comic Texan, Slingsby. The gunboat arrives opportunely; the Egyptians are defeated and Sadyk is hung from the yardarm of the *Arrow* to a roll of drums and British cheers.

Much of the militant imperialism and rampant patriotism of *Freedom* is conveyed through the characterization of Gascoigne, played without restraint by Harris himself. Throughout the play Gascoigne utters heroic sentiments of an extreme kind. At the end of act 1 he exults in the freeing of Sadyk's slaves: "These girls were slaves, they are free! England has decreed it, and in England's name I speak. Touch them at your peril! I defy you! [*Hurrah of sailors. Picture.*]" To Araf's reasonable statement that this is a dangerous situation for the English since they are heavily outnumbered, Gascoigne replies, "Odds! Were they a thousand to one I would stand up for my country's honour, till my last drop of blood was shed." In act 2 he hurries off from the consulate to rejoin his ship when trouble begins in the streets, telling Constance, "We, it seems, must go to our nuptials in true fighting fashion — when the decks are cleared for action the enemy comes athwart our bows, and we must cut our way to victory and each other's arms. God bless you! God bless you all! Come, my lads." Soon he reappears, "*his uniform torn — his face bloody,*" organizes the defense of the consulate and refuses to use the British flag to cover the body of the consul: "Haul down our flag, sir? No; rather nail it to the mast. We represent the name and honour of our native land. Let our enemies tear down our colours if they can; but they shall fly until the staff is shattered." In act 3 he saves Constance's honor at the crucial moment, climbing in through a window in Araf Bey's palace, having ascended the outer wall with rugged cliffs and the Nile below. This moment is classically perfect and demands quotation:

ARAF. The fire in your eyes inflames my purpose, Constance
    Loring, all the fierce passions of my Eastern blood rush
    to my heart and madden me. I have defied danger and
    law to possess you. Tempt my rage no more, but yield.

CONSTANCE. Never, Araf, never! [*He seizes her and flings her on the Ottoman. Music. With fury she clutches him by the throat with both hands.* ERNEST *appears at the window.]*
ERNEST. Ay! Never while I live. [*Flings* ARAF *away.]*
ARAF. Ah!
CONSTANCE. [*Rising and tottering towards him.]* Ernest, Ernest, my love!
ERNEST. My Life! Don't tremble, you are safe. [*Picture.]*

Gascoigne then vanquishes Araf in a duel with knives, magnanimously sparing his life only to fall prisoner to Sadyk. In act 4, entering on the point of collapse in Sadyk's slave caravan, he declares, with energy: "I have starved in Arctic seas, on wandering fields of ice, where the soul-killing cold congeals the blood; but the firm resolve and endurance that makes the power of Englishmen never deserted me till now." Against Sadyk's orders, an Arab boy gives him water. Sadyk threatens the boy and his mother, and Gascoigne of course has something to say: "I speak in her defence, as every true man should, when heroism and distress cry out for pity and respect."

Ernest Gascoigne is the popular imperialist hero *in excelsis*. The Arabs, on the other hand, are a miserable lot, cunning, treacherous, and despicable: Araf Bey, the rebellious villain; Sadyk, the cruel and savage slave dealer; Hassan, the greedy and cowardly middleman. Only the Arab women are good, and actively assist the English.

The plot of *Human Nature*, produced two years after *Freedom*, only incidentally concerns imperialist adventure; the second scene of act 4 is set in "The Desert City in the Hands of the Mahdists," an obvious allusion to Khartoum. During the run, an exhibition of "Egyptian and Sudanese Arms, Accoutrements & Relics" was held in the Grand Saloon of Drury Lane. In 1885 the forces of the Mahdi, after a long siege, finally broke into Khartoum and slaughtered General Gordon and several thousand others; a British relief column arrived three days late. Other dramatists had already seized upon the Sudan as a subject. The melodrama *Khartoum*, staged at Sanger's six weeks after Gordon's death, actually managed to present the Sudan disaster as a British victory. A disgraced officer enlists in the ranks and is killed in a native attack upon a heroic British square. The hero defies the Mahdi himself in the most satisfying manner:

MAHDI. I can see you are English by your faces.
JOCELYN. Naturally, for no enemy ever saw it by our backs.

The Mahdists attack Khartoum and the villain is blown up attempting to force the gates; the British are victorious.

This wilful perversion of history is not equaled by *Human Nature,* although it tries hard. As a relief force, headed by the hero, Captain Temple, approaches the beleaguered city, a disbelieving European prisoner doubts that it will succeed; another replies, "Do not forget they are Englishmen." As the battle commences, a despairing Arab cries out, "All is lost! The English are invincible." The English enter the city; the villain, a Frenchman who has been aiding the Arabs, slinks away to die in the desert. The most spectacular scene on stage was not the storming of the city, but the grand march-past of the victorious troops through Trafalgar Square, with Captain Temple on horseback at their head, "in the presence," said the *Times* (14 September 1885) "of a vast stage crowd, who swarm upon Landseer's lions and otherwise display a patriotic enthusiasm requiring to be restrained by the police."

The Sudan campaign of 1885 echoed in *A Life of Pleasure* (1893), the next drama to be considered. Act 4 presents a battle against Burmese "dacoits," dramatizing the continued British efforts to subdue the Burmese guerrillas years after the surrender of the King of Burma in 1885, in the last Burmese War. The *Times* (22 September) noted that "a prodigious quantity of gunpowder is burnt by scores of rifles and at least one genuine Nordenfeldt [a machine gun] which mowed the enemy down wholesale. Never has so much noise been heard in a theatre, and if further evidence of the reality of warfare were needed, it would be furnished by the stifling volumes of smoke which pervade the auditorium." Harris had consulted war correspondents and military experts about staging the battle. At its height, the hero, Lord Avondale, takes the rifle of a dead soldier and *"stands in a conspicuous place à la Captain Burnaby, coolly reloading and picking off the enemy."* Frederick Gustavus Burnaby was a noted traveler, author, and soldier who had already distinguished himself in the army. His heroic death at the battle of Abu Klea in the Sudan in 1885 struck one of those many powerful chords of public sympathy and emotion that resonated long after in a Britain that revered courage and bravery in the service of the crown above all else. His use as an iconographic figure in a melodrama eight years after his death is an interesting aspect of the relationship between the theatre and the unfolding drama of Empire.

Captain Burnaby's death was pictured in the popular illustrated papers, and certainly the pictorialization of the more thrilling and emotionally charged moments of Empire was common to both the press and the theatre. *Cheer, Boys, Cheer* (1895) —the title was taken from a song by Henry Russell —dramatizes and pictorializes just such a moment. The plot is as entangled and ponderous as is usual in the autumn dramas. All we need to know is that because of first- and second-act complications involving fraudulent speculation

in diamond mines in South Africa, the principal characters find themselves
there for the middle section of the play. It is Lady Hilyard, the mother of the
hero, who sits down at the piano at the end of act 2 and sings "Cheer, boys,
cheer" after declaring, roundly, "We'll turn our backs upon the old world,
its cant, its cruelty and its shame, and drop the heart-ache from us in that
new land beyond the sea, the Land of Good Hope!"—a not exceptional
motive for emigration and settlement in the colonies.

In act 3 the hero, George Hilyard, and his rival for the heroine's hand,
Chepstowe, army officers both, find themselves pursuing an impi of Matabele
after a massacre of the Mashonas. "And this," says George angrily of the anti-
imperialists, "is what some of the folks at home, the Little Englanders, would
let go on for ever! Thank Heaven out here we've men who'll put an end to
it." When asked what he will do with such a small detachment, George rises
to the occasion with a standard Drury Lane patriotic sentiment: "What
Englishmen have done before, sir—lick four times their own number when
they've got to defend the weak and helpless against the cruel and strong." He
refuses to wait for reinforcements because the lives of a few English civilians
at a mining station are in danger. As a result his men soon face a far larger
number of Matabele. The soldiers dig in and send one of the civilians for help;
he comes across Lady Hilyard's party headed for the mine, led by Boer
guides. When they know their danger, "*the* BOERS *slink off*" and Lady
Hilyard announces that "We are well rid of them—we are Englishwomen,
sir, and don't fear any danger they would skulk from." The heroine sets out
on a long, desperate night ride to find the reinforcements.

Act 3, scene 5 is entitled "The Last Stand." The English are surrounded.
Chepstowe addresses them: "My men, you see how it is with us—we've got
to die—and we're going to do it like Englishmen and sell our lives as dearly
as we can. Our fathers have died that our country might be great—it's our
turn to-day." The soldiers write letters home as the music of "Home, sweet
home" plays softly in the orchestra. The Matabele attack. When the ammunition is gone, the survivors rise and sing "God Save the Queen"; the
natives respectfully cease firing. Another attack comes, and only George
and Chepstowe are left alive, both wounded. At this moment "*Loud 'Hurrah'
off—scattered* MATABELE *rush in from R. A charge of* CAVALRY *sweep across
the stage. 'God Save the Queen' fortissimo from the orchestra.*" Chopin's Funeral
March succeeds "God Save the Queen" and Chepstowe considerably
expires. By now inured to such scenes of heroism and sentiment, all that
the *Times* reviewer (20 September 1895) could say was that they were
"stirring" and that "there is a welcome reduction in the amount of gunpowder consumed."

The scene of "The Last Stand" was based upon an actual episode in the campaign of 1893 against the Matabele, when Major Allan Wilson and a patrol of thirty-two men found themselves surrounded by several hundred Matabele on the bank of the Shangani River. According to the Matabele, when the ammunition ran out the survivors shook hands and sang "God Save the Queen" before being massacred to a man. A painting of this scene by Allan Stewart, entitled "There Were No Survivors," shows the soldiers under attack.[9] The scene at Drury Lane was an instance of a common phenomenon of the nineteenth-century stage: the merging of the arts of painting and stage production to incarnate the age and the historical moment in a striking, living image.

In October 1899 the second Boer War broke out and only two years after the gloriously patriotic and imperial Diamond Jubilee in 1897 the nation's mood began slowly to darken. The confident spirit of the Bishop of Wakefield's Jubilee hymn,

Where England's flag flies wide unfurl'd,
All tyrant wrongs repelling,
God make the world a better world
For man's brief earthly dwelling. . . .

gave way to a sort of Empire-induced fatigue, the mood of Kipling's "The White Man's Burden," written in 1899, a poem regarding the "new-caught, sullen peoples" with a sense of tired and endlessly repeated duty, a poem with quite a different character than Kipling's "A Song of the White Men" published in the same year:

Oh, well for the world when the White Men tread
Their highway side by side!

At the beginning of the war, however, Drury Lane reflected the fevered mood of the public at large.[10] On 18 December 1899, after two months of serious British reverses at the hands of the Boers, the idolized Lord Roberts, hero of the Indian Mutiny, Burma, and Afghanistan, was appointed commander in chief of the British forces in South Africa, with Kitchener as his chief of staff. Five days later he sailed from Southampton to take up his post, and war fever was at its height. The popular press, the music hall, and other places of entertainment positively foamed at the mouth in patriotic frenzy. The current exhibition at Olympia was entitled "Briton, Boer, and Black in South Africa" and included theatrical episodes, one of which culminated in a Boer defeat and immense applause from a huge audience when the British flag waved over the Boer position. At the Alhambra portraits of "prominent personages identified with the war" were thrown on a huge screen on the stage. The picture of Lord Roberts was received with a storm of acclamation, and "the patriotic spirit reached its highest pitch of expression when the portrait of her Majesty the Queen was shown. The audience sprang to their feet and indulged in wild cheers, which culminated in the singing of the National Anthem."[11]

All Drury Lane had to offer was its Christmas pantomime, *Jack and the Beanstalk*, but a last-minute change was made in the conception of the Giant, and he emerged on stage as Blunderboer, with a mask bearing the features of President Kruger. The 1882 pantomime *Sinbad the Sailor* had included a review of the victorious British troops returning from Egypt, but this was much exceeded in patriotic zeal by the eleventh scene of *Jack and the Beanstalk*, which the *Sketch* (27 December 1899) describes:

> After this mammoth Boer has fallen from his high estate, crushing several villages in his descent, a very extraordinary scene ensues. Not only does the Hero Jack stand upon the Giant's knee and warble an appropriately defiant patriotic ditty—while War-Correspondents, seated on his boots, prepare their copy—but from a pocket of the Giant Boer there issues forth a mighty army of British and Colonial troops, each one realistically uniformed and wonderfully trained.

Some of the troops—played by small children—were dressed in scarlet, others in khaki; some were sailors with a machine gun; some Australian lancers. All walked over the body of the fifty-foot Giant, and after they had emerged they raised their helmets on their rifles while "Rule, Britannia" rang out triumphantly in the orchestra.

By 1902 the attitude of the public and of the theatre had changed. At the end of May, after a protracted and bitter guerrilla war on the part of the Boers and an unpopular scorched-earth and internment-camp policy on the part of the British, the war finally ended. The confident, expansionist mood of the nineties had soaked away into the veldt with the blood of some 6,000 British and colonial dead and 23,000 wounded. Drury Lane's autumn drama for 1902 reflected this change in popular feeling. *The Best of Friends* was typical of Drury Lane melodramas in the size of its cast, its spectacle, and its leisurely rhythms—it lasted five hours on opening night (*Cheer, Boys, Cheer* took four and a half)—but different in its treatment of subject matter that a few years before would have thrown the audience into a jingoistic delirium. The principal characters are the Earl of Amesbury and a Boer, Paul de Lahne, students together at Oxford, and Paul's father, Michael, who visits his son in Oxford while actually on a secret mission to buy arms for the Boers. Michael de Lahne is fiercely independent and intensely anti-British. Early in the play he gets into an argument about war with the more tolerant Earl. Amesbury says that there may be occasions when "it isn't right and just to fight at all." He tells the hostile Boer that "fighting is the argument of savages," and the following exchange ensues:

> DE LAHNE. Eh? I thought all you English were proud of being fighting men?
> AMESBURY. Fighting men yes—bullies, no.

In act 3 the war is on. Amesbury, at the head of a Volunteer unit, has already won a Victoria Cross, and Michael de Lahne is much admired by the British for the skill and bravery with which he leads his Boer commando. Eventually the commando is surrounded and attacked by the British. The Boers lay down their arms; their flag is lowered; de Lahne dies of a heart attack, and the stage direction ending the act differs both in content and attitude from the usual upbeat patriotism:

> AMESBURY. . . . [*slowly advances and covers* DE LAHNE's *face with the Boer flag—as he does so a* SOLDIER *hoists the Union Jack over the Farm House. A distant cheer and bugles are heard and very distant band is heard playing the National Anthem.* BOERS, *all looking at DE LAHNE sorrowfully, take off their hats.* SOLDIERS *and* AMESBURY *look at flag and take off their hats.* AMESBURY *grasps* PAUL's *hand at same time,* PAUL *with bent head, sobbing.*]

The treatment of the Boers is restrained and sympathetic throughout; patriotic feeling is expressed, of course, particularly after the toast to the Queen—"Tremendous Cheers as Curtain falls"—at a farewell banquet for the Volunteers, but there is no beating of the imperialist drum, only a heartfelt desire that Boer and Briton should be "the best of friends."

The defense of their farm house by the Boer commando is de Lahne's last stand, and we are reminded of the extreme position of the British soldiers in *Youth, A Life of Pleasure,* and *Cheer, Boys, Cheer;* in all these plays there are "last stands." Indeed, the mythology of "the last stand," particularly from a British point of view, deserves investigation. Drury Lane was not the only English theatre to offer this rather specialized form of military entertainment. As far back as 1858, Dion Boucicault's *Jessie Brown; or, The Relief of Lucknow* was a hit in New York before it was staged in London. The play ends with the arrival of the Highlanders just as all hope is lost, and the stage directions recall the poster of *At Duty's Call* as well as the climax of several Drury Lane last stands: "BLOUNT, *standing on a disabled gun, deals ponderous blows right and left, with the rammer, and knocks over the* SEPOYS *as they appear.*" Finally, "*the* HIGHLANDERS, *with their piper, charge up the breast-work and crown it in every direction.*" In *Tommy Atkins* (1895) a British relief column in the Sudan (Kitchener was then moving against the Mahdists) arrives in the nick of time, and in *Midst Shot and Shell* (1899) the hero is instrumental in repelling a native attack while his colleagues sing "Soldiers of the Queen"—a song written during the Jubilee year of 1897. The last stand was a common subject in popular art, especially in illustrated magazines, as well as upon the stage; surely the British public also remembered the most famous last stand of all, that of Custer against the Sioux in 1876.

What was so immensely appealing about the last stand as a subject for fiction, art, and the theatre? Undoubtedly it presented, in a single powerful image, a microcosm of heroism, sacrifice, and love of country.

> *The sand of the desert is sodden red, —*
> *Red with the wreck of a square that broke; —*
> *The Gatling's jammed and the Colonel's dead*
> *And the regiment blind with dust and smoke.*

Did it also offer, more than any other single possible moment of nineteenth-century British history, a symbol of the essence, the best of Empire, of the bravery and sheer guts of the men who had made Empire possible? That verse of Henry Newbolt's "Vitai Lampada" concludes,

> *The river of death has brimmed his banks*
> *And England's far, and Honour a name,*
> *But the voice of a schoolboy rallies the ranks:*
> *"Play up! play up! and play the game!"*[12]

Whatever the answer to these questions, the last stand as a cultural artifact was perfectly suited to melodrama in the theatre.

The year 1899 and *Jack and the Beanstalk* marked the final frenzy of theatrical imperialism as exhibited at Drury Lane; it also marked the beginning of the end of an imperialist era. In terms of jingoistic sensibility and unshakable confidence in the righteousness of every British cause, *The Best of*

Friends in 1902 is a pale shadow of *Freedom* in 1883. Only once more was a Drury Lane autumn drama, or part of it, set in the Empire, and that was act 2 of *The Hope* in 1911, by Raleigh and Hamilton. The second scene of the act is laid in the officers' mess of the First Hussars at Delhi, and the third in the interior of the Dewan-i-Khas, where a splendid ball given by the Viceroy is in progress:

> [THE LADIES *wear their most beautiful dresses, mostly of cool-looking colours, and their most resplendent jewels.* THE MEN *are all in their fullest uniforms, wearing all their medals and orders.* SEVERAL NATIVE PRINCES, *gorgeously dressed, are present.* SENTRIES *and* ORDER-LIES *in brilliant native uniforms are dotted about here and there. A waltz is in progress when the lights go up and it continues for nearly a minute before it concludes.*]

However, this is all show; the splendor of the Raj merely serves as a background for the personal problems of the principal characters, and the setting is carefully calculated to take advantage of public interest in the great Durbar to be held in Delhi in December 1911 by George V.

When *The Hope* opened, the First World War was less than three years away, and the life of the schoolboy of "Vitai Lampada" would be extinguished in the trenches of the Somme. Along with him died an attitude and an ideal. If *Cheer, Boys, Cheer* was the distillation of popular beliefs about England and the Empire and war, R. C. Sherriff's *Journey's End* (1928), a rather different sort of play—which also contains a last stand—was the definitive theatrical expression of the First World War. It had no feeling for Empire. That sort of feeling, of popular sentiment and impassioned patriotism as articulated in the theatre, was most powerfully and strikingly expressed upon the stage of Drury Lane.

Notes

1. For further information on Drury Lane under Harris, see James Stottlar, "'A House Choked with Gunpowder and Wild with Excitement': Augustus Harris and Drury Lane's Spectacular Melodrama," in *When They Weren't Doing Shakespeare*, ed. Judith L. Fisher and Stephen Watt (Athens, Georgia: University of Georgia Press, 1989), 212-29. For the production style of these Drury Lane autumn dramas, see Michael R. Booth, *Victorian Spectacular Theatre* (London: Routledge, 1981), 68-74.

2. *Fortnightly Review,* 38, November 1885, 635.
3. *Era,* 29 September 1888, 14.
4. "Our play-box," *Theatre,* September 1882, 184.
5. See J. S. Bratton, "Theatre of War: The Crimea on the London Stage, 1954-5," in *Performance and Politics in Popular Drama,* ed. David Bradby, Louis James, and Bernard Sharratt (New York: Cambridge University Press, 1980), 119-37.
6. All quotations from the Drury Lane dramas are taken from typescripts submitted to the Lord Chamberlain for licensing purposes. They were never printed.
7. *Illustrated Sporting and Dramatic News,* 8 August 1881.
8. Dutton Cook, *Nights at the Play* (London, 1883), 466.
9. A more famous painting is Lady Butler's "The Defence of Rorke's Drift," which commemorated a heroic defence of their post against thousands of Zulus by one company of British soldiers. This occurred in 1879; the painting was commissioned by the Queen and exhibited at the Royal Academy. The film *Zulu* commemorates this particular last stand, and is a worthy filmic equivalent of Drury Lane patriotic spectacle.
10. Harris died in 1896 and was succeeded as lessee by Arthur Collins, but the policy of autumn drama followed by Christmas pantomime did not change.
11. *Times,* 27 December 1899.
12. Henry Newbolt, "Vitai Lampada," in *The Island Race* (London, 1898), 82. Alfred Tennyson's "The Revenge" (1878) is the most famous poetic treatment of a naval last stand.

2

THE EMPIRE RIGHT OR WRONG: BOER WAR MELODRAMA ON THE AUSTRALIAN STAGE, 1899–1901

JIM DAVIS

*N*INETEENTH-CENTURY MELODRAMA has increasingly been posited as a site of cultural negotiation, within which hegemonic and counter hegemonic discourses can be integrated and even resolved. J. S. Bratton, for instance, has argued plausibly that melodrama provided a useful basis for the negotiation and accommodation of imperialism within the British context, absorbing contradictory attitudes and values rather than imposing a simplistically pro-imperial ideology.[1] A reading of melodrama that allows for more complex interpretation of the performance and reception of the genre and for multiple and shifting perspectives in audience response certainly enables us to place it as a crucial rather than peripheral phenomenon of cultural history. It also raises interesting questions when the subject of investigation incorporates not only such issues as imperialism but also colonial relationships. The representation of the Boer War on the Australian stage is one such example, for it not only touches on imperialism, patriotism, and class, as do the equivalent English presentations, but also on the negotiation of imperial-colonial relationships at the point when Australia was moving rapidly towards federation.

Throughout the nineteenth century, melodramas based around military conflicts with external foes provided a particularly strong focus for both the validation and evaluation of national myths and national identities, while also giving scope for the spectacle and for the ethical contests essential to the genre. Such plays tended to encourage popular support for war, especially if they were specific to a contemporary conflict, yet also to reflect popular opinion as it changed or waned in enthusiasm. They also reinforced national stereotypes and sometimes redefined them, as was so often the case with the social stereotypes presented within melodrama. The hierarchies operational within the British army, for instance, provide an excellent source for the negotiation of social difference, so often a feature of the genre. Yet, while many of the Australian adaptations of English melodramas, to be discussed below, reflect these social divisions, the assertion of the worth of the Australian soldiers, regardless of class, often transcends such concerns. In other words, national difference replaces social difference as the category through which the status quo is destabilized yet, in keeping with the genre's ambivalence, reaffirmed, albeit from a slightly modified perspective.

The Boer War broke out on 12 October 1899, nominally over the status of the Uitlander population of the Transvaal. Many Uitlanders were British subjects, who had been flocking to the Witwatersrand goldfields since their discovery in 1886; they now outnumbered the Boers and wanted to be enfranchised and to enjoy full rights as citizens. President Kruger, the Boer leader, resisted their demands, since he was concerned that acquiescence would lead to British domination of the Transvaal. For Britain the real, if unspoken, issue was who would eventually control South Africa, especially if Kruger's stand led to a resurgence of Afrikaaner nationalism. There were undoubtedly strategic and financial gains to be accrued from a victory over the Boers. There was also a need to demonstrate that the British Empire was still an adversary not to be trifled with. In the event the Boer War lasted for over two and one-half years, until the Treaty of Vereeniging on 31 May 1902. For the first three months of the war, culminating in the notorious "Black Week" extending from 10 to 17 December, the British were less successful than they had expected, although it was to this period that most of the major engagements belonged. Then, until September 1900, a British counteroffensive led to the invasion and annexation of the Transvaal and the Orange Free State, made possible by reinforcements and colonial assistance, to which the Boers offered little resistance. From late 1900, after Lord Kitchener took over command of the South African field force from Lord Roberts, the Boers waged a sort of guerilla warfare. To oppose the Boer commandos the British and their allies resorted to an indiscriminate burning of Boer farms and crops, the destruction of stock, and the confinement of displaced women and children in concentration camps.

"It was to such a war," says L. M. Field, "that Australian colonists so unwittingly committed themselves and remained officially committed, although public enthusiasm for the venture waned rapidly as the novelty of troop departures wore off and the true nature of the war became

Registered at the General Post Office, Sydney, for Transmission by Post as a Newspaper.

Vol. 20—No. 1031.   SATURDAY, NOVEMBER 18, 1899.

FIGURE 2.   An illustration for "An Ominous Start":
front cover, *The Bulletin*, November 18, 1899.

apparent. . . ."[2] The phenomenal Australian response to the war was surprising, considering the growing tendency towards nationalism and federation during the previous decade. However, as both Richard Jebb and Barbara R. Penny have suggested, this war fever was a combined expression of nationalism and imperialism: "It was an assertion of self-reliance and a chance for colonials to prove their worth, even their superiority, to the imperial authorities and to the world."[3] Field suggests that there were three reasons for this eagerness to support Britain. Firstly, with Japanese, Russian, German, and French activity in the Pacific, Australia's continuing security depended on the British Empire's support. Secondly, there was the filial urge to stand by the Mother Country when she needed help. Thirdly, there was a strong desire within the army itself to demonstrate the competence of Australian Defence Forces.[4] Consequently, even before a shot had been fired, recruitment of Australians to fight in the Boer War had already commenced. Admittedly, when the New South Wales Legislative Assembly debated the issue in October 1899, William Holman, the Labour member for Grenfell, called the South African War the "most iniquitous, most immoral war ever waged with any race" and suggested that the English race had now "fallen on a time when apparently the utmost it can do is bully weak and struggling powers." To such views Edmund Barton, who was to become Australia's first prime minister after federation in 1901, responded: "When our Empire is at war with any other power whatever, it becomes our turn to declare the motto, 'The Empire Right or Wrong.'"[5]

Until late 1899 opinion was by no means united in Australia. Certain journals, such as the *Bulletin* and the *Worker*, were to maintain an antiwar stance even after the war's commencement, but most firmly supported British policy. "No individual colony could have possibly stood apart from the eager rush to support the Empire," writes Field, "and few politicians had either the conviction or the courage to oppose involvement in the Transvaal."[6] Australians had been volunteering to fight from as early as July 1899; by November contingents had departed from New South Wales, Western Australia, Victoria, Southern Australia, and Tasmania, to be followed by Queensland in December. Further contingents, including a number of Bushmen contingents, were to be raised throughout the war. The Australians proved a more resourceful match for the Boers than the British to begin with, particularly distinguishing themselves in the taking of Diamond Hill. Lord Roberts, the commander in chief of the British forces, praised the colonials for their intelligence and individuality and for the ease with which they coped with the South African terrain.

For the first half of the war the Australian involvement appeared to be fully justified.

The Boer War euphoria was soon reflected on the Australian stage in melodrama, pantomime, music hall, and patriotic concerts, not to mention in an increasing number of lectures and film shows as the war progressed. As in England there had been a growth in the popularity of military melodramas on the Australian stage towards the close of the century, while the music hall also echoed the British vogue for jingoistic songs and sentiments.[7] The Boer War provided scope for developing this tendency further, at least during the first fifteen months of the war. Even in September 1899 a number of military melodramas, all English in origin, could be seen in Australia. Sutton Vane's *For England* was playing at the Theatre Royal, Melbourne, where it was billed as an Anglo-African novelty, which, "in view of the present crisis in the Transvaal, possesses more than ordinary interest."[8] Meanwhile, at Sydney's Lyceum Theatre, the popular military melodrama *Tommy Atkins* was being performed, while in Brisbane *Under Two Flags* was in the Theatre Royal's repertoire. Back in Melbourne, Charles Holloway's company replaced *For England* at the Theatre Royal with *A Soldier and a Man,* a play set in South Africa during the Zulu War. "Given a wild outbreak of hostilities in South Africa, and the patronage of local warriors headed by a brass band," wrote the *Bulletin* (30 September 1899), "this tale of potted Zulu will supply a passing want." With its final tableau showing the triumph of the British flag, it could hardly fail, although the *Bulletin* (23 September 1899) drew attention to its formulaic nature in the following Kiplingesque verse:

> *"A Soldier and a Man" was constructed on the plan*
> *Of a dozen melo-dramas where the British flag comes in,*
> *And we knew the other night, when we saw the hero "tight,"*
> *He would have to fight for Hingland, and be cleansed of his sin*
> > *By the blood of many supers*
> > *Who presume to face the troopers*
> *Of the only blessed army that can ever hope to win—*
> *Of the blessed British army that is ever bound to win.*

When the Holloway company took the play to Brisbane, in February 1900, it had become even more topical. The South African scenery and the final tableau of a military battlefield after a fight elicited praise, but particularly memorable was a performance amid which news from the front was announced:

Throughout the proceedings the military spirit was uppermost, but
the enthusiasm reached its climax when just before the last act, Mr
Walter Rayham (the stage director) stepped in front of the curtain
and announced that the newspapers had just received a cable stat-
ing that a British flying column had got right at the back of the
Boers in Zulu-land. The announcement was the signal for one of
the most enthusiastic and inspiring demonstrations which it had
been the privilege of Brisbane playgoers to witness. Men waved
their handkerchiefs and hats and cheered vociferously; women
stamped their feet and clapped their hands. . . . It was some time
before the cheering ceased. . . .[9]

Such an audience, as can be imagined, was equally vociferous in its response
to the play's pro-Boer villain:

At one stage, when he denounced the British, saying—and intense
hatred could be traced in every word—"I hate these Britishers; they
want to plant their feet on every land," the indignation of the pit-
tites, and in fact of almost the whole house, was worked up to such
a pitch that the actor's voice was completely drowned in the chorus of hisses and groans . . . if there were any Boer sympathisers in
the audience on Saturday night, their hearts must have been making desperate attempts to get through the souls of their boots!"[10]

After the outbreak of the Boer War several Australian melodramas with
a Boer War setting also materialized. In December 1899 Lewis Scott's *A Tale
of the Transvaal* was performed at Sydney's Criterion Theatre by William
Anderson's Company. Anderson was well known for his programs of "bel-
low-dramas," more often than not drawn from English rather than
Australian sources. Founded on Rider Haggard's *Jess*, but updated, the
play included a Grand Tableau in which the British suffered reversal in conflict with the Boers, but achieved victory once Australian reinforcements
had arrived. *Briton and Boer*, by Alfred Dampier,[11] another version of *Jess*,
opened at the Alexandra Theatre in Melbourne in February 1900. The
Bulletin (24 February 1900) noted that it owed as much to "recent war
journalism and popular British theories of cause and effect in Krugerland"
as to Haggard. Jess's main function seemed to be to impede the progress of
the war, hampering the British advance on Pretoria and delaying the arrival
of the Victorian contingent, which is the signal for the Boer forces to surrender. Dampier, in the role of Charles Carrington, a British officer with a
speech impediment, served several functions within the plot, most significant of which was to make glowing remarks about the Australian troops.

"Thousands of the regular old bull-dog stock, the Australian contingent, will soon be here," he said, causing quite a sensation. Kruger was the villain of this piece, supported by Cronje and Joubert, and, when it played in Sydney in June, his proposal to drive the British into the sea was received "with yells of derision by the gallery."[12] *The Australasian* (24 February 1900), commenting on Edward Holloway's impersonation of Kruger, declared:

> Made up on the model of the pictures and supplied with a plentiful supply of Biblical allusions, the Kruger of melodrama is almost unlovely enough to merit the jeers and scorn with which he is greeted by the gallery. In a recent production of a similar type in London the actors who enacted the parts of Boers all demanded that their salaries should be increased, owing to the mental wear and tear caused by the detestation with which they were received by the audience.

Another Australian adaptation, this time of a drama rather than of a novel, was Bernard Espinasse's revision of the Harris, Meritt and Pettitt Drury Lane melodrama of 1881, *Youth*. The sensational battle scenes at the end of the play were transferred from the Khyber Pass to Kimberley, where a number of Australian troops were discovered: the *Bulletin* (24 March 1900) considered this" an outrage on history, seeing the Australians weren't there." Nevertheless, *Youth* enabled the J. C. Williamson management to mount a spectacular Boer War drama at Her Majesty's Theatre, Sydney, at a time (March 1900) when the Boer fever was still unabated.

In October 1899 the Alfred Woods–Maud Williamson Dramatic Company staged a play entitled *Transvaal Heroes* at Brisbane. Billed as "an exciting and realistic drama, bearing on the present Transvaal crisis in South Africa,"[13] it showed the rescue of a garrison by British troops and in the third act revealed the Boers about to shoot the hero, who is tied to a tree. The British consul, who had obviously learned the procedure from watching too many melodramas, covered him with the English colors and defied the Boers to fire upon them. Possibly *Called to Arms*, by the Australian dramatist Stanley Neville, performed by the same company at the Theatre Royal, Adelaide, in January 1900, is a retitled or revised version of the same play. Neville's play, which showed that Pretoria was as good as taken, also featured the by-now-obligatory appearance of President Kruger. When "he advises the killing of all wounded British soldiers, firing on the flag of truce, and the annihilation of all hospitals," commented the *Advertiser* (22 January 1900), "there is little wonder that the patriotic gallery boy rises to the occasion." Kruger's "mere make-up stamps him as a cheap invention of the enemy," commented the *Bulletin* (28 April 1900) when the play re-emerged in April at the Alexandra Theatre in Melbourne, under the title of *For Queen and Country*. Inevitably, an Australian contingent also made an appearance in this play. Indeed, the arrival of the Australian contingents just in time to relieve the British from certain annihilation became a recurring feature of these melodramas.

While some sort of reference to the Australian presence in South Africa was creeping into a number of military melodramas, there was also at least one play with a distinctly Australian base. On 23 February 1900, Dan Barry's dramatic organization advertised *Soldiers of the Queen* at the Theatre Royal, Brisbane. Beneath his Brisbane advertisement, which informed the public that over one hundred people were engaged in the production, including the full regimental band of the Queensland Volunteer rifles, was another, which stated: "WANTED 100 UGLY MEN To take the part of Boers in the play 'Soldiers of the Queen.' Apply Theatre Royal today."[14] According to the *Courier* (26 February 1900):

> The drama . . . is made specially to appeal to the prevailing Australian patriotism in the sending away of contingents to the seat of war. . . . The first act is set in Australia and deals with the incidents which lead to the sending away of a contingent which is joined by the hero, Harold Ponsonby. . . . The subsequent acts are laid in South Africa. . . .

The newspaper advertisement for the play's first performance was even more explicit:

> War between the British and the Boers is pictured in its actual, deadly and ghastly progress. Australia is represented as loyally answering to the Mother-country's call to arms by sending A CONTINGENT OF SOLDIERS to the seat of war, and the splendid Courage displayed by the AUSTRALIAN BOYS in the deadly struggle between the British and their foes is depicted in glowing language and gallant DEEDS OF HEROISM.[15]

This play was not in fact of Australian origin, but allegedly an adaptation of *The Roll of the Drum*, which had in turn been adapted from *Neck or Nothing*, a melodrama first performed at the Grecian Theatre in East London in the 1870s. In its new form it had already been performed in Victoria and New South Wales prior to its presentation in Brisbane.[16] When it had been performed in Maitland, New South Wales, in January 1900, the *Maitland Daily*

Mercury (31 January 1900) had praised the way in which it was punctuated by plentiful patriotic allusions to British bravery, Australian loyalty, England's greatness and "our beloved Queen, which cannot fail but find an echo in any but the breast of the most bitter pro-Boer."

The most acclaimed Boer War melodrama performed in Australia was not Australian in either background or authorship, but was from the pen of an English dramatist. Trading on the popularity of Kipling's famous poem, Arthur Shirley had fashioned a play, *The Absent-Minded Beggar,* first performed at the Princess's Theatre, London, on 25 November 1899. The drama commenced in a London flag factory, a setting that provided ample opportunity for patriotic comment. After the recruitment of a number of likely "absent-minded beggars" and a review of the troops in Hyde Park by Queen Victoria, the action moved to South Africa, where the machinations of a wicked Boer, a rescue of British passengers from an armored train, and a number of battle scenes, with the veldt on fire in the background, contributed further to plot and spectacle. It was first staged in Australia by Bland Holt, at the Theatre Royal, Brisbane, in May 1900, although the Theatre Royal's stage proved too small to accommodate all the auxiliaries deployed in the final battle scene. The production proved very popular when it moved to Sydney, although the *Herald* (16 July 1900) noted that the patriotic speeches met with little response from the gallery and that the play's appeal depended on action and spectacle. Indeed, it seems that patriotic sentiment was not quite at the "white heat" it had reached a few months previously. Nevertheless, when the play arrived in Melbourne in November, the *Argus* (5 November 1900) praised Bland Holt for the success of his "bold attempt" to put the Boer War on the stage and noted that:

> Before the final fall of the curtain the audience are treated to the sight of Pretoria thronged with regiments in war-worn khaki—the Australians prominent of course—and a famous trio of commanders ride side by side to the footlights. (Sir Redvers Buller, General Baden-Powell and Lord Roberts).

This was probably the most popular of the Boer War plays to be staged in Australia and signifies a peak in this sort of drama.

Such dramas tended to endorse pro-British sentiments not only through the vilification of Kruger and the Boers but also through what the Australian manager George Musgrove referred to as "their melodramatic claptrap about the British soldier against the world and a regiment of soldiers about to die giving cheers for the Queen."[17] A further element was the Australianization of such melodramas through the presence of Australian contingents arriving to save the mother country's troops in the nick of time. Australian support of British imperialism was thus compounded with national and patriotic sentiment, which enhanced the status of the colony through an implicit superiority in military prowess while at the same time upholding a notion of intense loyalty. Whether these plays were the more superior efforts of Bland Holt (*For England, Youth,* and *The Absent-Minded Beggar*) or the rougher efforts of Anderson or Barry, they inevitably carried the same message. Any tensions implicit in the colonial-imperialist relationship were subsumed and resolved, although both the nature of the representation and the ideological stance embedded in such plays were shortly to change.

Throughout 1900 and 1901 performances of military melodramas continued, although many now had no or very little connection with the Boer War. *On Active Service, The Ladder of Life, The Bugle Call, The Little Drummer Boys, The Second in Command, A London Arab,* and *The Death or Glory Boys* are examples of such dramas, all deriving from England, although there was a gradual decline in the popularity of the genre from mid-1900 onwards. *The Death or Glory Boys,* performed by William Anderson's company at the Sydney Criterion in August 1901, includes a scene in the South African desert in which Jack, the soldier-hero, provides a rather bleak (and far from euphoric) view of military life when he responds to the view that "bravery" is what makes a soldier fight:

> JACK. So the world says, but isn't it rather "desperation"—the
> choice between speedy delivery at the enemies' hands or the
> desperation of a long campaign, the uncertainty of life, the
> knowledge that we might never see the sun rise on the
> morrow, the longing for action brought on by forced marches
> and privation. The condemned Criminal walks without a
> struggle to the scaffold. Why, because he has to. We, we have
> to fight, and all for what the world calls bravery!
> NAT. But you forget Jack, we have our medals.
> JACK. Which many an old soldier has to sell to buy himself food.
> Then, where is the glory, the glory of the noble battles
> fought and won by our country's soldiers—the glory that
> leaves sorrowing wives and children—the glory that lays its
> warriors on a bed of pain and sickness—the glory for which
> we give our lives. [*Pause*] It's all very well in song, Nat—
> it's all very well in song.[18]

In the same month *Riding to Win,* which was staged at the Melbourne Theatre Royal, contained a comic Australian servant, Sam Flutter, who volunteers for military service in the Boer War, but comes home disillusioned with army life.[19] The role was played by Bland Holt, who was also responsible for the staging of the play. *A London Arab*, at Sydney's Lyceum Theatre in October 1901, based on a play first performed at the Surrey Theatre, London, in March 1899, actually retained a prewar scene set in South Africa, where its fugitive hero, Alfred, is working in the diamond mines:

> ALFRED. . . . Bah! I am sick of it all—this residence in a country where freedom is denied to strangers. We Uitlanders are bound hand and foot. We are muzzled, spied upon at every turn, practically prisoners at large. Let a word be breathed against any Englishman, and Heaven help him—let him be denounced as an enemy of the state, and his life may not be worth an hour's purchase.
>
> [*Voice heard in distance singing "Britons Never Will Be Slaves"*]
>
> This is the wrong place, mate, to sing that—a country where Britons allow themselves to be denied even a Briton's birthright—the freedom of speech. . . . Well, let's hope there are better times coming. It's our soldiers who have cleared the land of blacks for them—it's our money that has made the country what it is—they can't rule it for themselves, and sooner or later we'll have to rule it for them.[20]

Even if the *Bulletin* (12 October 1901) considered that "the gallery now takes this raving against the Boers in a dull and passive spirit," it is interesting that, as the Boer War dragged ignominiously on, a play containing a neat summation of the prima facie British argument for war should be preferred to a depiction of the current situation. Perhaps it was necessary, by late 1901, to be reminded why this extraordinary war had been declared in the first place.

There are a number of reasons for the declining representation of the Boer War on the Australian stage even while the war was still firmly in progress. The first of these was not specific only to Australia. John MacKenzie suggests that a taste for military spectacle on the stage was declining, since it was "now being satisfied by the real thing, particularly with the advent of newsreel film."[21] The Boer War, according to MacKenzie, provided a great stimulus for the commercial exploitation of film and many scenes from the front were shown. Much of this was faked anti-Boer propaganda:

These latter masterpieces, filmed in locations as diverse as London's
Hampstead Heath and a garden on the outskirts of Bolton, show
scruffy unwashed Boers sometimes attacking a hospital tent, or
shooting in the back a British soldier who has just given a wounded
Boer some water.[22]

The real thing (supposedly) replaced stage illusion. The *Bulletin* (24 March
1900), predictably less impressed than most other journals, complained
that many of the films were out-of—date by the time they arrived and cast
aspersions on their quality and veracity. Yet the taste for photographic representation of the war continued unabated, as witnessed by the enthusiastic attendance at Boer War lectures, many of which were illustrated by
lantern slides. Even the most competent of theatrical scene painters suddenly had their work cut out to compete with all this.

However, it would be misleading to suggest that film alone was responsible for a decline in live presentation of Boer War material on the Australian
stage. For, as the Boer War progressed, the films that were shown included
less and less war footage, concentrating instead on sporting and other current events. Perhaps those who had remained behind were beginning to be
bored by the war: it is interesting to note that the first group of invalids to
return from the war in May 1900 were enthusiastically received, but by
August of the same year such receptions were much more subdued. The reason for this is partly summarized by Field:

> Continuing enthusiasm for the departure and arrival of troops
> was possible only if those troops were fighting bloody battles in
> a noble cause, but the desperate fighting had ceased almost
> before the Australians had reached the field and feeling against
> the Boers had subsided once they ceased to pose a threat to
> Imperial prestige, and once the press was obliged to drop the fic-
> tion of an evil, grasping foe in the face of contrary testimony
> from such correspondents as the widely read and highly
> respected Patterson.[23]

Even conceding an undoubted need for escapist entertainment by an
audience satiated with an excessive diet of war, it is clear that the latter
stages of the war provided less glamorous scope for patriotic songs and military melodramas. The notorious "scorched earth" policy of the British
against the Boers had given rise to increasing indignation. "The Generals,"
wrote Corporal Thompson of the Queensland Bushmen, "will get a shock
if we have to go on burning houses over women and children. We will

mutiny some of these days and refuse to do it."[24] Burning homes and crops, destroying cattle, and placing women and children in disease-ridden concentration camps was hardly fit material for the contemporary stage. Nor was the poor showing of the British army, which had proved itself woefully inadequate in confrontation with a considerably less numerous foe. Admittedly, the Australian troops had proved their worth in the early part of the war, but their morale was soured by a number of incidents which occurred in 1901.

In June of that year a Victorian contingent was the victim of a surprise attack at Wilmansrust by Boers. Subsequently a British officer, General Beaston, accused the Victorian and Western Australian troops of cowardice, causing widespread offense. Shortly afterwards three Victorian soldiers were tried for incitement to mutiny; on 11 July they were all found guilty and sentenced to death, although their sentences were commuted to imprisonment. The federal Australian government first learnt of the sentences in September from a report in an Australian newspaper. If the news of the defeat at Wilmansrust had been bad, the news of the sentencing was even worse. "It provoked in Australia a sense of outrage tempered uncomfortably by guilt," writes Gavin Souter. "How could a British General be so grossly offensive to Australian troops, and how could the British army sentence Australians to death in such an arbitrary and secret manner? On the other hand, who could wholeheartedly defend what was said to be incitement to mutiny? . . . The Wilmansrust affair brought national pride into collision with imperial loyalty."[25] Additionally, there was the case of the Bush Veldt Carbineers. Three Australians, "Breaker" Morant, P. J. Handcock, and G. R. Witton, were charged with the murder of several Boer prisoners and of a German missionary who had witnessed the killings. Morant and Handcock, after secret court martials, were executed by firing squad in February 1902. This episode, says L. M. Field, "did more than anything else to foster Australian disenchantment with the war."[26]

Federation, which occurred on the first day of 1901, may also have deflected attention from the war, although it did nothing to diminish Australia's commitment. In fact, Australia's allegiance to and dependency on the British Empire remained very much intact: if federation was nationalist in impetus, it was certainly not anti-imperialist. Australians listened with equanimity to the English actor Wilson Barrett's farewell speech in Sydney at the end of 1901, in which he graced his audience at Her Majesty's Theatre with a few patronizing words about their new federal status and their ongoing commitment to the Boer War:

He then closed his valedictory with the words "Advance Australia."
(Cheers) And how wonderfully the country had advanced in that
brief space of time! They were now a people, a nation, young and
sturdy, not running fast at present, as in the plenitude of strength,
but beginning to walk with no uncertain step. (Cheers)[27]

He also informed his audience that at Colombo he had been told by some
exiled Boers that the British colonies would desert England:

But he replied, "Never will Australia or Canada or New Zealand
go back in their loyalty to the flag." (Loud cheers, and cries of
"Never!") And he would venture to add that never would the
Commonwealth Parliament say one single word that would cause
any serious difference with the Imperial Government. (Cheers)[28]

Yet, despite Barrett's laudations, a war that had been supported with such
enthusiasm by Australia at its commencement had more-or-less disappeared
from the forefront of public concern by the time it ended in 1902. Barbara
R. Penny suggests that "Australia's participation in the Boer War had been
a consolidating rather than a shattering experience."[29] Inexorably linked
with federation, it symbolized a coming of age, a rite of passage. But rites
of passage can be brutalizing experiences, as L. M. Field implies:

After 31 months of war peace came to South Africa. . . . The Boers
went back to their devastated farms to begin the long and heart-
breaking process of rebuilding. The British went home to enquire
into the poor showing of their cumbersome military machine. The
Australians went back to find their nation bent on forgetting the
whole thing. Peace came as a blessing to the Australian people, not
because it ended a period of national bloodshed and grief, but
because it closed an episode in their history which in their enthusiasm and ignorance they had elevated into a great national trial
and triumph; only to find, as their enthusiasm dulled and their
ignorance lifted, that they were embroiled in a war that brought no
national honor.[30]

If Field's conclusions are correct, they provide as good an explanation as any
for the evident decline of interest in the Boer War on the Australian stage
after 1900.

Consequently, it is hardly surprising that Australian melodrama moved
closer to the position advocated throughout the war by the republican
Bulletin. There had been opposition to the war both in Britain and Australia,

but whereas in Britain this had been influenced by class, pacifist, and anti-capitalist sentiment, in Australia it had depended more on the extent to which individuals identified with mother-country or colony. According to Professor Arnold Wood, who nearly lost his chair at Sydney University due to his opposition to the war: "It seems evident, then, that the minority against the war is very great, and . . . it is strongest in the most Australian parts of Australia."[31] Nevertheless, very little intrinsically Australian drama emerged in response to the war. The majority of the plays were adaptations of British sources, most of which originated in theatres such as the Whitechapel Pavilion, the Borough (Stratford), the Surrey, the Broadway Theatre (New Cross), or from the provinces. Only *Youth*, *The Absent-Minded Beggar*, and *The Bugle Call* had originated in London's West End. In other words, most of the melodramatic adaptations from British sources had first been performed in neighborhood theatres catering to working-class or lower-middle-class audiences.[32] Ironically, even if the colonial and imperialistic issues raised for Australians by the Boer War were negotiated through popular forms such as melodrama, it was through the adaptation of English material rather than through any home-grown product (a recurrent trait on the Australian stage throughout the nineteenth and early twentieth centuries) that such negotiations were transacted.

N o t e s

1. J. S. Bratton, *Acts of Supremacy: The British Empire and the Stage, 1790-1930* (Manchester: Manchester University Press, 1991), 22-27.
2. L. M. Field, *The Forgotten War* (Melbourne: Melbourne University Press, 1979), 2.
3. Barbara R. Penny, "Australia's Reaction to the Boer War: A Study in Colonial Imperialism," *Journal of British Studies* 7, no. 1 (1967): 129.
4. Field, *The Forgotten War*, 3.
5. Gavin Souter, *Lion and Kangaroo Australia, 1901-1919: The Rise of a Nation* (Australia: Fontana Collins, 1978), 64.
6. Field, *The Forgotten War*, 32.
7. The music halls in Harry Rickard's circuit were particularly patriotic, even importing singers like Tom Costello and Paul Pelham. According to Richard Waterhouse, "The Australian involvement in the Boer War engendered an initial wave of imperial patriotism here, especially amongst the middle class, and local songwriters adapted the English material to emphasise the particular Australian contribution to imperial security." *From Minstrel Show to Vaudeville: The Australian Popular Stage, 1788-1914*, (New South Wales: New South Wales

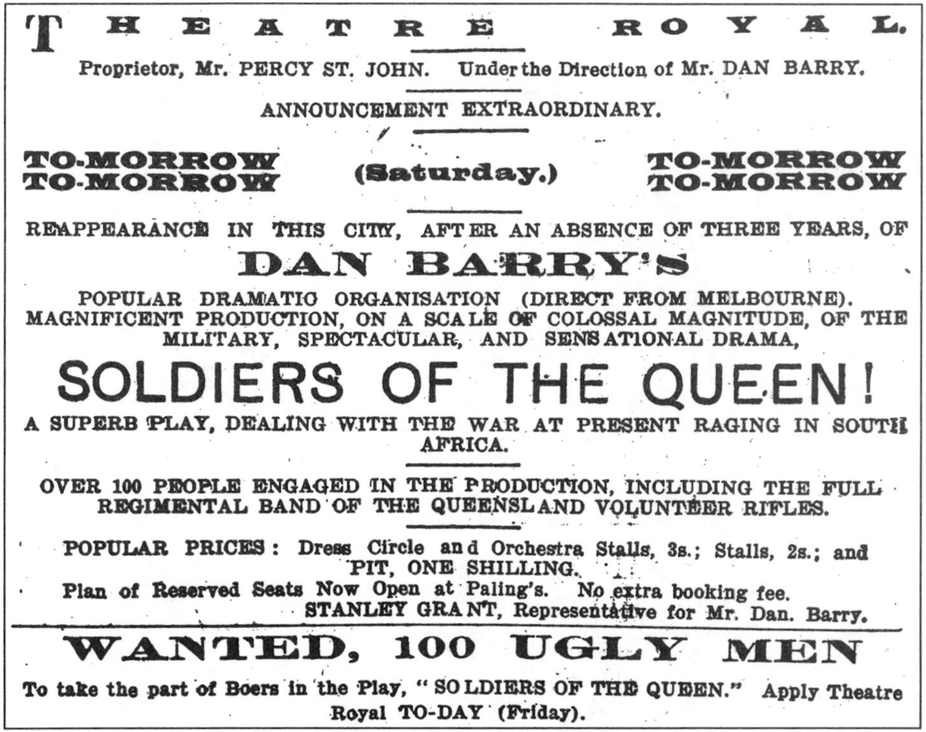

THEATRE ROYAL.

Proprietor, Mr. PERCY ST. JOHN.   Under the Direction of Mr. DAN BARRY.

ANNOUNCEMENT EXTRAORDINARY.

TO-MORROW
TO-MORROW   (Saturday.)   TO-MORROW
TO-MORROW

REAPPEARANCE IN THIS CITY, AFTER AN ABSENCE OF THREE YEARS, OF

DAN BARRY'S

POPULAR DRAMATIC ORGANISATION (DIRECT FROM MELBOURNE).
MAGNIFICENT PRODUCTION, ON A SCALE OF COLOSSAL MAGNITUDE, OF THE
MILITARY, SPECTACULAR, AND SENSATIONAL DRAMA,

SOLDIERS OF THE QUEEN!

A SUPERB PLAY, DEALING WITH THE WAR AT PRESENT RAGING IN SOUTH
AFRICA.

OVER 100 PEOPLE ENGAGED IN THE PRODUCTION, INCLUDING THE FULL
REGIMENTAL BAND OF THE QUEENSLAND VOLUNTEER RIFLES.

POPULAR PRICES : Dress Circle and Orchestra Stalls, 3s. ; Stalls, 2s. ; and
PIT, ONE SHILLING.

Plan of Reserved Seats Now Open at Paling's.   No extra booking fee.
STANLEY GRANT, Representative for Mr. Dan. Barry.

WANTED, 100 UGLY MEN

To take the part of Boers in the Play, "SOLDIERS OF THE QUEEN."   Apply Theatre
Royal TO-DAY (Friday).

FIGURE 3. An illustration for *Soldiers of the Queen,*
advertisement from *Brisbane Courier,* February 23, 1900.
COURTESY OF THE STATE LIBRARY OF NEW SOUTH WALES.

University Press, 1990), 128. Initially, the annual pantomimes, especially Bernard Espinasse's *Little Red Riding Hood*, also reflected a strongly patriotic bias.

8. *Argus*, 1 September 1899.
9. *Brisbane Courier*, 5 February 1900.
10. *Brisbane Courier*, 5 February 1900.
11. This was Dampier's third adaptation of the novel, on this occasion under the pseudonym of Adam Pierre.
12. *Sydney Morning Herald*, 25 June 1900.
13. *Brisbane Courier*, 14 October 1899.
14. *Brisbane Courier*, 23 February 1900.
15. *Brisbane Courier*, 23 February 1900.
16. The earliest copyright application for the play was made in Melbourne on 28 November 1899, claiming the play was first performed on 9 November 1899 at Her Majesty's Theatre, Ballarat. (Register of Copyright, Victorian Colonial Series, CRS, A2389, vol. 5, item 9270, Aust. Archives, Canberra). The earlier history of the play is traced by Stanley Grant, "Dan Barry Anecdotes," *Theatre Magazine*, 1 March 1916.
17. Quoted in Richard Fotheringham, *Sport in Australian Drama* (Cambridge: Cambridge University Press, 1992), 120.
18. Mitchell Library, MSS. 1412/3, William Anderson Collection.
19. Margaret Williams, *Australia on the Popular Stage 1829-1929: An Historical Entertainment in Six Acts* (Melbourne: Oxford University Press, 1983), 204.
20. Mitchell Library, MSS 1412/6, William Anderson Collection.
21. John MacKenzie, *Propaganda and Empire: The Manipulation of British Public Opinion, 1880-1960* (Manchester: Manchester University Press, 1984), 48.
22. M. D. Blanch, "British Society and the War," in *The South African War: The Anglo-Boer War, 1899-1902*, ed. Peter Warwick (London: Longman, n.d.), 232.
23. Field, *The Forgotten War*, 128.
24. Souter, *Lion and Kangaroo*, 65-66.
25. Souter, *Lion and Kangaroo*, 61.
26. Field, *The Forgotten War*, 174
27. *Sydney Morning Herald*, 23 December 1901.
28. *Sydney Morning Herald*, 23 December 1901.
29. Penny, "Australia's Reaction to the Boer War," 127.
30. Field, *The Forgotten War*, 178-179.
31. Quoted in Patricia Rolfe, *The Journalistic Javelin: An Illustrated History of the Bulletin* (Sydney: Wildcat Press, 1979), 156.
32. This may have had more to do with evasion of copyright payments than with the social composition of Australian audiences. Of the plays discussed in this essay *For England* (Sutton Vane) and *Tommy Atkins* (Shirley and Landeck) were first performed at the Pavilion, Whitechapel; *A Soldier and a Man* (Landeck) at Worthing, Coventry and Clapham; *On Active Service* at the Surrey Theatre; *The Ladder of Life* at the Borough, Stratford; *The Bugle Call* at the Theatre Royal, Haymarket; *The Death or Glory Boys* at Darlington; and *Riding to Win* at the Broadway Theatre, New Cross.

3

FROM MELODRAMA TO REALISM: THE SUSPECT HISTORY OF AMERICAN DRAMA

THOMAS POSTLEWAIT

INTRODUCTION

*T*HE BASIC HISTORY OF AMERICAN DRAMA, as we usually narrate it, is a success story, one that charts the somewhat slow but consequential development of drama into its "maturity" by the 1920s.[1] The process of change is easy to track: nineteenth-century entertainment — popular, romantic, sentimental, and quintessentially melodramatic — gives way to twentieth-century drama in the modernist mode, predominately realistic. This progressive shift from melodrama to realism, occurring between the 1880s and the 1920s, is usually seen as either a step-by-step transformation of American playwriting or a difficult struggle between two adversarial forms. Whatever the case, the American drama comes of age when modern realistic drama supplants melodrama as the definitive dramatic form. A "drama of sincerity," in Sheldon Cheney's words, emerges out of a popular theatre of sensationalism and sentimentalism.[2]

This progressive narrative has become the established history of American drama, even though it slights or sets aside poetic tragedy, comedy, satire, farce, burlesque, minstrel plays, revues, opera-drama, musicals, nationalistic drama, and pageant drama — a rather significant dramatic history to bracket or ignore.[3] We prefer, however, to focus primarily on melodrama and realism when we present a developmental history. Yet even within these constraints, the history has several problems. In the first place, despite the pervasive usage of the key terms—melodrama, melodramatic, romantic, romance, realistic, realism, naturalistic, naturalism—there is no agreement on how to define and use them. This problem of terminology is common knowledge (and much lamented).[4] Not only do we have trouble distinguishing melodrama from realistic drama (as genres, types, modes, methods, attitudes, or practices), we also have difficulty dividing them historically from one another, the one genre or practice supposedly located in the nineteenth century, the other in the twentieth. This historical opposition, whereby realism or realistic drama wins the genre wars, not only begs the question of whether the concept of realism can be defined as a genre but also posits a questionable idea of historical process. We must thus wonder if genre categories, derived from formalist analysis, serve adequately as a basis for charting this developmental or transformational history.[5]

Nonetheless, we cannot avoid using these terms, in part because they are established in our scholarly commentaries. Also, and this is probably most telling, these concepts were used by the major participants in the history itself. So we are caught in a dilemma. Unless we are prepared to ignore historical and scholarly practices (seeking instead a whole set of new concepts), we must use these familiar terms while recognizing that they are part of the problem we want to study.

Besides this essential matter of proper definition, we face difficulties in how we identify and interpret the historical evidence—the key facts, texts, performances, and figures. Part of the trouble stems from our tendency to take the "primary" evidence on its own terms, as if the initiating agents who produced the documents were objective observers and participants, without any self-serving or self-limiting motives, ideas, and purposes. For example, we have allowed the advocates for realism to determine many of the key terms and issues in our historical surveys. We grant these major figures, such as Henry James and W. D. Howells, the authority to pronounce the truth (which is to say, their truth becomes our truth). Also, we have established some questionable propositions on the generic and historical relations between melodrama and realistic drama. The issue here is not simply a matter of definition and evaluation but a procedural problem in how we chart and explain the processes of historical change for the two theatrical forms. Moreover, given our working assumptions on how and why dramatic realism emerged, we have privileged certain documents, events, and figures at the expense of other possible historical sources and contributing factors. Thus, over a period of three or four generations our scholarly commentary (both formalist and contextualist) has become not only circumscribed but distorted by a set of analytical procedures and interpretive ideas which shape our historical narratives. Perhaps at this time it is appropriate to review and reconsider our established history of American drama. We may be stuck with some of the key concepts, but we can still reconceive the organizational models and narratives.

PART I: SCHOLARLY CONSENSUS; OR, THE MAKING OF A HISTORICAL NARRATIVE

> *In the development of the American drama a promising feature is the tendency toward realism as opposed to conventionalism. By realism should be inferred not actualism, but the artistic representation of reality.*
>
> —WILLIAM GILLETTE
> playwright and actor
> "American Playwrights on the American Drama"
> *Harper's Weekly,* 1889

> *The realist . . . appears when the romanticist's . . . dreams are beginning to lose color.*
> —RICHARD MOODY
> historian
> *America Takes the Stage,* 1955

The major figure in the transformational history of American drama is of course Eugene O'Neill, who is credited with bringing American drama to its "maturity." He is, in the measured words of the *Cambridge Guide to American Theatre,* "the first U.S. playwright of major talent, the only one ever to win the Nobel Prize for Literature (in 1936), and still universally regarded as America's finest." Actually, the agreement on his talent is hardly universal; indeed, the debate continues to this day. But nonetheless we certainly identify O'Neill as the "imaginative and gifted" playwright who, more than anyone else, transformed American drama into a serious art form.[6]

Perhaps nothing serves better as an emblem of the decisive changes in American theatre than O'Neill's struggles with his father, James O'Neill, the famous actor who played the melodramatic lead in Charles Fechter's dramatization of *The Count of Monte Cristo.* Anyone familiar with Eugene O'Neill's great American masterpiece of realism, *Long Day's Journey into Night,* knows the standard version of the conflict. In the character of James Tyrone, modeled on his father, the playwright dissects the false ways and suspect authority of the aging patriarch. Set in 1912, the twilight days of the Gilded Age, the play thus represents two interrelated struggles. Autobiographically it portrays, in its harrowing family saga, Eugene O'Neill's personal revolt against his histrionic father; formally it offers, in its realistic technique and aesthetic agenda, a defiant rejection of the melodramatic heritage of American theatre. Thus both topically and structurally the play can be understood as an implicit indictment of a theatrical heritage of false fathers, epitomized by not only the melodramatic actor James O'Neill but such dramatists as Dion Boucicault, Augustin Daly, Bartley Campbell, Owen Davis, and David Belasco, those suspect crafters of an illusionary theatre that privileged grand actions and rhetorical posturing. The fathers—real and surrogate—are found guilty of bombast, shallowness, and lies.

Not surprisingly, given O'Neill's great achievement, we have turned him into the progenitor of modern American drama. (Perhaps the irony is appropriate: the slayer of fathers becomes the revered father figure.) Melodrama consequently slides into shadowy disregard, vanquished by O'Neill and his followers. His accomplishments, so substantial, eclipse the playwrights (including Howells, Herne, Moody, Fitch, Sheldon, and Crothers) who attempted to create a realistic drama in the decades before the arrival of O'Neill. They have become obscure figures in the history books, serving as mere precursors to his progressive genius. It is now a truism for us that the real history of American drama begins with him. The rationale is familiar, as Gerald M. Berkowitz expressed it recently:

> The American drama is, for all practical purposes, the twentieth-century American drama. There were plays written and performed on the American continent well before there was a United States, and during the nineteenth century the American theatre was widespread and active. But, as was also true in much of Europe, it was, with rare exceptions, not the home of a particularly rich or ambitious literature. . . . This is not to say that the playwrights of the nineteenth century were without talent, but that, like television writers, they were more likely to be artisans skilled at producing the entertaining effects that audiences wanted, than artists looking to illuminate the human condition or challenge received values.[7]

Here we have the terms of a familiar binarism. On the twentieth-century side of the great divide we find complex and ambitious drama, dedicated artists, and challenging plays about the human condition. On the nineteenth-century side we have derivative entertainment, theatrical artisans, and the constraining values of popular taste. The one is serious and complex; the other is frivolous and simple. Historically, then, the period between 1880 and 1920 becomes the age of transition—an awkward, adolescent age when the drama, struggling to shed its exuberant youthfulness, begins to achieve adulthood.

From our current perspective, shaped by the modernist canon and a century of theatrical innovation, few of us have trouble with Berkowitz's statement, which accords with almost all critical studies published since the 1930s.[8] Even critics and historians who are familiar with the earlier drama and recognize its social importance in American history agree that it lacks literary value. For example, C. W. E. Bigsby, clearing the way for his valuable and well-received study of modern American drama, announces that "American drama, as a serious form, is a product of the twentieth century."[9] He does note that Walter Meserve—in his series of books—shows that the American drama before O'Neill had "a long and fascinating prehistory." But the very term "prehistory" comes close to dismissing all early drama from required consideration. Meserve, an authority on nineteenth-century drama, seems to agree with this judgment: "No one need argue that the literary value of American drama during its first 200 years is very slight. That goes without saying."[10] With Meserve and Bigsby in apparent agreement, who wishes to disagree? Still, we must marvel at the power of the word "serious," which in this context can exile the American drama and culture of the eighteenth and nineteenth centuries into an ahistorical limbo.

Of course, there has been significant and praiseworthy scholarship on the earlier drama, including the work of Montrose J. Moses, Arthur Hobson Quinn, and Richard Moody. More recently, besides Meserve, both Jack Vaughn and Gary Richardson have surveyed the premodern terrain.[11] But almost without exception these consolidating studies rest upon the assumption that American drama, in its historical progression from the earliest days, finally grew up (approached maturity, achieved wholeness, attained seriousness) between 1880 and 1920. As Meserve argues, summarizing the standard viewpoint, the first important "milepost" in the "rise of realism" occurred in 1890 with James Herne's *Margaret Fleming.* And then by 1920, with "the creative work of the Provincetown Players and the imaginative genius of Eugene O'Neill" leading the way, "American drama was transformed into something more vital than it had been, but the result obtained was the product of forces at work in America since the beginning of the century." In brief, through a process of transformation, "realism on stage prevailed"—not only over melodrama but also over the theatrical conditions of commercialism that had limited the full development of American drama.[12] Given this narrative, some theatre historians and critics even seem to believe, as Gerald Bordman stated in 1994, that "melodrama disappeared from the

American stages" by World War I.[13] Apparently, once realistic drama attained dominance, melodrama retired in defeat.

To a great extent, these evolutionary and adversarial narratives now guide our research and analysis. Generic forms and their transformations provide the categorical order; developments and their directions serve as the historical imperative. The historian of drama thus looks for how and when realism contributed to what Barnard Hewitt, in *Theatre USA*, called the "fulfillment" of American drama and theatre.[14] Given this formal and historical argument, we try to locate a turning point or at least a series of key points in the development. Too readily, then, we reason backwards from O'Neill to his precursors, as if previous dramatists and theatre practices were but partial fulfillments of a manifest destiny. For example, Alan S. Downer, surveying the drama from 1860 to 1920, gives it the rubric of "Waiting for O'Neill."[15] The phrase captures our retrospective ordering of the past (and also our impatience with the long delay).

Perhaps the most important scholar in the making of this persuasive history has been Arthur Hobson Quinn. Since he published his definitive *A History of the American Drama* in the 1920s and 1930s, two generations of theatre scholars have followed his lead. Quinn's *History*, which is still the foundational study for most of us, solidified a canon and a tradition. In this multivolume work, well-researched and well-written, he described the development of a progressively realistic and "sincere" drama that emerged out of the matrix of nineteenth-century drama and theatre. It is important to note, however, that this historical understanding—as well as the formal categories that go with it—was not the creation of Quinn. He himself benefited from the writings of his near contemporaries, including Montrose J. Moses, Walter Prichard Eaton, Thomas H. Dickinson, and Sheldon Cheney.[16] And he was also guided by the crucial scholarship of J. Brander Matthews (to whom he dedicated his study).[17] In many ways, Matthews set the standard for Quinn's accomplishment.

For instance, an early essay by Matthews in 1875, misleadingly titled "The Decline of the Drama," raises the familiar complaint about the lack of good drama in America:

> American literature and American pictorial art are artistically in advance of the American drama. Most of the native productions of our stage are written by artisans and not by artists; by playwrights, not by dramatists; by men more or less expert in building pieces, but entirely incapable of creating a play.[18]

Matthews's lament (now our historical judgment) is a familiar one in nine-teenth-century commentary on the theatre, expressed by various writers, including, most famously, Edgar Allen Poe, W. D. Howells, Henry James, Hamlin Garland, and Walt Whitman. This critique of popular drama, extend-ing continuously from the nineteenth century to the present, is not merely the party line of the champions of high culture; it provides the necessary histor-ical condition for the belated yet required alternative: the realistic drama.

There is no question, of course, about the importance of modern realism and the campaigns for it. With the arrival of realism, manifesting itself in var-ious artistic forms and movements, a clear alternative to popular melodrama asserted itself—especially in the commentary of the advocates for realism. Today it is difficult, if not impossible, to measure and distribute all the many causes and credits for the emergence of realism in the modern arts. But in playwriting Ibsen was obviously the major force and influence, providing not only a model but the justification for change.[19] Consequently, no history of the emergence of American realism can be separated from the international origins of modern drama. (*A Doll's House* was published in 1879). Even the most provincial or independent developments in American drama show some signs of European influence, either directly or indirectly. Moreover, the progressive and evolutionary ideas that guided this historical narrative were also international, so the development cannot be limited to the particular events and ideologies of American culture (artistic and socio-political).

Still, of the American leaders in the campaign for realism in the late nine-teenth century, one of the most important figures is William Dean Howells.[20] In our historical view, Howells's commitment to realism matters far more than the fact that he attempted (in a search for profit) to write farces, comedies, and romantic melodramas for the popular theatre. His critical essays take pride of place. Part of his success in making the case for realism came from setting up melodrama as the adversary. As Brenda Murphy notes, Howells "became adept at separating the elements of realism from the old melodramatic con-ventions in . . . American plays, to praise the one and excoriate the other." In short, "melodrama became the *bête noire* of the realistic theatre critic."[21]

Supporting Howells, somewhat haphazardly, were several playwrights, including James A. Herne, Edward Harrigan, and William Gillette (not that any of them abandoned melodramatic conventions in their plays). Even Augustin Daly, a dramatist not usually associated with the realist movement, joined the rallying cry for the "future American dramatist" who would redeem the American stage.[22] And more forcefully, Herne argued for a theatre of truth that would become an alternative to the theatre of amuse-ment. As every history book now points out, his play *Margaret Fleming*

(1890) achieved aspects of this realistic drama (though his melodramatic sensibility still shaped character and situation). Not surprisingly, given our determination to write a history that privileges the key turning points in the victory of realism over melodrama, Herne and his play (and the documents generated by Hamlin Garland and others in support of the play) have become central to the narrative. We need him to be either the "American Ibsen," the decisive rebel with a cause, or the *figura* of a messiah in the person of Eugene O'Neill.[23]

So, the binarism of realism versus melodrama (or realism versus romanticism), articulated forcefully in the theatrical commentary of the late nineteenth century, has become the basis for our history of American drama. And why not? Obviously, *Margaret Fleming* appeared in 1890. More importantly, a series of playwrights, from Howells to O'Neill, set up melodrama as the Other, the blocking force against which realism had to struggle. Since the participants themselves saw the development in these terms, surely we must record their words, appreciate their insights, and honor their contributions. Accordingly, twentieth-century critics and historians, accepting this rhetorical and analytical heritage, have become advocates for realism, adjudicators of its key figures and plays, and justifiers of its triumph. In brief, Howells's campaign is our history.

This history—and its guiding principles—can also be charted in two other critical practices: the publishing of play anthologies and the collection of historical documents. For example, Arthur Hobson Quinn's famous anthology, *Representative American Plays*, which went through seven editions (1917, 1925, 1928, 1930, 1938, 1953, and 1957), established a tradition consistent with the argument in his *History of the American Drama*. Likewise, Richard Moody's important anthology (with its excellent introductions), *Dramas from the American Theatre, 1762-1909*, reflects his sympathetic analysis of the early theatre in *America Takes the Stage*. Moody expanded Quinn's canon, but did not change the tradition. These influential anthologies, which regrettably are now out of print, have guided teaching and shaped publication.[24]

Despite the fact that several scholars have provided detailed, extensive surveys of nineteenth-century American drama (George C. D. Odell, Richard Moody, Walter Meserve, David Grimsted, and Bruce McConachie among them), most critical and historical studies published today follow the standard anthologies, treating the collected plays as the canon. And they hold to the developmental thesis. For example, consider two well-received historical studies from 1993.

In *Melodrama and the Myth of America*, Jeffrey Mason focuses on *Metamora, The Drunkard, Uncle Tom's Cabin, My Partner,* and *Shenandoah* to present the history of American drama and culture in the nineteenth century. These are popular, important plays, studied with historical care, but they are also the usual suspects, regularly rounded up for display or indictment. In the process, the plays must carry the burden of representing a century of American drama and culture (portrayed in negative terms as a self-deceived age of sentimental vision and mythic ideology). Mason's abiding thesis is that "melodrama is a means of affirming a belief in a reductive perception of reality." This "construction" of melodrama, though expressed in the current terms of cultural studies, accords well with the standard attacks on melodrama by the advocates for realism (yet they probably would not have constructed the idea of America in quite the same critical manner).[25]

Somewhat surprisingly, few critical and historical studies today take advantage of the most important collection of early plays, Barrett H. Clark's *America's Lost Plays* in twenty volumes. To his credit, Gary Richardson, in *American Drama: From the Colonial Period through World War I*, attempts to open up the canon by analyzing some of the plays in the Clark volumes.[26] But for the most part he too holds to the representative plays in Quinn and Moody. Richardson's critical and pedagogical aim is "to prompt a wholesale rethinking of [the] attitude" that there is no worthy drama before O'Neill. Accordingly, he purposefully tries to avoid offering "a totalizing, teleological narrative tracing the development of the national drama." Nonetheless, Quinn's key plays and shaping argument on the progressive change from melodrama to realism remain the central line of investigation. For example, at the end of his crucial chapter on "the development of realism," Richardson praises the accomplishments of the transitional playwrights:

> As America rang in the new century, the ascendancy of realistic drama was not yet at hand, but the first tentative steps had been taken. A new generation of playwrights — more comprehensive in their vision, more daring in their techniques, and, in some instances, more artistic in their expressions — would continue along the path that their precursors had blazed.[27]

This narrative, with its familiar metaphors, points yet again to the arrival of O'Neill. Teleological narratives are hard to suppress.

Thus, on the one hand, the major anthologies have placed the premodern American drama before us for educational and scholarly study; yet, on the other hand, they have helped to establish the idea that these plays, the lost heritage, are forerunners of a more important drama that emerges in the twentieth century. The anthologies, despite their editors' intentions to honor the early drama, signal and sanction the trajectory toward realism. They thereby document the developmental struggle of American drama to achieve maturity. As for the collection of documents, consider *The Dawning of American Drama: American Dramatic Criticism, 1746-1915*, edited by Jürgen C. Wolter. Wolter's title reveals the organizing principle: the most important documents are those that illustrate the awakening of American drama, its progression toward the full light of day. The giant slumbers until realism stirs its imagination. Consequently, this collection features various essays and articles that complain about melodrama, jeremiads alternating with polemics. And most importantly, it gathers together many of the documents on the campaign for realism, "the prolonged dawning of the American drama."[28] Wolter has collected many valuable essays, but once again the familiar binarism provides the organizing principle, as if the advocates for realism were making the selections.

This is our abiding history. And if a figure such as Howells slips out of sight, as he did by the 1950s, our scholarly job is to pull him back into the limelight so that the narrative remains in place.[29] This kind of scholarship, often first-rate in its documentary aspects, provides a crucial historical record. But it also reminds us that the academic field of theatre studies has become in large measure the caretaker of an established version of American dramatic history. For this reason, scholars such as Quinn, Moody, and Hewitt are doubly important; not only did they produce the scholarship that shaped our historical understanding, they also trained the next generation of scholars who now refine and maintain the tradition. The dissertations become articles and books, as these scholars continue to consolidate the standard history of American drama. Though hardly an ordained gospel (or a conspiracy cooked up by bearded men in tweed), this received standard version has attained its own hegemonic charm.

Perhaps, however, a more dialectical understanding—and less rhetorical polarization—might help in our history of realism and melodrama. The key question is this: is it necessary today, from our historical perspective, to frame and explain the changes in American dramatic history either in the pejorative manner of the advocates of realism or in the defensive and recuperative manner of contemporary scholarship? Specifically, is melodrama to be categorized as either an opposing form that realism defeated or an embryo out of which the modern drama emerged? Should our understanding of melodrama's place in American dramatic history be conditioned and controlled by these narratives? Also, should we continue to perceive melodrama not only as the mere forerunner of realistic drama but as a lesser kind of drama? I think not. But in order to reconceive melodrama and its relation to realism we need to understand how and why this narrative was formulated and continues to be so convincing.

Obviously, there is an important history to tell on the emergence of realism in American drama and theatre (told well recently by Brenda Murphy), but it cannot be contained satisfactorily within our standard narratives of either the theatre of growth or the theatre of revolt. If we are not careful, we end up writing the typical history of the winners, whereby the modernist trajectory is all that finally matters. Moreover, we seem determined to celebrate the artistic rebel, an endearing figure from romanticism through postmodernism. Ironically, then, we tend to arrange the history of American drama according to melodramatic conventions—a primary conflict between good and bad drama, high and low culture, innovative art and retrograde tradition, enlightened critique and false consciousness.

In other words, we have decided to side with Eugene O'Neill against James O'Neill. In this sense, as historians, having accepted a pejorative definition of melodrama, we read the history of American drama with a melodramatic imagination. Of course, we continue to perceive *Long Day's Journey into Night* as a realistic play; indeed, we go another step and treat it as a historical document (given its realistic and autobiographical conventions). Then, making a paradoxical turn, we derive a melodramatic message from it. We smooth out the ambiguities and ironies so that the rebellious son triumphs—in our minds and hearts—over the delusory, canting father.[30] The son has our sympathy and our judgment, for we see the father as the villain. The son is right, the father is wrong. Realism delivers the indictment, the cross-examination, and the judgment. Melodrama is found guilty. Isn't that what history shows?

PART II: MANIFEST DESTINY; OR, THE EVOLUTIONARY NARRATIVE

The man on a trapeze recalls the ancestral monkey who swung by his tail from the forest tree; and the realist cannot all at once forget the romanticist.
　　　　　　　　　　　—WILLIAM DEAN HOWELLS
"The Moral Reformation of the Stage," 1891

The drama must pass through its evolution, through its periods of types and conditions.
　　　　　　　　　　　—MONTROSE J. MOSES
The American Dramatist, 1911

To reconfigure this history, we need to examine key assumptions and ideas that have guided the narrative for the last hundred years. One such concept, readily apparent, is the idea of evolution. And closely tied to it is the idea of progress. In the nineteenth century a series of related ideas on development, expansion, improvement, and progress permeated all aspects of American life and culture. The concepts as well as the rhetoric had become part of American values and experience.

Thus, subsequent to the religious attacks on theatre, which declined substantially by midcentury, much of the criticism on popular drama was articulated in the discourse of development and improvement. Whether moral or aesthetic (or a mix of the two), these critiques written by theatre reviewers and literary figures (and in time by scholars) presupposed that conditions should and could improve. The early religious warnings on the inherently corrupt and degenerative nature of theatre and drama were replaced by hopeful, optimistic polemics proclaiming that theatre and drama could be beneficial — and thus should evolve, with the country itself, toward greater complexity and quality. A flowering of culture must occur — if only melodrama did not retard development.

Similarly, the realistic dramatic theories of Howells, Garland, Herne, and others, including European observers of American drama such as William Archer, depended upon an evolutionary and progressive thesis about historical and aesthetic development. Evolutionary theory and American political philosophy easily merged. For example, James Herne, a believer in the ideas of Henry George and Herbert Spencer, proclaimed that "art is a corner stone of progress and liberty."[31] Howells likewise became an advocate of Spencer's popular theories of cultural Darwinism. Especially important were Spencer's theories on the evolutionary development of forms from simple to complex, the transformation of one organism into another, the teleological movement of history, and the struggle between individuals (and groups) within social and political systems.

Actually, as one reads the many complaints, laments, polemics, and manifestos written by advocates for a new, improved American drama in the realistic mode, several contradictory arguments emerge. One recurring argument mixes evolutionary ideas with assessments of literary value. Nineteenth-century melodrama, spreading throughout the nation, is seen not only as a simpler (earlier, cruder, incomplete, or primary) form but also as a pervasive presence that limits or resists the development of realism, which must fight for its niche. Being of superior quality, realistic drama must eventually triumph, but the battle is a difficult one. Melodrama thus became, in these arguments, the form that must give way to (or transform into) the maturing realistic drama with its social themes.

Two arguments, one about evolutionary progress and another about greater literary value, became fused (and confused) by the advocates for realism. They assumed that because realistic drama is supposed to be inherently more significant and sophisticated than melodrama (primarily because it focuses on social issues), it is therefore the historical end towards which the form of American drama must evolve. Adding to the confusion, the historical process was seen both as a progressive growth toward maturity (part of the ordained march of American culture) and as a struggle of the fittest—a battle between an entertainment behemoth of territorial ambitions and its brave if small adversary—the Theatre Syndicate on one side, the Little Theatre movement on the other.

And yet, despite the appeal of this simple to complex scenario, another recurring argument demanded just the opposite: a complex to simple historical development so that American drama could advance itself. Repeatedly in the nineteenth century, melodrama was identified with an overly complex and decadent European culture. Accordingly, if only American drama would throw off the yoke of European drama (all of those elaborate French, German, and English adaptations), it could redeem itself by becoming simple, honest, and artless, just like the popular Yankee characters. Native characters, local scenes (especially in the frontier), and simple virtues—here we find the true American drama. For example, in 1889 Bronson Howard placed *Davy Crockett, Rip Van Winkle,* and *My Partner* "among the characteristically American plays."[32] And Hamlin Garland's one major complaint about *Margaret Fleming* was that "it lacks the simplicity of life."[33] Thus, by the second half of the nineteenth century, as the calls for an American drama recurred as frequently as the calls for realism, the two campaigns joined, but this led to yet another contradiction. Ironically, in order to achieve its pure, plain identity, American drama had to return to "an effete European source," as Boucicault warned.[34] Which is to say, the American drama saved itself from European decadence by embracing European realism, the best form for representing decadence. So much for the logic of advocacy and the logic of historical progress.

In the twentieth century few critics and historians fell into jingoistic campaigns for American drama and American virtue, and so most avoided some of the contradictions noted here. But the comparison between a jaded Europe and a wholesome America still resonated. As Quinn remarked in 1927, comparing the development of modern American drama to the modern drama of the "older civilization" in Europe: "What our drama lacked in maturity it made up in a freshness and a progressive quality which distinguish it from the drama of pessimism."[35] Today, few critics and historians of

American drama feel a need to praise it at the expense of European drama, but almost all of them have accepted and carried forward the basic argument that melodrama developed (grew, matured, transformed) into realistic drama. This understanding depends in great measure upon the same generic categories and upon similar assumptions about historical process and literary value that we find in the nineteenth-century commentaries. The explicit language of cultural Darwinism may have disappeared from more recent scholarly studies, but the presuppositions about development and social drama have remained prominent.[36] Even academic defenders of the earlier American drama find themselves using the language and the logic of evolutionary development to describe these premodern works, thus partially undercutting their own attempts to give serious consideration to the dramatic heritage.

In other words, both the advocates for realism and many of the theatre historians and critics of American drama have made interpretive mistakes similar to the misjudgments that O. B. Hardison Jr. identified in the assumptions and practices of certain scholars of medieval drama.[37] These scholars, including E. K. Chambers and J. M. Manly, depended upon a false analogy derived from cultural Darwinism. They assumed that the various types and manifestations of medieval drama were to be interpreted in one of two ways: (1) as developmental pieces in a historical process that achieved its fulfillment in the subsequent drama of the sixteenth century or (2) as the constricted works of a religious culture that finally gave way to an emerging secular culture in which great tragedy and comedy were able to develop. Sometimes both of these arguments—the developmental and the adversarial—were joined, just as they have been in the scholarship on American drama.

As Hardison shows, while the documentary value of this medieval scholarship has proved most valuable, the historical arguments are terribly flawed. For example, on the one hand, J. M. Manly, supposing the medieval dramatists were driving at Elizabethan drama but lacked the skills, conditions, and understanding to achieve this complex form, deemed their plays "pre-Shakespearean." Their artistic significance, then, was placed within a teleological history: they created plays that evolved, in the fullness of time, into the comedies, histories, and tragedies of the Elizabethan stage. Yet, on the other hand, Chambers saw the Renaissance as a break from the medieval heritage, a new secular age and movement. In this case, the liberation of drama from religious constraints made possible the flowering of genius in the Renaissance. So in these various studies of medieval and Renaissance drama by Chambers, Manly, and others, a developmental argument alternates with an adversarial view of the relation between two types of drama and the two eras of literature.

Thus, in the history of medieval drama as well as the history of American melodrama, the two generic forms, lacking their own integrity and significance, are perceived as incomplete, lesser forms that give way to or turn into their opposites. Historical change occurs within a polarized field of developmental energy. The argument seems almost unavoidable, in part because the period concepts (medieval versus Renaissance, nineteenth-century versus twentieth-century, premodern versus modern) prescribe a binary shape to history, which then gets articulated as either a developmental transformation or an adversarial conflict between opposites (sacred versus secular, European versus American, melodrama versus realism, mythic imagination versus critical judgment).

We need to recognize the limitations of these kinds of evolutionary and antagonistic narratives, tied to misleading period concepts. Whatever the rhetorical advantages of tracing the history of American drama according to a progression from crude to sophisticated, from frivolous to serious, from amusement to social commentary, and from superficial to vital art, the disadvantages are more substantial. Quite simply, we cannot organize a satisfactory history of American drama on the basis of a thesis about the evolution of genres, especially an argument that posits the growth and transformation of melodrama into modern realistic drama.

PART III: CONCLUDING POLEMIC; OR, A RETURN TO THE BEGINNING

> If one held the belief that there is any very intimate relation between the stage, as it stands in this country, and the general cause of American civilization, it would be more than our privilege, it would be our duty, as vigilant observers, to keep an attentive eye upon the theatres.
>   — HENRY JAMES
> "Some Notes on the Theatre," 11 March 1875

> . . . perhaps the thought begins to dawn upon us that there is fine melodrama and poor melodrama.
>   — Arthur Hobson Quinn
>   A History of American Drama
> from the Civil War to the Present, Vol. 2, 1927

Historically, melodramatic and realistic dramas developed during the same period in the nineteenth and twentieth centuries. So if we wish to define two genres, we need to recognize that right from the beginning they shared and traded traits, forms, and practices. Like twins, they were separate yet joined identities. And they were mutually influential, so much so that it is close to impossible historically to keep them separated. Accordingly, separate genre definitions, though an analytical need, do not actually fit the changeable (often confusing) historical process of cultural interpenetration and transformation. We are confronted with a number of manifestations of realism and melodrama. More to the point, we are confronted with numerous joinings of melodramatic and realistic forms and functions. So, we make a categorical and historical mistake when we attempt to fix their identities (as if each had a controlling genetic code) or to create an evolutionary development (as if any formula, such as simple to complex or A replacing B, explained the matter). The changes are open ended, within and across boundaries.

Also, as international forms of art, melodramatic and realistic drama cannot be contained by matters of national origin or identity, even though the two genres (as we may formally identify them) helped to articulate various nationalist agendas. They thus often responded to and were shaped by similar socio-political conditions in the modern industrial and imperial age of nationalism, capitalism, population explosion, urban growth, rapid change, technological advancements, massive migrations and resettlements, ethnic conflict, enslavement, massacres, revolutionary movements, authoritarian controls, and terrible wars. Here in these complex conditions both art forms found their many topics and themes.

Still, to discuss melodramatic and realistic drama we require generic definitions, even though the process of fixing identities goes against the historical grain. This tension between formal categories and historical processes is an abiding problem for critics and historians. Identity and change pull against one another, whether we are defining a genre, a person, an artistic movement, or a period. To proceed, however, we stipulate certain traits, tendencies, typologies, themes, and so on, for the genre. In turn, we set up comparisons and contrasts (melodrama and realism, popular and elite). In this manner, we perceive (define, categorize, analyze, and respond to) melodramatic and realistic drama as separate forms that not only can be distinguished from one another but also, as the campaign for realism demonstrated, can be set in opposition to one another in historical commentary and practices.

But this separation should not mislead us. Melodrama may be defined as a theatrical form of polarized excesses, articulating and resolving primary conflicts, but this does not mean that its relation to realism is equally polarized. Most of the time we can find melodramatic elements in realistic drama and realistic elements in melodramatic plays. This interpenetration of dramatic traits, attitudes, practices, and so on, is a process that goes on while the two forms, as we characterize them, also follow parallel developments, a process of both/and rather than either/or. Our genre categories serve us poorly if they keep us from seeing this historical and generic condition of mutuality. We might say, therefore, that over the last two hundred years melodramatic and realistic dramas have shared some similar effective and material causes, if not always formal and final causes. Such a perspective on them suggests a quite different history than the one we keep trying to write about American drama.

At the very least, given these working definitions, we might entertain the idea that melodrama is not an early stage of modern realistic drama (or any other kind of drama). Nor does it take its basic meaning in an agon with realism. As a concept and a practice, it has its own achieved form, fully developed and immensely popular since the end of the eighteenth century. Of course it has gone through changes, as do all art forms, but this does not mean that, like a child or a rudimentary organism, it grew or developed into realism, in accordance with some kind of germ theory or teleological law of causality. Though the melodramatic form has developed a number of kinds, modes, or subtypes over the last two hundred years—gothic, domestic, nautical, western, detective, adventure, fantasy, horror, science fiction—it has remained, within its own expansive generic form, as artistically whole or complete as any other genre. And as artistically adaptable. So, we must realize what should be obvious: It did not come to an end or evolve into something else at the beginning of the twentieth century. It has continued to take many forms. And various melodramatic traits, as we define them, can also be discovered in other genres because the concept of pure or exclusive form is misleading, even irrelevant.

Yet assuming we grant melodrama a serious status as a genre, what difference would this make in a history of American drama? In the first place, it should help us to overcome our confusion of the formal categories of drama with a progressive or evolutionary idea of history. In turn, we may even find ways to distinguish these formal categories and historical ideas from social definitions of high and low (elite and mass) culture and from aesthetic categories of literary value. Then, perhaps, we could look at melodrama and the various other forms of modern drama as sometimes different, sometimes similar, but almost always interrelated expressions of American experiences, wishes, fears, values, narrative strategies, and mythic consciousness. We will not see this, however, if we stay confined within generic categories of definition and narrative models of history that posit an evolutionary history moving from melodramatic craft to realistic artistry.

Despite the rhetoric of the campaign for realism, melodrama is not a retrograde form of popular entertainment that stands in the way of progress, liberty, true culture, and enlightenment. Our initial task, then, is to get beyond the pervasive dichotomies: melodrama distorts, realism reports; melodrama offers escapism, realism offers life; melodrama is conservative, realism is radical; melodrama delivers ideologies (as false consciousness), realism deconstructs ideologies. The neat polarities multiply rapidly in our historical and critical analysis. In fact, both melodrama and realism distort and report, conserve and criticize. And both articulate and challenge the ideologies of the time.

So, when Henry James complains that audiences have gone to melodrama "to look and listen, to laugh and cry—not to think," we might reply respectfully that this statement is yet another of those false dichotomies delivered to us by the advocates for realism (each of whom was also a closet melodramatist). Instead, we should note that, first, audiences cannot avoid thinking at a melodrama (though their thoughts may not satisfy a particular critical judgment) and, second, the pleasures of looking, listening, laughing, and crying belong to all the theatrical arts, including *Long Day's Journey into Night*, that great melodrama wearing the mask of realism.[38]

Notes

1. The concept of maturity, used by Arthur Hobson Quinn, Walter Meserve, C. W. E. Bigsby, and many other historians of American drama, can be traced back to the nineteenth century. Dion Boucicault, for example, used similar terminology in 1890 when he called contemporary plays the "baby drama of the future." Metaphors of growth and evolutionary development dominate the last hundred years of commentary on American drama, as I will show.

2. Sheldon Cheney, "The American Playwright and the Drama of Sincerity," *Forum* 51 (April 1914): 498–512; reprinted in *The New Movement in the Theatre* (New York: Mitchell Kennerly, chap. 1 (part), 34.

3. Of course, no one denies that these various forms of entertainment are part of American theatre history. But when we come to write the history of drama (as opposed to the history of theatre) we prefer to tell a developmental story, one that moves from melodramatic excess to realistic accomplishment. This is a story of literary attainment not theatrical variety. We want order and direction.

4. For example, on the many usages of the concept of realism in American literary study, see two recent surveys: Amy Kaplan, *The Social Construction of*

American Realism (Chicago: University of Chicago Press, 1988); and Michael Davitt Bell, *The Problem of American Realism: Studies in the Cultural History of a Literary Idea* (Chicago: University of Chicago Press, 1993). The problematic concept of melodrama has received much less attention in literary study.

5. I should make clear that my aim in saying this is not to dismiss formalist study of drama, but to identify some possible problems in a pervasive method of analysis. In turn, as I hope to show, even most studies that attempt to provide a social history of American drama remain tied to many of the same questionable assumptions that we find in the formalist studies.

6. Don Wilmeth and Tice L. Miller eds., *Cambridge Guide to American Theatre* (New York: Cambridge University Press, 1993). The entry on O'Neill is written by Louis Sheaffer, the respected biographer of O'Neill.

7. Gerald M. Berkowitz, *American Drama of the Twentieth Century* (London and New York: Longman, 1992), 1. Berkowitz tries to overcome the opposition between the terms "realistic" and "melodramatic" by defining the style of twentieth-century American drama as "realistic contemporary middle-class domestic melodrama." This is a promising but undeveloped idea in his study.

8. Two key studies at the end of the 1930s: Eleanor Flexner, *American Playwrights: 1918-1938* (New York, 1938) and Joseph Wood Krutch, *The American Drama Since 1918* (New York, 1939). More recent works have followed these models, including John Gassner's *The Theatre in our Times* (1954) and Bernard Dukore's *American Dramatists, 1918-1945* (1984).

9. C. W. E. Bigsby, *A Critical Introduction to Twentieth-Century American Drama, 1900-1940* (Cambridge: Cambridge University Press, 1982,) vii. Bigsby understands, however, that the earlier drama often expressed a mythic idea of American identity. The plays, for instance, often dramatize, "with political rhetoric and fast-congealing myths, the opening of a continent and the creation of a national identity" (vii). Vital issues, indeed.

10. Walter J. Meserve, "Preface" in *An Outline History of American Drama*, 2d ed. (New York: Feedback Theatrebooks and Prospero Press, 1994), viii (p. xiii in the original edition).

11. Montrose J. Moses, *The American Dramatist* (1911; rev. ed, 1925); Arthur Hobson Quinn, *History of the American Drama from the Beginning to the Civil War* (1923); *History of the American Drama from the Civil War to the Present* (1936, 1943); Richard Moody, *America Takes the Stage* (1955); Walter J. Meserve, *An Emerging Entertainment: The Drama of the American People to 1828* (1977); *Heralds of Promise: The Drama of the American People During the Age of Jackson, 1829-1849* (1986); Jack A. Vaughn, *Early American Dramatists: From the Beginnings to 1900* (1981); Gary A. Richardson, *American Drama from the Colonial Period Through World War I* (1993).

12. Walter J. Meserve, *Outline History of American Drama*, 18, 147, 218, 319. See also "American Drama and the Rise of Realism," *Jahrbüch für Amerikastudien* 9 (1964): 152-200. A similar argument runs through his essay on the history of American Drama in Walter J. Meserve, Richard Moody, and Travis Bogard, *The Revels History of Drama in English*, vol. 8, *American Drama* (London: Methuen, New York: Barnes and Noble, 1977).

13. Gerald Bordman, *American Theatre: A Chronicle of Comedy and Drama, 1869-1914* (New York: Oxford University Press, 1994), 742. In contrast to Bordman, Meserve knows that melodrama continued: "The theatre could not exist without melodrama and farce, and a good part of American drama written between the World Wars fits into one or the other of these categories or has some of its characteristics" (*Outline*, 296).

14. Bernard Hewitt, *Theatre USA, 1668-1957* (New York: McGraw-Hill, 1959), 331.

15. Alan S. Downer, "Waiting for O'Neill," in *The American Theatre: A Sum of Its Parts* (London: Samuel French, 1971), 25-40. Downer's title is unfortunate because in the essay he recognizes that realism and melodrama are often joined together in nineteenth-century theatre.

16. Moses, *The American Dramatist;* Walter Prichard Eaton, *The American Stage To-Day* (1908); *At the New Theatre and Others* (1910); Thomas H. Dickerson, *The Case of American Drama* (1915), *The Insurgent Theatre* (1917), *Playwrights of the New American Theatre* (1925); Sheldon Cheney, *The New Movement in the Theatre* (1914); *The Art Theatre* (1917; rev. 1925).

17. J. Brander Matthews, *Studies of the Stage* (1894); *The Historical Novel and Other Essays* (1901); *The Development of the Drama* (1903).

18. J. Brander Matthews, "The Decline of the Drama," *Galaxy* 19, no. 2 (New York, February 1875); 225-31; reprinted in *The Dawning of American Drama: American Dramatic Criticism, 1746-1915*, ed. Jürgen C. Wolter (Westport, CT: Greenwood Press, 1993), 182-83.

19. Ibsen's drama was soon taken up by supporters and advocates, including William Archer, whose campaign for Ibsen and realism spread from London to New York. I have charted Archer's role in the campaign for realism in Thomas Postlewait, *Prophet of the New Drama: William Archer and the Ibsen Campaign* (Westport, CT: Greenwood Press, 1986). Often taking Archer's view, I tended to see the history of this era as a struggle between realism and melodrama. Ten years later I see the historical process, if not the historical issues, somewhat differently.

20. Both Walter Meserve and Brenda Murphy have demonstrated that Howells was a guiding figure in the campaign. Walter J. Meserve, ed., *The Complete Plays of William Dean Howells* (New York, 1960). Brenda Murphy, ed., *A Realist in the American Theatre: Selected Drama Criticism of William Dean Howells* (Athens: Ohio University Press, 1992).

21. Brenda Murphy, *American Realism and American Drama, 1880-1940* (New York: Cambridge University Press, 1987), 5.

22. Augustin Daly, "The American Dramatist," *The North American Review* (1886); reprinted in Wolter, *Dawning of American Drama*, 191.

23. There is little evidence that *Margaret Fleming*—seen by few people and unpublished until many years later—had much direct influence on playwrights between 1890 and 1920. The general campaign for realism, engineered as much by Garland as Herne, probably was more influential. For a standard theatre biography that features Herne as a key figure in the evolution of American

realism, see John Perry, *James A. Herne: The American Ibsen* (Chicago: Nelson-Hall, 1978). For the history of the manuscript of *Margaret Fleming*, see John Perry and Arthur Hobson Quinn, eds., *Representative American Plays*, 7th ed. (New York: Appleton-Century-Croft, 1953). Also see Herbert J. Edwards and Julie A. Herne, *James A. Herne: The Rise of Realism in the American Drama* (Orono: University of Maine Press, 1964).

24. Perry and Quinn, *Representative American Plays*; Richard Moody, *Dramas from the American Theatre, 1762-1909* (Cleveland: World Publishing, 1966). For a list of the various play anthologies, see Walter J. Meserve, *American Drama to 1900: A Guide to Information Sources* (Detroit: Gale, 1980), 15-21. The other important editors of anthologies were Montrose J. Moses and Barrett H. Clark.

25. Jeffrey Mason, *Melodrama and the Myth of America* (Bloomington: Indiana University Press, 1993), 153.

26. Barrett H. Clark, ed., *America's Lost Plays*, 20 vols. (Princeton: Princeton University Press, 1940-41; reprint, Bloomington: Indiana University Press, 10 vols., 1963-65).

27. Gary Richardson, *American Drama: From the Colonial Period through World War I* (New York: Twayne, 1993), ix, 204.

28. Wolter, *Dawning of American Drama*, 3. Wolter's metaphor of "dawning" echoes writers of the time. For example, John Corbin published an essay called "The Dawn of the American Drama" in *Atlantic Monthly* in 1907 (reproduced partially in Wolter).

29. Besides the collections of plays and essays by Walter Meserve and Brenda Murphy mentioned above, see George Arms, Mary Bess Whidden, and Gary Scharnhorst eds., *Staging Howells: Plays and Correspondence with Lawrence Barrett* (Albuquerque: University of New Mexico Press, 1994).

30. Or in O'Neill's metaphoric terms, the conflict is between the consuming performer (low culture) and the consumptive artist (high culture). In accordance with the conventions of melodrama, the victory goes to the suffering son rather than to the self-aggrandizing father. Art is redeemed through suffering and struggle (a basic narrative that ironically melodrama and romanticism first perfected).

31. Quoted in Perry, *James A. Herne*, 215.

32. Bronson Howard, "American Playwrights on the American Drama," *Harper's Weekly* (1889); quoted in Wolter, *Dawning of American Drama*, 201.

33. Hamlin Garland, "Mr. and Mrs. Herne," *The Arena* (1891); quoted in Wolter, *Dawning of American Drama*, 219.

34. Dion Boucicault, "The Future American Drama," *The Arena* (1890); quoted in Wolter, *Dawning of American Drama*, 211.

35. Quinn, *American Drama from the Civil War*, vol. 2, 251.

36. Of course, when confronted on this matter, almost all drama critics and historians today would deny that they believe in historical progress, cultural Darwinism, the germ theory of history, or any other such theory of aesthetic and historical development. But their metaphors, nouns, and verbs often still express the assumptions of Darwinism and progressivism.

37. O. B. Hardison, Jr., "Darwin, Mutations, and the Origin of Medieval Drama,"
    in *Christian Rite and Christian Drama in the Middle Ages* (Baltimore: Johns
    Hopkins University Press, 1965), 1-34. Hardison also points out that
    Chambers was drawn to a polarity between Christianity and the folk, whereby
    the "clergy is consistently cast in the role of the villain who opposes the
    'mimetic instinct,' which is associated with such terms as 'healthy,' 'human,'
    and 'pagan'" (15). This adversarial approach is similar to the way Howells and
    others set up the opposition between melodrama and realism. Just as
    Christianity is seen as the retarding force in the development of drama, so
    melodrama and its villainous producers are seen as the restraints on realism
    and its development.
38. Henry James, "Some Notes on the Theatre," *Nation* (11 March 1875);
    reprinted in *The American Theatre as Seen By Its Critics, 1752-1934*, eds. Montrose
    J. Moses and John Mason Brown (New York: W. W. Norton, 1934), 123.

4

MELODRAMATIC CONTINGENCIES: TENDENCIES IN THE BULGARIAN DRAMA AND THEATRE OF THE LATE NINETEENTH CENTURY

Kornelia Tancheva

*A*MONG THE STUDIES that have claimed to anchor melodrama to a specific historical context, Peter Brooks's *The Melodramatic Imagination* can probably be singled out as the one that has had the most consequential impact. Ironically, his elaboration of a "melodramatic imagination" that is a constant of the literary imagination has been so successful that many subsequent studies have ignored his attempts to take into account the historicity of the genre.[1]

Recently, however, renewed interest in the historical specificity of melodrama—coupled with contemporary political and ideological considerations—has emerged forcefully in studies that focus on particular melodramatic contexts. Thus, Gabrielle Hyslop considers French "classic" melodrama to have been one of the earliest and most powerful forms of mass media. Pixérécourt's melodramas "were presented in order to impose the values of the dominant social class on the common people. Melodrama expresses the conservative, patriarchal ideas of the middle class who aim to control the opinions and life-styles of the men and women they regard as inferior."[2] In a similar vein, Julia Przybos remarks on the "uncanny coincidence between dramatic social changes and the appearance of melodramatic elements in theatre" and the final conservative message of melodrama in the French context.[3]

Clearly though, the ideological and political uses to which melodrama was put varied considerably depending on the cultural context. According to several critics, for instance, melodrama in England and America served to create a social space where artisans and working-class audiences could assert their cultural presence.[4] Furthermore, as Michael Hays has argued, popular theatre and melodrama in England could also be pitted against the novel and "literature," and often presented a challenge to mainstream ideology. Melodrama is a marker of and participant in the politically charged transformation of British society in the nineteenth century that led to a unified imperial discourse, yet, in its early stages, melodrama registered the incompleteness of this discourse whereas its full coalescence is more evident in the narrative forms of the time.[5] American melodrama, on the other hand, has been regarded as an expression of American society and national character, shaping the popular imagination and the perception of self and country.[6]

These efforts to examine the specific ways in which melodrama functions in its cultural environment stand in pronounced contrast with attempts to elaborate a universally valid "melodramatic" world-view whose constitutive principle is poetic justice. This view assumes that melodrama presented an idealized picture of human experience: a black-and-white world, a universe devoid of fatality and inevitability, an expression of unflagging faith in human equality and in the power of innocence and the triumph of virtue over vice.[7]

What needs to be recognized more fully is that most of the moral premises in melodrama are directly contingent upon a play's participation in the debates proper to its specific cultural context. Thus, discussions of "melodrama" should necessarily take into account not only the specifics of the genre and the way in which it elaborates a "melodramatic" world-view, but its reception and interpretation, and the ways in which it is used to express specific ideological formations.

Bearing this in mind, I would like to contribute to this larger discussion by examining the way in which melodrama functioned in the Bulgarian context at the end of the nineteenth century during the National Revival. I will argue that the melodrama, its reception, and its evaluation were all caught up in the cultural wars of the period, which were themselves a measure of the political and economic developments Bulgaria was going through. What may be most interesting about the Bulgarian situation is that there was an active consciousness of the strategic value of using melodrama to construct an idea of nationhood within the context of the National Revival.

For the sake of readers who are not familiar with Bulgarian history, I will first provide a brief outline of the situation. In the mid-nineteenth century, the country was still under the domination of the Ottoman Empire but had

already entered what is traditionally considered the final stage in the protracted and excruciating process of national unification and economic,
social, and cultural revival.[8] The Ottoman rule of almost five centuries was
drawing to a close (Bulgaria would finally celebrate her national liberation
in 1878) and unrest in the country increased dramatically in preparation for
what would turn out to be a decisive, albeit unsuccessful, attempt at a
national uprising in April 1876.

The Crimean War (1853-1856), which Bulgarians had viewed as a tangible
opportunity for their freedom, had ended with the victory of the Ottoman
empire and its allies, and there was a growing sense that an armed uprising
in the Bulgarian territories was Bulgaria's sole option. Other Balkan portions
of the empire had already broken away or were in the process of doing so,
thereby providing comparatively safe havens for Bulgarian revolutionary
activists. In the late 1860s, the arrival of militia troops organized outside the
country was expected to supply the expertise needed to train the voluntary
members of the local revolutionary committees within. The latter were organized by special envoys called *apostles* who had been sent by the Bulgarian
Revolutionary Central Committee headquartered in Rumania.

The move toward revolutionary insurgence was complicated by the dire
economic and political consequences of the Crimean War. The gradual and
very painful recovery of internal and external commercial ties and the slow
revival of Bulgarian villages and towns led to significant class stratification.
On one side were the socially mobile artisans, some of whom were newly
impoverished and, thus, little better off than the poor peasants, while others
had amassed substantial capital; on the other side was the consolidating
Bulgarian bourgeoisie, the *chorbadzhi*, who were fundamentally ambivalent
in their attitudes toward social unrest. Elements among the well-to-do
Bulgarians openly sided with the Ottomans, others were content to endorse
an autonomous state under the sultan, and still others whole-heartedly supported the struggle for national liberation.

Nonetheless, in the second half of the nineteenth century, the interests of
all the strata of the Bulgarian society began to converge in the need for
national independence and a Bulgarian state, although the different groups
proposed substantially different ways of attaining this goal. These ranged
from a collaboration with the Ottoman authorities in the hope of certain economic self-sufficiency—a collaboration that would eventually guarantee
the nation-state advocated by all concerned—to a general national uprising.[9]

Since most of the historical documents dealing with earlier Bulgarian culture had either disappeared—hidden in monasteries or suppressed by the
Ottoman authorities—or were at best available only to very small commu-

nities, and since new historical narratives had only recently begun to weave the story of a past Bulgarian greatness and a future promise, the interpretative possibilities were practically unlimited. At its core, the new Bulgarian culture was constructed as the successor to a magnificent pre-Ottoman culture and as an element in a Pan-Slavic spiritual awakening. Both of these perspectives were further deployed within the more general framework of a conflict between Christianity and Islam.

In this historical context, it is hardly surprising that the theatre was called upon to participate in the ideological struggles of the time. The amateur stages in the country were given the task of disseminating the discourse and image of Bulgaria's glorious past, thus providing incentives for a national uprising.[10] Ivan Vazov, the most influential Bulgarian writer after the Liberation, claimed that, prior to 1876, the drama was not considered a "work of art, meant to occupy a certain place in the literary production of the time, but rather an easy and practical tool for influencing the minds and emotions of the audience."[11]

To examine the historical ground for this and similar assessments of the role of the theatre and the melodrama during this period, the best place to start would be with *Mnogostradalna Genoveva* (Long-Suffering Genoveva), an adaptation of Ludwig Tieck's *Leben und Tod der heiligen Genoveva* (1799) and the most popular play staged during the first two decades of the modern Bulgarian theatre. The play was written by Pavel Todorov in 1856, drawing on Vasilie Jovanovic's Serbian translation *Siegfried and Genoveva*.[12]

It recounts the story of Siegfried, a German count, who goes to fight the Moors in Spain, leaving his young wife, Genoveva, at the mercy of an unscrupulous steward, Golos. Golos propositions her, and when she refuses his advances he first kills her faithful servant Drako and then accuses her of having had an affair with him. When the count sends orders to kill his unfaithful countess, the executioner takes pity and lets her and her young child find refuge in a forest cave. Seven years later, the count returns and, discovering Golos has betrayed him, punishes him and bitterly mourns for his wife. One day while hunting in the forest he accidentally comes across the cave in which she and their child are hiding. They recognize each other and return to the castle where they live happily ever after.

Between 1856 and 1878, *Genoveva* was invariably among the first plays to be produced on the bills of community centers, or *chitalishte*—places for reading, supported by the community and local schools, which combined the functions of a public library and a headquarters of the local revolutionary committee and later served as centers housing the first theatrical companies.[13] The play was produced throughout the Bulgarian lands and was regarded as the ultimate criterion of truth, justice, and honor by audiences that surrendered unconditionally to its emotional appeal.[14]

This sort of emotional surrender caused some uneasiness among contemporary commentators as well as later scholars of the Bulgarian theatre. There were also ideological objections to this and other such plays. For example, the Bulgarian émigrés' revolutionary press targeted the melodrama in particular as inadequate for revolutionary propaganda, and Hristo Botev, a revolutionary poet who later died in the struggle for liberation, specifically denounced *Genoveva* in his newspaper *Zname*. He thought it was a conservative endorsement of the interests of the Ottoman authorities and their well-to-do Bulgarian collaborators.[15]

A later, "pro-revolutionary" interpretation maintained that performances of *Genoveva* were meant to inspire compassion for the unfortunate and those who had been deprived of their liberty. This view assumed that the Bulgarian public identified with the suffering of the heroine.[16] The performance context also justified the production of specific melodramas. Thus, it has been argued that the staging of *Genoveva* in Lom (1856) was meant to divert the attention from the much more subversive *Belisar*.[17]

This sort of abstract judgment tells us little, however, about the ways in which the melodrama in general and *Genoveva* in particular were construed and put to use by contemporary and later commentators. To get a better understanding of the functional work of the drama and its significance in the Bulgarian situation we might turn to Ivan Vazov's novel *Pod Igoto* (Under the Yoke), (1887-1889), which contains an extensive reinterpretation of *Genoveva* that elaborates on both ideological and contextual considerations. The book is also of importance because it is thought to be the definitive narrative of the struggle of the Bulgarians for national independence—the "quintessential" expression of Bulgarian national identity and the national experience that culminated in the April uprising of 1876.

In Vazov's account, the whole town of Byala cherkva eagerly awaits the performance of *Mnogostradalna Genoveva*, the immensely popular melodrama whose plot they are thoroughly familiar with:

> This naive and touching plot had drawn tears from all the old ladies and young matrons of the town. Even to that day everyone remembered the legend of Genoveva, while many ladies knew the play by heart. That was why this evening's performance had provoked general excitement for many days past. Everyone looked

forward to it impatiently as a great event which would add pleasant variety to the monotony of life in Byala Cherkva. One and all
made ready for the theatre.[18]

In the course of the performance, the audience becomes totally wrapped
up in the vicissitudes that befall the characters, and it constantly transfers
emotions triggered by the action and the characters onto the actors. After
shedding heart-rending tears for the distressed heroine, all the spectators are
overjoyed to witness the reunion of husband and wife and "the triumph of
good over evil is complete" (93).

Meanwhile the chief representative of the Turkish authorities is also at the
performance and has an interpreter, especially chosen for his ingenious
expression and quick wit, to help him follow the action. The interpreter's
imagination often gets the better of him and he recounts a number of similar accidents from all over the world, but he gets the main idea across pretty
accurately. The play is supposed to end with a song sung by the count, the
countess and their retinue: "Count Siegfried, Now Rejoice!" Instead,

> after the first two verses of this virtuously joyful song, the strains
> of a revolutionary march rang out on the stage:
>   Blaze up in us, oh love, so bright,
>   Against the Turks we'll go and fight. . . .
> It was as if a thunderbolt had struck the hall. At first only one sang
> it, then the song was taken up by a few of the actors on the stage,
> then by all of them, and at last the audience itself took up the refrain.
> A wave of patriotic fervor swept over everyone. The brave tune of
> this song grew like an invisible wave, filled the hall, flowed over into
> the yard and burst out into the night. . . . The song rent the air,
> stirred up and exhilarated people's hearts. These martial notes
> struck a new chord in the audience. Everyone who knew the song
> began to sing it, both men and women; it united all souls, it made the
> stage merge with the hall, and rose heavenward like a prayer (93).

The Bulgarian-Turkish interpreter rises to the challenge and renders the
forbidden revolutionary song as follows,

> The song . . . expressed the great love of the Count for the Countess.
> The Count says to her, 'I love you a hundred times more now,' and
> she says to him, 'I love you a thousand times more now.' He says
> that he will build a church where the cave had stood in memory of
> it, and she says that she will sell all her diamonds to give alms to the
> poor, and she will build a hundred marble fountains (94).

The revolutionary song was begun by a member of the audience, one of the *apostles* of the revolution, who happened to be in Byala cherkva at the time. Later, he explains his actions to the lead actor, a teacher in the town, who is both an *apostle* and organizer of the revolutionary committee in the town thus:

> I just couldn't help it, brother. I got sick of all those tears and that chicken-hearted lamentation over your long-suffering lady. We had to bring all those people to their senses somehow. And then it came into my head to get onto the stage. . . . You saw what a brilliant effect it had. (94)

Thus, the production of the popular melodrama, which had been chosen (according to this narrative) because it was bound not to antagonize the Ottoman authorities and the wealthy Bulgarians who were providing most of the financial backing, serves as an occasion for revolutionary propaganda and the dissemination of a feeling of national community in opposition to the Ottoman rulers.

Whether this account even remotely corresponds to any actual performance of *Genoveva* is a moot point. What matters is the play's position of prominence in the narrative. The episode is allotted central significance in the structure of the novel, which is built on the gradual formation of the popular consciousness. As such it is placed on a par with the establishment of revolutionary committees and the open dissemination of revolutionary ideas for armed resistance; in other words, the melodramatic representation is interpreted here as a full participant in the dominant discourse of national liberation and cultural and political nationalism.

Of course, this is not an interpretation grounded in the play itself, but it is a perfect example of narrative restructuring of the melodrama. The narrative's desire to transform a popular melodrama into an element of a full-fledged, nationalistic, revolutionary discourse can be seen as an instance of the same sort of ambiguity and usefulness for the power struggles of the time that Michael Hays uncovers in the melodrama in England in the second half of the nineteenth century.

Indeed, the events of the play itself suggest such transforming interpretations. The count is, after all, at war with the Moors—Moslems attacking a Christian country—and is finally victorious. This plot line could furnish audiences and critics with a meaningful allegorical parallel to the innermost desires of a Christian population longing for liberation from its Moslem ruler. Equally significant is the ultimate moral of the melodrama: the belief that our Lord the Savior will restore personal and social justice for all.

Some commentators actually denounced this particular aspect of the play because they considered it an attempt at Roman Catholic proselytizing among Eastern Orthodox Christians, whose Holy See was based in Constantinople.[19] Contextually speaking, however, the opposition at the time was not so much Rome versus Constantinople, as Christianity versus Islam; hence a victory of the Christian soldiers and Christian morality could allegorically refer to the plight of the audience and promise salvation in clearly recognizable, morally oppositional terms. What is more, all the virtues of the characters endorsed by the play participate fully in the value system of the Bulgarian society of the period.

While *Genoveva* could only provisionally be inserted into this context, later melodramas offered greater possibilities for integration into the canon of Bulgarian national drama, especially if they could be deployed within the context of the opposition between Bulgarian (Christian) virtue and Ottoman (Moslem) vice. Such plays were Dimiter Shishmanov's *Dobriyat ɜin* (The good son) (1857; 1868); Dobri Voinikov's *Stoyan voivoɜa* (Stoyan, the voivode) (1866) and *Dimanka ili vyarna purvinɜka lyubov* (Dimanka; or, faithful first love) (1876); Stoiko Yordanov's *Altunlu Stoyan voivoɜa* (Golden Stoyan, the voivode) (1866); Bogdan Manchov's *Izgoubena Stanka* (Lost Stanka) (1870); Bacho Kiro's *Siromah Tancho* (Poor Tancho) (1874); Atanas Ouzounov's *Dobur haiɜoutin* (Good rebel) (1874-1875) and *Tɜvyatko voivoɜa* (Tsvyatko, the voivode) (1876); and Nikola Zhivkov's *Ilyu voivoɜa* (Ilyu, the Voivode) (1876). These plays invariably showed courageous and virtuous Bulgarians pitted against inhumanly cruel aggressors.

Shishmanov's *Dobriyat ɜin*, for instance, presents a typical figuration of the conflict between the moral fortitude of the Bulgarians and the depravity of their Ottoman rulers. It depicts the misfortune of an honest Bulgarian family: the father dies, two of his sons are killed by robbers, two others are kidnapped by the Turks and forced to work for them, and only the youngest son, Yovan, remains free. He is passionately in love with Maria, but the local aga, Hassan, who himself covets the beautiful Maria, kills him. While she is mourning his loss, the Turk tries to rape her, causing her to go mad. A friend, Raina, then saves her by killing Hassan.

The play's motif—the Bulgarian maiden at the mercy of a Moslem violator—was a common one. In Manchov's *Izgoubena Stanka*,[20] plundering Tartars kidnap the beautiful Bulgarian girl, Stanka. Peter, her betrothed, and her brother Vassil seek the help of the Bulgarian outlaws Zhelyu and Nikola to save her. The latter—very much in the Robin Hood tradition—are legendary defenders of the poor Bulgarians against the atrocities of their Ottoman oppressors. They succeed after several skirmishes, Stanka and Peter marry, and the traditional morality of the patriarchal family is celebrated with a folk song. The moral is unambiguous: The lost maiden, who is almost ravished by the infidel, personifies the suffering of her country at the hands of non-Christian oppressors; she is saved thanks to the bravery of her brother and future husband. The same imagery appears in folk songs, where the outlaws are often betrothed to Bulgaria rather than to women and dedicated to fighting for her liberation: the native land saved by a faithful male figure.

The religious motif must also have struck a powerful chord in the hearts of Bulgarian audiences, since folk songs and tales had already constructed the narrative of the worst plight that could befall a Christian maiden — to be taken into the harem of the local Moslem official and forced to renounce her own faith. In one of the most popular of these folk songs, "Davash li, Davash, balkandzhi Yovo" ("Are You Prepared to Renounce, Yovo"), the male hero gladly accepts having his arms cut off, his eyes plucked out, and every other imaginable physical pain before he is finally beheaded rather than give his sister to the Moslems. Meanwhile, to be sure, the maiden always remains faithful to her Bulgarian betrothed (much as Genoveva remains faithful to the count), or to her family and her faith if there is no betrothed to be faithful to. This is one of the typical melodramatic tropes that will be carried over into other genres as well. Physical atrocities usually involved a Bulgarian maiden, or, better, a Bulgarian princess, as in Voinikov's *Stoyan voivoda* (1866, Brăila), in which Princess Raina is tortured by Zinan Pasha, who wants her to renounce Christianity and convert to Islam. It is only through the miraculous interference of Stoyan, the outlaw, and Prince Vladimir, the lawful heir to the Bulgarian throne, that she is saved.

Sometimes poor Bulgarians are victimized by the local *chorbadzhi*, who is necessarily in alliance with the authorities — a further complication in the melodramatic structure, this one the result of class stratification. The wealthier members of the community were often seen as collaborators, so both in the popular melodramas of the time and in the didactic historical dramas meant to enlighten the people and incite them to an open confrontation with the oppressors a second story line frequently appears — that of personal merit rewarded regardless of social position as defined by family ties and wealth.

Of course, there is also something ahistorical and contradictory about this plot construction and its narrative framework, since in reality most of the revolutionaries came from wealthier families, which had the means to send them abroad to study, most often in Russia. Although many revolutionaries renounced their conservative fathers, they understood both the significance of an overall national coalition and the importance of the financial means available in the wealthier strata of society. The potential conflict inherent in these contradictory orientations was resolved by elaborating an opposition between a nationalist and a pro-Turkish Bulgarian bourgeoisie. The former supported the national revolutionary cause and was, therefore, celebrated. The latter, content with a peaceful integration in a supposedly more "evolved" Ottoman Empire or, worse, with the preservation of the status quo, could only be seen as perfidious and treacherous.

The nation's virtues are often embodied by a poor girl, who, in a twist of the classic Cinderella plot, represents both conventional feminine integrity and the positive aspects of the national character. Often she also carries the revolutionary message. Naturally, and despite all obstacles, she will eventually be appreciated by the progressive son of a well-to-do Bulgarian merchant: Virtue is rewarded while vice punished. Voinikov's *Dimanka* presents exactly this kind of heroine yet also captures the actual social tensions of the time by depicting the confrontation between a poor girl, Dimanka, and the local *chorbadzhi*, whose unbridled exploitation of the poor has turned him into an enemy far worse than the Turks. She invokes images of Bulgarian women who fought in the past for their rights and their national identity in order to present the play's message and its endorsement of the moral construct framed by honesty, enterprise, and responsibility to the community — terms corresponding to the new, historically progressive, national bourgeoisie that opposed the feudal Ottoman rule and its native servants. The melodramatic structure itself promoted an unambiguous polarization of the characters into heroes and villains, young and old, physically attractive and repulsively deformed, morally commendable or depraved according to nationality and/or social status and, thus, worked towards transforming the theatrical event into a parable of national destiny and a mediated construct of a specific national identity.

Similar confrontations between virtuous poor Bulgarians and wealthy traitors are dramatized in Ouzounov's *Dobur haidoutin* (published after the Liberation, in 1880, but written between 1874 and 1875) and Nikola Zhivkov's *Svetoulka* (The Firefly), performed in Ploiesti in 1877. In *Svetoulka*, the poor and unjustly suffering Bozhana and her children are finally rewarded while the evil *chorbadzhi*, Mihalaki, is punished. In Dimiter Fingov's *Nagradenü podvig* (Exploit rewarded) (1871), the impoverished family of Bogdan is plagued both by the wealthy local *chorbadzhi*, who had driven Bogdan's father away because of his struggle against the Greek priests, and by Stoyanka's mother. Stoyanka and Bogdan are in love, but her mother would rather have her marry Marko, who has recently arrived from Constantinople and is reputedly very wealthy. Stoyanka refuses — she can recognize the viciousness in Marko at first sight. Marko kidnaps her, Bogdan comes to her rescue and, thanks to the sudden return of his father, also turns out to be extremely well off.

Of course, despite their failings, and in contrast to Turkish and Moslem villains, Bulgarians who had sinned against the accepted morality were not beyond redemption. Sometimes they could be reclaimed by virtue, as in Dimiter Shishmanov's *Dobrodetel i zloba* (Virtue and Spite) (1871), Todor Stanchev's *Yustina* (1871), or Krustyu Pishourka's *Ispadnal turgovets* (The Ruined Merchant) (1870).[21]

Returning to Vazov's narrative in *Under the Yoke* about the production of *Genoveva*, it should be noted that the revolutionary appeal of a melodrama was further facilitated if the spectators were familiar with the actors in some off-stage capacity. The lead actor in this instance is the chairman of the revolutionary committee in Byala cherkva, who has already approached most of the members of the audience on behalf of the revolutionary movement. Even some of the Turkish military officials already suspect him of subversive activities. What is more, the overall production environment—the performance space, which is the local school, the props supplied by the audience or improvised by the performers symbolically significant to everyone involved, the possibility for a direct communication between the audience and the actors, and the paucity of theatrical exposure among the spectators—further contributes to the significance of the revolutionary song as an ultimate communion of spirit desired by the revolutionary workers. This brings the closure of reconciliation—an act of absolute selflessness in the face of the real or imaginary retaliation expected from the Turks.

Throughout the performance, the audience must have been additionally drawn into the action by the costumes used. They were, Vazov informs his readers, "the same ones used three years before when Princess Raina was performed" (87). *Raina knyaginya* (Princess Raina) was written by Voinikov in 1866 and was almost as popular as *Genoveva*,[22] but it stands between "classical" melodrama and the historical dramas that were soon to oust foreign and domestic melodramas altogether. As such it is of great interest here. The primary aim of the play is to denounce foreign intrigues against the Bulgarian kingdom and to show that the Kiev prince Svetoslav is the friend of Bulgaria, thus responding to the widespread hope that Russia would turn out to be Bulgaria's liberator.

The melodramatic structure of the play gives ample space for the sudden turns and revelations specific to the historical moment depicted in the work. It is set in the time of Tsar Peter (927-969), whose reign was quite long despite the frequent schemes and plots of the nobility that undermined the kingdom and made it easy prey for foreign invaders after Peter's death. Even Svetoslav, the prince of Kiev, attacked the country en route to Constantinople. He captured the capital but was later driven from Bulgaria, only to make room for the invaders from the Byzantine Empire, who ruled Bulgaria from 1018 to 1185.

At the time the play was written, tradition held that the noblemen and Peter himself were to blame for not standing up to defend the past glory of the country and for having sold out to the enemy. In this there was a clear parallel drawn between the conditions existing immediately before Bulgaria fell under Byzantine sway and the gradual surrender of the country to the Ottoman Empire in the fourteenth century. The play makes no reference to the "Turkish yoke," as it was popularly called; it was not possible to draw such parallels openly. Instead, it tells the story of Peter's daughter, Raina, who is caught in the web of the noblemen's betrayals, the first councilor's treacherous politics, and the assassination of Peter by Samouil, the councilor's son, who wants Raina for himself.

Raina, with mother long dead, father perfidiously murdered, and brothers held hostage in Constantinople, has only a devoted maid and her exiled uncles to protect her. In this context, the most significant element of the plot is the historical reconfiguration of Svetoslav's invasion. In the play he is initially presented as an unwitting victim of the cunning intrigues of the first councilor, who has sold out to Constantinople, but once he invades Preslav, the Bulgarian capital, he comes to know, sympathize with, and love the Bulgarian people, appreciate the beauty of the land, and admire Raina's grace and charm. He vows eternal friendship and assistance in driving away the foreign enemies. Raina's uncles, in the wisdom of their years, are the first to trust him:

> OBREN. Yes, Princess, the Russian Prince Svetoslav has
> conquered most of the Bulgarian kingdom and is
> today in Preslav where I am now coming from. Yet,
> hark — he does not seem an enemy to us; quite to the
> contrary, he has already given up his friendship with
> the Greeks and wants to be our ally, leaving your
> brother Boris to rule his father's lands.[23]

Svetoslav not only offers his help against the arch enemies of the Bulgarian kingdom, he also arranges for a lawful succession to the Bulgarian throne. This theme must have been quite dear to the hearts of a people who had long lost their royalty and who, in a decade or so, would actually seek out a European prince to rule their country. Svetoslav himself never misses a chance to point out his conversion to loyal friend of an unfortunate people whose land is so fertile and whose princess so charming: "I wouldn't crave somebody else's right and lands. Raina's brother will have the kingdom and rule it" (131), "Oh, how unfortunate the children of a King who left them all alone in the world must be. . . . I will help them and bring them happiness again—I'll give them their father's throne, it shall be theirs to enjoy" (132). Svetoslav does not limit his support to mere words; he goes on to aid his prospective in-laws directly. After enabling the legitimate heir to succeed to the throne, Svetoslav also helps him fight against the Greeks, thus adding a further curious twist to the play's interpretation and reconstruction of history. In fact, of course, right after Svetoslav's actual invasion Bulgaria fell under Byzantine domination. But here is the revision offered in the play:

> SVETOSLAV. . . . let me quickly leave to nip the danger
> in the bud before it would befall your kingdom; I'll
> fight with all my might, as if I am fighting for my
> own land, and help me, Lord, I will not let your
> enemies succeed (136).

Why should a Russian prince be so conceptualized and be chosen as the person to grant Princess Raina and her people this long-overdue release? The classic melodramatic trope that provides for the recognition of personal virtue and its ultimate reward is put to use here to figure the larger promise of a reward for the virtuous nation as a whole that will include the restoration of justice for all. Not surprisingly, the justice proposed is a victim's justice, one that allows the implied audience to enter vicariously the world it must long for. This makes it all the more interesting that the medium for justice is a foreign power.

Clearly, the play responds to and operates within the popular contemporary belief that Bulgarian liberation would stem from a holy crusade by Russia on behalf of the Christian population in the Ottoman Empire: salvation in the play arrives in the form of a Russian prince who requires a miraculously short span of time to appreciate deeply this poor Slavic people in distress.

Needless to say, I have underlined only one representational line from the play here. The piece is much more complex and, at times, even contradictory both in terms of its melodramatic structuring of experience and its gestures toward historical reality. One of the most fundamental melodramatic conventions is violated in the final scene, despite its overall structure as a formal tableau. After the culminating, melodramatic recognition(s) and reconciliation(s), when Princess Raina is ready to leave for Russia with Svetoslav— presumably to live in safety while the Bulgarian kingdom is reestablished (after the healing has begun and social order is about to be restored)—an unexpected scene (xiii) is inserted. In a moonlit field, the Russian troops fight the traitor Samouil, whose mercenaries kill Princess Raina, one of her uncles, and Svetoslav; her maid disappears, and "*Samouil triumphs*" (138).

As has already been indicated, *Princess Raina* stands halfway between melodrama and the romantic historical dramas that were soon to assume center stage. *Princess Raina* preserves the usual melodramatic plot contrivances as well as the strong emotionalism of pieces like *Genoveva*, but also breaks away from a clear-cut polarization of characters into heroes and villains. More importantly, it questions the inevitability of a reward for virtue. This displacement corresponds to a shift in sensibility within the genealogical development of the National Revival as well. While at first it was unanimously assumed that the country could be liberated only with outside help—through an act of "divine justice" as it were—it later became of paramount importance to advocate liberation from within. Self-reliance was the credo of those revolutionaries who denounced the earlier belief in an eventual triumph of justice due to "divine" intervention. Consequently, the anxieties of the times found their theatrical corollary in the representation of a more "Romantic" hero—neither villain nor saint—who took his fate into his own hands.

In this same manner, the historical plays of the National Revival period preserved certain melodramatic tendencies in their plots and resolutions but focused attention more closely on the immediate goal of national liberation, thus ensuring their place within the canon of modern Bulgarian drama. Ivan Vladikin's *Velikii knyaz Boris* (Great Prince Boris) (1871), for instance, has a typical melodramatic structure. Boris has been exiled by his father, Tsar Peter. Because Boris, his wife, and his son are starving in a forest hut, Boris's faithful servant Dragan robs an unknown rider in hopes of alleviating their suffering. The rider turns out to be Peter himself, happy to find his son and sorry to have exiled him unjustly. They all return to the palace, and Boris is guaranteed succession to the throne. This could be interpreted as the typical virtue-rewarded-and-vice-punished plot, but it takes on a different significance insofar as it promises stability in the succession to the Bulgarian throne. This same aura of "historical justice" as might be delivered by Bulgarians themselves envelops Konstantin Velichkov's *Nevyanka i Svetoslav* (Nevyanka and Svetoslav) (1874).[24] The plot is again melodramatically conventional—the protagonists' love is temporarily hindered by the political climate, but is finally triumphant. Since Svetoslav's father, Vladimir, has been wrongly accused of betraying the late Tsar Peter, the young couple is convinced that neither the current tsar, nor his first councilor—Nevyanka's father—will authorize their marriage, so they elope. Meanwhile the throne is threatened by the pretender, Ivanko, who is victorious in a battle against the lawful tsar. At this juncture, Nevyanka and Svetoslav's volunteer troops come to the aid of the besieged tsar, who grants them his permission to marry; Svetoslav is forgiven and justice has its day. What matters most here, though, in terms of the overall movement of the play is that the kingdom is maintained because of the active involvement of honest Bulgarians.

Although melodrama had almost completely disappeared from the Bulgarian stage by the 1880s and only certain melodramatic tendencies were preserved in sentimental drama, its brief popularity (and its complex reinterpretation within the canon of the modern Bulgarian theatre) can be best explained in relation to the formation and consolidation of a national consciousness in Bulgaria in the second half of the nineteenth century. It seems clear that the representational and communicational strategies employed in dramatic and performance texts, as well as the plays' theatrical and dramatic reception and interpretation, and the often contradictory ways in which melodramatic traditions (both foreign and domestic) unfolded in the emerging Bulgarian theatre, were necessarily tied to the contemporary audiences' ideological affiliations within the larger cultural context of the struggle for national liberation and the creation of an independent Bulgarian state.

N o t e s

1. See Peter Brooks, *The Melodramatic Imagination: Balzac, Henry James, Melodrama, and the Mode of Excess* (New Haven: Yale University Press, 1976), esp. 11-44. For studies based on Brooks's notion of a "melodramatic imagination," see, for instance, Jeffrey N. Cox, "Melodrama, Monodrama and the Forms of Romantic Tragic Drama," in *Within the Dramatic Spectrum*, ed. Karelisa Hartigan (Lanham, MD: University Press of America, 1986), 20-34; Ann E. Kaplan, *Motherhood as Representation: The Mother in Popular Culture and Melodrama* (London, New York: Routledge, 1992); and William R. Morse, "Desire and the Limits of Melodrama," in *Melodrama*, ed. James Redmond (Cambridge: Cambridge University Press, 1992), 17-30.
2. Gabrielle Hyslop, "Deviant and Dangerous Behavior: Women in Melodrama," *Journal of Popular Culture* 19, no. 3 (1985): 66. See also Hyslop, "Pixérécourt and the French Melodrama Debate: Instructing Boulevard Theatre Audiences," in *Melodrama*, Redmond, 61-85. "Classic" melodrama refers to Pixérécourt's body of work in France at the turn of the nineteenth century.
3. Julia Przybos, "Melodrama as Social Ritual," *French Literary Studies* 15 (1988): 86. She maintains that at the end of melodrama a new order superior to the one reigning before is established, and that this connects melodrama to the rites of passage and purification rituals. The conservative message is associated with a pleasant emotional state resulting from the reduction of cognitive dissonance.

On the conservatism of Pixérécourt's early melodrama see also Bruce McConachie, "Pixérécourt's Early Melodramas and the Political Inducements of Neoplatonism," in *Melodrama*, Redmond, 87-103.

4. See, for instance, Jim Davis, "The Gospel of Rags: Melodrama at the Britannia, 1863-74," *New Theatre Quarterly* 7 (1991): 369-89; Daniel Gerould, "Representations of Melodramatic Performance," *Browing Institute Studies* 18 (1990): 55-71; Michael Booth, "Melodrama and the Working Class," in *Dramatic Dickens*, ed. Carol Hanbery MacKay (New York: St. Martin's, 1989), 96-109; and Mel Gordon, "The Yiddish Theatre in New York: 1900," *New York Literary Forum* 7 (1980): 69-74. In terms of structure, the genre has also been seen as progressive because it allows for social change. See William Sharp, "Structure of Melodrama," in *Melodrama*, Redmond, 269-280. Recent genre criticism has set itself the task of deconstructing the illusion of the completeness of a genre and of analyzing the layers of sedimented ideologemes constructed into a seemingly distinct genre. See Mitsuhiro Yoshimoto, "Melodrama, Postmodernism, and Japanese Cinema," *East-West Journal* (Special Issue on Melodrama and Cinema) 5, no. 1 (1991): 28-55.

5. See Michael Hays, "Representing Empire: Class, Culture, and the Popular Theatre in the Nineteenth Century," *Theatre Journal* 47 (1995): 65-82.

6. See Daniel Gerould, "The Americanization of Melodrama," in *American Melodrama*, ed. Daniel C. Gerould (New York: Performing Arts Journal Publications, 1983), 7-29.

7. See Robertson Davies, *The Mirror of Nature* (Toronto, Buffalo: University of Toronto Press, 1983); Maurice Wilson Disher, *Blood and Thunder: Mid-Victorian Melodrama and its Origins* (London: Frederick Muller, 1949) and *Melodrama: Plots that Thrilled* (London: Rockcliff, 1954); and Ira Hauptman, "Defending Melodrama," in *Melodrama*, Redmond, 281-89.

8. The event that launched the National Revival was the appearance of the first Bulgarian history in 1762, compiled by the monk Paisii Hilendarski. For typological reasons, the National Revival is regarded as having passed through three stages: education, struggle for an independent national church, and revolutionary efforts for political independence.

9. As much as I appreciate the importance of completely historicizing the argument I am going to present, and of providing adequate background information on the developments characterizing Bulgarian society at the time, only a very sketchy and necessarily impoverished picture of the complex and contradictory forces and agendas vying for supremacy and people's affiliations can be provided. For an overview of Bulgarian history in English see R. J. Crampton, *A Short History of Modern Bulgaria* (Cambridge, New York: Cambridge University Press, 1987) and Glenn Curtis, ed., *Bulgaria: A Country Study*, 2d. ed. (Washington, D.C.: Federal Research Division, Library of Congress, 1993) and, in Bulgarian, Dimiter Kossev, ed., *Istoriya na Bulgaria*, vols. 5 and 6 (Sofia: Izdatelstvo na Bulgarskata Akademiya na naoukite, 1979-).

Bulgarian names have been transcribed following the Library of Congress system, with some variations for the sake of backtracking and consistency.

10. See, for instance, the way Zahari Stoyanov, one of the revolutionary *apoštleš*, describes amateur stages in the country in his *Zapiški po bulgarškite vuštaniya* [Records of the Bulgarian uprisings] (1879, Sofia: Naouka i izkoustvo, 1981), 166. He even believed that the theatre was among the immediate incentives for the April uprising (245-46, 737).

11. Ivan Vazov, "'Ilyu Voivoda'": Drama v pet deistviya ot Nikola Zhivkov," *Narodnii glaš* 140, no. 25 (1880): 3.

12. Jovanovic's adaptive translation was also based on Christoff von Schmid's novelette *Genoveva*, while Tieck's play followed the *Volkšbuch von der Pfalzgräfin Genoveva* (1647), which derives from a French legend. The story circulated in Bulgaria in at least two variants. It was first introduced among the Catholic minority around 1830. The different variants of the Genoveva text and their genesis are described in detail by Nadezhda Andreeva-Popova in "'Mnogostradalna Genoveva.' Ot srednovekovna legenda do bulgarskata vuzrozhdenska stsena. Kum vuprosa za avtora na bulgarskata 'Mnogostradalna Genoveva,' *Godišhnik na VITIZ "Kruštyu Sarafov."* 5 (1960): 284-285. See also Stefan Karakostov, *Bulgarškiyat teatur: Srednovekovie, Renešanš, Prošvešhtenie, 865-1858* (Sofia: Naouka i izkoustvo, 1972) 246ff, hereafter *BT.*

13. The first modern performances in Bulgaria were in the schools, usually at the end of the school year. After the struggle for independent Bulgarian schools in the 1830s and 1840s had culminated in the official adoption of Bulgarian and the opening of the first Bulgarian high school in Gabrovo in 1835, new Bulgarian schools were founded throughout the Bulgarian lands, as well as in other Balkan countries where there were sizable Bulgarian colonies. By 1876 there were 1479 elementary Bulgarian schools and 50 high schools.

The first community centers were established in Shoumen, Lom and Svishtov in 1856. By 1876 their number had grown to 130. The first amateur theatrical companies appeared in 1856 in the cities of Lom and Shoumen organized by the members of the community centers there. The first documented theatre performances in Bulgaria were those of *Mihal* (14 August 1856, Shoumen) staged by Sava Dobroplodni and *Genoveva* (12 December 1856, Lom) staged by Krustyu Pishourka.

The first theatrical society was organized in 1865 by Dobri Voinikov in Brăila, Rumania after he had been exiled from the country.

For further information on the development of Bulgarian theatre, see Nikola Popov, "Nashiyat naroden teatur," *Novo Vreme* 16-17 (1915): 515-27; Dobrin Vassilev, *Opit za ištoriya na bulgarškiya teatur* (Varna: Grafiza, 1942); Stefan Karakostov, *BT,* 150-279, and his *Bulgarškiyat vuzrozhdenški teatur na ošvoboditelnata borba* (Sofia: Naouka i izkoustvo,1973), and Yulian Vuchkov, *Bulgarška dramatourgiya, 1856-1878* (Sofia: Bulgarski pisatel, 1989) in

Bulgarian. In English, the materials are quite scarce and old — see, for instance, Krassimira Popova, *The Bulgarian Theatre* (Sofia: Sofia Press, n.d.), and Lyuben Shaoulov, *The Bulgarian Theatre* (Sofia: Foreign Language Press, 1964). More recently, a number of journal articles and collections of essays have appeared in English, but they all deal with specific aspects of chiefly contemporary theatre.

14. *Genoveva* was performed in the community centers in Lom, Pleven, Shoumen, Plovdiv, Kazanluk, Svishtov, Veliko Turnovo, Sliven, Stara Zagora, Samokov, Yambol, Gabrovo, Kalofer, Panagyurishte, Byala cherkva, Moussina, Edirne, Sopot, Lyaskovets, Tryavna, Harmanli, Svilengrad, Kotel, Koprivshtitsa, Perushtitsa, Elena, Troyan, Lovech, Shipka, Gorna Oryahovitsa, Karlovo, Razgrad, Sevlievo, among others. See Karakostov, *BT,* 523-690.

15. *Zname* 12, 28 March 1875, also 15, 9 May 1875.

16. See Vassilev, *Opit za istoriya na bulgarskiya teatur,* 42 ff.

17. See Karakostov, *BT,* 257, 261. *Belisar* was an adaptation after *Trautzschen* (1843) by A. S. Kipilovski, published in Leipzig in 1844. Two other adaptations appeared later. It was performed in Shoumen, Veliko Turnovo, and Rousse, among others.

18. Ivan Vazov, *Under the Yoke,* trans. Marguerite Alexieva and Theodora Atanassova, ed. Lilla Lyon Zabriskie (New York: Twayne, 1971), 86. Further references to this work are included parenthetically in the text. Vazov's version of the plot is consistent with Todorov's translation.

19. Karakostov, *BT,* 245-51.

20. Manchov dramatized Iliya Bluskov's novelette of the same name, first published in 1865 in Bolgrad and in 1867 in Rousse. *Izgoubena Stanka* was performed in Rousse (1872) and Moussina (1873), among other places.

21. The latter is an adaptation of a Serbian play, probably Mihailo Vitkovic's *Zhertva na smert* (1830), in its turn an adaptation of Kotzebue's *Der Opfertod.*

22. *Raina knyaginya* (1866) was after Veltman's novel *Raina, korolevna bolgarskaya* (1843), translated into Bulgarian by Elena Mouteva in 1852. It was performed in Shoumen, Kazanluk, Svishtov, Gabrovo, Rousse, Panagyurishte, Varna, Lovech, Lyaskovets. It was also performed by the emigrant Bulgarian colonies, in Brăila, Bucharest, Giurgiu, and Constantinople.

23. Dobri Voinikov, "Raina Knyaginya," *Suchineniya,* vol. 1 (Sofia: Bulgarski pisatel, 1983), 122. All excerpts have been translated by me. I have tried as much as possible to preserve the stylistic register and the distinct archaic flavor that the Bulgarian originals exhibit. Further references to this work are included parenthetically in the text.

24. *Nevyanka i Svetoslav* is taken from Stefan Zahariev's short story *Nevyanka, boyarska dushterya* (Nevyanka, boyar's daughter), in its turn an adaptation of F. Karamzin's story of the same name (1867).

P l a y w r i g h t s   C i t e d

Fingov, Dimiter. *Nagradenii podvig. Drama v pet deistviya. Vienna,* 1871.

Manchov, Bogdan. *Izgoubena Stanka.* Bucharest: Narodna knigopechatnitsa, 1870.

Ouzounov, Atanas. *Dobur haidoutin. (Nasila ozhenvane.)* Sofia: Tsentralen dom za narodno tvorchestvo, 1966.

Pishourka, Krustyu. *Ispadnal turgovets ili smurtna zhertva. Pozorishtna igra, v tri deistviya.* Vienna: L. Sommer and Co., 1870.

Shishmanov, Dimiter. *Dobrodetel i zloba. Fantaziya v tri deistviya.* Rousse: Knigopechatnitsa na Dounavskata oblast, 1871.

Velichkov, Konstantin. *Nevyanka i Svetoslav. Drama v pet deistviya.* Constantinople, 1874.

Vladikin, I.S. "Velikii knyaz Boris." *Pozorishtni dela.* Bucharest, 1870-1871.

Voinikov, Dobri. "Dimanka, ili vyarna purvinska lyubov. Drama v pet deistviya." *Bulgarskata Dramatourgiya do Osvobozhdenieto.* Ed. Pencho Penev. Sofia: Bulgarski pisatel, 1964, v.II.

Voinikov, Dobri. "Stoyan voivoda. Sled padenieto na bulgarskoto tsarstvo. Tragichesko predstavlenie v tri deistviya." *Suchineniya,* v. 2. Sofia: Bulgarski pisatel, 1983, 267-97.

Zhivkov, Nikola. *Svetoulka. Drama v chetiri deistviya s ssteni iz Bulgarskii zhivot.* Rousse: V. Slavyanin, 1880.

Part II

Generic Patterns
and Social Constructs

5

ON THE ORIGINS OF THE ENGLISH MELODRAMA IN THE TRADITION OF BOURGEOIS TRAGEDY AND SENTIMENTAL DRAMA: LILLO, SCHRÖDER, KOTZEBUE, SHERIDAN, THOMPSON, JERROLD

LOTHAR FIETZ*

I.

*T*HAT THE TRIVIAL CAN PRODUCE LITERATURE OF SIGNIFICANCE was known long before things trivial and popular became objects of critical inquiry. Of course, the fact that critical interest in the trivial has grown sharply in the past two centuries in no way alters its triviality. Rather, it reflects a new relationship to the context and significance of the trivial, one that has resulted in valuable insights into the history of the mind set governing a broad segment of the public in the nineteenth century. This history has opened to view the substratum that more refined literature sought to transcend precisely because of its discomfort with this basic mindset.[1] Without a picture of this bedrock of popular literature—which a more inquiring literature reacted to and went beyond—any description of the epoch will remain incomplete. This is precisely why the growing critical interest in the melodrama can pave the way to a substantially more accurate understanding of the nineteenth century.

A number of recent works on the nineteenth-century English melodrama,[2] especially Johann N. Schmidt's *Aesthetik des Melodramas*,[3] have shed welcome light on production techniques and on the contingent nature of the rhetorical and thematic structures imposed on the work by artistic intention and audience expectation during the heyday of the melodrama. This essay has a somewhat narrower focus: the beginnings of the melodrama in the sentimental drama into which the bourgeois tragedy declined in the eighteenth century, and in which the exchange between national cultures intensified to an unexpected degree.

George Lillo's *The London Merchant* marks the beginning of a developmental process that moves through and links the French and German translations and adaptations of his play to August von Kotzebue's sentimental dramas. These in turn were widely performed in England in the last decade of the eighteenth century.[4] In order to show that Kotzebue's sentimental plays prefigure essential elements of the English melodrama, I will first look at his *Die Spanier in Peru* and Richard Brinsley Sheridan's adaptation, *Pizarro* (1799),[5] and then move on to *Menschenhaß und Reue* (Misanthropy and Repentance) and Benjamin Thompson's translation, *The Stranger* (1798). These plays will, in turn, be the starting point for a comparison of Kotzebue's work with an early example of the English melodrama, Douglas Jerrold's *Black-Ey'd Susan* (1829).[6] My goal is to show not only the intercultural paths leading to the birth of a genre, but the structural isomorphy inherent in this process.

II.

The fascination that Lillo's *London Merchant* worked on German dramatists around the middle of the eighteenth century is so well known there is no need to document it in any detail here.[7] Gottfried Lessing's *Miß Sara Sampson* (1755) and Bassewitz's *Der Kaufmann von London* (1757) offer sufficient initial evidence of the connection. The most obvious and concrete dramatic elements foreshadowing the melodrama then emerge some twenty years later in the changes that Friedrich Schröder made when he adapted Louis-Sébastien Mercier's French translation of *The London Merchant* as *Die Gefahren der Verführung* (Temptation's dangers) (1778).[8]

Lillo's "domestic tragedy" reflects the status and role that the bourgeoisie assigned to a "literature of its own" in the process of finding itself. The time for comic renditions of the bourgeois as nobleman was past. The middle class had matured to the point that it was a worthy subject for the middle genre, the novel, but it still lacked the legitimation offered by the highest genre—tragic dignity. The anthropology and the mechanisms of prebourgeois, heroic tragedy continued to operate in Lillo's work. Barnwell—who is so completely under the spell of the courtesan, Millwood, that "natural" ties and rules of behavior mean nothing (he murders his uncle)—clearly echoes those Shakespearean heroes who are slaves of passion, no longer guided by reason.[9] Lillo constructed his bourgeois protagonists on the basis of a model of the individual that assumed a dualism between mind and body, passion and reason—precisely the conception that the bourgeoisie was about to give up in favor of a sociological model. But thanks to this connection to pre-bourgeois anthropology, the bourgeois protagonist of the play achieved tragic status. Lillo's basic approach makes it appear that his protagonist is intimately related to the tragic hero of the pre-bourgeois era, except that, because of his lower social position, he can no longer unleash the kind of tragedy that Shakespeare's sovereign figures could—a tragedy that could also affect the social collective.

When Schröder takes up the material of Lillo's bourgeois tragedy almost a half-century later, a decisive change of attitude emerges. The bourgeois sense of self-worth no longer seems to need tragic confirmation. This marks the beginning of a process in which the bourgeoisie's consciousness of individual self-worth, which had first been heightened by tragedy, enters a new phase in which an untragic view of the self develops, a view that reflects the bourgeoisie's confidence in the power of its virtues and their ability to eliminate the tensions and conflicts that had been calculated into tragedy—those that pitted the passion-driven individual against the superindividual norms of reason. Within the framework of a closed system of private entities such as the family, this could contribute to a resolution of the tragic nexus. Once this point is reached, the tragic conflict can be replaced by actions that portray temporary moral confusion and that end with the reinstatement of the individual within the harmony of the bourgeois order.

In Schröder's adaptation, Adolph Millhof is, like Lillo's Barnwell, urged on to murder by the courtesan, Lina von Marin:

> LINA. Your happiness and mine. Now you must prove your
>   love to me. I demand from you the death of the man who
>   is persecuting me.
> ADOLPH. My father's brother? Lina! Horrors, what a
>   thought!—
> LINA. Weak, cowardly man! who has not the courage to make
>   his own happiness. Tomorrow you will have nothing
>   more to fear, you will be free, rich, and master of your
>   Lina.
> ADOLPH. Dreadful thought! God is my witness; I had no wish
>   to purchase a throne with the blood of this old man . . .
>   what right do I have over the days of his life.[10]

But Adolph does not murder his uncle; instead, at the decisive moment, he puts himself under the protection of his employer, Woldemar, and his uncle, Paul Millhof. This saves him from guilt and condemnation.

> **WOLD.** [*to Millhof*] Dear friend! Were you really in danger?
> **MILLH.** Not just a little. — It was only a question of my life —
> **WOLD.** [*to Adolph*] What should I call you? a recovered, or lost youth?
> **ADOLPH.** A repentant, one who has seen the light. . . .
> **MILLH.** . . . Well, I've had a bit of a fright. But tomorrow we can celebrate the happy way in which God turned away temptation.[11]

In this closing construct, events that pertain to a class — the bourgeoisie — are modulated down to the private level of the family, which thereby becomes the guarantor of the idea of order, able to protect and "save" a George Barnwell from his tragic conflict.

The title itself signals the distance between Schröder's play and *The London Merchant*. At this point, its privacy seems to have given the bourgeoisie powers of self-healing, and these powers have, in turn, become the source of self-satisfied and pleasurable emotions about the strength of its morality. In this sense, Schröder's play marks the transformation of bourgeois tragedy into bourgeois sentimental drama. In *Das bürgerliche Drama, seine Geschichte im 18. und 19. Jahrhundert* (1898) — a book that is still worth reading — Arthur Eloesser characterized this emerging tendency toward privatization and toward a "reductio ad familiam" as follows:

> The cadre for this art is supplied by the narrowest sphere of family life. There is no talk here of public life or affairs of state. At no time are the institutions of marriage and the family called into question as such; instead, exceptions that crop up within this order are rectified. The burgher is conceived of entirely in private terms. He is not linked to the wider world or dependent on economic forces.[12]

In the hermetic world of private life no consciousness of the surrounding public sphere remains, or still less of things having cosmic or transcendental dimensions. Only if viewed historically — against the background of the progressive narrowing of the prevailing frame of reference that started in the Middle Ages — is it clear to what degree the world has been reduced in the sentimental drama and the melodrama. Though the Middle Ages and the Renaissance still maintained categories of thought derived from a *world-view*, one that comprehended immanence and transcendence, a progressive banishing of the divine from this world-view slowly narrowed it to a *view of society*. And in a third phase, the one under examination here, this idea of society was further reduced to an image of the *family*, the collapse of which led to the emergence of a communicationless juxtaposition of private, isolated individuals. Then, finally, in the provisional end phase of this evolution, a dissecting, "microscopic" analysis begins to focus only on the discontinuous inner life of the individual. Within the progressive narrowing of the model of reality sketched here, the sentimental drama and the melodrama hold a middle position. In the course of this evolution the literary image of the bourgeois individual changed. Since the norms of the old, transbourgeois society were no longer sufficient, in the second half of the eighteenth century the burgher was refigured as someone able to take personal responsibility for justice. After Lenz's court tutor (*Der Hofmeister oder die Vorteile de Privaterziehung* [The tutor], 1774)[13] seduces Gustchen he enacts this sense of personal responsibility by castrating himself. Unlike Sophocles's Oedipus, who blinds himself in a tragic act of self-despair when he realizes that he has killed his father and slept with his mother, this seducer, unable to control his sexual urges, carries out preventative justice on himself. This act of self-mutilation as "self-deliverance" allows a conflict in the public sphere to be resolved in the private sphere. Echoes of classical tragedy are still perceptible, but even this *Sturm und Drang* work anticipates the sentimental drama and melodrama. The conflict between a self-willed individual and social institutions and between passion and reason is no longer draped as tragedy. And although painful human relations are represented, their pathos has demonstrably lost its initial tragic potential. This change in the relationship of the bourgeois individual to larger powers and to him/herself manifests itself as a shift from tragic to unfortunate but untragic existence.

III.

Although the initial direction of influence was from England to Germany—as is demonstrated by the German reception of Lillo, Richardson, Fielding, and Sterne—toward the end of the eighteenth century the situation was reversed. The bourgeois tragedy, which had metamorphosed into the sentimental drama in Germany, was reexported to England in this revised form. Kotzebue played a key role in this movement. Kotzebue (who, according to Goethe, loved whatever appealed to the public) took up the tendencies discussed above and developed them further. And the reception of his plays in England shows that the changes in the horizon of expectation proper to the bourgeois era in England followed one another in much the same way they did in Germany.

In the 1790s an astounding number of Kotzebue's plays were produced in translation on the English stage. After an artistic hiatus of more than twenty years, Richard Brinsley Sheridan (1751-1816), who in the 1770s had achieved great success with comedies of manners such as *The Rivals* (1775) and *The School for Scandal* (1777), adapted a translation of Kotzebue's *Die Spanier in Peru* for the English stage under the title *Pizarro* (1799). The reviewer who discussed the play in *Public Characters* did criticize Sheridan for his betrayal of the aesthetic principles he had laid down in *The Critic*, but he also had to acknowledge that

> *Pizzaro*, with all its defects, recommended by the joint reputation of Kotzebue and Sheridan, attracted more numerous and fashionable audiences than have ever attended an English theatre . . . . The genius of the German dramatist is unquestionably of the first order. In conducting a passion through its most intricate mazes, he is, perhaps, unequaled, and he seldom fails to produce emotions of the most agonizing kind. But probability, the genuine source of concern and dramatic feeling, is too frequently violated.[14]

Sheridan's adaptation of the play went through twenty printings in 1799 alone and by 1840 the play had been reprinted thirty times.[15]

On the surface, Kotzebue's *Spanier in Peru* seems to be a historical drama. Francisco Pizarro was a Spanish conquistador who led an expedition to Peru in 1532 in hopes of finding a hoard of gold. His greed, ambition, and cruelty were exceptional even by the standards of the conquistadors, but this historical information, like the political background and the problems surrounding these events, was more or less irrelevant to Kotzebue. A close look at the play reveals that behind the trappings of a *Haupt und Staatsaktion* (a play dealing with leaders and affairs of state) a world defined by the values of the bourgeois sentimental drama is in evidence.[16]

A 1799 review of the play mentions Kotzebue/Sheridan's ability "to produce emotions of the most agonizing kind," and adds that this achievement came at the expense of mimetic probability in the world represented by the play. The suggestion is that plays such as this aim primarily at generating emotional responses in the spectators. That the mimetic principle was seldom compatible with the intended effects in this type of play is a sign of the literary status of the genre.

IV.

Earl Bargainnier and John Cawelti have suggested that trivial literature in general—and the melodrama in particular—is formulaic in structure, and *Pizarro* seems to fit this description perfectly.[17] The thematic code in *Pizarro* upholds an unwavering formula, one that pervades the entire play: the antagonistic confrontation of good and evil. This formula initially manifests itself on the level of the play's key metaphors. On the one hand there is the vulture, which the ancient bestiaries presented in the double aspect of a two-headed bird of death because it first foretold the number of deaths in battle to augurs, and then took the fallen soldiers as its booty.[18] On the other hand, three images with overlapping significance are juxtaposed to the vulture: the lamb, the cygnet (young swan), and the dove (37, 62),[19] images that have since become formulaic clichés, shot through with sentiments about innocence, powerlessness, meekness, and purity.

The thematic code evidenced in the imagery of the play also regulates the world depicted in *Pizarro*. The vulture, here equated with the Spanish forces, is mentioned in association with representations of oppression, betrayal, and baseness, and is interpreted in terms of a catalogue of vices including "insatiate avarice" and "pride" (26, 37). These vices are not simply named in the play, they appear on stage in the actions of the characters.

Clearly, the world represented in *Pizarro* is not derived from actual political or cultural history. Instead it depends on a dualism between good and evil that can only be understood from a moral standpoint, a dualism in which the Peruvian side is presented as the "lambs." This basic idea of innocence and powerlessness is constantly reinforced by additional interpretive sallies. The Peruvians are referred to as "our innocent and unoffending brethren" (24), as "children of innocence" who receive their guests with "eager hospitality and confiding kindness" and "generosity" (26). Las Casas, the Spanish priest who sympathizes with humanity in general and with the Peruvians in particular, pleads for "pity," "compassion," "forgiveness," and "humanity" in the face of Pizarro's Machiavellian villainies. There also seem to be echoes of Marlowe's Tamburlaine in the play. Pizarro is "self-taught, self-raised, and self-supported" (22). Everything he does stems from his self-centeredness and his need to make himself absolute. He is a "slave of passion, avarice, and pride." (37)

Here, the fundamental thematic code of the play is expanded through a second antithesis: an extreme self-centeredness is juxtaposed to a mastery of self through sympathy and pity—a self that, according to Christian tradition, has pronounced ungodly tendencies. These antithetical positions derive from the medieval system of virtues and vices, but overlaying the medieval Christian perception of the Good as self-mastery in obedience to God are attitudes that belong to the eighteenth-century sentimental tradition stemming from Schaftesbury. The Peruvians emerge as embodiments of uncorrupted human nature, their inner and unfailing ethical sense still intact. For example, Rolla, the Peruvian leader, has an opportunity to kill Pizarro, "the scourge of innocence, the terror of the Peruvian race, the fiend," but, in a truly sentimental and "naturally" enlightened gesture, he instead chooses an alternative referred to as "Peruvian vengeance" (68).

> ROLLA. The God of Justice sanctifies no evil step towards good.
> Great actions cannot be achieved by wicked means (66).

In the sentimental drama such spiritual nobility stands in contrast to the villain's nobility of birth. Moral aristocracy is no longer tied to a single class. So, in the sentimental drama and in the melodrama, there is more and more opportunity for the bourgeois individual to play the role of the—untragic— hero. The theme of the classlessness of moral aristocracy is closely linked to the theme of altruistic unselfishness and self-denial, and this thematic linkage provides the stimulus for a culinary-narcissistic enjoyment of the virtues that the bourgeoisie attributed to itself. The enlightened Puritanism and sentimentalism that developed in the eighteenth century supply the medieval Christian notion of virtue with a new content. Thus, "self-denial"—individual denial of self before God with all its religious implications, including fear of God and contempt for the worldliness and transitoriness of the self—takes on decidedly secular dimensions in the bourgeois era.

The vulture/lamb code that governs the choice of characters in *Pizarro* also implicitly regulates the action: the lambs and doves must be victimized by the vultures. And here a problematic aspect of sentimentalism's notion of virtue begins to emerge, one that comes fully to the fore later, in the nineteenth-century novel. As literary sentimentalism evolves, it soon becomes apparent that the specifically altruistic virtues typical of the "man of feeling"—self-denial, sympathy, pity, and caritas—can also be interpreted as weakness or even as impotence in the sentimental character.[20] Towards the end of the century these virtues were, in general, still presented in a quite positive light in the sentimental drama, but they had also begun to be viewed as weaknesses that would almost certainly provoke "vultures" into sacrificing lambs. Here, the culinary emotions that arose when the virtues characteristic of one's own class were depicted began to mix with the emotions that crop up when a representative of these virtues is pursued or even destroyed. Self-indulgent emotion was tinged with feelings of mourning and of fear. This specific linkage of affects intended for the spectator is typical of the sentimental drama in the transitional period at the end of the eighteenth and the beginning of the nineteenth century. A sense of fear could be stimulated by portraying the difference in power that exists between villains and the virtuous, that is, between the principles of evil and good. In terms of the action, there was no longer a struggle; instead the traditional dramatic agon was increasingly replaced by events involving pursuit and annihilation, and by the victimization of virtue through evil.

Sentimental drama of the type represented by *Pizarro* stands at the threshold of the nineteenth century, a time when precisely those virtues cherished by enlightened sentimentalism were recast as weaknesses within the capitalist economic system, weaknesses that turned the sentimental hero into a victim.[21] The extent to which a mimetic deficit plagues the sentimental drama at the beginning of the nineteenth century is evident in the fact that the characters embodying the bourgeois virtues are always the victims of an unqualified evil. By comparison, the history of the industrial revolution clearly indicates that segments of the bourgeoisie had long since let positive notions of "self-reliance" deteriorate into individualistic self-assertion and a competitive mentality at the expense of the altruistic virtues. They had, in other words, gone over to the side of the "victimizers." So, as the desire to provoke culinary anxiety in the spectator emerges, the etiology of the suffering presented on stage fades into the background and the private souldrama of persons tormented by villains comes to the fore.

At the same time that the world represented in the play is reduced to the dimensions of the private and the familial, a complementary internalizing and psychologizing of the characters occurs. Beyond these realms no larger political and economic system seems to exist. Thus, the Peruvians in *Pizarro* do not embody a society *(Gesellschaft)*, they represent a community *(Gemeinschaft)* founded on the basis of power-free, private relations. Of course, the Peruvians have a king, but his authority is grounded in the principles of partnership and love:

> ROLLA. . . . We serve a Monarch whom we love—a God
> whom we adore—. . . . The throne we Honour is the
> PEOPLE'S CHOICE—the laws we reverence are
> our brave Fathers' legacy—the faith we follow teaches
> us to live in bonds of charity with all mankind (37).

The State and social body are held together by the idea of brotherhood. Cora gives expression to this idea when she poses the rhetorical question: "are not all men brethren?" (34).

If one links these various historical and conceptual elements together, the syncretic philosophy in a sentimental drama like *Pizarro* becomes clear: the mystic belief that no man is an island, that he is fundamentally linked to others, fuses with the democratic ideas of equality and fraternity that led to the French Revolution, and with fellow feeling and pity, empathy and sympathy—the concepts fundamental to enlightened sentimentalism. Although these ideas derive from different traditions of thought, they meet and even interpenetrate in the sentimental drama. When brought on stage together, their presence leads to a pronounced emphasis on private and personal connections as the basis for community. The members of such a community *(Gemeinschaft)*, in contrast to those in a society *(Gesellschaft)*, are not bound together by public functions and roles but by compassion. Indeed, large sections of *Pizarro* are given over to depicting aspects of private, triangular relationships. For example, Rolla, the Peruvian general, and Alonzo, the Spaniard who switches sides and joins the Peruvians, love the same woman:

> . . . Rolla, the kinsman of the King, is the hero of our army; in war
> a tiger, chafed by the hunter's spear; in peace as gentle as the
> unweaned lamb. Cora was once betrothed to him, but finding she
> preferred Alonzo, he resigned his claim, and, I fear, his peace, to
> friendship and to Cora's happiness; yet still he loves her with a
> pure and holy fire (30).

Rolla, the spotless hero of this play, is a "man of feeling," unselfish and self-denying. Instead of pursuing his own fortune, he wishes only to make others happy. Because of this, he gives Cora to his friend Alonzo, to whom he remains bound by friendship and brotherliness. In order to achieve the effect aimed at by the sentimental drama, this basic idea is played up as much as possible. Alonzo, aware that he may die in the war with the Spanish, asks his friend Rolla to be his heir: "Be Cora thy wife—be Thou a father to my child" (32). And later, when Alonzo is taken captive by the Spaniards, Rolla does not waver in his dispassionate altruism; he takes Alonzo's place in prison so that this father and husband can escape and make Cora happy again.

The sentimental drama is one of those literary sites at which the basic ideas of sentimental philosophy, as a philosophy of humane consideration, decline into pure sentimentality. The foundations for the private relationships between the "good" characters in the sentimental play are unselfishness and self-denial—even to the point of self-sacrifice when it is a question of making one's fellow beings happy. But the "bonds of charity" sublimate potentially impassioned relationships, turning them into partnerships "of . . . toil . . . feelings and . . . fame" (37). Only dispassionate and sentimentally sublimated relationships can grow in the pan-caritative soil of brotherhood and mystic solidarity, relationships that become a source of maudlin pleasure. Within the framework provided by the world-view in this sort of sentimental drama, the sublime—a source of fear, reverence, and admiration—is displaced by the sublimated—here a source of culinary feelings about the possibility that human nature, passionate in its raw form, can be open to altruistic transfiguration and sublimation.

V.

In addition to sublimated male/female, male/male, and female/female relationships, Kotzebue/Sheridan also dramatizes the connections between mother and child or father and child as a means of creating culinary affect. In literature in general, and in the drama in particular, children had not previously been assigned this kind of key role. According to Elisabeth Badinter and others working on the social history of sentiment, a new attitude toward children developed around 1760, one that the sentimental drama used to the full: "Beginning in the eighteenth century, a new image of the ideal mother began to emerge, and the features would be molded into increasingly accentuated forms over the next two centuries. The era of 'proofs of love' had begun. The baby and the child would become the center of the mother's attention. The woman would agree to sacrifice herself . . . so that her little one could live."[22]

Kotzebue was quick to take up this trend and exploit it for the sentimental drama. Cora is modeled after the new image of the mother. Despite the sublimation of all her libidinal instincts, she has managed—God knows how—to have a child. The child in turn becomes the source of the mother's sentimental joys as Mother. And this intimate, mother-child relationship becomes a source of the feelings the sentimental drama will instill in the spectator. Sentimental plays even develop a specific rhetoric for the bliss that the child engenders in the mother:

> **CORA.** The ecstasy of his birth I pass; that in part is selfish: but
> when first the white blossoms of his teeth appear,
> breaking the crimson buds that did encase them; that is
> a day of joy: next, when from his father's arms he runs
> without support, and clings, laughing and delighted, to
> his mother's knee; that is the mother's heart's next
> holiday: and sweeter still the third, whene'er his little

stammering tongue shall utter the grateful sound of,
Father, Mother! — O! that is the dearest joy of all! (33).

In a world that has been reduced to the dimensions of the family, the child
is something akin to an emotional catalyst that enables the sublimation of
feelings.

CORA. . . . a mother's love for her dear babe . . . is a new delight
that turns with quicken'd gratitude to HIM, the author
of her augmented bliss (33).

What Cora suggests is that the child has enhanced the quality of the hus-
band-wife relationship. Of course, what she has in mind is not erotic pleasure. Rather, and fully in accord with the decorum of the sentimental drama,
the father of the child becomes the "cause" of the increased bliss of the
mother as Mother.

The child emerges here as a literary figure with a quite specific function,
but to see how this happens one must begin with the new attitude toward
the child that came to the fore in the Romantic movement. What was needed
was a new set of expectations and fears regarding the child and the dangers
that could befall it. Once this new perspective was in place the child could
be further stylized in the sentimental drama and used as a figure meant to
stimulate emotions whenever it was endangered.

VI.

When Diderot spoke of the villain as the "stage-setter" *(machiniste)* of the
drama, he had in mind the way in which the villain functions as the motor
for the action. If one retains Diderot's image as a means of describing the
way in which plays in general — and the sentimental drama and melodrama
in particular — function in terms of aesthetic affect, then one could say that,
on the whole, they serve as "stage machinery" *(Maschinerien)* for the production and stimulation of the spectator's emotions. As part of this machinery, the child is just one of several figures that keep things "moving." The
emotional potential built into a situation in which a child is ill-treated or separated from its mother is obviously considerable, but, if one looks at these
situations in terms of actantial models, it is evident that the figure of the child
is interchangeable with, for instance, that of the innocent young woman.[23]
In both cases, the desired agitation in the spectator is stimulated by con-
templation of innocence, powerlessness, chastity, and persecution. Whatever

displacement there is from one to the other has mainly to do with the figures as individualized *acteurs*, and much less to do with the deep structure and the function of the *actant*. What this means is that—on the actantial level—even when shifted from the German to an English context the basic mechanisms of stimulation remain the same.

Kotzebue's *Menschenhaß und Reue* (1790) had appeared in four different English translations by the end of the eighteenth century, one of which was *The Stranger* by Benjamin Thompson.[24] Since this translation remained immensely popular on the English stage up to the middle of the nineteenth century, it will provide the evidence for this part of my analysis.[25] *The Stranger* is a play about adultery, about the separation of a married couple and their ultimate reunion. The betrayed husband hides from the world behind the protective mask of a misanthrope, but this misanthropy actually only serves to conceal his still intact, altruistic kindness. Once again, virtues stemming from the sentimental tradition—brotherliness, caritas, altruism, and self-denial—enable culinary enjoyment of morality. But the play moves off on a different tack, toward the tension-filled moment at which the audience will see whether the protagonist of a sentimental play can sustain his "moving" behavior when he confronts his faithless wife. There is a pause when the former husband and wife, who have lived near each other without knowing it, meet and recognize each other. At this point the betrayed husband's benevolence is not sufficient for a reconciliation.

At the high point of this test of virtue, Kotzebue—well aware of the emotional potential offered by such figures—brings their children into the game. They have been kept from their mother and, at their father's behest, are being cared for somewhere nearby. The mother, already plagued by old feelings of guilt, is also filled with fear that something may have happened to her children:

> MRS. H[ALLER]. Oh! but one minute more! An answer to
> but one more question. — Feel for a mother's heart! —
> Are my children still alive?
> STRA[NGER]. Yes, they are alive.
> MRS. H. And well?
> STRA. Yes, they are well.
> MRS. H. Heaven be praised! William must be much grown?
> STRA. I believe so.
> MRS. H. What! have you not seen them! —And little Amelia, is
> she still your favorite? [*The Stranger, who is in violent
> agitation throughout this scene, remains in silent contention
> between honour and affection*] Oh! let me behold them once

again! — let me once more kiss the features of their
father in his babes, and I will kneel to you, and then part
with them forever (71).

This activates the emotional potential inherent in a situation in which a married couple has separated at the expense of "innocent children" — the same
potential that, even today, determines the strategies of the trivial press and
trivial literature when they aim at stirring their reader's emotions. The liberation of this emotional potential reaches its high point when the children,
the victims of this shattered marriage, are brought on and give stammering
but eloquent evidence of the importance of an intact marriage for the wel-
fare of children:

[. . . *as they are going, she encounters the* BOY *and he the* GIRL]

CHILDREN. Dear father! Dear mother!

[*They press the* CHILDREN *in their arms with speechless affection
then they tear themselves away — gaze at each other — spread their arms,
and rush into an embrace. The* CHILDREN *run, and cling round their*
PARENTS. *The Curtain falls*] (72).

The play ends with the restoration of a lost order. Like the melodrama, the
sentimental play is marked by a characteristic, though undeclared, urge
toward harmony in the construction of its final moments: poetic justice prevents the tragic, ineluctable demise of the hero or heroine. And unlike
tragedy, in which the hero moves from ignorance to knowledge at the
moment of his downfall, and in defeat gains wisdom, the sentimental play,
though it manages to broach metaphysical, existential, and social problems,
generally does so only momentarily, to kindle emotions and specific moods.
The absence of a tragic conflict — which is replaced by actions centering
around pursuit and persecution — does not signify that the sentimental drama
or the melodrama is without tension, but it is a tension of ". . . and then?"

The conceptual closure of the "little world" of the sentimental drama and
melodrama becomes most obvious in the fact that the main question — about
the source of evil — and questions about social and political factors are neither asked nor pursued. Thus, in *Menschenhaß und Reue,* the fact of adultery
is explained neither in terms of human nature nor as an upshot of social circumstances — just as there is little or no insight into the political forces behind
the figure of Pizarro in *Die Spanier von Peru.* Their obvious narrowing of perspective and the limitations placed on the problems to be dealt with lead to
a reduction of the locus of problems to the individual, to the family, or to some

ahistorical "human condition." These narrow perspectival nodes are symptoms of the absence of a consciousness of larger connections.

The sentimental plays that were exported to England—that were adapted there and then enjoyed an enduring popularity—show surprising isomorphism with the later English melodrama. If one compares Jerrold's *Black-Ey'd Susan* (1829) with plays like *Pizarro* or *The Stranger*, there are, needless to say, some displacements at the level of the *acteurs*, but there are also obvious correspondences, both in terms of their key thematic images and the underlying deep thematic structures. For example, Jerrold develops the thematic code of his play by means of a series of images in a dream:

> GNATBRAIN. Aye; I dreamt that a young lamb was set upon
>   by a wolf, when, strange to say, a lion lept upon it, and
>   tore it piecemeal; at this moment a band of hunters came
>   up, and secured the noble brute; they were about to kill
>   the lion, their guns were pointed, their swords drawn,
>   when a thing, at first no bigger than my hand, appeared
>   in the sky—it came closer and I saw it was a huge
>   vulture; it went wheeling round and round the victim
>   lion, and appeared to anticipate the feast of blood—and
>   with a red and glaring eye, and grasping talons, seemed
>   to demand the carcase, ere the lion yet was dead.[26]

Though the play offers what seems to be a different set of dramatic characters, the structural analogy to *Pizarro* is unmistakable. The basic formula is even repeated in the selection of the images that pit the lamb against the vulture. There is a slight difference in the way the formula is structured, but this has little impact on the basic conception of the play. In contrast to *Pizarro*, the predator's camp is differentiated—wolf, lion and vultures— meaning there is greater variation in transposing the fundamental *actants* into various *acteurs* with the same or comparable functions. Nonetheless, the relationship between the opposing sides is the same as in *Pizarro*. In Jerrold's melodrama, too, the action implicit in the formula unfolds as an act of persecution. If one looks at the surface structure, the level on which the *acteurs* operate, the victim is not a child as in *Pizarro*, but Jerrold's heroine bears similar traits: she is an "orphan child," "poor and unprotected" (9), and has been separated from her husband by an intrigue. By playing on the image of "a caged nightingale" (8), thereby invoking the Philomela–Tereus myth, the conception of the melodramatic heroine as victim is deepened. This also allows the motifs of power and defilement to be brought into play as variants on the theme of victimization.

The actantial function of the persecutor figure—here transcribed on the metaphorical level in the images of the wolf, the lion, and the vulture—is implemented through two *acteurs* in this play. Due to his name, the first of these, Hatchet, the captain of the Redbreast, is characterized negatively from the start. But the usual persecution plot is given an erotic twist here. As might be expected, Hatchet pursues Susan—the heroine destined to be his victim. However, his libidinal instincts appear to be sublimated in a peculiar way by the decorum of an era that, although by and large hostile to the senses, was nevertheless keen on erotic sensations—as, for example, when Hatchet emphatically repeats, "I'm going to be married. . . . I must marry Susan. . . ." (7). Melodramatic decorum keeps the steam of the melodramatic machine from getting too hot. The *machiniste* (using Diderot's term for the villain) pursues his erotic intrigues under the guise of bourgeois respectability and repeatedly conceals his libidinal instincts behind the euphemism of "marriage." Here—via the figure of the "rake" and under the impact of Victorian decorum—the pathetic hero of tragedy is transformed into the villain of melodrama: the villain disguised as a respectable citizen.

After Hatchet leaves the stage, Crosstree appears. He serves the same actantial function, but his intentions are somewhat more evident:

> **CROSSTREE.** I know it is wrong, but I will see her —and come what may. I must and will possess her (21).

> I know I may be wrong, but passion hurries me —the wine fires me —your eyes dart lightening into me, and you shall be mine! [*Seizes Susan*] (30).

This analysis could be extended to the other main characters as well as to the secondary figures, since they serve instrumental functions as helpers or opponents in building the tension necessary to the intrigue and pursuit. It could also be expanded to include later melodramas such as Boucicault's *The Colleen Bawn* (1860), Hazlewood's *Lady Audley's Secret* (1863), Taylor's *The Ticket-of-Leave Man* (1863), and so on, plays that have at least survived in various anthologies. However, such detailed investigations would hardly provide other relevant new in sights. In his thoroughgoing study of the nineteenth-century melodrama, J. N. Schmidt appraised a number of relatively unknown texts without coming across a comparable set of structural displacements. That he presented his analyses in a systematic, typological format and not as a history of the melodrama in the nineteenth century is due to the consistently formulaic nature of this popular genre.

The aim of the present work is to offer a genealogy that can stand alongside a systematic presentation of the aesthetic and the typology of the melodrama in the nineteenth century. The initial assumption here has been that—in the course of its reception in Germany—Lillo's bourgeois tragedy underwent a transformation due to the bourgeoisie's own changing attitude toward itself, and that it reappeared as the sentimental drama. Then, in England—as the reception of Kotzebue's work demonstrates—this drama encountered a set of expectations that determined the positive reception of the sentimental drama, the preservation of the actantial constellations typical of the genre, and the characteristic course of action along with the strategies that steer emotion and sympathy. The structural history of the English melodrama in the nineteenth century is a history of variations on a fundamental and amazingly constant thematic code, variations that operate on the malleable surface structure of these plays.

Notes

* Translated by Michael Hays.
1. See, for example, Thackeray's polemical discussion of the melodrama *The Stranger*: "Those who know the play of the 'Stranger' are aware that the remarks made by the various characters are not valuable in themselves, either for their sound sense, their novelty of observation, or their poetic fancy. Nobody ever talked so. If we meet idiots in life, as will happen, it is a great mercy that they do not use such absurdly fine words. The Stranger's talk is a sham, like the book he reads, and the hair he wears, and the bank he sits on, and the diamond ring he makes play with—but, in the midst of the balderdash, there runs that reality of love, children, and forgiveness of wrong, which will be listened to wherever it is preached, and sets all the world sympathising." W. M. Thackeray, *The History of Pendennis* (Oxford, New York: Oxford University Press, 1994), 47. See also "French Dramas and Melodramas," in *The Works of William Makepeace Thackeray*, vol. 5 (New York: Harper and Brothers, 1898), 235-52.
2. Michael Booth, *English Melodrama* (London: H. Jenkins, 1965); Robert Bechtold Heilman, *Tragedy and Melodrama: Visions of Experience* (Seattle: University of Washington Press, 1968); Charles G. Bird, *The Role of the Family in Melodrama, 1797-1827* (Visalia, Ca: Jostens, 1976); Robert Leach, *Victorian Melodrama* (London: Harrap, 1978); Kurt Tetzeli von Rosador, "Myth and Victorian Melodrama," *Essays and Studies* 32 (1979): 97-114 and "Das Idyllische im englischen Melodrama des 19. Jahrhunderts," in *Idylle und Modernisierung in der europäischen Literatur des 19. Jahrhunderts*, ed. Hans Ulrich Seeber and Paul Gerhard Klussmann (Bonn: Bovier, 1986), 24-36.

3. Johann N. Schmidt, *Aesthetik des Melodramas: Studien zu einem Genre des populären Theatres im England des 19. Jahrhunderts* (Heidelberg: C. Winter, 1986).

4. See L. F. Thompson, *Kotzebue, A Survey of his Progress in France and England* (Paris: Champion, 1928); Marcella Gosh, "Translators of Kotzebue in England," *Monatshefte für den Deutschen Unterricht* 31 (1939): 175-83; Doris Maurer, *August von Kotzebue: Ursachen seines Erfolges: Konstante Elemente der unterhaltenden Dramatik* (Bonn: Bovier, 1979), esp. the section on Kotzebue's success in England, 239ff; Walter Sellier, *Kotzebue in England: Ein Beitrag zur Geschichte der englischen Bühne und der Beziehungen der deutschen Literatur zur englischen Bühne* (Leipzig: O. Schmidt, 1901). *The Stranger* was performed regularly every year up to 1842. The last recorded performance was in 1872.

5. *The Plays and Poems of Richard Brinsley Sheridan*, vol. 3, ed. R. Crompton Rhodes (New York: Macmillan, 1929).

6. August von Kotzebue, *The Stranger*, trans. Benjamin Thompson, in *The British Theatre*, vol. 24 (London: Longman, Hurst, Rees, Orm, and Brown, 1808), and Douglas William Jerrold, *Black-Ey'd Susan*, in *Nineteenth-Century Plays*, 2d ed., ed. George Rowell (London, New York: Oxford University Press, 1972).

7. *The London Merchant; or the History of George Barnwell: A Tragedy* (1731), trans. by Henning Adam von Bassewitz as *Der Kaufmann von London oder Begebenheiten George Barnwells: ein bürgerliches Trauerspiel* (1752), ed. Klaus-Detlef Müller (Tubingen: Niemeyer, 1981). See Horst Albert Glaser, *Das bürgerliche Ruhrstück* (Stuttgart: J. B. Metzler, 1969), and Peter Szondi, *Die Thorie des bürgerlichen Trauerspiels im 18. Jahrhundert: Der Kaufmann, der Hausvater, und der Hofmeister*, ed. Gert Mattenklott (Frankfurt a. M.: Suhrkamp, 1974). Cf. Arthur Eloesser, *Das bürgerliche Drama: Seine Geschichte im 18. und 19. Jahrhundert* (1898; reprint, Geneva: Slatkine Reprints, 1970).

8. *Die Gefahren der Verführung: Ein Schauspiel in vier Aufzügen. Nach Mercier's* Jenneval, in *Friedrich Ludwig Schröders Dramatische Werke*, ed. Eduard von Bülow with an introduction by Ludwig Tieck (Berlin: G. Reimer, 1831), 157-98.

9. See Lily Campbell, *Shakespeare's Tragic Heroes: Slaves of Passion* (New York: Barnes and Noble, 1952). The problematic nexus—bourgeoisie, puritanism, capitalism—first raised by Max Weber in *The Protestant Ethic and the Spirit of Capitalism* and then further developed by Szondi in his discussion of *The London Merchant* (see note 7) needs no further elaboration here. But the notion of passion deserves a note, since the ever greater reduction of the term to its sexual aspect hides the many other facets that were still operative in the eighteenth century and that applied to all sorts of selfish behavior: the will to power and to money, etc. and erotic passion all had in common the will to satisfy egoistic ends.

10. Schröder, *Die Gefahren der Verführung* (IV, vii), 191.

11. Ibid. (IV, xiii), 195, 198.

12. Eloesser, *Das bürgerliche Drama*, 59.

13. An English translation of the play is available in J. M. R. Lenz, *The Tutor and The Soldiers*, trans. William E. Yuill (Chicago: University of Chicago Press, 1972).

14. Sheridan, vol. 3, 7.

15. The play was translated under various titles in England: M. G. Lewis, *Rolla, or the Peruvian Hero* (1797), which had been reprinted twenty-six times by 1800; T. Dutton, *Pizarro in Peru, or the Death of Rolla* (1799); R. Heron, *Pizarro in Peru* (1799). In connection with these plays, see Mayron Marlaw, "English Versions of *Die Spanier in Peru*," *MLQ,* 16 (1955): 63-67.

16. See Eloesser, *Das bürgerliche Drama,* 193.

17. Earl F. Bargainnier, "Melodrama as Formula," *Journal of Popular Culture,* 9 (1975): 726-33, and John G. Cawelti, "The Concept of Formula in the Study of Popular Literature, *Journal of Popular Culture,* 3 (1969): 318-90.

18. See T. H. White, *The Book of Beasts, Being a Translation from a Latin Bestiary of the Twelfth Century* (London: Jonathan Cape, 1954), 109-110.

19. This and further parenthetical references to Pizarro are from *Plays of Sheridan,* vol. 3. A similar encoding process is evident in *The London Merchant,* which draws on the images of the "hawk" and "partridge." See Lillo, *The London Merchant* (Lincoln: University of Nebraska Press, 1965), 22.

20. See Henry Mackenzie, *The Man of Feeling* (1771), ed. Brian Vickers (London, New York: Oxford University Press, 1967).

21. See Wolfgang Herrlinger, *Sentimentalismus und Postsentimentalismus: Studien zum englischen Roman bis zur Mitte des 19. Jahrhunderts* (Tubingen: Niemeyer, 1987).

22. Elizabeth Badinter, *Mother Love: Myth and Reality* (New York: Macmillan, 1980), 169.

23. On this topic, see Vladimir Propp, *Morphologie des Märchens* (Munich: Karl Hanser, 1972) and Algirdas J. Greimas, "Actantial Models," in *Structural Semantics: An Attempt at a Method* (Lincoln: University of Nebraska Press, 1984).

24. The translations were: G. Papendick, *The Stranger* (1798); A. Schink, *The Stranger* (1798); J. Hemet, *Misanthropy and Repentance* (1799); and B. Thompson, *The Stranger* (1800).

25. Kotzebue, *The Stranger,* trans. Thompson, in *British Theatre,* vol. 24. Further references to this work are included parenthetically in the text. On the popularity of Thompson's translation of *The Stranger,* see note 4.

26. Jerrold, *Black-Ey'd Susan,* in *Nineteenth-Century Plays,* ed. Rowell, 32. Further references to this work are included parenthetically in the text.

6

THE RETURN OF MARTIN GUERRE IN AN EARLY NINETEENTH CENTURY FRENCH MELODRAMA

BARBARA T. COOPER

CHARLES HUBERT'S *Le Faux Martinguerre, ou la Famille d'Artigues* (The false Martinguerre, or the d'Artigues family), a three-act *mélodrame à grand spectacle*, was first performed at the Théâtre de la Gaîté in Paris on 23 August 1808 and drew large crowds to that theatre for approximately one month.[1] As was common in that era, initial publication of the piece followed closely on the heels of its successful opening. Later reprintings, in 1813 and 1824, point to the work's continued appeal.[2] Said to be drawn from the pages of the *Causes célèbres*, a collection of celebrated court cases published by François Gayot de Pitaval in the eighteenth century, the play recounts an episode in the life of Martinguerre [sic], count of Artigues, a Frenchman whose identity and property are temporarily appropriated by a lowly born impostor named Arnaud du Tilh. According to historian Natalie Z. Davis, however, the drama grossly deforms the true story of the sixteenth-century French peasant Martin Guerre, whose family and friends were duped into believing that Arnaud du Tilh was in fact their long absent kinsman and neighbor.[3] Davis's reaction to Hubert's distortion of the historical record is, of course, understandable given her disciplinary perspective and her extensive archival research. Unlike history, though, drama is under no obligation to respect the facts. On the contrary, for a theatre piece to be effective and persuasive, truth must often bow to dramatic convention and the tale told must generally fall within the parameters of audience expectations. It is not surprising, therefore, that while borrowing the broad outlines of a well-known judicial case for the framework of his piece, an early-nineteenth-century

French playwright might decide to transform a complex legal matter into a simplified, archetypal tale of the conflict between honesty and deception, virtue and villainy. More important, then, than the matter of the play's historical accuracy is the question of *why* Hubert elected to dramatize the story of Martin Guerre and *why* he transformed that celebrated case of impersonation in the way he did.

Although we have no preface, letters, or other documents that directly explain Hubert's choice of subject, we do know something of the historico-aesthetic context in which the dramatist made his decision. As early as 1773, Louis-Sébastien Mercier emphasized the didactic goals of drama in a volume entitled *Du Théâtre, ou Nouvel Essai sur l'art dramatique* (On the Theatre, or New Essay on dramatic art). "A theatrical performance offers a tableau," Mercier wrote in the introduction to his study; "One must make that tableau useful, that is to say, [one must] put it within reach of the greatest number [of people], so that the image it presents might serve to bind people together through victorious feelings of compassion and pity. It is therefore not enough that the soul be engaged or even moved; it must be drawn to good; the moral goal [of the play], without being hidden or too obvious, must capture the heart and establish its influence there."[4] Considering it the role of the theatre to serve as a place where evildoers are judged and punished, where those "monsters" who sully good names and violate sacred duties can be brought before the court of public opinion, Mercier signals the interest celebrated court cases hold for those dramatists who wish to make a contribution to society.

> After the courts have pronounced their verdicts against the unjust father, the unnatural child, the unfaithful agent, the traitor, the hypocrite, the titled thief, the liar, the blackguard in favor, etc., if the poet then decided to produce those social monsters on the stage and to seek confirmation of the triumph of the law in the public's applause, how much force, radiance, and power that second verdict born of genius would have! With what strength the novelty of current events would bolster his talent! How quickly minds, barely freed from that sway in which they had been held by the equal eloquence of the two opposing attorneys, would side with truth! . . . And what a positive benefit would be derived from this second [judicial] apparatus! The guilty party would tremble that crimes brought to the attention of the tribunal would no longer remain buried and lost in the dust of the court clerk's office, but would come out of the shadows and be immortalized on the stage.[5]

In a footnote appended to this observation about what can be gained from the dramatization of legal controversies, Mercier notes that he had once read the *Causes célèbres* compiled by Gayot de Pitaval. While condemning the diffuseness and pedantic style of that work, Mercier nonetheless insists that he had never read anything that fascinated him so completely. "The hallmark of truth impressed upon those singular and extraordinary recent events sparked an interest in my heart that the most brilliant fictions by the greatest poets and the best novelists had never managed to produce," he declares.[6]

Some thirty years later, Pierre-Louis de Lacretelle, the elder, wrote in the preface to his dramatic novel *Le Jeune Malherbe, ou le Fils naturel* (The young Malherbe, or the illegitimate son) that "There is a greater connection than one might think between the celebrated events of a judicial nature and those that might prove touching on stage."[7] Echoing Mercier's declarations on the moral and social purpose of drama, Lacretelle, too, insists that "It is the finest attribute of the theatre to condemn those vices and disorders that gain acceptance thanks to certain laws and opinions; it is in the theatre that the conscience of virtuous people, shored up by the authority of public censure, can be heard."[8] Lacretelle distinguishes, however, between the accuracy required in the depiction of individuals in historical documents, personal memoirs, and judicial records and the license afforded those engaged in the aesthetic (re)production of action and character. He believes that, when representing individuals on stage, one may "heighten and even exaggerate their character, provided that by preserving their principal distinguishing features, one takes care to assure that the subjects [depicted] do not fall outside of their known parameters."[9]

A journalist named Jacques-Barthélemy Salgues espouses a similar opinion in his review of *Le Faux Martinguerre* published in the *Courrier de l'Europe et des spectacles* in 1808. Like Mercier and Lacretelle, he believes that

> The *Causes célèbres* can become a fecund source [of inspiration] for authors of melodramas. They will find therein singular adventures, combinations that are all the more rare in that, for the most part, they are the product of a profound meditation and of often ingenious calculations. These subjects will at least have the merit of recalling some interesting memories, of presenting facts that are more plausible, less bizarre, and less monstrous that those customarily offered us.
>
> Doubtless the author must allow himself to violate history to some degree, to raise his subject upon the stilts of the [melodramatic] genre, and to pump up his characters to make them appear more important, because melodrama likes larger than life figures and puffed up heroes.[10]

It is not only against the background of these theoretical statements on the moral, social, and aesthetic benefits to be derived from the transformation of well-known legal cases into popular drama that we should read Hubert's adaptation of the Martin Guerre story, however. Beginning in 1807, Count Maurice Méjan started publishing a series of volumes entitled *Recueil des Causes célèbres, et des arrêts qui les ont décidées* (Collection of celebrated cases, and the verdicts by which they were resolved). This new *Collection*, although modeled on the earlier volumes by Gayot de Pitaval, drew its material from contemporary court records and presented conflicts that, to one degree or another, had the French Revolution for a backdrop. The case known as the "Affaire de Madame de Douhault," published in volume 3 of the *Collection*, thus relates the story of a woman who may or may not have usurped the identity of a marchioness. In the introduction to his summary of the legal briefs and proceedings, Méjan outlines the affair as follows:

> Did a brother, inspired by the most sordid type of greed and assisted by some of his close relations, have his sister, a virtuous and estimable woman, locked up in a loathsome place, in the Salpêtrière prison, by means of a *lettre de cachet*? Did he deprive her of all means of appeal against such a tyrannical act by burying her in that place of opprobrium under a name other than her own? Lastly, to hide the disappearance of that sister, did he, in his perfidiousness and heinousness, go so far as to fake her death and have it legally certified with the help of false witnesses?
>
> Or did a woman without morals, backed by witnesses who were seduced or deceived, attempt, by means of a diabolical plan, to take the place of a dead woman, to usurp her name and rights which were not hers, to introduce herself into [a] distinguished family in order to seize a part of its property, and thus to renew the bold claims of Martin-Guerre [sic], of the false Caille and of the beggar of Vernon which the old collection of *Causes célèbres* recounts?[11]

It was apparently this same well-publicized, much prolonged affair that inspired Jean-Baptiste Dubois and Montgobert to write *La Fausse Marquise* (The false marchioness), a three-act melodrama that premiered at the Théâtre de la Porte-Saint-Martin on 28 June 1805. In that piece, the marquise de Senneville is impersonated by a woman named Nicole who, with the aid of a male accomplice, Lafleur, initially manages to convince everyone but Mathurin, the virtuous caretaker of Senneville castle, that she is the long-absent noblewoman whom they all cherished and missed. The success of Nicole's plan is jeopardized, however, by the unexpected appearance of the real marchioness's now remorseful brother who, years earlier, had had his sister imprisoned and knows that she is long dead.

The local judge, Dorsemont, is called upon to decide the validity of the conflicting claims advanced by the opposing parties. In order to unmask the woman who, by virtue of her physical resemblance to the marchioness, has assumed his sister's identity and hopes to take possession of her property, Senneville appeals to Dorsemont in the following terms: "Your Honor, men's perfidiousness is incalculable, but must not frighten honest people. I repeat, Madame is not my sister, and however great the crime that hangs over my head, I fear nothing so much as the postponement of my justification . . . [which] I wish to see promptly come to light, and to that end I turn myself in as your prisoner. Assemble the local magistrates; I shall explain myself before them, and before them I shall prove that Madame is as little suited to be a lady of quality as Lafleur is to be the interpreter of virtue."[12] In act 3, scene ii, Nicole and Senneville each convincingly recounts the story of the marchioness's disappearance and arrest, but when Senneville advances the deliberately false claim that his sister is still alive and a prisoner in her own castle, Nicole appears flustered. Dorsement urges her to "Think about the penalties in store for a guilty person such as yourself, think about the fact that by playing the role of an impostor before the court you persist in your crime, and you lose all right to the indulgence of your judges."[13] When Nicole fails to heed the judge's warning and her true identity is discovered, Dorsemont declares himself unable to treat her mercifully. He insists that "To take the name of an esteemed individual and to profane it in order to seize that person's property is a double crime which must be punished in the interest of virtue and for the tranquility of society."[14]

The magistrate's observation, which not only bears the full weight of the law and morality within the context of the drama but also serves as the epigraph to the play, is of major importance. On the one hand, it highlights the social and ethical purpose of Dubois's and Montgobert's text. (That the play seeks to educate as well as to entertain its audience is also made apparent in the final line of the drama when Senneville, addressing the peasants who had prepared a celebration in honor of the false marchioness, tells them: "Never forget that appearances can be deceiving; for often no one [seemingly] resembles an honest person so much as a scoundrel.")[15] On the other hand, the judge's statement provides some insight into early-nineteenth-century French attitudes regarding the false appropriation of a person's identity and property. Indeed, proof that the magistrate's declaration coincides with contemporary law can be found in the French Civil Code, often called the Napoleonic Code, which specifically declares that "No one may claim a status at odds with that to which one is entitled by birth and birthright; And conversely, no one may contest the status to which a person is entitled by birth."[16]

Given the fact that the play recreates a notorious legal case involving issues of identity and property, *La Fausse Marquise* surely must be considered as a precedent and a possible stimulus for Hubert's dramatized revision of the Martin Guerre story. Indeed, I would argue that Martin's social promotion from peasant to count of Artigues and his acquisition of an accomplice in Hubert's *Faux Martinguerre* is in part the result of a kind of intertextual contamination by the story of the false marchioness.[17] This hypothesis seems all the more likely given that, in Hubert's piece as in *La Fausse Marquise*, the impostor acts generously toward the locals the better to dupe them and a character willingly surrenders to the authorities in order to persuade a judge of the merits of his case. (In the *Faux Martinguerre*, however, Arnaud du Tilh's intention is to deceive the court rather than to bring the truth to light.)

Nonetheless, despite the statements by Mercier, Lacretelle, and Salgues regarding the dramatic potential of the *Causes célèbres* and despite the concrete illustration of that potential in *La Fausse Marquise* and other works,[18] it is possible that *Le Faux Martinguerre* might not have been written had historical circumstances been different. In the first decade of the nineteenth century, however, France was still recovering from its revolutionary past and was engaged in far-flung military conflicts. Emigration and war sent many from their homes for extended periods of time and created opportunities for financial chicanery as well as a multitude of personal and legal problems.[19] It was doubtless in response to these circumstances that an entire section of the Civil Code adopted in 1804 was devoted to the absent.[20] The expropriation and sale of property during the revolutionary period, followed by the gradual return to France of many dispossessed aristocratic landowners, likewise created the potential for endless litigation and social turmoil. Given Napoleon's need for military recruits and his interest in the establishment of domestic political stability, it is perhaps only a slight exaggeration to suggest that one of the primary aims of the Civil Code promulgated in his name was to provide a means to define and verify personal identity and to fix the terms of legal property ownership. When considered against this backdrop, it is not surprising that the age-old tale of Martin Guerre — a man who, after an extended absence, comes home to reclaim his place in his family and to recover his property — might appeal to an early-nineteenth-century French melodramatist and to his audience. It is, at any rate, surely no coincidence that Hubert's play, like the Napoleonic Code, seeks to impose order and clarity in the face of uncertainty and to defend certain kinds of rights and values.

Having set Hubert's choice of subject in its historico-aesthetic context, we can now turn to the *Faux Martinguerre* itself and attempt to determine whether the distortions of fact that Davis finds so objectionable can be explained by the playwright's adherence to well-established melodramatic conventions.[21] We have already noted that Hubert transforms the historical Martin Guerre, a peasant-soldier of the sixteenth century, into Martinguerre, count of Artigues. Such a social promotion, as Salgues suggested, was perfectly consonant with the "larger than life" requirements and the standard practices of the genre in which the play was written.[22] Indeed, few early-nineteenth-century French melodramas depict peasants as heroes. Naive and easily duped, country folk are instead generally relegated to secondary, oftentimes comic, roles. On those occasions when peasant characters are granted some measure of nobility, the term must be understood to reflect their moral rather than their social status and is most often applied to persons of mature years.[23]

But Hubert's play does more than simply elevate its eponymous hero to the ranks of the nobility; it also provides him with a new, historically unattested motive for absenting himself from his family's estate. The drama sets aside any notion of a voluntary, perhaps premeditated, departure and instead explains Martinguerre's disappearance as the result of his victory in a duel unexpectedly occasioned by his marriage. It further suggests that politically powerful and morally unscrupulous men deliberately misrepresented the death of the count's opponent in that affair of honor as an act of premeditated murder. The then eighteen-year-old Martinguerre was thus forced to flee his home and to abandon his ten-year-old bride in order to avoid arrest and execution (I, i, 4-5). Thus, in *Le Faux Martinguerre*, persecution and injustice—those key components of melodramatic villainy—serve to explain the young man's absence in ways that boulevard theatre audiences would find both persuasive and comfortingly familiar.[24] That the exiled hero's return home was postponed by an ill-fated encounter with Barbary Coast pirates only makes the conventional nature of the antecedents to the play's action more apparent and (in generic terms) more "plausible" (II, ii, 21) to the theatregoing public.

In addition to the changes wrought in Martinguerre's status and the new explanation given for his lengthy absence, Hubert's drama also modifies the character of the historical Martin Guerre's wife. Whereas both Martin and his impersonator, Arnaud du Tilh, retain recognizable versions of their actual names in the play, Martin's wife, Bertrande de Rols, is given an entirely new name in the play: Adèle de Monval. More "feminine" and aristocratic than Bertrande (Adèle means "of noble birth" and, unlike Bertrande, has no masculine equivalent), Adèle was a name very much in fashion at the time of the drama's composition (see, among others, Victor Hugo's wife Adèle, born 1806, and the comtesse de Boigne, born Adèle d'Osmond in 1781). Perhaps more importantly, though, "Adèle" was, according to Jean-Baptiste Goureau, a name inherited from the heroines of eighteenth-century novels and was commonly used in melodramas as a device to help audience members recognize certain young, innocent women as the intended victims of the traitor's felonious plot.[25] In addition to the examples Goureau provides, I would cite Louis-Charles Caigniez's 1807 melodrama *Le Faux Alexis, ou le Mariage par vengeance* (The false Alexis, or the vengefully [imposed] marriage). That play, like *Le Faux Martinguerre*, turns on the impersonation of a nobleman (in this case, the son of Peter the Great) by a scoundrel of lowly birth. Not surprisingly, the ingénue-victim of the villain's treachery bears a "Russified" version of the name Adèle: "Adelna."[26]

I would also argue that there is also a melodramatic precedent to account for Hubert's historically inaccurate depiction of Adèle's prolonged post-nuptial virginity. Although Bertrande de Rols and Martin Guerre were initially unable to consummate their marriage (he was allegedly under a spell that left him unable to perform his conjugal duties), the young woman eventually bore both the real and the false Martin Guerre a child. In contrast, in *Le Faux Martinguerre*, Adèle is sent to a convent immediately after her marriage and remains there until the moment the play's action begins. The young woman thus remains pure and unsullied by any experience of sexual congress. Moreover, when a cousin of the real count d'Artigues denounces Arnaud du Tilh as an impostor, it is Adèle herself who tells the man claiming to be her husband: "Sir, for your honor and my peace of mind, you cannot refuse the explanation you have been asked to furnish. Bound by an indissoluble tie [marriage], you place me in the strangest situation a woman has ever known; and if, after what I have just heard, you waver about proving to us who you are, I shall not hesitate [a moment] longer to consider you the most deceitful of all men" (II, v, 25).[27] Adèle's insistence on a public proof of her husband's identity not only constitutes an attempt to guarantee her virtue, but also alerts the spectators to the fact that she is in no way a party to Arnaud's deception. They would expect no less of a melodrama's heroine.

This display of the young woman's innocence can thus, in part, be explained by audience expectations and generic convention.[28] It is also likely that Hubert chose not to elaborate a complex scenario of female guilt and repentance both because it would unduly complicate his plot and because it would force an unsustainable comparison between *Le Faux*

Martinguerre and René-Charles Guilbert de Pixérécourt's well-known and highly successful play of 1802, *La Femme à deux maris* (The woman with two husbands).[29] Instead, the dramatist appears to have adopted and adapted a scenario that Pixérécourt used in another of his long-running works, *L'Homme à trois visages* (The man with three faces). In that play, as in Hubert's piece, a man, unjustly accused of a crime and sentenced to death *in absentia*, is obliged to abandon his bride and flee his home immediately after their wedding.[30] In both pieces, the plot is male-centered and the focus is on the injustice and persecution suffered by a virtuous man. What is more, in *L'Homme* as in *Le Faux Martinguerre*, the hero, who has returned home in disguise to avoid prosecution, is eventually pardoned for the crimes of which he was falsely accused and is able to recover his good name, his bride, and his place in society. The usurper-impostor is then of course condemned and punished for his misdeeds.

As disturbing to Davis as the changed names and status Hubert attributes to Martinguerre and Adèle is the fact that it is Arnaud's own father, the tenant farmer Pierre du Tilh, who denounces his son's imposture in *Le Faux Martinguerre*. Here, again, however, the explanation can be found in the conventions of the melodramatic aesthetic. Although occasionally misguided,[31] birth parents—and especially fathers—in early-nineteenth-century French melodramas are typically paragons of virtue and founts of wisdom; they are the exemplars and the personifications of divine justice. (If they have serious moral flaws or are guilty of criminal behavior, the characters presumed to be the hero's or heroine's biological parents are generally discovered to have usurped that title.) It is not surprising, therefore, that when faced with incontrovertible evidence of Arnaud's unscrupulous behavior, Pierre du Tilh should attempt to set his son back on the path of virtue.

Rejecting Arnaud's brazen and persistent assurances that he is Martinguerre, du Tilh first appeals to those feelings of honor and decency that nature supposedly plants in the hearts of all human beings. "Rest assured," he tells his child; "I have not come, armed with the total authority granted me by the law, to deal ruthlessly with an ingrate who dishonors me. However guilty he may be, I still love my son; I want to bring him gently back to those feelings for which he need not blush" (III, ii, 36-37).[32] When Arnaud continues to deny his true identity, however, du Tilh sternly warns him: "Don't you know that a child who repudiates his father is a monster society abhors, that he sets himself apart from humanity, and that, by dedicating himself to public loathing, he draws the curse of heaven down upon himself" (III, ii, 36-7).[33] When his third appeal (the New Testament echoes are unmistakable here) for recognition and reform fails to sway his son, du Tilh finally gives up. "Your

hardheartedness disgusts me," he tells Arnaud. "Heaven, so fearsome in dealing with perjurers, is inflexible toward unnatural children; tremble lest in its
anger [divine providence] fulfills the curse that I now call down upon your
head" (III, ii, 37).[34] Still, du Tilh does not immediately denounce his son, no
doubt hoping that Heaven will spare him that sad duty. When it later becomes
apparent that his testimony alone can prevent a further injustice and allow the
judicial authorities to distinguish the true Martinguerre from the impostor,
virtue and his conscience compel him at last to reveal the truth (III, ix, 46–47).
His action may be a historically inaccurate and dramatically dubious way to
bring about the play's necessary conclusion.[35] It is, however, perfectly consonant with the moral purpose and the generic conventions of melodrama.

As represented in *Le Faux Martinguerre*, the character of Arnaud du Tilh
likewise owes more to melodramatic norms than to history. Only recently
arrived at the d'Artigues estate, Arnaud and his unsavory accomplice feign
virtue and imitate its spoken and gestural discourse with uncanny accuracy,
given their disreputable pasts and their criminal designs. Flattery, gifts,
and noble sentiments are proffered in artful ways that persuade the count's
more naive and unwary vassals, as well as Adèle's misguided father, that the
true Martinguerre has returned. Like the physical resemblance to the count
on which he trades, Arnaud's apparent morality is, however, only skin-
deep.[36] In conversations with his confederate and with his father, the impostor's true nature and purposes are made obvious. Not content merely to
occupy a place that is not legitimately his, he also intends to dishonor Adèle
and to deplete Martinguerre's fortunes. What is more, he brazenly repudiates his father, rejects the opportunity to tell the truth, and is unrepentant
of his misdeeds. In the world of melodrama, such crimes and deceptions are
a sign of contempt for the moral and social order and, as such, are a source
of scandal. They brand Arnaud as a subversive, irredeemable villain who is
fully deserving of his punishment.[37] Heaven (via the intervention of Pierre
du Tilh) and the law (personified by the unnamed judge) expel the dis-
sembler from an otherwise virtuous community at the very moment when
his treachery seems assured of success.[38] As is true in most other melodramas of this period, the scoundrel's exclusion leads to the restoration of an
idyllic world order and patriarchal control in a microcosmic universe meant
to serve as a paradigm for society.

By replacing *Le Faux Martinguerre* in its historico-aesthetic context and
offering generic convention and intertextual "contamination" as the most
likely explanations for some of the differences between the historical
account and Hubert's dramatized depiction of the celebrated case of Martin
Guerre, my goal has been to determine whether Natalie Davis's summary

dismissal of this early-nineteenth-century play was well considered. This is not because I wished to argue that *Le Faux Martinguerre* ought to be resurrected as a great or unjustly neglected example of melodramatic dramaturgy. Perusal of the play by no means supports such a thesis. Instead, I hoped to show that, precisely because of its departure from recorded facts, Hubert's piece affords us an opportunity to learn something about early-nineteenth-century France, and as such is deserving of close attention. Our study of that drama has indeed called attention to the aesthetic and didactic synergy that theoreticians and critics felt might be achieved by playwrights who chose to draw their inspiration from the *Causes célèbres* and has allowed us to recover some sense of how the anxiety about identity and property that surfaced in early-nineteenth-century France in the Napoleonic Civil Code and contemporary legal proceedings was depicted on stage.

In an unsigned editorial note appearing in a recent issue of *Romantisme*, one scholar has suggested that, during the nineteenth century, identity was a concept marked by uncertainty and instability and repeatedly probed by writers, philosophers, scientists, and others.[39] If that is true, and there is no reason to call the matter into question, then one would have to say that *Le Faux Martinguerre* at least to some extent participates in that century-long investigation. It also strikes me as true, however, that whereas such masterpieces of nineteenth-century French dramaturgy as Musset's *Lorenzaccio* and Alfred Jarry's *Ubu roi* problematize identity and explore its breakdown, thus pointing the way toward modernism, Hubert's play, along with other melodramas of its period, expresses a nostalgic yearning for the restoration of past certainties and comforting hierarchies.

One cannot, of course, deny that *Le Faux Martinguerre* takes liberties with the judicial case from which it draws its subject matter. But is the meaning of such poetic license so very different for social historians and theatre scholars? I would venture to argue that it is not. Historians may seek archival documentation for their representations of the past, but they at times also examine the way ideological biases have inflected the depiction of historical individuals and events. For theatre scholars, too, ideological manipulations of form and content have become a legitimate area of investigation and a frequent source of interpretative insight. Rather than deploring the factual distortions in Hubert's play, then, perhaps we should be grateful for the opportunity they afford us to further explore the intersection between past and present and the connections between legal and theatrical discourse which growing numbers of studies of gesture, declamation, and rhetoric have already shown to be frequently linked.

Notes

1. See "Théâtre de la Gaîeté, *Le Faux Martinguerre*, mélodrame en trois actes," *Magasin encyclopédique* 5 (1808): 419 regarding the play's initial reception. While not equal to the "blockbuster" status achieved by some of Pixérécourt's dramas, *Le Faux Martinguerre*'s run of twenty-nine or thirty performances marks it as a substantial success in early-nineteenth-century terms.

2. Unless otherwise noted, I shall be quoting from the 1813 edition of the play: Charles Hubert [Philippe-Jacques Laroche], *Le Faux Martinguerre, ou la Famille d'Artigues*, 2d ed. (Paris: Barba, 1813). All in-text page references in this chapter refer to this work. This second edition contains some modest changes and revisions and has a different pagination than the original. In 1824, the play was published again, this time along with other *Chefs-d'oeuvre du répertoire des mélodrames* (Paris: Veuve Dabo). All translations from this and other texts are my own. It is likely that the 1813 edition, and perhaps that of 1824 as well, coincides with a revival of the play on stage.

3. Natalie Zemon Davis, *The Return of Martin Guerre* (Cambridge, MA: Harvard University Press, 1983), 131.

4. Louis Sébastien Mercier, *Du Théâtre, ou Nouvel Essai sur l'art dramatique* (Amsterdam: E. van Harrevelt, 1773), 1: "Le Spectacle est un tableau; il s'agit de rendre ce tableau utile, c'est-à-dire de le mettre à la portée du plus grand nombre, afin que l'image qu'il présentera serve à lier entr'eux les hommes par le sentiment victorieux de la compassion et de la pitié. Ce n'est donc pas assez que l'âme soit occupée, soit même émue; il faut qu'elle soit entraînée au bien, il faut que le but moral, sans être caché ni trop offert, vienne saisir le coeur & [sic] s'y établisse avec empire." I am indebted to Sarah Maza, *Private Lives and Public Affairs: The Causes Célèbres of Prerevolutionary France* (Berkeley and Los Angeles: University of California Press, 1993), 263-311, for pointing me in the direction of Mercier and of Lacretelle, cited at notes 7-9.

5. Mercier, *Théâtre*, 153-54:

> Et quand les tribunaux ont prononcé leurs arrêts contre le père injuste, l'enfant dénaturé, le dépositaire infidèle, le fourbe, l'hypocrite, le voleur titré, le violateur de ses sermens, le scélérat en faveur, etc. si le poëte venoit à son tour produire sur la scène ces monstres de la société, et confirmer par les applaudissemens du peuple le triomphe des loix [sic], que ce second arrêt émané du génie auroit de force, d'éclat & de puissance! comme la nouveauté des faits encore récens prêteroit un solide appui à ses talens! comme les esprits à peine sortis de cette balance où les retenoit l'éloquence égale des défenseurs des deux adversaires, se porteroient rapidement du côté de la vérité! . . . Et quel fruit avantageux résulteroit de ce second appareil! Le coupable frémiroit de porter à la face des tribunaux des crimes qui ne demeureroient pas ensevelis & confondus dans la poussière du greffe, mais qui sortiroient de l'ombre pour être immortalisés sur le théâtre.

6. Mercier, *Théâtre*, 157:

> J'ai lu une fois dans ma vie les *Causes célèbres* de Gayot de Pitaval. On sait que l'ouvrage est écrit d'un style diffus, pédant, qu'il est mal fait, mal digéré & [sic] d'une prolixité insupportable, & cependant je n'ai jamais rien lu qui m'ait aussi pleinement attaché. Le sceau de la vérité empreint au milieu de ces événemens singuliers, extraordinaires & récens, jettoit dans mon âme un intérêt que les plus brillantes fictions des plus grands poëtes & des meilleurs romanciers n'ont jamais sçu [sic] produire.

> Mercier uses the word "recent" here as the opposite of "ancient" (dating from antiquity) and not as a synonym of "contemporary." The story of Martin Guerre is one of the first recounted in Gayot de Pitaval's account of celebrated court cases.

7. Pierre-Louis de Lacretelle, *Le Jeune Malherbe, ou Les Fils Naturel*, vol. 2 of *Oeuvres diverses de P. L. Lacretelle (aîné)* (Paris: Trentelle and Würtz, 1802), 175: "Il y a plus de rapport qu'on ne croit entre les faits célèbres de l'ordre judiciaire et ceux qui peuvent émouvoir sur la scène."

8. Pierre-Louis de Lacretelle, *Roman théâtral*, vol. 4 of *Oeuvres de P. L. Lacretelle (aîné)* (Paris: Bossange frères, 1823-24), 199: "C'est le plus bel attribut du théâtre de faire justice des vices et des désordres, qui prévalent à la faveur des certaines lois, de certaines opinions; là se fait entendre la conscience des gens de bien, avec le poids d'une censure publique." Despite the date of publication, the texts quoted here were written in 1802.

9. Lacretelle, *Roman théâtral*, 62:

> J' aurais à expliquer . . . ce qu'on doit entendre par un *caractère* dans la peinture des hommes, soit qu'on les contemple et les reproduise tels qu'ils se sont montrés, et c'est là l'emploi de l'histoire, des mémoires particulières, et même de certaines causes judiciares . . . soit enfin qu'on les place dans la perspective de la scène, pour les rehausser et même les exagérer par cet idéal, où l'objet ne doit sortir des mesures connues, qu'en conservant ses traits principaux et distinctifs.

10. Jacques-Barthélemy Salgues, "Théâtre de la Gaîté: *Le Faux Martinguerre*," *Courrier de l'Europe et des spectacles* 442 (25 août 1808): 3:

> Les *Causes célèbres* peuvent devenir une source féconde pour les auteurs de mélodrames. Ils y trouveront des aventures singulières, des combinaisons d'autant plus rares, qu'elles sont pour la plupart, le produit d'une méditation profonde et de calculs souvent ingénieux. Ces sujets auront au moins le mérite de rappeler quelques souvenirs intéressans, de présenter des faits d'une nature plus vraisemblable, moins bizarre et moins monstrueux que tous ceux qu'on a l'habitude de nous offrir.

> Il faudra bien sans doute que l'auteur se permette de faire quelques violences à l'histoire, qu'il élève son sujet sur les échasses du genre et qu'il gonfle ses personnages pour les faire paroître plus grands; car le mélodrame aime les tailles fortes et les héros bouffis.

11. Maurice Méjan, "Affaire de Madame de Douhault," in *Recueil des Causes célèbres, et des arrêts qui les ont décidées*, vol. 3 (Paris: P. Plisson, 1808), 5-6:

Un frère, poussé par la cupidité la plus sordide, aidé de quelques-uns de ses proches, avait-il fait renfermer, par une lettre de cachet, sa sœur, femme estimable et vertueuse, dans un lieu infâme, à la Salpêtrière? Lui avait-il enlevé tout moyen de réclamation contre un acte aussi tyrannique, en l'ensevelissant dans ce lieu d'opprobre sous un autre nom que le sien? Enfin, pour couvrir la disparition de cette sœur, avait-il poussé l'atrocité et la perfidie jusqu'à feindre sa mort, jusqu'à la faire légalement constater à l'aide de faux témoins?

Ou bien une femme sans moeurs, soutenue par des témoins séduits ou trompés, avait-elle tenté par une intrigue infernale, de se substituer à une femme morte, d'usurper son nom et des droits qui n'étaient point les siens, de s'introduire dans cette famille distinguée, pour lui arracher une portion de son patrimoine, et de renouveller ainsi les prétensions audicieuses de Martin-Guerre, du faux Caille et du Gueux de Vernon, dont l'ancien Recueil des *Causes célèbres* nous retrace l'histoire?

12. Jean-Baptiste Dubois and Montgobert, *La Fausse Marquise* (Paris: Barba, 1805), II, xx, 45:

> Monsieur le Juge, la perfidie des hommes est incalculable, mais elle ne doit point effrayer les gens honnêtes. Je le répète, madame n'est point ma soeur, et quelque grand que soit le crime qui pèse sur moi, je ne crains rien que le retard de ma justification . . . je veux donc qu'elle éclate promptement, et pour cela je me constitue votre prisonnier; assemblez les magistrats du lieu, devant eux je m'expliquerai, et devant eux je prouverai que madame est aussi bien faite pour être dame de qualité, que Lafleur pour être interprète de la vertu.

13. Dubois and Montgobert, *La Fausse Marquise*, III, xii, 61: "Pensez aux peines qui attendent un coupable tel que vous, pensez que jouer devant la justice le rôle d'un imposteur, c'est montrer de l'audace dans le crime, et c'est n'avoir plus aucun droit à l'indulgence de vos juges."

14. Dubois and Montgobert, *La Fausse Marquise*, III, xiii, 62: "Prendre le nom d'une personne estimable, et le profaner pour s'emparer de ses biens, c'est un double délit qu'il faut punir pour l'intérêt de la vertu et le repos de la société."

15. Dubois and Montgobert, *La Fausse Marquise*, III, xiv, 64: "N'oubliez jamais qu'il faut se défier des apparences; car, souvent, rien ne ressemble plus aux honnêtes gens, que les fripons."

16. *Le Code civil* (Paris: GF=Flammarion, 1993), 151: "Nul ne peut réclamer un état contraire à celui que lui donnent son titre de naissance et la possession conforme à ce titre; Et, réciproquement, nul ne peut contester l'état de celui qui a une possession conforme à son titre de naissance." This article was originally part of a decree dated 21 March 1803 and remains unchanged to this day. According to Davis (*Return* 87) no such law existed in sixteenth-century France.

17. I would further argue that echoes of *Le Faux Martinguerre* can, in turn, be found in Planard's three-act comedy *Le Faux Paysan* (The False Peasant), which premiered 10 December 1811 at the Théâtre de Sa Majesté l'Impératrice (Odéon). In that play, Count Médina, condemned to death *in absentia* for having killed the Duke de la Plata's son in a duel, is hiding at a family estate near Cadiz

under the name of Mr. Pérès. In love with Caroline Lopez, whom he has known since childhood, "Pérès" secretly draws his beloved's portrait from memory. An unlikely possession for a man who claims to be a peasant, the drawing puts the count's life at risk. Thanks to Lopez's intervention, however, Médina's outstanding arrest warrant is revoked, he is pardoned by the king, and he recovers his property via his marriage with Caroline. In the *Faux Martinguerre*, too, there is a warrant, condemnation *in absentia*, exile that comes as a result of a duel, a secret portrait of a woman loved since childhood, and, of course, a royal pardon and restitution of property.

18. In Odile Krakovitch, "La Censure théâtrale sous le Premier Empire (1800-1815)," *Revue de l'institut Napoléon* 158-59 (1992): 52-53, another play, *La Cause célèbre, ou L'Épouse enterrée vivante* (The celebrated case, or the wife buried alive), based on a contemporary divorce proceeding is cited. Destined for performance at the Théâtre de la Porte-Saint-Martin in 1807, the work was rejected by the government's theatre censors, who not only condemned it as a mediocre drama but also worried that the real-life models for the fictional characters might object to the representation of their story and that the boulevard public might learn a dangerous lesson from the piece.

19. See, for example, Balzac's *Le Colonel Chabert*, vol. 3 of *La Comédie Humaine* (Paris: Gallimard, 1976). In that novel, Chabert, a colonel in Napoleon's army who is believed to have died in the battle of Eylau, returns home years later only to discover that his wife has remarried, his fortune is no longer his own, and his very identity is questioned.

20. *Le Code Civil*, 68-72.

21. For background on early-nineteenth-century French melodrama and audience expectations, see, among others, Jean-Marie Thomasseau, *Le Mélodrame sur les scènes parisiennes de "Coelina" à "L'Auberge des Adrets"* (Lille: Service de reproduction de thèses, 1976); Peter Brooks, *The Melodramatic Imagination* (New Haven and London: Yale University Press, 1976); Julia Przybos, *L'Entreprise mélodramatique* (Paris: Corti, 1987); Marie-Pierre Le Hir, *Le Romantisme aux enchères: Ducange, Pixérécourt, Hugo* (Amsterdam and Philadelphia: John Benjamins, 1992); J. Paul Marcoux, *Guilbert de Pixérécourt: French Melodrama in the Early Nineteenth Century* (New York: Peter Lang, 1992); and Gabrielle Hyslop, "Pixérécrout and the French Melodrama Debat: Instructing Boulevard Theatre Audiences," in *Melodrama*, ed. James Redmond (Cambridge: Cambridge University Press, 1992). Krakovitch likewise reminds us of the censors' fear of the potential moral corruption of popular audiences that might result from the depiction of unpunished criminal behavior at boulevard playhouses.

22. Salgues, "Théâtre de la Gaîté." When he first appears on stage in II, i, Martinguerre is designated by the didascalia as Count d'Artigues and refers to himself by that title; Hubert, *Le Faux Martinguerre*, 18-19. In subsequent scenes, the didascalia consistently refer to him as "the Count," while in the dialogue he is called Martinguerre, M. le Comte, d'Artigues, etc.

23. As we shall see later, this is precisely what happens in the case of the tenant farmer Pierre du Tilh.

24. In II, i, 18, the real Martinguerre, dressed in tatters, returns to his family seat and exclaims:

> At last, here I am at my estate, in this place so dear to my childhood and witness to my youthful pleasures! What a contrast between my present situation and that period so rich in delightful illusions! Outlawed, exiled from my homeland, forced to disguise myself in order to avoid death, must I also be obliged to fight a scoundrel who usurps my name and takes over my possessions? . . . What shall I do? Shall I present myself at the castle? Shall I unmask the traitor? What do I have to fear? . . . If death is to strike me in the midst of my undertaking, at least I shall prevent my paternal inheritance from falling into the hands of a scoundrel. [Enfin, me voilà dans mes domaines, dans ces lieux si chers à mon enfance, et témoins de mes premiers plaisirs! Quel contraste entre ma situation présente et cette époque si riche en illusions délicieuses! Proscrit, exilé de ma patrie, forcé de me déguiser pour me soustraire à la mort, faut-il encore que je sois obligé de lutter contre un scélérat qui usurpe mon nom, et se pare de mes dépouilles? . . . Que faire? Me présenterai-je au château? Irai-je démasquer le traître? Qu'ai-je à craindre? . . . Si la mort doit me frapper au milieu de mon entreprise, j'empêcherai du moins que l'héritage de mes pères ne passe entre les mains d'un intrigant.]

The conventional nature of the melodramatic situation and style employed here is, of course, unmistakable.

25. Jean-Baptiste Goureau, Preface to *Antony*, by Alexandre Dumas (Paris: La Table Ronde, 1994), ix.

26. Louis-Charles Caigniez, *Le Faux Alexis, ou le Mariage par vengeance*, 2d ed. (Paris: Barba, 1811), 4: "Yes, Pougatcheff; that is, they say, the real name of the ferocious adventurer who, by the grossest imposture, and by means of a vague [physical] resemblance with Alexis, wants people to believe that he is the son of Peter the Great . . . who died ten years ago." [Oui, Pougatcheff; c'est, dit-on, le véritable nom de ce féroce aventurier qui, par la plus grossière imposture, et à la faveur de quelques traits de ressemblance avec Alexis, veut faire croire aujourd'hui qu'il est ce fils infortuné de Pierre-le-Grand . . . dont un sort funeste a, depuis dix ans, terminé les jours.] To punish her father, who rejects the false Alexis's claims, Adelna is forced to marry against her will. In the end, however, she is spared any dishonor.

27. "Monsieur, pour votre honneur et ma tranquillité, vous ne pouvez vous refuser à l'explication qu'on vous demande. Enchaînée par un noeud indissoluble, vous me placez dans la situation la plus étrange où une femme se soit trouvée; et, après ce que je viens d'entendre, si vous balancez à nous prouver qui vous êtes, je n'hésite plus à vous considérer comme le plus fourbe des hommes." For the debate surrounding Bertrande's possible complicity in Arnaud's plot and other matters, see the exchange between Robert Finlay, "The Refashioning of Martin Guerre," *American Historical Review* 93 (1988): 553-71; and Natalie Zemon Davis, "On the Lame," *American Historical Review* 93 (1988): 572-603.

28. What is more, as Krakovitch, "La Censure théâtrale," 49, reminds us, during the Napoleonic era, "The government's theatre censors" adhere completely to the "defense of established values such as respect for wealth and property and for marriage and fidelity." [Les censeurs . . . adhèrent complètement à la défense de valeurs sûres, telles le respect de l'argent et de la propriété, ou encore du mariage et de la fidélité.]

29. This drama recounts the story of a woman who, convinced by falsified documents of the death of the villain she had married without her father's permission, has wed for a second time. When she discovers that her first husband (who is the father of her child) is still alive, she fears that her good and noble second husband will think she knowingly and deliberately deceived him, and that he will consequently despise her. In the end, however, the scoundrel dies and everyone lives happily ever after.

30. Set in Venice and revolving around a political plot, Hubert's borrowing from this play might have been less immediately obvious to audiences than any reminiscences of *La Femme*. This is all the more likely in that *L'Homme* does not involve the impersonation of one individual by another, but a villain pretending to be virtuous while actually engaged in treacherous behavior.

31. Among the misguided, one can cite Adèle's father, Monval, and Clara's biological father in Hubert's 1808 melodrama *Clara, ou le Malheur et la conscience*.

32. "Rassure-toi, je ne viens point, armé de la toute puissance que me donne la loi, sévir contre un ingrat qui me déshonore. Tout coupable qu'il est, j'aime encore mon fils; je veux le ramener par la douceur à des sentiments dont il n'ait plus à rougir." The Civil Code did indeed grant fathers extensive powers and authority over their children. See "De la puissance paternelle," *Le Code civil*, 191-92.

33. "Ne sais-tu pas qu'un enfant qui renie son père est un monstre en horreur à la société; qu'il s'exclut lui-même du rang des hommes, et, qu'en se dévouant à l'exécration publique, il attire sur lui la malédiction du ciel."

34. "l'on endurcissement me révolte. . . . Le ciel, si terrible au parjure, est inexorable envers les enfans [sic] dénaturés: tremble que sa colère n'exauce la malédiction que dès cet instant j'appelle sur ta tête."

35. See the opinion expressed by the reviewer for the *Gazette de France*, who writes: "One must admit that the means the author uses to confound [Arnaud] and to bring about the dénouement [of the play] is no better than others, and that the false Martinguerre might continue to brush aside the testimony of his father, as he had already successfully done." [Il faut même convenir que le moyen que l'auteur emploie pour le confondre et amener le dénouement n'est pas plus fort que les autres, et que le Faux Martinguerre pourroit continuer à repousser le témoignage de son père, comme il l'a déjà fait avec succès.] The critic concludes, however, that the play still has merit. "Théâtre de la Gaîté, *Le Faux Martinguerre*, mélodrame en trois actes," *Gazette de France* 240 (29 août 1808): 959.

36. One cannot help recalling here Senneville's already cited words of caution at the conclusion to Dubois and Montgobert, *La Fausse Marquise*: "Never forget that appearances can be deceiving; for often no one [seemingly] resembles an honest person so much as a scoundrel." See, too, the conclusion to *Le Faux*

Martinguerre, where the Count tells the assembled peasants who attempt to return the gifts Arnaud had given them: "Keep [them], my friends, keep these presents. While I detest the hand that gave them, I approve their destination, and I double the sum." [Gardez, mes amis, gardez ces présens. Tout en détestant la main qui les a faits, j'en approuve la destination, et j'en double la somme] (III, xi, 48).

37. In this way the play stands in marked contrast to the 1982 French film "The Return of Martin Guerre" ('Le Retour de Martin Guerre') and the 1993 American remake, "Sommersby." In those retellings, as well as in the version Montesquieu recounts in letter 141 of *Lettres persanes* (The Persian Letters) (Paris: Garnier, 1960), the impostor never entirely loses audience sympathy, even when he is found out. Perhaps that is because his crime is presented as having at last brought happiness and pleasure to a woman's life. That aspect of the story is entirely absent here, since it would not be consonant with the representation of Adèle as an unfailingly virtuous melodramatic heroine. On the relationship between the Martin Guerre case and *Lettres persanes,* see Dena Goodman, "The Martin Guerre Story: A Non-Persian Source for Persian Letter CXLI." *Journal of Intellectual History* 51, no. 2 (1990): 311-16.

38. It is perhaps no coincidence that Pierre-Paul Prud'hon's luridly melodramatic painting of "Law and Divine Vengeance Pursuing Crime" ('La Justice et la Vengeance divine poursuivant le Crime') likewise dates from 1808. Although the crime portrayed in that tableau is murder and the avenging figures therein are depicted in a conventionally allegorical manner, Prud'hon's painting and Hubert's play share a common message about the inevitabilty and the source of punishment for criminal misdeeds. (The nudity and pose of the murder victim's body are no doubt meant to recall artistic representations of Christ's crucifixion and thus to heighten the viewer's sense of his innocence and the villain's treachery.)

39. "Identitiés," *Romantisme* 81 (1993): 128.

7

HISTORICAL DISRUPTIONS: THE WALTER SCOTT MELODRAMAS

ANASTASIA NIKOLOPOULOU

Given the historical basis of the new historicism in art, why did the latter produce the historical novel and not the historical drama?
—GEORG LUKÁCS, *The Historical Novel*

GIVEN LUKACS'S BROAD INTEREST in the works of Walter Scott, it is rather surprising that he insists there was no historical drama in the nineteenth century. Of course, Lukács, like many other later critics—particularly those interested in positioning realism as the first step toward a weightier, modernist canon—may have assumed that the melodrama was unworthy of the appellation "historical," but it is nonetheless the case that, by the end of the century, upwards of 4,500 productions of "Scott" melodramas and operatic adaptations had been mounted.[1] The discrepancy between Lukács's critical claim and the reality of this theatrical activity deserves closer examination, since it can open the way not only to a better understanding of the reasons behind Lukács's misprision but, more important, to a clearer grasp of the cultural dynamics behind the emergence of the historical melodrama in nineteenth-century England and of the degree to which the ideological complexities of early melodrama were, in fact, grounded in contemporary history.

The years 1810 to 1830, during which Scott melodramatizations proliferated, coincided with the formation of a new sector of the theatre public, comprised of artisans, middle-class radicals, and manufacturing workers, who were part of what the *Crisis* later called the "radical public"—people who were well aware of current street activism, machine breaking, and the ideas of Thomas Paine and William Cobbett.[2] Artisans and manufacturing workers were especially prominent in the minor theatres of London, such as the Surrey and the Olympic, as well as in the theatres of other industrialized cities, such as Manchester, Leeds, Liverpool, and Birmingham, where Scott's melodramas were quite popular. Artisans also comprised the majority of pit and gallery audiences at the monopoly theatres Drury Lane and Covent Garden and were, of course, at the forefront of the Old Price Riots at Covent Garden in 1809.[3]

Thus, rather than approaching the question of historical drama from the outside, as a literary-critical problem, it might be worthwhile to look directly at the cultural wars that were waged between minor and monopoly theatres in early nineteenth-century London and especially at the melodrama itself as markers of an artisan cultural practice and aesthetic that was first excoriated and, finally, erased by the cultural paradigms favored by the middle and upper classes. In this sense, the early history and function of the melodrama can readily be linked to storytelling, which Walter Benjamin calls the "artisan university." And in its demise the early artisan melodrama also reminds us of Benjamin's description of the fate of storytelling: the move from storytelling to the novel destroyed the former's capacity to bring the community together, to introduce information "from afar," whether the "spatial kind from foreign countries or the temporal kind of tradition," which possessed an authority, and, therefore, a validity, even when it was not subject to verification.[4] Although the melodrama in many ways fulfilled this storytelling function in the early years of the century, its importance in this regard has been rendered invisible by a number of factors, including the emphasis critics such as Lukács and Bakhtin have placed on the literary and cultural significance of the narrative emplotment of the novel.

In this essay I will try to sort out some of the ways in which the Scott melodramatizations embody the elements of artisan storytelling that were largely suppressed in the historical novels of the era—the ways in which they not only brought the community together but also reenacted some of the material conditions, social conflicts, and political opposition that had been diluted or suppressed by the overproduction of historical detail in the narratives of Scott's and other novelists' works.

The relationship between melodrama and storytelling goes beyond sharing generic and formal affinities, such as episodic structure, use of popular legends, abrupt breaks in time, and characters that morphologically resemble each other.[5] The significance of melodrama's kinship to storytelling needs to be sought in their emotional economy. In reviving the performativity of

Scott's narrative, the melodrama also redirects the emotional responses produced in the reader, who, according to Benjamin, wants to "devour the novel" and make it "his own" in order to enliven his solitude. By freeing plot and character from the closed narrative space of the novel and the privatized realm of reading, the melodramatizations reopen the possibility of constructive interplay between the now fragmented action and the spectator, thus reproducing the artisan economy of "counsel," the "useful instruction" of storytelling.[6] The Scott melodramatizations intensify the social and material aspects of the story as well as the obstacles surrounding the characters, thus applying a certain pressure on the text and using it as a medium to address social issues that were relevant to the audiences. This emphasis toward the everyday and the material conditions that emerge in the melodrama of life is not really surprising if one examines the social status of the melodramatist as a factor in the development of the cultural function of the form itself.

Unlike the storyteller, whose culture was agricultural-artisan, the melodramatist was integrated within the activity of the industrialized city, where he found himself caught between a booming artisan economy and a nascent capitalist market with attachments to patronage. Not surprisingly, the melodramatist found himself early on in the midst of censorship and political propaganda.[7] The dominant belief was that he not only violated the laws (literary and judicial) governing the drama and its production, but did so for the purpose of propagating subversive ideas. To these forms of pressure the melodramatist responded in a marginal but dissonant manner, raising his voice against monopoly and challenging the rules of tragedy and great narratives. Interestingly, the melodramatist's role in appropriating and modifying other genres aligns him with Benjamin's concept of the materialist historian—a collector or scavenger *(Lumpensammler)* of great narratives who mixes them with local material (songs, dance, local references), thereby bringing them closer to the experience of the audiences.[8]

By eliding references to historical dates and great political events, the melodramatist disrupted the novel's grand narrative and made it available for use in addressing the daily experiences of "ordinary" people, affirming their capacity to produce their own history and language. The playwrights who adapted Scott's and other novels may have favored action at the expense of the situation (thereby inverting Scott's subordination of character to "external incidents"), but rather than rejecting these revisions as "melodramatic" and "unrealistic" perversions we might instead examine them more closely to see in what ways they embody a spirit that was antithetical to the literary and cultural artifacts embraced by the readerly (bourgeois) public and sustained by the industrial culture of print. The rest of this essay should be understood as an opening moment in this sort of exploratory effort.

According to Philip Bolton, several productions of Scott's novels became known in the provinces well before his novels circulated in the market. In 1816 and 1817, news about Terry's melodramatization of *Guy Mannering*, titled *Guy Mannering; or, the Gypsy's Prophecy*, spread so quickly from London to Newcastle, Durham, York, Bath, Exeter, and other cities that sometimes the play would be moved from one city to another in a few weeks or less. It is therefore possible to suggest, as Bolton notes, that many readers of Scott's novels and poems had seen their melodramatizations first.[9] And according to Elizabeth Macauley, who adapted *Marmion* for a production in Dublin (1812), Scott's popularity was increased by staging of his works rather than the other way around.[10] This is a sign of the relative interest the public actually assigned to the content of these works, although Scott would probably have resented the suggestion. He did not hold the melodramatists who revised his plays in very high esteem—except, perhaps, Daniel Terry, whom he knew, and for whom Scott contributed a ballad to the adaptation of *Guy Mannering*. Speaking of one of the melodramatic adaptations of *The Lady of the Lake*, Scott wrote (without too much enthusiasm) that it was handled by two "play carpenters in ordinary to Covent Garden [who] are employed in scrubbing, careening, and cutting her down into one of those new-fashioned sloops called a melodrama."[11]

Scott's ambivalent critical inscription of melodrama is also demonstrated in his discussion of Ann Radcliffe's gothic novel, which he compares to melodrama in its capacity to evoke fear:

> The species of romance which Mrs. Radcliffe introduced, bears nearly the same relation to the novel that the modern anomaly entitled a melo-drama does to the proper drama. It does not appeal to the judgment by deep delineations of human feeling, or stir the passions by scenes of deep pathos. . . . And yet [it] has, notwithstanding, a deep, decided, and powerful effect, gained by . . . an appeal . . . to the passion of fear, whether excited by natural dangers, or by the suggestions of superstition.[12]

There are several aspects of this commentary that are of interest for the rest of this discussion; they should pave the way for a fuller appreciation of the elements that distinguish the work of his adapters from Scott's own. The first is the way in which Scott elevates his commentary on these forms to the level of a set of judgments about abstract literary modes. Scott does not offer any examples of well-known melodramas but instead introduces the term "melo-drama" in a way that makes it useful for his discussion of gothic narrative and fear. On the surface, this is a seemingly innocent manipulation of the word, yet it clearly enables an aesthetic discussion of the melodrama and other genres that could only be of interest to a certain "literary" public while cleansing the "melo-drama" of the everyday reality of its content and performance situation.

Considering that many early melodramas were suspect because they seemed to promote "subversive" and Jacobin messages thinly disguised within the actions and statements of their "outlaw" characters,[13] Scott's distaste for both the adaptations and the adapters of his works no doubt participates in the then current effort to denigrate the "inferior" and Jacobinical taste of the audience, but it also reinscribes the melodrama in a rhetoric that disassociates it from the public, theatrical sphere and the cultural dynamics associated with it, by assigning it aesthetic properties and narrative affinities that transform it into something abstract and malleable—and safe. Refiguring the melodrama in relation to the novel and the rhetoric of literary narrative removes it from the realm of the quotidian and the political and minimizes its capacity to become available for what Michael Hays refers to as the dangers of interpretive revision and role-playing.

In his recent discussion of the melodrama and imperial culture in England, Hays uses Jane Austen's *Mansfield Park* to suggest the way in which the narrative closure of the novel stands in marked contrast to the potential for cultural and political openness and revision embodied in the melodrama. Focusing on the section of the novel in which Sir Thomas Bertram burns the unbound copies of Kotzebue's *Lovers Vows*, Hays suggests that the importance of these scenes lies in the fact that Sir Thomas not only removes the material necessary for the performance of the play but, more importantly, interferes with and, finally, preempts the interpretive role playing and revision inherent in the performance situation. His gesture emblematically repeats the history of the novel's displacement of the drama as cultural paradigm, a process in which the novel, which is "bound" and, hence, "secure," displaces plays like Kotzebue's which, as vehicles for performance—for interaction rather than readerly abstraction—could become the site of concrete cultural interplay and revision: "It would seem that what secures the physical as well as the discursive form of the novel here is that it is bound. The play, on the other hand, as performance, is figured as unbound, open to the dangers of revision and role playing, alternative orders and practices."[14]

Sir Thomas has not banished bound copies of Kotzebue's play, but they would take their place in the library, the physical space of "readerly knowledge" and narrative closure, and, thus, the library replaces the stage as the site of knowledge. An abstract, binding order "removes from the hands of others both the task and the materials for either independent or interdependent construction of alternative spaces or meanings."[15]

Although Scott's disparaging remarks about the melodrama do not act quite this fully in relation to the melodrama, they do reenact the movement toward a system of dispassionate literary judgment and cultural values that leaves no space for the impassioned and unstable action of the melodrama. This seems to be particularly evident in Scott's reference to melodrama as a genre that evokes fear—a term that might otherwise remind us of the anti-Jacobin rhetoric of the period, which cast the melodrama as subversive agent, teaching "immorality," "rapine," and "murder."[16] This is the same rhetoric that Coleridge took up in 1816 in his critique of Maturin's *Bertram; or, the Castle of St. Aldobrand* and it clearly addresses something far more disquieting than the aesthetic fear about which Scott muses in his comments on Radcliffe's novels.[17]

Of course, fear was a sentiment shared not only by members of the British literati or the British bourgeoisie, it was experienced daily by the many British weavers and unskilled workers who feared they might starve to death, such as the Lancashire weavers who smashed power looms in 1826 and who, after seeing some of their own members arrested, were "so frightened that many durst not go to be in their own houses. Some left the country; others hid themselves for weeks, some in one place, some in another, some in coal pits."[18] Scott's notion of fear in the romance and the melodrama does not take up these sociopolitical realities; rather, it transforms fear into an enjoyable aesthetic response—the reader's playful reaction to the semi-hidden meanings and "shadowy semblances" that he or she is expected to "resolve" into their "ordinary form and commonplace meanness of reality."[19]

In Scott's own work, the possibility for this readerly response is secured by the subordination of his characters to the historical situations in which they are placed: Narrative power, according to Scott, resides in the "delineation of external incident, while the characters of the agents, like the figures in many landscapes, are entirely subordinate to the scenes in which they are placed."[20] Thus, it seems that his narrative theory sanctions control in the production of the novel in ways that are similar to Sir Thomas's activities in *Mansfield Park*. Indeed, Scott's interest in the aesthetics of "subordination" and in the value of "fear" are already evident in his early experiments with the gothic form (secret subterranean spaces, political authoritarianism, violence) in his first historical drama, *The House of Aspen*, an adaptation of a dramatic romance called "Der Heilige Vehme" ("The

Secret Tribunal").[21] The main character, George of Aspen, is accused by the Tribunal of the Invisible Ministers of Justice of trying to conceal the involvement of his mother in the murder of her first husband, Arnolf of Ebersdorf. Summoned to attend the Tribunal in the "subterranean chapel of the castle of Greifenhaus," he quietly submits to the charge of violating the Tribunal's laws. Although George knows that he is the victim of a political conspiracy against his family, he passively accepts his fate, follows an elderly member behind a "sacristy," and the last we hear of him is his body falling "heavily" on the stage floor.

> ELDER JUDGE [*from behind the scene*]. Dost thou forgive me?
> GEORGE [*behind*]. I do! [*He is heard to fall heavily*]
>
> [*re-enter the old judge from the sacristy. He lays on the altar the bloody dagger.*]
>
> RODERICK. Hast thou done thy duty?
> ELDER JUDGE. I have. [*He faints*]
>
> [*He is assisted off the stage. During this four members enter the sacristy, and bring out a bier covered with a pall, which they place on the steps of the altar. A deep silence*].[22]

In a later preface to the play, Scott tried to explain the reasons that prompted John Philip Kemble to reject the play by appealing (in a somewhat ambivalent manner) to his youthful interest in the plays of Schiller (whose *Robbers* had been attacked by the *Anti-Jacobin Review* as a radical play that propagated "infractions of law").[23] Yet, despite his claim to have propagated radical ideas, Scott's first historical drama actually celebrates conformity in a manner that is in line with Lessing's "victimized innocence on the stage," a mode of delineating character that Peter Szondi has shown is typical of bourgeois aesthetics: "As long as the middle-class spectator wants to feel pity in the theatre, the model hero of bourgeois tragedy will be the helpless victim of an absolute . . . arbitrary power."[24]

Given Scott's disclaimer, it is worth noting that a quarter of a century later a production of *The House of Aspen* failed to attract the attention of the Surrey audience, which was noted for being quick to defend its in-house rights and which happily responded with an "uproar" to the melodramas it favored.[25] This audience probably found little to appreciate in George's passive submission. Similar reasons may underlie the failure of Scott's last play, *Auchindrane; or, the Ayrshire Tragedy* to attract attention when it was performed in Edinburgh in 1830. Written in a period that marked a turning point in "antagonistic forms of class consciousness,"[26] when middle- and working-class writings such as James Mill's *Essay on Government* (1824) and Thomas Hodgskin's *Labour Defended* (1825) had begun to appear, *Auchindrane* sends a problematic message about social conflict. In the antagonistic relationship between a naive youth, Darlymple, and his ruthless patron, Muir of Auchindrane, that Scott sets up, the victim does not even know who his opponent is, so it is impossible for him to confront his adversary. Darlymple is assassinated by Muir of Auchindrane's son when he goes to meet his patron for what he assumes will be a friendly meeting.

Scott does give this victim a chance to fight back here though—from the dead. Darlymple's body is to be buried on a beach, but because the incoming water prevents the murderers from concealing the corpse in the sand, they decide to throw it in the sea. Instead of sinking, Darlymple's body resurfaces and begins to follow them:

> PHILIP. I struck him overboard,
> And with MacLellan's aid I held his head
> Under the waters . . .
> As in defiance of the words we spoke,
> The body rose upright behind our stern,
> one half in ocean, and one half in air,
> And tided after as in chase of us.
> AUCHINDRANE. It was enchantment!
> ....
> 'Twas Hell's own work! —[27]

The climactic moment in the play is a confrontation between oppressor and dead victim—a poetic but not very useful form of socio-political opposition as far as the victim is concerned. Indeed, Scott's historical dramas are striking in their absence of any direct conflict, a trait that carries over into many of his novels and poems, where characters seem to be more subject to natural laws than to the realities of political economy. A character is not primarily a landlord or a yeoman, a Norman or a Saracen, but a "villain," a "dark and tyrannical count," "a heroine, subjected to all manner of hazards," or "an aged crone of a housekeeper."[28]

Although Scott's narrativized characters are not all victimized in the way George of Aspen and Darlymple are, they are all subjected to "historical forces" but are allowed little awareness of their source. The minor characters in Scott's novels are, on the other hand, allowed to recognize the presence of these overarching forces and foresee impending crises (Alice in *The Bride of Lammermoor*, Meg Merrilies in *Guy Mannering*, Allan Bane in *The Lady of the Lake*, or an anonymous minstrel in *Marmion*), but their social powerlessness prevents them from communicating the problem or doing anything to prevent the catastrophe. The main characters appear unaware of these negative conditions. For example, the Master of Ravenswood in *The Bride of Lammermoor* is a passive youth whose need to withdraw into the woods surrounding his dilapidated castle is greater than his passion to seek revenge for the injustice committed upon his father, and he appears equally oblivious to premonitions about his impending death. Yet Scott's contemporaries found that his novels had a special dramatic quality.

Hans Robert Jauss claims that "what so impressed Augustin Thierry, Guillaume de Barante, and other historians . . . was . . . , above all, the new form of the 'drama'" — one of Scott's major claims to fame — by which his contemporaries meant not so much the dramatic plot-weaving as the still unfamiliar dramatic form of the narrative: "as the narrator of the historical novel remains completely in the background, the story can unfold itself like a play, giving him the illusion that he is present in the drama."[29] Some twentieth-century critics, Lukács among them, have claimed that Scott's novels expressed the "democratic forces of his era," because his narrative gave an unprecedented degree of freedom to the reader, the capacity, as it were, to become an actor and a maker of history.[30] However, this freedom is as illusory as the reader's "presence" in the novel. Indeed, this illusion actually conceals the ideological complexities embedded in the work. These complexities can only be teased out of such elements in the novels as that of anachronistic tableaux, that is, the construction of multiple scenes that refer simultaneously to different historical moments and which, taken all together, generate a sense of panoramic impression of "historical process."

According to Diderot, a tableau ought to organize a picture depicting an authentic moment of nature, of truth, such as motherhood.[31] As Jay Caplan points out, every such tableau must have a hidden code, a "missing fragment," which usually appears in the form of a potential disorder threatening to subvert the "natural" order of things (such as a mother in distress or a wife mourning a husband). Speaking of the peasant woman mourning her dead husband in Diderot's *Entretiens sur le fils naturel* (1757), Caplan suggests that the beholder is called upon to stand in for the husband, thereby "conjuring away the loss."[32] But where Diderot's tableau signifies a timeless moment, the multiple tableaux in Scott's work signify intersecting temporalities. One example among many can be found in Scott's *Marmion* in the Elfin Knight episode, where a reference to the Elfin Knight's appearance at the time of Alexander III foreshadows the encounter between Marmion and de Wilton and causes four distinct temporalities to collapse into one: ca. 1260 (the time of Alexander III), 1563 (Marmion's time), 1808 (the time of the publication of Marmion), and ancient Egypt, represented by the anachronistic dress of the wizard Gifford.[33]

Given this "optical" effect of historical depth, the reader who "enters" Scott's narrative also seems to "enter" history as a process. The reader is, in effect, invited on an illusory journey into the "barbaric" feudal past, which, upon his or her return to the present, will reinforce the belief that the modern world (and, by extension, industrialization and capitalism) offers a great improvement over the past. It is really in this rejection of the past and in his securing of the status quo that Scott becomes, in Lukács's view, a spokesman of progressive forces. As Scott suggests elsewhere, the modern world that he favored was itself in some danger and, therefore, needed to be protected—from unspecified dangers—in order to prevent it from falling back into the violence of our "feudal ancestors:"

> There is not, perhaps, upon record, a tale of horror which gives us a more perfect picture than is afforded by the present, of the violence of our ancestors, or the complicated crimes into which they were hurried, by what their wise, but ill-enforced laws, termed the heathenish and accursed practice of Deadly Feud. . . . Yet if we look at modern events, we must not too hastily venture to conclude that our own times have so much the superiority over former days as we might at first be tempted to infer.[34]

Of course, it was not the feudal forces of the barbaric past that threatened modernity but the radical movements that had erupted among artisans and manufacturing workers who sought universal suffrage and a public space in which to voice their concerns about unemployment, inflation, wages, and their absorption by crowded factories.[35] Scott's novels, because they use the past to demonstrate the importance of securing the present, actually contain and suppress the historical reality of the present, especially that related to the cultural and political revisions desired by the lower classes. A simulacrum of historical "drama" replaces the real drama of the streets, just as the novel displaces the theatre as the scene of significant cultural action.

The resistance that Scott's novels manifest to the question of the dynamics underlying the historical antagonisms of the moment marks an irreparable rupture between contemporary oral traditions and the emerging historical novel. Contrary to the assertions of Lukács and others that the historical novel is the "modern epic," Scott's novels and poems are detached from the cultural and political dimensions of the storytelling traditions, ballads, and legends he appropriated in his works. His narrative reproduction of popular heroes—not only Rob Roy and Ivanhoe, but almost every outlaw, renegade, or rogue character, such as Dick Hatteraick, Meg Merrilies, Dominic Sampson, and Caleb—ends up, as Michel de Certeau suggests, unavoidably "removing it from people's reach and reserving it for the use of scholars and amateurs."[36] Narrativized, the tales that are the stuff of storytelling became a commodity for the newly emergent reading public and a cultural artifact for the museum. Earlier on, Hazlitt had already referred to Scott's narrative poems as "history or tradition in masquerade."[37]

Scott's sources were located not among the popular audiences who listened to storytellers but in the Advocates Library in Edinburgh, where he could also consult the antiquarian compilations of T. Percy's *Reliques of Ancient English Poetry* (1765) and George Ellis's *Specimens of Early English Metrical Romances* (1805). So, despite his seeming interest in the performative aspects of storytelling, Scott's literary theory and practice prevented him from experiencing either its communicative character or its dialectical relationship to the past—the capacity, as Wlad Godzich puts it, to contain the new, as though it had been a prediction of the old.[38] Because they could be enacted, stories, legends, and ballads were also an important carrier of codes of political opposition. "Popular poetry," as Edward Barry called the Robin Hood ballads in his *Thèse de littérature sur les vicissitudes et les transformations du cycle populaire de Robin Hood* (1832), constituted an "alternative political history" because it was performed. "In order for popular poetry to truly draw inspiration from contemporary history and identify with it, the people (le peuple) must make the history they sing, must be actors in the drama they recount to us."[39] Permeated by its own "modern history," popular poetry "modified in its own way the old historical ground on which it superimposed itself."[40]

The emergence of the historical novel on the other hand signaled the loss of the pre-dictive character of storytelling because it suppressed the latter's capacity to question social conflict. By reproducing popular traditions, the historical novel could claim it was representing the popular democratic forces of its era, but as long as it secured history's compliance by silencing its material traces (its bodies, sites, localities, oral traditions), it remained isolated from the public sphere of action, from the real drama of the public stage. It is in the context of the historical novel's problematic and abstract rendering of storytelling traditions that the ideological and formal complexities of the melodramatic adaptations of Scott's works also become apparent. At first sight, the Scott melodramas seem to sacrifice historical detail for the sake of conciseness. Especially apparent is the absence of the illusion of historical depth. Indeed, the playwrights who dramatized Scott's works often kept only the historical outline of the story. Such an adaptive

operation did require confident craftsmen-writers who did not feel threatened by the (often inaccurate) encyclopedicisms that are interspersed in
Scott's historical narrative. Yet behind what some critics have passed off as
poor substitutes for the original lies a very specific achievement: By elimi-
nating the historical layers in which the characters were encased, the Scott
melodramas produce a condensed dramatic action that foregoes a degree of
psychological analysis in favor of an intensification of the representation of
the material conditions in which the characters operate; political conflict,
price increases, hunger, and the dangers of poverty are brought to the fore
in ways that also addressed the social conditions of the audiences.

In his popular adaptation of *The Bride of Lammermoor*, which was first
performed in Edinburgh in 1822 and later in London, Dublin, Leeds, and
many other industrialized cities, John William Calcraft skips the historical
disquisition on the affairs of Scottish aristocracy following the departure of
James VI from England and moves directly to the near-riot during the
funeral of Ravenswood's father. In this episode, an armed Ravenswood
demands that the Scottish Episcopal priest whom he had invited officiate at
the funeral service rather than the Presbyterian priest appointed by the
Privy Council (of which Lord Ashton, Ravenswood's opponent, was a
member). In the novel, Ravenswood's opposition has little resonance in
the midst of the many historical references and local details—ranging from
the gloomy weather to the gothic architecture—and the nefarious role
played by Lord Ashton remains hidden. In Calcraft's play, the opening
conflict points directly at Lord Ashton as the man who wants to get rid of
Ravenswood. Having taken possession of Ravenswood's estates after
Ravenswood's father was accused for his involvement in the Civil War in
1689, Lord Ashton is now determined to prevent Ravenswood from reclaim-
ing the estates:

> SIR W. My orders, sir, were positive; and, if the young Master
> of Ravenswood dared oppose, force should have
> compelled obedience.
> LOCKHART. It was impossible, my lord, to execute your
> orders, surrounded as we were by all the kinsmen of the
> family: the Master drew his sword, and threatened the
> clergyman with personal violence unless he proceeded
> with the ceremony.
> SIR W. Did the rest second this resolution?
> LOCKHART. All, my lord; an hundred weapons were
> displayed in an instant. . . . We were happy to leave the
> chapel, happy to escape with our lives.[41]

These opening lines demonstrate not only the direct nature of the Ashton-Ravenswood conflict but also raise the possibility that individuals like Ravenswood can resist political and economic oppression by speaking up, and, if necessary, by taking arms and calling on others to do the same.

A similar intensification of the material conditions surrounding the characters can be found in Terry's melodrama *Guy Mannering; or, the Gypsy's Prophecy.* Terry skips the first fifteen chapters of the novel and the astrological predictions about Harry Bertram's fate and introduces us directly to the financial difficulties Godfrey Bertram's daughter experiences:

> MRS. McCAN. And then, sir, his distresses broke his heart, and
> he died, leaving his poor daughter, pennyless and
> unprotected, in the wide world!
> BAILLIE. His affairs in utter disorder, and twenty-seven pounds,
> six shillings, and eightpence halfpenny, in my books.[42]

Although Terry omits a great deal of information about Glossin's schemes to get possession of the Ellangowan estates, the dissonant tone of the play is clear in the way it transforms the old gypsy, Meg Merrilies, into a principal agent of the action, bringing her closer to the prototype Scott had used for his novel, a staunch Jacobite woman known for her political outspokenness.[43] Meg's chieftain-like leadership in rescuing Harry Bertram from Glossin's machinations also shows how early melodrama, far from being always complicitous in the creation of gender and ethnic stereotypes, could empower marginal characters by giving them the chance to become voices of opposition.

The description and presentation of the material obstacles that the characters face never reaches the pitch of radical rhetoric, yet the performative gestures in these plays clearly suggest that an important part of their "melodramatic" development involved aspects of the contemporary struggle for survival: in Dibdin's *Ivanhoe*, Wamba, the minstrel-outlaw, sings a "Parody of an Old Song," which can best be understood as a commentary on the rising food prices and poverty that were very much part of the audiences experience: "An ox very lately was worth eighteenth-pence, / Now they charge half-a-crown, without any pretense; As to bread, we to eat it must very soon cease. . . . Oh! well-a-day, what shall we do, / In this year, eleven hundred and ninety and two." The moment turns into a crisis when Wamba announces to the audiences that he will die and leave his possessions to his pretty Elgiva: "Since times are so bad, and all things so awry, And as there's no living — 'tis better to die. . . . Dear me, how she'll weep, when my fate she shall hear — and find herself worth two pounds seven a year." Immediately after this statement, Wamba resumes his. minstrel persona and playfully addresses the audience: "Oh! well-a-day, what shall we do, / In this year, eleven hundred and ninety and two," thus inviting the spectators to find an answer of their own.[44]

We see a similar playful and, at the same time, potentially tragic moment in Calcraft's *The Bride of Lammermoor* in the episodes surrounding Caleb's lies about the meal he had prepared for his honorable but unexpected guests, the Ashtons. To create the scene, Calcraft juxtaposes an episode from chapter 8 of Scott's novel in which Caleb justifies the absence of food in Wolf's Crag by explaining that "thunner came down the chimney," with an episode from chapter 11, in which Caleb warns Ravenswood that if he visits the Ravenswood estates he will die: "In the halls of his father his blood shall flow / And his names shall be lost for evermoe!"[45] This linkage of death to a lack of food is not, however, accompanied by an invitation to the audiences to identify with Ravenswood (who, despite his riotous temperament, never asks his elderly servants how they feed themselves) or with Caleb (whose attachment to Ravenswood borders on foolishness). What the "thunder" scene brings forth is a "dry" juxtaposition of the conditions of hunger and death. These conditions did not have to be psychologized or demonstrated in order to be understood by the audiences because the fear of starvation and death could readily be understood by the majority of the artisan spectators. That such material conditions are limned rather than demonstrated indicates another of the affinities between a Scott melodramatization and storytelling. The former, like the latter, was "penetrated by the present in which it existed, expressed this [present] without choosing, often without intelligence. It hints at it more than it shows it, offering a few more or less fixed features, a few more or less precise indications."[46] The compact and dry form of representation in Scott's melodramatizations also reveals another affinity with storytelling: "allegorical" renditions of the place and moment of production that are "masks . . . for political satire."[47] This same characteristic allows for easy transformation as the locale of the performance changes. It is, therefore, not surprising that performances of these melodramas in Dublin and Philadelphia were adjusted according to the sociopolitical reality of their respective audiences. This possibility was proper to the form itself.

In the preface to her melodrama *Marmion*, performed in Dublin in 1812, Elizabeth Macauley explains how she changed the character of Constance de Beverley (which she acted herself) from a victim of seduction to a woman struggling against religious oppression so that she could become a metaphor for the "plights of women" and the oppression of Catholics "bending beneath a bitter Yoke imposed by the Sister Land."[48] For an American production of *Marmion* (ca. 1816), J. N. Barker omitted all references to monasteries and monks, so that the play would become a parable for the oppression of the Americans by the English: "England did sack the peaceful border, even while pending negotiation was protracted by her evasions. . . . such was England to Scotland in the sixteenth century; and such, precisely such, has she recently been to America."[49] What is common to all of these productions is a clear sense that the play should be the site of a conflict that was politically and economically charged, that the genre called for this usage.

But if melodramatists wanted to represent pressing economic or political issues, why turn to a historical novel or narrative poem instead of writing a melodrama that focused on the present? The Scott melodramas suggest that communication on issues of politics or economics and the possibility of suggesting the need for actions that might develop out of this communication could, for obvious reasons of censorship or worse, most readily emerge within a historical setting that could limn the present while remaining within the culturally secure framework of Scott's (and others') antiquarian monuments.

Despite the fact that the melodrama's emergence coincides with an explosion of historical representations (from Byron's historical tragedies such as *Marino Faliero* to the Robin Hood almanacs sold in the markets), history, or rather a heroic vision of history that brought to life the rise or fall of great military generals, senators, or kings, could not be a goal for early melodrama. As a genre that was allowed to exist at the cultural borders of the theatrical market and legitimate drama, the melodrama and its authors were constrained, but also free to, offer tales in a form that was culturally and economically suited to this position on the margins—not "grand epic" or heroic tragedy, but works that hark back to an oral tradition that, as Barry reminds us, becomes "popularized" by gradually breaking up larger stories into "small episodes," which then multiply by appropriating characteristics of rural and regional localities: "Nottingham, Sherwood Forest, Barnsdale."[50] By virtue of its fragmented form, early melodrama repeats this relocation of the past.

Often produced from materials the melodramatist collected from the great tragedies, from novels, narrative poems, sentimental dramas, legends, and oral traditions, the melodrama represented history as a procession of small, localized episodes rather than as grand, unifying process. Instead of trying to represent a secure totality, the melodramatist worked by collecting materials from different sources which were put together with the eagerness of a craftsman-artisan rather than with the mastery of the "poet-artist" hailed by the literati. According to Robert William Elliston, this was precisely what differentiated melodrama from regular, "legitimate" drama.

When he was accused by the Covent Garden and Drury Lane managers in 1818 of having produced a legitimate drama (Henry Hart Milman's *Fazio*) at the Olympic, Elliston defended himself by asserting that the difference between a tragedian (Milman in this case) and a melodramatist (Thomas Dibdin, who wrote the melodramatic adaptation of *Fazio*, entitled *The Italian Wife*) is that whereas the former is an "ingenious gentleman" whose plays remain unused, the latter simply mixes the gentleman's plays with other material and makes them actable: "A license, my lord, was certainly granted for a melo-dramatic piece performed at the Olympic Theatre, called the "Italian Wife;" and . . . this piece was formed, in part, of matter collected from the published, and then unperformed, tragedy of "Fazio". . . . It was nothing more than the description of mixed performance, long exhibited, at the minor Theatres."[51]

In his analysis of Walter Benjamin's materialist historian, Irving Wohlfarth provides us with some concepts that are striking in terms of the way in which they recapture the role of the melodramatist as described by Elliston. What especially stands out in Wohlfarth's analysis is his portrait of the materialist historian as a collector, a scavenger of great histories, which he cuts up and mixes with "local" material, such as stories about streets, cities, buildings, and sites. Like the materialist historian, the melodramatist emerges as a "minor figure," a "rag-picker," a "*Lumpensammler,*" an "expert cameraman," a master-craftsman of stories made out of materials that he fashions "sharply:"

> The first step of the way will be to apply the principle of montage to history. To erect large constructions from the tiniest, sharply fashioned *(scharf und schneidend konfektioniert)* materials. . . . To grasp the construction of history as such. By way of commentary. The refuse of history.[52]

What the materialist historian removes from history is its silence, its antiquarianism, its mystified monuments. No longer a silent spectacle, history resumes its noise and becomes a spectacle for hearing too. What the melodramatist gives back to history is its voice, its street music, its market noise. Although incorporated into the character of a minstrel or an outlaw, the singer or balladeer in the melodrama could still evoke the dissonance and disruptive character of broadsides and popular songs, which often drew attention to injustices (broadsides and songs, were, for example, instrumental in sustaining the Old Price riots). And although the melodramatist did not consciously retain the materialist-historical consciousness of Benjamin's

Lumpensammler historian, he was, nonetheless, aware of his status as a lumpen-playwright, a literary scavenger surviving by collecting material from legitimate literary figures, a Walter Scott or a Byron. Being under the gun of the monopoly shareholders who safeguarded their property jealously, the melodramatist could not claim a central place in the theatre. Not surprisingly, his history ended up as an incomplete or marginal chapter in the grand history of nineteenth-century literature.

In his defense of *The Italian Wife*, Elliston vehemently refused to define what melodrama "does" —a difficult and potentially dangerous task in any case. He simply answered on the grounds of what "melo-drama" (or burletta, as he calls it alternatively, clearly playing with words to avoid as much as possible the word "drama") does not do: illicitly enact tragedy. But what melodrama did in the early part of the nineteenth century was evident to its antagonists: melodrama destabilized and disrupted the cultural models embedded in tragedy and the novel. In Scott's case, the melodramatist "blasted" (to use Benjamin's term) the life of the characters out of the historical forces controlling their actions and gave them a chance, if not to reach the tragic heights, at least to confront their opponents in the flesh, even if they failed in the attempt.

So, for example, in Calcraft's version of *The Bride of Lammermoor*, Ravenswood dies in a duel with Colonel Ashton, Lucy's brother, who has accused Ravenswood of causing her death. This confrontation between a wealthy bourgeois and a disinherited man, whose poverty and marginality could have established, in the eyes of the audiences, his affinity with legendary disinherited outlaws, fails to materialize in the novel although a duel is arranged. It doesn't take place because Ravenswood conveniently vanishes in the Kelpie's Flow as he is galloping toward his meeting with Ashton. Paradoxically, this moment is, however, foreshadowed in the novel in an introductory chapter when Scott introduces an interesting character named Tinto, a painter, who is drawn from the early nineteenth century. Tinto announces proudly to his friend Pattieson that he has in his possession a manuscript with the story of the bride of Lammermoor, and that he has used it to create a painting that "lifts the veil to futurity":

> The sketch . . . represented an ancient hall, fitted up and furnished in what we now call the taste of Queen Elizabeth's age. The light . . . fell upon a female figure . . . who, in an attitude of speechless terror, appeared to watch the issue of a debate betwixt two other persons. The one was a young man, in the Vandyke dress common to the time of Charles I., who . . . seemed to be urging a claim of right, rather than of favor, to a lady, whose age . . . pointed her out as the mother of the younger female.[53]

The moment is anachronistic because it evokes the late seventeenth century but clothes the Ashtons in the style of Charles I and thus places them seventy or so years earlier than in the novel (which is supposed to take place in the period of the Act of Union, 1707).[54] Further, the painting foreshadows the crisis that will ensue several pages later in the "future" of the novel, when Lady Ashton refuses to endorse the marriage of Lucy and Ravenswood. Tinto's anachronistic insight needs some attention, for he represents a historian who not only can see the past from the vantage point of the future but can also foresee the future from the past — a historical understanding closer to storytelling, which, unlike the historical novel, does not have to provide a "progressive" narrative that leads to a closure. But with Tinto's death at the end of the introductory chapter Pattieson inherits the manuscript and becomes the narrator, one who is accustomed to "creeping details."[55] Nonetheless, Tinto's brief appearance in the novel sketches the possibility of another kind of novel, and the possibility that Scott himself was aware of the way in which that other novel might address the present. This other novel also floats, specter-like, in the mist above the Kelpie's Flow.

Just minutes before Ravenswood vanishes in the Flow, Caleb (who is in Wolf's Crag) sees Ravenswood from afar, galloping to meet Ashton. "The prophecy at once rushed on Balderstone's mind, that the Lord of Ravenswood should perish on the Kelpie's Flow, which lay half way betwixt the tower and the links, or sand knolls, to the northward of Wolf's hope. He saw him accordingly reach the fatal spot, but he never saw him pass further." Immediately thereafter, we get a second perspective, this time from Colonel Ashton, who sees a horseman riding towards him: "At once the figure became invisible, as if it had melted into the air. He rubbed his eyes, as if he had witnessed an apparition, and then hastened to the spot."[56] The disappearance of Ravenswood is represented as an optical trick, an illusion of historical perspective. The more Ravenswood disappears from Caleb's view, the more he appears in Ashton's view. The more he moves away from his home (his "past," his "feudal" origins), the more "visible" he becomes in the range of Ashton. But this suggestive double perspective vanishes in the final tableau along with Ravenswood, and the novel invites the reader to forego questions about social conflict in favor of the greater fear and pleasure afforded by the mysterious aesthetics that surround the Kelpie's Flow.

This situation stands in marked contrast to the events in Calcraft's melodrama. There, Ravenswood (acted by Calcraft) bursts into his former estates demanding to speak to Lucy:

[*Enter* **RAVENSWOOD**, *bursting open the folding doors, and coming forward; his dress is much disordered, and partly enveloped in a large riding cloak, his hat slouched, his face haggard and pale. They all start with astonishment.*

LUCY *raises herself, and stands gazing on him, as if petrified. A pause.*]
RAVENSWOOD. I must and will hear the truth from her own mouth: without this satisfaction I will not leave the spot. Murder me by numbers, you possibly may; but I am an armed man — I am a desperate man — and I will not die without ample vengeance. . . . [*Taking out two pistols. All draw as he presents them.*] Now choose whether you will have this hall floated with blood, or grant me the decisive interview with my affianced bride, which the laws of God and the country alike entitle me to demand.[57]

As a desperate man sustained by the "laws of this country," Ravenswood lives up to the promise he had made during his father's funeral to oppose Ashton — he is there not only for Lucy but also for the estates that have been taken away from him. But Lucy, his fated bride, fails to awaken to the historical significance of the moment and, dazed by the events, proceeds to die in Ravenswood's arms. Instantly, Ravenswood finds himself surrounded by the Ashtons, Lucy's would-be husband Bucklaw, and their servants, all with swords drawn. Colonel Ashton insists that he alone confront Ravenswood. Yet the moment fails to achieve its promised potential:

CO A. Hold! I command ye all. To me, to me alone, his blood is
due. By my hand he falls, or here completes the ruin of
my family. Ravenswood arise, and singly meet me; rise
murderer! coward, rise! [RAVENSWOOD *starts up,
draws, and engages* COLONEL ASHTON. *At the first
pass,* RAVENSWOOD *runs upon his sword.*]
RAVENSWOOD. Thus I provoke my fate. [*Falls, c.*] 'Tis past!
the prediction is fulfilled; the blood of Ravenswood
flows in the hall of his ancestors! Accursed race,
contemplate and enjoy your savage triumph — we are
beyond your malice. Lucy, I come; — in life they severed
us, but in death we are united. [*Dies*][58]

Ostensibly, Ravenswood's decision to run upon Ashton's sword stems from his despair at Lucy's death. This abrupt reversal of the action, however, occurs so rapidly and in the midst of so many explosive moments that the spectator is given little time to reflect on the psychology of Ravenswood's motives. In the end, the spectator is left in a state of suspension. The only possible caption for this moment would be an exclamation mark, such as the ones that bombarded the viewer from nineteenth-century playbills: "Marriage ceremony of Hayston by Bucklaw and Lucy Ashton, prevented by the sudden appearance of THE FATAL AVENGER!"[59] We see a similar twist of the final moment in Dibdin's version, *The Bride of Lammermoor; or, the Spectre of the Fountain* (Surrey, 1819), where Ravenswood is killed by a servant as he is ready to confront Ashton. These abrupt closures to an otherwise rapid exchange of explosive episodes inevitably raise the question: "What would have happened if . . . " Although the plays cannot offer an answer, they nonetheless suggest the question and thereby direct the audience to further ask if it has to be so. No longer caught in the optical tricks of the narrative tableau and the mystical power of the Kelpie's Flow, the spectators of the Dibdin and Calcraft melodramas are left with an image of an unrealized possibility: Ravenswood's actions, despite his death, were fully in accordance with his desire to survive in a hostile environment where he is overtaken by forces that are not mystically, but politically and economically, stronger.

Like many other melodramatizations produced before the 1830s,[60] the Dibdin, Calcraft, and Terry melodramas announce that social conflict exists and that one may have no choice other than to confront one's antagonists. Without clothing their heroes in revolutionary rhetoric, they made these questions relevant to an audience that was in urgent need of a space as well as a language in which to portray the material conditions of their lives. The production of these early Scott adaptations coincides in this sense with the rise of the language of radicalism fostered by the Owenites and trade unionism. It was there that the question of power and the economics of labor began, for the first time, to appear and develop into a combustive language that captured the attention of theatre audiences for more than a century in London, Edinburgh, Manchester, Newcastle, Durham, Glasgow, Bath, Dublin, Paris, New York, Philadelphia, and elsewhere.

Notes

1. For the melodramatizations of Scott's works, see Philip Bolton, *Scott Dramatized* (London: Mansell, 1992), vii; Richard Ford, *Dramatisations of Scott's Novels* (Oxford: Bodleian Library, 1979); and Henry Adelbert White, *Sir Walter Scott's Novels on the Stage* (New Haven: Yale University Press, 1927).

2. Jon P. Klancher, *The Making of English Reading Audiences, 1790-1832* (Madison: University of Wisconsin Press, 1987), 101-102.

3. For the Old Price riots, see Michael Hays, "Comedy as Being/Comedy as Idea," *Studies in Romanticism* (summer 1987): 221-30; Marc Baer, *Theatre and Disorder in Late Georgian London*, (New York: Oxford University Press, 1992); and Anastasia Nikolopoulou, "Artisan Culture and the English Gothic Melodrama," (Ph.D. diss. Cornell University, 1990).

4. Walter Benjamin, "The Storyteller," in *Illuminations*, ed. Hannah Arendt, trans. Harry John (New York: Harcourt, Brace, and World, 1968), 89.

5. For generic affinities between melodrama and storytelling, see, for example, Vladimir Propp's *Morphology of the Folktale* (1958) and *Theory and History of Folklore* (1984).

6. Benjamin, "Storyteller," 86.

7. See, for example, the prefaces to Joseph Holman's *The Red Cross Knights* (1802) and Matthew Gregory Lewis's *Adelmorn, the Outlaw* (1801), where both playwrights protest the accusations that their plays were promoting subversive ideas. Coleridge's famous attack on Maturin's *Bertram; or, the Castle of St. Aldobrand* as a "modern Jacobinical drama" also shows how melodramatists were suspected of having Jacobin ideas (see note 17). The Larpent Collection at the Huntington Library includes dozens of plays that were censored during the late eighteenth and early nineteenth centuries.

8. See Irving Wohlfarth, "Et Cetera? The Historian as Chiffonier," *New German Critique* 39 (fall 1986): 144.

9. Bolton, *Scott Dramatized*, 56.

10. Elizabeth Macauley, *Marmion* (Dublin, 1812), ix.

11. Bolton, *Scott Dramatized*, 12.

12. Walter Scott, *On Novelists and Fiction*, ed. Ioan Williams (New York: Barnes and Noble, 1968), 114.

13. See, for example, such outlaw plays as M. G. Lewis's *Adelmorn the Outlaw*, William Robert Elliston's *The Venetian Outlaw*, Charles Robert Maturin's *Bertram; or, the Castle of St. Aldobrand*, and J. Robinson Planché's *The Brigand*.

14. Michael Hays, "Representing Empire: Class, Culture, and the Popular Theatre in the Nineteenth Century," *Theatre Journal* 47 (March 1995): 68.

15. Hays, "Representing Empire," 68.

16. George Canning, John H. Frere, and George Ellis, *The Rovers: Poetry of the Anti-Jacobin* (London: J. Wright, 1799); reprinted in *Burlesque Plays of the Eighteenth Century*, ed. Simon Trussler (New York: Oxford University Press, 1969), 327.

17. Samuel Taylor Coleridge, *Biographia Literaria*, in *The Collected Works of Samuel Taylor Coleridge*, ed. James Engelle and W. Jackson Bate, vol. 7, part 2 (Princeton: Princeton University Press, 1983).

18. John Stevenson, "Social Control and the Prevention of Riots in England, 1789-1829," in *Social Control in Nineteenth-Century Britain*, ed. A. P. Donajgrodzki (New Jersey: Rowman and Littlefield, 1977), 45.

19. Scott, *On Novelists and Fiction*, 116-17.

20. Scott, *On Novelists and Fiction*, 110.

21. Walter Scott, "Advertisement," (1826), *The House of Aspen*, in *The Poetical Works of Sir Walter Scott* (Boston: Tichnor and Fields, 1864), 229.

22. Scott, *The House of Aspen*, 297.

23. Canning, Frere, and Ellis, *The Rovers*, 327.

24. Peter Szondi, "Tableau and Coup de Théâtre: On the Social Psychology of Diderot's Bourgeois Tragedy," in *On Textual Understanding and Other Essays*, trans. Harvey Mendelsohn, foreword Michael Hays (Minneapolis: University of Minnesota Press, 1986), 132.

25. Theatrical Scrapbook 10, 1830-1840, Folger Shakespeare Library.

26. Gregory Claeys, "Radicalism and Society in Nineteenth-Century Britain: An Introduction," in *Radikalismus in Literatur und Gesellschaft des 19. Jahrhunderts* (Frankfurt am Main: Peter Lang, 1987).

27. Walter Scott, *Auchindrane; or, the Ayrshire Tragedy* (New York: J. J. Harper, 1830), 328-29.

28. Scott, *On Novelists and Fiction*, 110.

29. Hans Robert Jauss, *Question and Answer: Forms of Dialogic Understanding* (Minneapolis: University of Minnesota Press, 1989), 33.

30. Georg Lukács, *The Historical Novel* (Lincoln: University of Nebraska Press, 1983), 89-170.

31. Szondi, "Tableau," 116.

32. Jay Caplan, "The Esthetics of Sacrifice," *L'Esprit Createur* 24 (spring 1984): 101.

33. Walter Scott, *Marmion* (Chicago: Scott, Foresman, 1903), 148-55.

34. Scott, preface to *Auchindrane*, 179-80.

35. Klancher, "Making," 113.

36. Michel de Certeau, *Heterologies: Discourse on the Other* (Minneapolis, University of Minnesota Press, 1986), 120.

37. William Hazlitt, *Lecture on the English Poets*, quoted in Hermann Fischer, *Romantic Verse Narrative: The History of a Genre* (Cambridge: Cambridge University Press, 1991), 105.

38. Wlad Godzich and Jeffrey Kittay, *The Emergence of Prose. An Essay in Prosaics* (Minneapolis: University of Minnesota Press, 1987), 104.

39. "Pour que la poésie populaire s'inspire véritablement de l'histoire contemporaine et s'identifie avec elle, il faut que le peuple fasse l'histoire qu'il chante, qu'il soit acteur dans le drame qu'il nous raconte." Edward Barry, *Thèse de littérature sur les vicissitudes et des transformations du cycle populaire de Robin Hood* (Paris, 1832), 49.

40. "C'est l'histoire du temps où les ballades subissaient leurs rédactions dernières, et cette histoire toute moderne modifiait à sa manière le vieux fond historique au-dessus duquel elle se superposait." Barry, *Thèse*, 60.

41. John William Calcraft, *The Bride of Lammermoor* (London: G. H. Davidson, 18—?), 9.

42. Daniel Terry, *Guy Mannering; or, the Gypsy's Prophecy* (London: M. R. Denham, 1845), 10.

43. Walter Scott, *Guy Mannering* (Boston: DeWolfe and Fiske, n.d), 18.

44. Thomas Dibdin, *Ivanhoe*, in *Cumberland's Minor Theatre*, vol. 1 (London: John Cumberland, ca. 1830-55), 42.

45. Calcraft, *Bride*, 25; see also Scott, *The Bride of Lammermoor* (Oxford University Press, 1991), 185.

46. "Pénétrée du présent au milieu duquel elle vit, elle l'exprime sans choix, souvent sans intelligence. Elle le laisse deviner plutôt qu'elle ne le montre par quelques traits plus ou moins arrêtes, par quelques indications plus ou moins précises." Barry, *Thèse*, 60-61.

47. Barry, *Thèse*, 47-8.

48. Macauley, *Marmion*, ix.

49. J. N. Barker, *Marmion; or, the Battle of Flodden Field* (New York: D. Longworth, 1816), v.

50. Barry, *Thèse*, 21, 34-5.

51. Robert William Elliston, *Copy of a Memorial Presented to the Lord Chamberlain by the Committee of Management of the Theatre Royal, Drury Lane and by the Proprietors of the Theatre-Royal, Covent Garden, Against the Olympic and Sans Pareil Theatres* (London, 1818), 26-30.

52. Walter Benjamin, *Gesammelte Schriften*, ed. Rolf Tiedemann and Hermann Schweppenhauser, vol. 5 (Franfurt am Main: Suhrkamp, 1974-1982), 575; quoted in Wohlfarth , "Et Cetera?" 144.

53. Scott, *Bride*, 23.

54. Scott, *Bride*, ed. notes, xvii and xxxv.

55. Scott, *Bride*, 24.

56. Scott, *Bride*, 327.

57. Calcraft, *Bride*, 44.

58. Calcraft, *Bride*, 44.

59. Bolton, *Scott Dramatized*, 303.

60. Later melodramas, such as J. P. Simpson's *The Master of Ravenswood* (Lyceum, 1865) and H. Merivale's *Ravenswood* (Lyceum, 1890), written after the defeat of Chartism and when an attempt was made for the incorporation of the working class within Victorian morals, return to the narrative strategy of Ravenswood's "disappearance." In Simpson's melodrama Ravenswood is engulfed by waters while carrying Lucy away from the chapel, whereas in Merivale's melodrama Ravenswood sinks into the Kelpie's Flow (off stage). Ford, *Dramatisations of Scott's Novels*, 8.

Part III

Radicalism
Contained

8

HE NEVER SHOULD BOW DOWN TO A DOMINEERING FROWN: CLASS TENSIONS AND NAUTICAL MELODRAMA

MARVIN CARLSON

*T*HE GILBERT AND SULLIVAN OPERETTAS occupy a peculiar and quite unusual place in the history of dramatic literature, since they draw much of their plot and story construction from popular entertainments of their period—various varieties of melodrama, fiery extravaganzas, and so on—which have now almost totally disappeared from the acquaintance of anyone but historians of British popular culture. And yet the charm of Sullivan's melodies and the wit of Gilbert's scripts have proven so enduring that audiences still flock to these bright entertainments, providing the curious spectacle of parodies that continue to delight audiences who have almost totally lost any acquaintance with the original object of the parody.

Thus even a quite sophisticated theatregoer today will almost certainly know the tradition of the British nautical melodrama only through its witty parody in *H.M.S. Pinafore,* perhaps the most beloved and frequently produced of all of the Gilbert and Sullivan entertainments.[1] Such a theatregoer very likely will recognize those parodic elements in the *Pinafore* plot that tie it to a general Western comedic tradition reaching all the way back to classic Rome—the babies switched at birth, the young lovers separated by parents or guardians who place considerations of rank or wealth above those of the heart, the grotesque alternate suitor, the surprising revelations and reversals that make possible the happy ending, crowned by the union of the lovers. But unless the theatregoer has an unusual knowledge of the tradition of nineteenth-century popular theatre, he or she is unlikely to realize that all of the nautical material is not simply an exotic device for reinvigorating the old

Plautus/Molière classic comedy structure, but is the ingenious grafting of that structure into another highly codified and predictable form, the nineteenth-century nautical melodrama.

When *H.M.S. Pinafore* was first produced at London's Opéra Comique in 1878, however, the nautical melodrama had been one of the most popular forms on the British stage for more than forty years, and there is little doubt that those first audiences saw it much more as a comic variation on that familiar dramatic world than as the traditional comic imbroglio we see in it today. The enduring popularity of *Pinafore,* and the almost total disappearance of the genre that was its inspiration, leaves us, somewhat paradoxically, with the parody as the only really familiar example of the sort of work we propose to discuss. Beginning our observations with a genre's parody is, however, by no means beginning with a disadvantage. The operations of parody are often in fact an aid to analysis, since the parodist like the genre critic is interested in discovering and highlighting the distinctive features of the genre under consideration. As it happens, concern about rank and social class — and, even more specifically, tensions about rank and social class experienced within the society — were in fact so strongly and typically woven into the fabric of this popular dramatic form that they are faithfully reproduced in Gilbert and Sullivan's parody, where they become as essential to the dynamic of the play as the traditional comedic structure itself.

The subtitle of *H.M.S. Pinafore* expresses its central dilemma: *The Lass that Loved a Sailor.* The dilemma, it will be recalled, is that while Josephine loves Able Seaman Ralph Rackstraw and he loves her, she is the daughter of the captain of his ship and therefore quite beyond his social sphere. The difficulties caused by the whimsical power of love to strike those of unequal social ranks has been one of the mainstays of comedy since classic times, and many interchanges in the play turn precisely upon such difficulties. Ralph, with the encouragement of his messmates, tries to convince himself that in the face of true love, rank must give way to common humanity:

> RALPH. Is not my love as good as another's? Is not my heart as
> true as another's? Have I not hands and ears and
> limbs like another?
> ALL. Aye, aye! (114).

In fact Josephine reciprocates his love, as she confesses to her father, but in the manner of a Corneillian heroine she recognizes that while one cannot prevent the heart from being attracted to an improper object, one can by force of will choose not to follow the heart's inclinations. She thus resolves "to carry my love with me to the tomb" and never allow Ralph to know of it, a decision warmly approved by her father.

Josephine's resolve is maintained even in the face of Ralph's profession of love to her, but her hesitations are overcome in an unexpected way. Sir Joseph Porter, the first lord of the Admiralty, seeks her hand in marriage, and takes her reluctance for timidity in consideration of his exalted social position. Her father helpfully suggests that Sir Joseph inform her "that it is a standing rule at the Admiralty that love levels all ranks," in the hope that "her respect for an official utterance" might overcome her hesitation (124). Sir Joseph follows this advice, resolving the ancient conflict between love and social expectations by an "official" pronouncement that "love is a platform upon which all ranks meet," thus of course unwittingly making the case for his rival (125).

This strategy, of releasing pressure on a system of social legislation by legislating certain situations in which the controlling principles of that system are declared inoperable or unenforceable, operates in the predictable contradictory manner of such strategies. The introduction of liminal possibilities relieves pressure by relaxing the rigidity of the law, but at the same time it introduces the danger of a subversion of the governing structures through this opening. Those concerned with protecting authority attempt to control the range of the exception represented by inclinations of the heart by suggesting that only the strongest and truest love can be permitted this liberty, but in fact the play in general, and the characters' specific observations concerning this matter, are haunted by a rhetoric much more potentially subversive of the social fabric. What is most feared is not simply that seemingly ill-sorted people might fall in love because love is whimsical and irrational, but rather that anyone might fall in love with anyone because there is ultimately no essential difference between people of one rank and people of another. The apparent threat posed by true love to social stratification and the ambivalence felt about its power in *H.M.S. Pinafore* masks a more basic threat and ambivalence, and that is about the threat that democratic ideals, strictly followed, pose to rank, position, and power.

Of course the denouement of *H.M.S. Pinafore*—the revelation that Buttercup switched the captain and Ralph at birth—and the easy switching of their roles as soon as this is discovered expresses at the very center of the play's dramatic action the instability and arbitrariness of traditional social roles. Perhaps even more striking, and certainly more thoroughly worked into the ongoing action of the play, are the comments of various characters on this matter, which follow a highly predictable and revelatory pattern. We find most of the leading characters at one time or another staunchly upholding democratic ideals until these come into conflict with the antidemocratic facts of conventional social stratification and power relationships, at which point the characters retreat into hasty qualifications. A succinct and typical example of this ambiguity is the captain's observation: "I attach but little value to rank or wealth, but the line must be drawn somewhere" (Act I).

A far more extended and comically developed example is Sir Joseph's attempt to instill a democratic spirit on shipboard. Speaking more truly than he knows, he insists that the captain treat his crew with respect, for "That you are their captain is an accident of birth. I cannot permit these noble fellows to be patronized because an accident of birth has placed you above them and them below you" (112). After praising Ralph for his bearing and enthusiasm, Sir Joseph bestows upon him the manuscript of a song he has "composed for the use of the Royal Navy" designed "to encourage independence of thought and action in the lower branches of the service, and to teach the principle that a British sailor is any man's equal, excepting mine" (113). Like the captain, Sir Joseph strongly supports the ideal of independence, up to a point. But the line must be drawn somewhere, and it is drawn of course at the point where such independence would threaten the privilege of Sir Joseph's own position.

The song Sir Joseph leaves with the sailors is one of the operetta's most familiar, its two stanzas lauding, as its author promised, the proud independence of the "British tar":

> A British tar is a soaring soul,
>   As free as a mountain bird,
> His energetic fist should be ready to resist
>   A dictatorial word.
> His eyes should flash with an inborn fire,
>   His brow with scorn be wrung;
> He never should bow down to a domineering frown,
>   Or the tang of a tyrant tongue (114-115).

What such sentiments necessarily overlook is that on shipboard a sailor is hardly "free as a mountain bird." On the contrary, his every action places him at the bottom of a power hierarchy supported by an entire legal system, and the "dictatorial word" or "tyrant tongue" most likely to be encountered is that of a legal superior, the commanding officer, while the resistance of "an energetic fist" would be a crime, an act of mutiny. Only poor Dick Deadeye, the plain-speaking Thersites of the play, sees this inconsistency, remarking that while Sir Joseph may mean well, "when people have to obey other people's orders, equality's out of the question." One is reminded of the passage in Ibsen's *Enemy of the People*, when Billing, rather fatuously praising democratic government, remarks that a community is like a ship; everyone ought to be prepared to take the helm. Captain Horster, the only one there with experience in such matters, dryly remarks: "Maybe that is all very well on shore; but on board ship it wouldn't work."[2]

All recoil at Deadeye's comment, but it expresses a serious problem. The disjuncture between the rhetoric of democracy and independence and the fact of social differences, especially in the highly ordered and disciplined world of the military (enforced in this case not only by social pressure but by such legalized coercive instruments as the ship's hold and the cat-o-nine-tails), provides a tension in any democracy, and is a constant concern of *H.M.S. Pinafore*. Given Gilbert's obviously parodic tone, one might be tempted to assume that after a century of popular but patriotic melodramas, this work represented at least in part a corrective debunking of a tradition built upon an unquestioned acceptance of the paradox represented by the patriotic tar, as free in his opinions as in his demeanor, who in fact represents the lowest rung of a rigid and highly codified social system, punishing by pain, degradation, and even death the slightest challenge to its authority. In fact, however, the historical dramatic situation is both more interesting and more complex. *H.M.S. Pinafore*, for all its comic exaggeration, is more faithful to its sources than one might expect, and the tension that permeates its world of social construction is actually deeply embedded in the tradition of the nautical melodrama itself, a tradition to which we now turn.

Although *H.M.S. Pinafore* provides indirect evidence of its continued popularity into the 1870s, the nautical melodrama's great age was the 1820s and 1830s, when London's melodrama houses offered countless works of this sort, and certain actors, most notably Thomas Potter Cooke, built flourishing careers on such entertainments. England's national dramatic tradition, the product of a seafaring nation, has from the beginning prominently included plays dealing with the sea, and the bluff and honest, if somewhat roughhewn, British seaman appears, only slightly disguised, in such Shakespearian characters as Antonio in *Twelfth Night* or in less exotic guise as Ben Jonson's Captain Otter or Ben in Congreve's *Love for Love*.

The great sea battles and victories of the Napoleonic Wars provided a major new impetus for theatricalization of nautical themes now more closely than ever tied with national pride, patriotism, and civic and social virtue. Particularly associated with such entertainments was the Royal Circus, opened in 1782 in a working-class neighborhood south of the Thames. As an unlicensed theatre, the Royal Circus was permitted to present only pantomime works, and although it regularly tested this legislation, it did have a strong motive to emphasize visual spectacle. During the 1790s, this turned increasingly to military subjects, but patriotic and military fervor occupied both major and minor theatres at this time. The Haymarket utilized the talents of the Royal Circus's James Cross to create *Britain's Glory; or, A Trip to Portsmouth* celebrating a royal review of the fleet in 1794, and Covent Garden itself followed this patriotic extravaganza with *England's Glory; or, The British Tars at Spithead* the next year and *England's Glory; or The Defeat of the Dutch Fleet* in 1797.

In 1804 Sadler's Wells installed a water tank on its stage particularly for the production of reenactments of such naval engagements as the Siege of Gibraltar (1804), the Battle of Trafalgar (1806), and the Battle of the Nile (1815), but these, like the earlier Royal Circus pantomimes, stressed visual spectacle over plot. More typical melodrama characters and situations, though still with a strong patriotic overlay, began to dominate nautical melodramas in the next decade, beginning, according to most scholars, with William Moncrieff's *Shipwreck of the Medusa* in 1820. Here, as in *Pinafore*, the Captain's daughter loves a simple seaman, and indeed disguises herself as a sailor to be near him, but no class difference hinders their eventual match, especially after the seaman, Jack Gallant, saves the lives of father and daughter after the shipwreck. His heroic credentials are specifically tied to his nation's recent naval triumphs:

> We won the Nile and Trafalger, aye, and single-handed too, and we will again whenever old England chooses to give the word, for British heart of oak stands firm for ever![3]

Such expressions of bravery, pride, defiance, and patriotism are almost universal in such plays, and compatible enough with the reputation of the victorious English navy. The early nautical dramas almost invariably showed seamen and officers united against a common foe — Frenchmen, Americans, pirates, smugglers. So Jack Gallant and his captain in *Shipwreck of the Medusa* or Captain Barnstable and his faithful coxswain Long Tom Coffin in Edward Fitzball's *The Pilot* (1825) feel no class tensions in their common devotion to the British cause. During the major years of the popularity of nautical melodrama after 1820, however, these more-or-less straightforward exultations of patriotic fervor began to be colored with the darker tones of social conflict. There seem to have been a variety of reasons for this. Such melodrama houses as the Royal Coburg, featuring a "Marine

Saloon" with frescos of British naval victories and tritons bearing admiralty flags, and the favored home of nautical melodrama, the Surrey (as the Royal Circus was renamed in 1810), were both located on the South Bank, in a district with close ties to the sea and shipping. Thus they attracted many off-duty sailors to their productions, an audience that doubtless enjoyed the flattering portraits of brave British tars, but recognized also that actual life on board ship was hardly a round of patriotic speeches and dancing horn-pipes. Tom Topreef, the seaman hero of Edward Stirling's *The Anchor of Hope*, given at the Surrey in 1847, ends the play by begging a hearty "salute from your hands" from the "messmates perched up aloft" in the inexpensive gallery, as well as from "friends stationed in the cabin," the pit and stalls, and "patrons in the quarterdeck," the boxes.[4]

Other London theatres, whose audiences had less direct experience with actual life aboard ship, nevertheless were now more than a generation removed from the patriotic fervor of the Napoleonic Wars and Lord Exeter's triumph over the pirates at Algiers. A series of famous mutinies and well-publicized court trials alerted the more general public, even at the height of that enthusiasm, that English seafaring life had its dark side; that many a British tar undertook his duties not out of patriotism but as the unwilling victim of a press gang or as a means of buying himself out of debtors' prison, and once on board ship might find little evidence of British heart of oak and more of inadequate rations, unfeeling or even sadistic superiors, and a life of grinding oppression, enforced by flogging. The new democratic ideals from the Continent undoubtedly added to a growing resistance to such practices, as can be clearly seen in a 1797 pamphlet, putting the case of mutinous sailors before a larger public: "Shall we, who in the battle's sanguinary rage, confound, terrify, and subdue your proudest foe, guard your coasts from invasion, your children from slaughter, and your land from pillage — be the footballs and shuttlecocks of a set of tyrants who derive from us alone their honors, their titles, and their fortunes? No, the Age of Reason has at length evolved. Long have we been endeavoring to find ourselves men. Now we find ourselves so. We will be treated as such."[5] The famous Bounty, Spithead, and Nore mutinies contributed as significantly to the British mental image of its navy as did Trafalgar and the Nile, and, as the patriotic enthusiasms of the early century waned, made a competitive claim upon the dramatic imagination.

Equally important was the increasing interest in class conflict within the developing domestic drama, very often played out in variations of the paradigmatic situation of a virtuous but poor young woman, loved by a virtuous but poor young man but pursued by a corrupt and ruthless aristocrat, landed

gent, factory owner, etc. who uses his superior power, wealth, and social position to advance his own suit. Sexual rivalry thus became the common
dynamic for the playing out of class conflict. The enormous popularity of this
theme virtually guaranteed that it would affect the nautical melodrama, as it
did the whole world of English melodrama in this generation, but for the nautical melodrama it posed a problem of particular delicacy. Captains and
superior officers, previously the natural allies in patriotic fervor with common seamen, often became in this new dramatic configuration rivals and enemies. The proud peasant defying the local squire or landlord, however,
raised much less ambiguous reactions, since he was not necessarily by that
defiance itself breaking the law, while the seaman challenging his captain was
committing an act of mutiny, and thus threatening the very military order that
grounded his reputation and appeal to the public.

   Black-Ey'd Susan by Douglas Jerrold, which premiered at the Surrey in
1829, was the most popular and famous of all the nautical melodramas.[6] It
was also the first important example of this genre to shift the major concerns
of nautical drama from the dramatic structure of the patriotic extravaganza, centering upon a confrontation between the heroic British tar and a
variety of miscreants from pirates to foreign nationals, to the dramatic
structure of domestic melodrama, placing the tar in the actantial role of the
lower-class hero defending his wife or love against the financial and/or sexual oppression of lustful and rapacious social superiors. Both author and
leading actor, it might be noted, were steeped in the material they represented. Both had gone to sea at the age of ten, Jerrold as a midshipman and
his actor T. P. Cooke as a crewman, and had spent their teenage years in the
Napoleonic Wars. *Black-Ey'd Susan* admirably illustrates, in its somewhat
scattered focus and moral concerns, the generic tension between the domestic and nautical actions that it weaves together, but also the moral tension
between the nautical drama's respect for class order and discipline and the
domestic drama's deep suspicion of rank and privilege. Poor William must
best a variety of villains to protect his wife Susan, and they represent a variety of generic concerns. In the opening scene we meet two of these.
Doggrass, Susan's heartless uncle, is a familiar figure from domestic melodrama, the landlord of the humble home of Susan and her sick, widowed
mother, who is about to turn them out for arrears in rent. The other,
Hatchet, comes from nautical drama, the captain of a band of smugglers
who hopes to supplant William by giving his wife a false report of his death.
William confronts, and with little difficulty bests, both of these, but then a
new threat appears that introduces a far more complex situation—William's
own captain, Crosstree.

When Crosstree first sees Susan he is fascinated, even when a sailor tells him she is already married, and to another sailor. In fine villainous fashion, Crosstree observes: "Wife of a common seaman! why, she's fit for an admiral. I know it's wrong, but I will see her—and come what may, I must, and will possess her" (I,iv). Later, leaving the inn, intoxicated, he encounters Susan and seizes her. William, coming upon the scene and having already recently rescued Susan from the smugglers, assumes that these outlaws have returned and with a cry of "Susan! and attacked by the buccaneers! Die!" stabs Crosstree, who is revealed as the captain as the curtain falls on the first act.

The entire second act is taken up with the court-martial trial of William, who finds himself, as do playwright and audience, caught between generic codes and social codes with conflicting claims. As man and husband William must defend his wife, but as sailor and patriot he must bow to the wishes and commands of his superior officer. Jerrold calculatedly softens the dilemma by making William unaware, as he strikes, that his enemy is his captain and his act a mutinous one. In his trial he points out that he is not guilty of an attempt to kill the captain, but he goes on to admit his guilt in striking to defend his wife. The distinction is an important one emotionally in terms of the choice William makes but William himself eventually admits that even had he known Susan's assailant to be "the first lord of the Admiralty, I had done it." Under the circumstances he can only plead for his judges to "condemn the sailor," but "respect the husband," a hopeless plea in the fact of the "twenty-second Article of War," which clearly prescribes death for lifting one's hand against a superior officer, whatever the cause (II, ii). This grim situation is happily resolved by an ending quite worthy of Gilbert and Sullivan: a surprise legal quibble. The wounded captain arrives to confess that his actions drove William to attack him, but, more important, that he had earlier applied for a discharge from the Navy for William, which had arrived just before the attack, so that William was not in fact a sailor attacking his superior, but an aggrieved common citizen.

The actual spectre of civil disobedience within the rigidly controlled ranks of the military is thus raised only to be skirted around in Jerrold's popular play, and mutiny becomes at last only a titillating possibility, not a reality. The power of William's presumed dilemma clearly appealed to Jerrold, however, because within a year he was represented at the Pavilion, a melodrama house in the East End, and at the Surrey's major rival, the nearby Royal Coburg, by *Mutiny at the Nore*.[7] Its central conflict takes up the same problem as that of *Black-Ey'd Susan*, but confronts it directly, avoiding *Susan*'s palliatives [such as William's ignorance of the mutinous implications of his act and the surprising legal turn that unexpectedly saves him from actually confronting the consequences of his challenge to rank and authority]. Jerrold followed the common practice earlier in the century of basing his nautical drama upon a well-known historical incident, but instead of using a great victory, such as Trafalgar, to celebrate British loyalty and patriotism, he picked one of the navy's darkest hours, when a fleet at anchor rose in rebellion during the French wars,[8] to develop a darker exploration of the tensions suggested but not really directly confronted in his previous play.

The specific details of the Nore and Spithead mutinies of 1797 and their subsequent trials were probably only dimly remembered by audiences thirty years later (perhaps rather like the collective memories Americans had today of such major political events of thirty years ago as the governmental confrontations in Selma, Alabama, or the Cuban Missile Crisis), but on the whole this worked to Jerrold's advantage, since he wanted to use the Nore mutiny primarily to give an historical cachet and authority to his real concern, which was to explore, in a more extreme situation than in *Black-Ey'd Susan*, the dramatic implications of a conflict of personal and class loyalties and expectations in a nautical setting. Instead of the standard swashbuckling tar represented by William, he took as his protagonist Richard Parker, the actual historical leader of the Nore mutineers, who, as Jerrold's audience could be expected to know, encountered no theatrical salvation, but was tried and hanged for his activities.

Jerrold thus clearly sought to raise the dramatic and emotional stakes in *Mutiny at the Nore*, but the dramatic action and characters remain far closer to those of *Black-Ey'd Susan* than to anything resembling the actual Nore Mutiny. Like Jerrold's hero, the original Robert Parker was a sailor on board the flagship *Sandwich*, was elected president of the Court of Delegates that represented the mutinying fleet, and was later tried and hanged. The backgrounds and motives of the two are however, quite different. Jerrold's Parker, like his William, is a long-time veteran, seven years in the service. The actual Parker had been aboard the *Sandwich* only six weeks when the mutiny began, and his relationship with the service was far more complex.

A British military ship was a self-contained society, regulated and controlled in extreme detail, with every section of the ship social coded and subject to its own set of intersocial regulations. There were three major social divisions, reflecting the ranks and (since ranks were tied closely to social class) the social position of their inhabitants. The front third of the ship was the domain of the sailors, their deck the forecastle, its symbol the foremast. The middle part of the ship was for the "midshipmen"—the lesser officers, such professionals as the cooper, carpenter, sailmaker, gunner, and surgeon, and the master of arms and marines, in charge of keeping order. Above the middle deck rose the quarter-deck, the domain of midshipmen and officers. For a sailor even to appear on this deck without authorization was tantamount to mutiny, and the strictest regulations covered any such appearance. The sailor had to touch his cap while speaking, keep his eyes lowered, and always stand on a lower portion to the deck than an officer. Jerrold's Parker accurately remarks that stepping on the wrong side or answering in a tone too high or too low was a mutinous crime and exposed the culprit to the pain and disgrace of flogging (I,ii). Behind the quarter-deck was the still higher poop deck, beneath which lived the captain, admiral, and other high officers.

The historical Parker, a man of some education and the son of a merchant, served during the American War not as a "humble foremast lad" but as a midshipman and petty officer. His career was a stormy one; he quarreled with his captain and indeed challenged him to a duel, an unthinkable action for a common sailor. After the war he settled in Scotland and married a farmer's daughter. When war broke out he enrolled again, and served as a petty officer, but was court-martialed for refusing to obey a superior. He returned to Scotland as a schoolteacher, but ended in debtors' prison and bought his way out by accepting a bounty to re-enlist as a quota man. The quota men, with some education and a rather ambiguous social position, often served as centers for dissatisfaction with the rigid social organization aboard ship, as one captain later noted in his memoirs. The quota men represented a "new class of persons" in the service, "whose minds were infected with the prevailing sentiments of the times, and whose pursuits and habits were consequently by no means congenial to the good order and general peaceableness of the seamen who had been brought up in the profession, when confined to their duty."[9]

Thus Parker's education, his attitudes, his background as a petty officer, and his assignment to the flagship all probably contributed to his selection as a mutiny leader, but aside from a history of resistance to authority he had no personal stake in rebellion, unlike Jerrold's simpler sailor, who, like William, turns against his captain as a result of sexual rivalry.

Instead of the open, almost accidental confrontation in *Black-Ey'd Susan*, the rivalry here is acknowledged, long-standing, and driven underground to a festering resentment on both sides. The actual social rank of Jerrold's Parker is unclear. Though a "common sailor" now, he was brought up a "genteel, high-spirited young man," though so poor that a match with him enraged his wife's father, who turned her out. Fortune has now placed him on a ship commanded by the higher-born Captain Arlington, an unsuccessful rival, who has lost no occasion to make Parker suffer. Falsely accused of a theft and flogged, Parker sought to desert, was captured and lashed through the fleet, and now burns with a desire for vengeance on his tormentor.

Parker in his public pronouncements addresses general grievances — short rations, poor pay, tyrannous treatment — but his expressions of democratic ideals have a personal edge: "my mind may be as noble, my heart as stout, as are the minds and hearts of those who strut upon the quarter-deck and are my masters" (I, ii), and it is clear that his quarrel with the captain is in the end a personal one. His triumph comes not in forcing wrongs to be addressed but, as he tells Mary, in beholding "the tyrannic blackhearted Arlington writhing like a crushed worm at my foot" (I, ii). Interestingly enough, while William argues that his attack on his rival, a personal act, might be forgiven but his mutiny could not, Parker's assumption is quite the opposite, that mutiny may be forgiven but not murder. He goes to the scaffold calling for his mates to remain loyal to the king, faithful to the nation, and just to themselves.

While Parker's resolution is admirable, he is a much more suspect hero than William, marked physically and morally by the wrongs he has suffered, and the drama is filled with strategies to mediate his defiance of authority. The most complex of these is the character Jack Adams, a fellow mutineer and a kind of double of Parker, who is much closer to the traditional stage tar in language and attitude. He defends the mutiny but works constantly for reconciliation between the parties, and the lass he loves in port is not a source of friction with authority, but the reward of the reestablishment of order, since Adams plans to marry her as soon as he sees "the admiral's flag flying, and all the men returned to their duty" (I,i). Adams deserts Parker when the rebellion breaks out on board the ship, but then saves Parker's son when his head is about to be blown off as a result of his father's belligerence. Later, as patrols seek Parker to arrest him for his leadership in the mutiny, Adams chooses friendship over duty by attempting to spirit off the condemned Parker and save him from death. At the play's end Adams becomes the surrogate father for Parker's son. Uncontaminated by the poison of revenge, he provides a more positive negotiation of naval abuses: representing grievances, pursuing redress in good faith, and expecting (and ultimately obtaining) fair and just treatment in the end from his superiors. Parker is both a victim and a product of the flawed older system, suffering from but also corrupted by it. Justice demands his death, as he himself recognizes, but he also recognizes, or at least hopes, that the old order passes with him, and that his son, under the stout tutelage of Adams, will restore the family name in a more just and wholesome society.

After the 1820s and 1830s the nautical melodrama was gradually replaced in the public's favor by other entertainments, but for the rest of the century examples continued to appear, almost invariably dealing not only with the patriotic exuberance that traditionally has been associated with this genre, but also with darker, and often tragic themes of mutiny, duty, and sexual rivalry. C. A. Somerset's *The Sea*,[10] presented at the Olympic in 1842, provides a striking example of this, as well as the generic adaptability of melodrama, since here the nautical melodrama, closely allied with the domestic melodrama for much of the previous generation, adds to this mixture a gothic plot as well. Like Jerrold's William and Parker, Somerset's honest seaman, Harry Helm, begins the play already married ("spliced" is the favored term) to his sweetheart, Mary, a former Portsmouth barmaid. This contract does not, however, spare her from the unwanted attentions of Harry's captain, Mandeville, when she comes on board to provide refreshments for the female passengers (this already elevating her above the sexual connotations of her profession were she to be taking orders from the men).

When the captain nevertheless begs a kiss from her, Harry interferes in the manner and with the vocabulary of the traditional heroic tar: "Avast there, captain! Steer clear of my tight little frigate of a wife there, if you please; or damme, you'll force me to scuttle you in the turning of a handspike" (I, i).

Such a threat, noble and justified as it may be in human terms, is nevertheless an act of mutiny if directed toward a superior officer, as Mandeville immediately announces, seeking to stab Harry with a cry of "Audacious mutineer! This to thy heart." Mary throws herself between the men, averting the blow, and leading the captain to announce that for her sake he will "overlook the indignity of being insulted by a common sailor." Harry immediately responds to this challenge as well:

> A common sailor! Many's the swob rated high on the ship's books, while the good and able seaman is suffered to go to leeward all his life. — A common sailor, indeed! Not quite so common, but he has courage to stand up for the woman of his heart, against an emperor, if he dare insult her (I,i).[11]

One might expect Mandeville to resist these democratic sentiments, but he in fact apologizes to Harry for his impetuosity, while informing the audience in an aside that this is "only in dissimulation," until his plans "reach maturity." It is of course the persona of the stage villain speaking here, and hardly that of the military superior, who had every authority to hold Harry to account for his intemperate words as well as for his threatening actions. He even agrees to Harry and Mary's request for a bit of shipboard celebration that afternoon on the deck of his ship, the *Windsor Castle*, in honor of the christening of their first-born child that morning by the ship's chaplain. In the midst of the ceremony, Mandeville pursues his plans by sending Harry as messenger to a nearby sister ship, the *Grosvenor,* with a sealed note to its captain to detain Harry, leaving Mandeville free to pursue his wife.

On board the *Grosvenor,* Harry finds himself again in the position of defender of the oppressed, but here the appeal is not to his personal interests but his common humanity. Captain Sturdy of the *Grosvenor* has discovered the dangers of teaching "Negroes" to read, for his black servant Snowball is entranced by the story of a negro slave who stabs his master, a "white negro," when the slave's wife and children are sold. When Sturdy inquires what Snowball means by a "white negro," the servant replies that there are plenty such in the world, with white faces, though "him heart be as black as a coal," and expresses the wish that Sturdy had a glass breast so that the color of his own heart might be seen. The outraged Sturdy begins beating his servant just as Harry appears. Asked to identify himself, he replies that he is:

> A man, who never yet beheld a suffering, degraded fellow-creature, writhing beneath the lash of tyranny, without extending to him the hand of friendship and protection (I,iii).

Harry's challenge to the "lash of tyranny" draws, in this context, upon a complex web of associations. Central to military discipline of the early nineteenth century was "punishment," that is flogging, which was not merely punishment, but one of the service's most important ceremonial occasions. It was designed to be impressive, painful, and degrading, and was all three. The entire ship attended the punishment, which took place on the main deck, with the officers standing above on the quarter-deck in full uniform. Lashings of a hundred strokes or more were not uncommon and although few victims actually died from this experience, permanent scars were left, physical and emotional. Actual sadists among captains were few, but flogging was almost universal, and was surely the most hated and feared aspect of naval life. Jerrold's Parker, it will be remembered, is driven to his fatal course of mutiny and revenge by an unjust sentence of five hundred lashes, and he horrifies his wife by recounting scenes of this practice:

> I have seen old men, husbands and fathers, men with venerable gray hairs, tied up, exposed, and lashed like basest beasts; scourged, whilest every stroke of the blood-bringing cat may have cut upon a scar received in an honourable fight (I,ii).

The "cat-o-nine-tails," amusingly threatened but of course never employed in *H.M.S. Pinafore,* was no laughing matter. It represented ultimately the power as well as the potential for cruelty and enforced injustice of those in authority, and when it appears in the nautical melodramas it is almost invariably associated with abuse of power and rightfully resisted, though occasionally suffered, by the sailor heroes.

Although Harry's trope of the "degraded fellow-creature writhing beneath the lash of tyranny" inevitably arouses echoes of shipboard flogging, the circumstances here are more private, and involved with another potential tyranny, that of race. Although as it happened in 1834 Parliament considered bills to both to outlaw the practice of flogging in the military and to outlaw the practice of slavery in the colonies, the latter was passed and the former defeated. This still of course left profitable slave markets elsewhere, most notably in the United States. So both flogging and slavery continued to appear as concerns in the nautical melodrama, flogging as a continuing national concern and slavery as the activity of less humane and civilized people, and thus the target, along with smuggling and piracy, for the patriotic and humanitarian zeal of British seamen. Harry Hallyard, the seaman hero of John Haines's popular *My Poll and My Partner Joe* (1835),[12] leads in the liberation of a slave vessel and exults:

> Dance, you black angels — no more captivity; the British flag flies over your head, and the very rustling of its folds knocks every fetter from the limb of the poor slave (II,ii).

Such expressions, however well-meaning, are never free of a certain paternalism, since the negro, like the tender maiden, primarily serves as the helpless victim of villainous oppression, thwarted only by the valor of the heroic seaman. For all the talk about suffering fellow-creatures, neither the seamen themselves nor their playwright-creators are inclined to provide members of other races (or genders) with much real positive agency in the dramatic action. *The Sea* provides two striking examples of this. The first is merely visual. When the party scene on the *Windsor Castle* deck begins, the stage directions note that the Crew is "*grouped variously, the native* Indian Seamen *apart from the* Europeans" (II, ii). This grouping seems insignificant during this scene, since the native Indian Seaman have no lines (indeed, we would not know there were any such without the stage direction), but this scene prepares for a subsequent and far more important use of them.

That scene results from Harry's surprising return to the *Windsor Castle.* Captain Sturdy orders him detained and if he resists, flogged, but Harry leaps into the sea, and in a spectacular feat of strength swims back to his ship. He arrives exhausted and his companions, ignoring the captain's orders to leave him to his fate, work to revive him. Coming to himself, Harry charges the captain with arranging his detention on the *Grosvenor* to pursue his "base design" on Harry's wife. The crew all cry "Shame," which the captain takes as rebellion:

> This looks like mutiny, and I must check the evil in the bud. Seize
> on that daring rebel, Harry Helm! and let the cat teach him respect
> for his superiors (I, iv).

This tyrannical act produces a rebellion indeed. The crew, with their stout Irish spokesman, Dennis O'Trott, refuse to deliver Harry up for punishment. The captain seems checked, but now matters take an unexpected turn. He appeals to the hitherto uninvolved native seaman for aid:

> Natives of India, I appeal to you to assist me to suppress this
> mutiny, and liberally shall you be rewarded, the instant we in
> safety reach Bombay (I, iv).

The natives rally behind the captain, causing Dennis, hitherto as liberal as Harry with pity for his "suffering fellow-creatures" to challenge the natives as "black, ugly-looking spalpeens." Harry makes a final appeal:

> Remember, Captain; before we proceed to this desperate extrem-
> ity, that it is your cruelty forces us to transgress the laws. [*To the
> Crew.*] Now, my boys, here goes—for female innocence, victory or
> death! (I, iv).

Unhappily, after a hard struggle, as the stage directions report: "*the Europeans are subdued by superior numbers*" (I, iv). The captain pardons all but Harry, who is condemned to walk the plank. One final agonizing turn is wrung from his execution, however. Sinking into the sea, Harry grasps an iron ring in the ship's side and might still be saved. At the captain's command however, "*A Malay carpenter runs with an axe to the ship's side, and severs the hand*" (I, iv), whereupon Harry sinks dying into the sea.

The ship's carpenter, like the cooper, sailmaker, and surgeon, was a mid-shipman and in mutinies almost invariably joined the officers, but such midshipmen were most unlikely to be Indian or Malay. Clearly Somerset needed another "native" to perform so odious a task—another native who, like the Indian seamen, has no voice in the play, even as a part of a chorus, but is utilized only to support the villain in actions no respectable British seaman would undertake. Clearly there is a large space between abolishing slavery and seeing non-Europeans as capable of acting with the same moral responsibility as Europeans.

Like Robert Parker, Harry Helm goes to his death as a condemned leader of mutiny, and again like Parker, Helm leaves behind in the care of a trusted messmate a son, who, it is assumed, will remove the stain on the family name. Somerset's *The Sea* cannot, however, end with the death of the mutineer as does Jerrold's *Mutiny at the Nore,* because the higher moral order so essential to the universe of melodrama has not been served. Despite his provocations, Parker understands and accepts his sentence and goes to his death praising king and country. He has, moreover, exacted his revenge on his tormentor. Helm goes to a shameful and ignominious death, struggling to survive, and with the agent of his shame and his destruction apparently triumphant. Another act is therefore needed to right these wrongs, and it takes place eighteen years later, when Harry's son, named Jack Neptune and raised by Dennis O'Trott, is old enough to take his father's place at the moral center of the play.

Harry continues to participate in the action, but now necessarily as a spirit, and so the prevailing tone of this act is gothic rather than nautical. Mary Helm is now a wandering lunatic. Captain Mandeville, retired and his name changed, frequents a rude tomb raised to Harry's memory and is haunted by his deed. Eventually Mary and Jack track him down, aided by a shipmate who has kept Harry's severed hand in a box. Mandeville, confronted with this physical evidence of his crime, confesses and commits suicide. Jack and his own sweetheart kneel with Mary as the backscene opens and the spirit of Harry arises in apotheosis from the sea.

Framed by these thrilling and spectacular events on land, the second act contains one extended sea sequence showing how young Jack Neptune operates in this element, and it serves as a useful recapitulation of the nautical themes and tensions of the earlier act and of earlier works in this tradition. Jack Neptune is now aboard the frigate *Antelope,* working by preference on the masthead, the most dangerous post on the ship. Captain Worthyman decides to make a public example of a sailor for drunkenness, one of the most common of shipboard offenses. Lieutenant Jack Manley comes forward with a petition "in the name of the whole ship's company," asking the captain to pardon the seaman, as this is his first offense.

The captain notes that Jack Neptune's name is not registered, and calls him down from the masthead, as the most reliable of the crew, and "a true British seaman, every inch of him," to gain his opinion. Jack at first seems to support the captain, saying that insubordination cannot be tolerated and discipline must be maintained. Yet he too argues that the first offense might be overlooked, and strengthens his argument with a plea to common humanity:

> From the Lord High Admiral down to the poorest loblolly-boy, there's not a man but is sometimes overtaken by a fault. Lord bless your honour's fine, noble, florid countenance, do you not occasionally, your honour, deviate a little from the strict rules of sobriety, and indulge in an extra glass or so now and then? Why, we are all sinners, your honour, and ought to be merciful to our fellow-creatures (II, v).

A certain punishment is indeed merited, Jack feels, but not that conventionally given, which is flogging. He goes on to deliver a spirited condemnation of this practice, which might as easily have come from Jerrold's Robert Parker:

> Punish him, your honour, but not with that instrument of torture, the cat; it is cruel, degrading, and unnatural. The man who has been once publicly whipped, if he possess one spark of manly feeling, sinks too low in his own estimation ever again to rise; and, I trust, the day is not far distant, when so foul a stain to our national character, as the laceration of a fellow-creature's flesh, will be blotted from old England's naval and military code for ever! (II, v).

One can surely assume that the audience as well would have joined at least in spirit in the common shout of "Bravo, Jack Neptune!" that greeted this proclamation, and even the captain does not hesitate to add: "A sentiment in which I most cordially concur" (II, v).

As these examples from some of the most popular representatives of the genre demonstrate, social commentary, and indeed social critique, was as important and familiar a component of the nautical melodrama as the seagoing vocabulary and the declarations of patriotic pride that most chroniclers cite as the distinctive features of these plays. To be sure, the critiques could be ambiguous from play to play, or even within the same play, but that is often because they were dealing with social and class problems about which the society itself had mixed feelings, and the theatre, as a social expression, mirrored those tensions. Even such cruel institutions as the press gang, lashing, and flogging were widely condemned, but protected by British law and accepted, as unpleasant military practices often are in democratic states, as necessary for the maintenance of a strong and disciplined force to protect the nation.

Harry Hallyard, pressed into service in *My Poll and My Partner Joe*, calls the press service an idea conceived and advocated "by fiends":

> What! force a man from his happy home, to defend a country whose laws deprive him of his liberty? But I must submit; yet, oh, proud lordlings and rulers of the land, do ye think my arm will fall as heavily on the foe as though I were a volunteer? No! (I, iii).

And yet the press service was widely tolerated as necessary to fill the ranks of the military at times of national peril, and indeed was often considered quite positively as a means of clearing the streets and roads of real or potential criminal elements. Nor was this attitude confined to monied landmen. Even Jerrold's swashbuckling hero William in *Black-Ey'd Susan* applauds the actions of a press gang when it removes two villains who have been pursuing Susan and indeed looks forward to their rough treatment aboardship:

> If they are drafted aboard of us, all I wish is that I was boatswain's mate, for their sake! Oh, wouldn't I start 'em! (I, v).[13]

Sentiments of this sort are not common in these plays, whose heroes are more likely to be threatened by lashing than to threaten it, but outright condemnation of flogging, like that of Jack Neptune's, is as uncommon as defense of it. Flogging is almost always considered as an abuse of power, an unjustified punishment, rather than as a punishment unacceptable in all circumstances. Tensions about practices like the press service or flogging are displaced into considerations of the abuse of these practices.

Class tensions are similarly displaced, almost invariably into the familiar configuration of sexual rivalry. The number of actual admirals and common sailors in love with the same woman would obviously have been infinitesimal, but judging from the nautical melodramas it was a standard concern of British shipboard life. The dramatic trope of the peasant girl wooed by a young man of her class and sought by an aristocrat is an ancient one, first extensively explored in the European pastoral tradition. In the nineteenth century, however, it became particularly favored in the domestic melodrama as a means of expressing the power of love over social position and the frequent moral superiority of the Rousseauesque lower classes over their monied superiors. In the limited confines of an English village, the poor heroine, her lover, and the wealthy landlord formed a not unlikely configuration, but the process of transposing this triangle onto a British man-o-war presented formidable obstacles to verisimilitude. The fact that nevertheless

a long tradition of works were based upon this unlikely confrontation testifies both to the power and popularity of the dramatic arrangement itself
and to the continued fascination with the class tensions it represented.

Notes

1. William S. Gilbert and Arthur Sullivan, *H.M.S. Pinafore; or, The Lass that Loved
   a Sailor* (London: Chapell and Co., 189 — ?). Further references to this work
   are included parenthetically in the text.
2. Henrik Ibsen, *Ghosts and Other Plays*, trans. R. Farquharson Sharp (Dent:
   London, 1964), 114.
3. Quoted in Michael Booth, *English Melodrama* (Herbert Jenkins: London,
   1965), 104.
4. Edward Stirling, *The Anchor of Hope; or, The Seaman's Star* (London: S. French,
   18 — ?), II, iv.
5. Quoted in Jonathan Neale, *The Cutlass and the Lash* (London, 1985), 62.
6. Douglas Jerrold, *Black-Ey'd Susan; or, All in the Downs* (London: T. H. Lacy, 18).
   Further references to this work are included parenthetically in the text.
7. Douglas Jerrold, *Mutiny at the Nore* (London: T. H. Lacy, 18 — ?). Further references are included parenthetically in the text.
8. See James Dugan, *The Great Mutiny* (London, 1966); Conrad Gill, *The Naval
   Mutinies of 1797* (Manchester: Manchester University Press, 1913); G. E.
   Manwaring and Bonamy Dobree, *The Floating Republic* (London, 1935).
9. Rear-Admiral Charles Cunningham, *A Narrative of the Occurrences that Took
   Place During the Mutiny at the Nore* (London, 1829), 9.
10. C. A. Somerset, *The Sea* (London: T. H. Lacy, 18 — ?). Further references to
    this work are included parenthetically in the text.
11. Sailors, when speaking to officers, were required to stand on the leeward side
    of the ship so that their heads would be lower than the officers', to windward.
    Harry's comments closely reflect the complaints of other democratic voices of
    the time. Samuel Leech's *A Voice from the Main Deck*, published in London the
    year after Somerset's play, complained that "The difficulty with naval officers
    is, that they do not treat with a sailor as a *man*," and remarked further that:
    "There is often more real manhood in the forecastle than in the wardroom."
    Quoted in Neale, *The Cutlass*, 157.
12. John Haines, *My Poll and My Partner Joe* (London: T. H. Lacy, 18 — ?). Further
    references to this work are included parenthetically in the text.
13. "Starting" the crew was one of the standard responsibilities of the boatswain
    and his mates. This consisted of awakening the crew and driving them to their
    morning's work by repeated lashing with pieces of rope. Neale, *The Cutlass*, 27.

9

THE IDEOLOGICAL TACK OF NAUTICAL MELODRAMA

JEFFREY N. COX

*T*HE HISTORY OF NINETEENTH-CENTURY BRITISH DRAMA is usually told as a tale of the slow but inevitable victory of realistic theatre over a failed romantic poetic drama. The melodrama appears in this story as an innovative form suited to a new era, paving the way for the domestic drama, the well-made play, the "Adelphi Drama," and finally the plays of Shaw. The praise of melodrama in such "Whig" theatrical histories is echoed in literary analyses of its content: for the melodrama's representation of such subjects as alcohol abuse, factory conditions, and absentee landlordism can be seen as dealing seriously with the issues confronting people living in working-class neighborhoods and attending theatres such as the Coburg or the Surrey or the penny gaffs of Victorian London.[1] Melodrama thus appears to some as a precursor of bourgeois realistic drama and to others as a kind of proletarian theatre. Poised in both views against Elizabethanizing romantic verse plays and grandiose Gothic tragedies, the melodrama can be discovered as the most progressive form of its day.

Despite its innovative stage techniques, however, and despite any "modern" or "realistic" or "popular" content, the melodrama nevertheless functioned within the institution of the theatre and the hierarchy of dramatic forms as a reaction against the Gothic and romantic drama and ultimately as a vehicle for a reactionary ideological vision. Imported from revolutionary France in *A Tale of Mystery* (Covent Garden, 1802) by the "Jacobin" writer Thomas Holcroft, the melodrama may have revolutionized the British stage, but it supported conservative values. On the one hand, the melodrama offered fantasies—often orientalist or militaristic—and, on the other hand, in its domestic form, packaged accounts of working-class life within a sentimental frame of family values and a conventional social order. Even an examination of the plays offered at working-class theatres shows that these plays were either escapist or participated in a hegemonic ideology of what Hegel calls in his discussion of the melodramatist Kotzebue "conventional morality."[2] The melodrama could place any formal innovation or controversial content within a safe vision, much as television can render everything from slavery to AIDS a safe topic: melodrama created the form of the "Made For TV" problem drama long before the invention of television itself. The challenge to familial, social, and even providential orders that the romantic drama offered in such works as Shelley's *The Cenci* and Byron's *Cain* and the perceived threat of what Coleridge called "the modern jacobinical drama"[3] found in such Gothic plays as Matthew Lewis's *Castle Spectre* and Charles Robert Maturin's *Bertram* were countered by the melodrama. There is a disjunction between a "progressive" history of aesthetic or stage techniques and a history of cultural reaction in which potentially radical forms are routed in the post-Napoleonic theatre by the domestic melodrama.

I would like to begin the project of exploring this disjunction in the history of nineteenth-century drama by revisiting a moment in the history we have constructed for the melodrama itself. Michael Booth, our best historian of British melodrama, argues that there are three divisions within the melodrama that succeed one another in rough chronological order: the Gothic (which contains the Eastern), the nautical, and the domestic.[4] As the middle form that converts the melodrama from the supernatural to the domestic, the nautical melodrama, I will argue, most clearly reveals the process of ideological transformation by which the melodrama pacifies the potentially radical charge of the earlier Gothic form. While the turn from the Gothic to the nautical and then to the domestic melodrama might appear as a move from "fantasy" to "realism," the ideological function of the nautical melodrama is to replace potentially radical dramatic representations and the revolutionary history that they gestured towards with a reactionary myth.

Often considered the first nautical drama, J. C. Cross's *The Purse; or, The Benevolent Tar,* which premiered at the Haymarket on 8 February 1794 (this being a period when the "Little Theatre" was being used by the Drury Lane company), was revived at Drury Lane in 1797, opening February 16 and being offered seven times before the theatre closed for the summer; the musical was then staged at the Haymarket, running there from June 26 for seven performances until the theatre closed in September. At the same time, the Arnolds's opera *The Shipwreck,* another early version of the nautical drama, which premiered at Drury Lane on 10 December 1796, was being offered, achieving twenty-one performances during the 1796-1797 season. What is intriguing about the presence of these two plays on stage during the spring of 1797 is that it is precisely at this moment that England faced the naval mutinies at Spithead and the Nore, as well as overseas mutinies, the most famous being that of the *Hermione*. That is, the myth of the Jack Tar was being created at the very moment when history offered another, more dangerous image of the British sailor. The development of the nautical *melo-drama*—which does not really arrive on the stage until the 1820s—out of both the history and the theatre of the late eighteenth and early nineteenth centuries can, in one sense, be seen as an attempt to counteract the historical fact of the naval mutinies, to offer a reactionary countermyth to the history of resistance. The melodrama's success at translating history into myth will be signaled when the mutinies themselves can become the subject of a melodrama in Jerrold's *Mutiny at the Nore* of 1830.

David Mayer has said of naval pantomimes offered around the turn of the century that "many of them testify to the unflagging enthusiasm of the British for their fleets, the shadow of Nore and Spithead mutinies never darkening the general approval,"[5] but the image of the seaman and the navy circulating within British culture at the time was actually more conflicted than this suggests. In the early years of the war, when the army was neither particularly effective nor popular, the fleet did win key victories for England at Camperdown in 1797, at Cape St. Vincent and the Battle of the Nile in 1798, and later at Trafalgar in 1805. England delighted in the Jack Tars manning its "wooden walls." Nelson, England's greatest naval hero, was celebrated in paintings, prints, and plays, including the anonymous drama *Battle of the Nile* (1799), which drew upon Aeschylus's *Persae*, and Thomas Dibdin's interlude *The Mouth of the Nile; or, The Glorious First of August* (Covent Garden, 25 October 1798), which was acted over thirty times. We can see how this popularity could be put to use by the Tory government when we note that Canning wrote a song for Pitt's birthday during the 1802 Peace of Amiens called "The Pilot that Weathered the Storm"; or when we look at a print such as "Jack's return after Lord Howe's Glorious Victory," in which all of British society, from those safely at home to the lowly sailor just returned, can celebrate the "Glorious First of June" 1794, as Admiral Howe's victory over the French off the coast of Brittany was called.[6]

Nevertheless, there was another side to these images of the jolly Jack Tar, defender of king, home, and country, just as the mutinies revealed the oppression that lay behind England's naval victories. If there were naval heroes such as Admiral Howe, it was the radical politician Sir Francis Burdett who would be hailed during elections in 1802 and 1806 as the "sailor's friend," because he championed the rights of some of the 1797 mutineers along with other inmates of Cold Bath Fields Prison in an effort that gave rise to the slogan "Burdett and No Bastille."[7] Breaks in the war such as the Peace of Amiens not only brought sailors home but also allowed shipyard workers to press for higher wages, as in an 1802 strike that provoked violent government intervention and an attempt to burn down the Woolwich yards;[8] and disturbances would arise after the close of the war as we can tell from John Frier's *A Poem, With Remarks on the Late Disturbance in Shields, Occasioned by the Ship-Owners Refusing to Man Their Ships Properly, and Endeavouring to Lower the Seamen's Wages After the Commencement of Peace* (1816). If there was the hero Admiral Nelson, there was also Richard Parker "Admiral" of the "Floating Republic." If there were plays celebrating naval successes, there were also attacks by the opposition press suggesting that such celebrations were used — in a fashion we are used to from the Falklands or Grenada — to divert attention from other difficulties; take, for example, the *Morning Chronicle's* "A Loyal Song" attacking Pitt's government:

> *If your Money he take — why your Breeches remain;*
> *And the flaps of your Shirts, if your Breeches he gain;*
> *And your Skin, if Your Shirts; and if Shoes, your bare feet.*
> *Then, never mind TAXES* — We've beat the Dutch fleet![9]

If Canning wrote a song in favor of Pitt, there were also songs supporting the 1797 mutineers, such as the ballad *Injur'd Freedom; or, Brethren Unite:* "Then rouse from your sloth and resolve to be free, / Be firm, yet be moderate too; / In your SEAMEN a noble example you see / Their conduct a pattern for you."[10] If, as we will see, many patriotic nautical plays offered a scene in which the British flag is raised and *Rule Britannia* is sung, mass demonstrations, such as that at Peterloo, were known to raise the black flags identified with those villains of the nautical drama, pirates.[11] Part of the cultural work done by the nautical melodrama was to consolidate a pacified image of the loyal British sailor and to use this figure of Britain's military victories at sea to underwrite a vision of the status quo at home.

As Booth points out,[12] the nautical drama has one of its key sources in the military spectaculars staged at the Royal Circus, Astley's, Sadler's Wells, and even the major patent theatres. Interestingly, the first of these spectaculars were representations of the taking of the Bastille: for example, *Paris in an Uproar; or, The Destruction of the Bastille* at Astley's (then the Royal Grove, 5 August 1789), John Dent's *The Bastille* (19 October 1789) at the Royal Circus, and a banned play prepared for production at Covent Garden. A year later, the minor theatres were still offering celebrations of events in France, with the Royal Circus providing *The French Jubilee* (3 August 1790) and Sadler's Wells staging *Champ de Mars; or, The Royal Federation* (2 August 1790). While there continued to be some works that were sympathetic to the Revolution, it became increasingly difficult, as events in France progressed and particularly as England entered the war against the revolutionary government, to get theatre managers (let alone the examiner of plays, John Larpent) to allow any representation of revolutionary history.[13] In the place of revolutionary spectacles came military, particularly naval, ones.

After Admiral Howe won on "the Glorious First of June," Sadler's Wells offered a series of patriotic plays such as *Sons of Britannia; or, George for Old England* (4 June 1794) showing the "Triumph of British Loyalty over Gallic Madness,"[14] and *Naval Triumph; or, The Tars of Old England* (July, 1794). Sheridan staged at Drury Lane (2 July 1794) an entertainment called *The Glorious First of June* as a wildly successful benefit for the widows and orphans of the sailors lost under Howe.[15] Covent Garden also offered plays such as *England's Glory; or, The Defeat of the Dutch Fleet by the Gallant Admiral Duncan, on the Memorable Eleventh of October* (18 October 1797). The Haymarket staged Robert Benson's *Britain's Glory; or, A Trip to Portsmouth* (20 August 1794) inspired by the king's review of the fleet. It is important to note that these spectaculars occur directly after the event, making part of their power reportorial, part of it celebratory. The immediacy of these pieces indicates that, while they contribute to the tradition out of which the nautical melodrama grew, they are still distinct from melodramatic naval plays, which became popular only when these events could be viewed at a sentimentalizing distance.

Sadler's Wells, long a favorite theatre for sailors and under the patronage of the duke of Clarence, the future Sailor King William IV, gave a new twist to nautical spectaculars when in 1804 Charles Dibdin the younger — part of an important theatrical family, known for writing nautical songs — added to the accoutrements of the theatre a tank, three feet deep, ninety feet long, and as wide as twenty-four feet, which could be filled with water from the New River. Whereas other theatres had to stage their climactic sea battles using so-called dry effects, Dibdin put scale model boats into real water. His first "aqua-drama," *The Siege of Gibraltar* (2 April 1804), used 117 ships designed by the Woolwich Dockyard shipwrights (the same shipyards that had seen violent strikes in 1802) and capable of firing their guns; for drowning Spanish sailors saved by the British, Dibdin used children, "who were instantly seen swimming and affecting to struggle with the waves."[16] Staging as many as three new "aqua-dramas" each season, Dibdin would use his water effects in a variety of plays from the melodramatic *An Bratach; or, The Water-Spectre* (July 1805) to the pantomimical *Fashion's Fools; or, The Aquatic Harlequin* (1809). Naval spectaculars would continue to be popular during a period when the navy was the key source of England's military successes. Thus, we find Sadler's Wells staging *The Battle of Trafalgar* (14 April 1806) and *The Battle of the Nile* (28 March 1815).

Another source of the nautical melodrama was the theatrical laboratory run at the Royal Circus by J. C. Cross, a key unheralded innovator in the theatre at the close of the eighteenth century. Drawing upon dumbshow, scrolls providing the audience with key bits of information, and spectacular effects, Cross created a vital drama in spite of the ban on the spoken word at "minor" theatres. Cross offered his own brand of naval spectacular at Covent Garden when he staged *The Raft; or, Both Sides of the Water* (31 March 1798), in which the French attempt to cross the English Channel on a gigantic raft. At the Royal Circus, he turned to less recent history in his *Sir Francis Drake, and Iron Arm: A New Naval Spectacle* (4 August 1800), composed a shipwreck play, *The False Friend; or, Assassin of the Rocks* (25 August 1806), and offered one of the first and most successful of the pirate plays in his *Blackbeard; or, The Captive Princess* (Easter Monday, April 1798), which ran for over one hundred nights its first season. Cross also wrote *The Purse; or, The Benevolent Tar,* considered by some, as noted above, to be the first nautical play.

There are, then, a number of different kinds of nautical dramas: the nautical spectaculars already discussed; pirate plays ranging from Cross's *Blackbeard* to Thomas Dibdin's adaptation of Scott's novel as *The Pirate; or, The Wild Woman of Zetland* (Surrey, 26 December 1822) or Edward Fitzball's adaptation of Cooper's novel as *The Red Rover; or, The Mutiny of the Dolphin* (Adelphi, 9 February 1829); dramas about wreckers such as Samuel Arnold's opera *The Shipwreck* and Edward Fitzball's *The Inchcape Bell; or, The Dumb Sailor Boy* (Surrey, 26 May 1828); plays about famous shipwrecks such as W. T. Moncrieff's *The Shipwreck of the Medusa; or, The Fatal Raft* (Coburg, 19 June 1820); mutiny plays such as Douglas Jerrold's *The Island; or, Christian and his Comrades* (Sadler's Wells, 1823) based on Byron's poem on the Bounty; and supernatural nautical plays such as Edward Fitzball's *The Flying Dutchman; or, The Phantom Ship* (Adelphi, 1 January 1827).

The nautical melodrama arose in the 1820s out of this varied tradition. Within the institution of the theatre, the arrival of the nautical melodrama can be seen as the replacement of earlier, at times almost improvisatorial, stage forms with a more polished (but also pacified) theatrical vehicle that could cross the boundaries from "major" to "minor" theatres, offering to the patent theatres royal a way of drawing upon "illegitimate" spectacular effects and to the minors access to a form made "legitimate" by its inclusion on the major stages. Within the hierarchy of genres, the nautical melodrama was instrumental in domesticating and displacing the Gothic drama which had been a major form since the 1790s. Most importantly, the high point for the nautical melodrama—marked by such successes as Fitzball's *The Pilot; or, A Tale of the Sea* (Adelphi, 31 October 1825) and Douglas Jerrold's *Black-Ey'∂ Susan; or, All in the Downs* (Surrey, 8 June 1829) —occurs not during the war years, not when nautical victories were being actually fought and then celebrated in spectacular plays, but a full decade after the challenges of the revolutionary and Napoleonic years were past. As Booth puts it, "Nautical melodrama recreated rather than reflected glories, and its recreations were acceptable to audiences nourished on the triumphs of the past. . . . The melodramatic tar was a conscious and mythic reworking of history."[17] It is important to see this conscious myth as a perhaps unconscious ideological transformation of history that performs two key pieces of cultural work: By rendering the potentially troubling figure of the sailor as the tar, defender of conventional order, the nautical melodrama both cleanses naval history of its radical elements and transfers the cultural authority of past British naval victories onto a vision of domestic order in the present. As it moves the melodrama from its Gothic to its domestic modes, the nautical melodrama steers its characters and its audience from the violence of the Napoleonic era to the peaceful order that was supposedly won by British victory.

We can perhaps see better the transformations wrought by the nautical melodrama if we look at a group of plays that hinge upon a similar plot device, which ultimately has roots as far back as the *Odyssey*: a key character has returned after many years at sea to reclaim his love and his place in society.

It will be useful first to examine this device in a Gothic play that offers interesting parallels and contrasts to the nautical melodrama, Charles Robert Maturin's *Bertram; or The Castle of St. Aldobrand* (Drury Lane, 5 September 1816).[18] Prior to the opening of Maturin's play, Bertram has won the love of Imogine and the patronage of his king to become the "darling of his liege and of his land" (II, i), only to lose them due to some vague but apparently Luciferian revolt (he is referred to as the "apostate" and "the coiled serpent" [IV, ii]). As an outcast, a rebel, and the leader of a band that has gained control of a portion of Italy, he returns to Sicily to find that his place in the king's favor and in Imogine's bed has been usurped by his enemy St. Aldobrand. A romantic Coriolanus, Bertram banishes the society that would ostracize him, rejecting the authority of the state in the figure of St. Aldobrand, whom he kills, and of the church in the figure of the prior, whom Bertram ignores while overwhelming with his demonic charisma. A romantic Othello, he is consumed by jealousy over Imogine, until he forces her to prove her love through adultery. With Aldobrand dead and Imogine dying insane, Bertram commits suicide rather than be taken by the law officers of the society that has rejected him. The play traces the ever deepening isolation brought on by Bertram's revolt as he finally defines himself beyond the claims of society, love, or morality.

Whereas Bertram finds he cannot go home again, the nautical melodrama enacts just such a return, as can be seen as early as Cross's *The Purse*.[19] Edmund—the son of the baron—has gone to sea eight years before the play opens, only to suffer shipwreck and then capture by an Algerian slaver. During his trials, he has befriended a common seaman, Will Steady, who—like his precursor Ben in Congreve's *Love for Love*—speaks in nautical jargon; this specialized form of speech would mark the "tar" throughout the history of the nautical drama. Both Edmund and Will are concerned about their return, for Edmund does not know whether his betrothed Louisa is alive and "true," and Will worries about his wife, his "pretty pinnace" who might have "foundered in a hard squall of adversity" (ii). During Edmund's long absence, his father has given up hope of his return and is ready to adopt Theodore, his steward, as his heir and as Louisa's mate; little does the baron know that Theodore has betrayed his trust and used his money recklessly. Theodore decides to cast blame upon a page serving the baron. His plot gets accidental help when Will Steady, not knowing the page is his son but moved when he hears of the boy's devotion to his mother, places a purse full of gold in the boy's pocket, which he is then accused of having stolen. The boy is about to be driven from the castle when Will Steady arrives to reveal the truth, with Sally, his wife, and Edmund appearing in a moment to second him. Money and mates end up in the proper hands.

This short piece—which, according to John Genest, "met with more success than it deserved"[20]—is important for it suggests how the nautical melodrama could convert Gothic elements into a paean to domesticity, as can be seen in its handling of a number of apparently tangential elements. The play, in telling us that Edmund has been shipwrecked and captured by slavers, engages two motifs also found in *Bertram*. Maturin's play opens with a spectacular shipwreck, which appalled Coleridge because of its lack of any providential significance: "It is a mere supernatural effect without even a hint of any supernatural agency."[21] This questioning of providential order—which we might more readily identify with Byron's *Manfred*, a play influenced by *Bertram*—is a mark of much of the Gothic drama's engagement with the supernatural, but it is exactly such questions that the nautical melodrama refuses.

The Algerian slavers engage another motif, that of the robber band. In *Bertram*, the Gothic villain-hero is accompanied by "banditti," a term that links them back through various Gothic gatherings of brigands to Schiller's revolutionary band in *The Robbers* (1780). Bertram's comrades thus still offer on stage visual traces of the people in revolt. However, in the nautical melodrama, pirates, slavers, smugglers, and wreckers replace Schillerian bands of noble robbers, as revolt is redefined as crime. We cheer, for example, when the crew of wreckers and smugglers are captured in *Black-Ey'd Susan*, and we tremble when the wrecker-smugglers of Fitzball's *Inchcape Bell* cut loose the bell warning ships of danger. Bertram can pursue his revolt in the company of his band, but Edmund, of course, wants only to return home from capture by slavers.

We can find an emblem for the domestication that goes on in Cross's *The Purse* in its treatment of the standard Gothic devices—already established by 1793—of a gloomy "Gothic hall," mistaken identity, and betrayals within the castle—all of which become the stuff of financial and familial struggles as concern focuses upon fiscal responsibility and sexual propriety, both perhaps alluded to by the title, if we remember the innuendoes in Iago's speech about stealing his purse. While the Gothic raised questions about providential order and revealed the oppression of human order, in this play, the social order—represented by the benevolent baron—is based on a domestic model, grounded in female chastity and fiscal security and presumably backed by a patriarchal providence. The play's ethos is perhaps best indicated when the page, after confronting the devious Theodore in a "Gothic Hall," sings a song, the burden of which is "Lords and ladies me much caressed, / But still I love my mother best" (iii).

The invocation of the domestic is not merely a change of subject, a move from the public to the private, from the dangerous collectivity of revolt to the tamed unity of the family. The family, domesticity, traditional family values were then, as now, invoked to grant an acceptable form to a larger set of ideological claims. While the move from the solidarity of revolutionary ties to the bonds of the family might in itself suggest a reactionary move, it is also the case that the family was frequently invoked as *the* counterrevolutionary image, from Burke's famous evocation of Louis XVI and Marie Antoinette as models of marital bliss as well as social order to Hannah More's use of the patriarchal family in *Village Politics* (1795) as the image of the orderly state, from the promonarchist ideology that promoted the counterrevolutionary George III as the "father" of his country to the antifeminist celebrations of the maternal woman that arose in the wake of the firestorm over Godwin's publications of Wollstonecraft's *Memoirs* (1798).[22] The family is used to cloak constructed sexual, social, and political relations in what claims to be a natural order. This domestic ideology would assert as natural male domination of women. It would pit against "unnatural" collectivities such as the revolutionary mob or the drama's robber band the organic order of the family. It would defend power—that of the boss, the captain, and the king—as merely an extension of the "natural" authority of the father. Patriarchalism may have always have been with us, but it is in its assertion over against the sexual, social, and political upheavals of the revolutionary years that it takes on its modern virulent form. The melodrama was the key means in the theatre of promoting this ideology of the domestic, an ideology that had been contested in romantic tragedies such as Shelley's *The Cenci,* with its assault upon familial, political, and religious patriarchy, and in Gothic dramas such as *Bertram,* with its less systematic satanic revolt against the law of the father and its turn to a robber band, adultery, and demonic self-assertion over against the state, the family, and the church.

The function of the nautical melodrama in the larger discourse of domesticity was to provide a model for the return of the wanderer or the prodigal to the fold, for the conversion of potentially revolutionary and at best nonsocial energy into socially acceptable forms, roughly conjugal sexuality and work. As we can see in the most famous of nautical plays, Douglas Jerrold's *Black-Ey'd Susan; or, All in the Downs,*[23] the tar, as the emblem of an energy exercised outside normal social bonds, enacts this conversion as he is subjected to two institutional moments: marriage and the court-martial.

In this play, it is William—played by T. P. Cooke, the most renowned nautical actor, who acted this part more than 800 times—who is returning home from the wars against France (only vaguely invoked), having saved his captain's life and hoping to see his wife Susan and win his discharge from the navy. During his absence, his wife has faced both financial and sexual threats—her uncle, having driven William into the navy, threatens her with eviction, while her uncle's ally, the smuggler Hatchet, hopes to exploit her fiscal distress in a seduction plot. Susan is saved from Hatchet's designs not only by William's bravery but also by the action of Lieutenant Pike, who, disguised as a French officer escaped from the prison hulks, has infiltrated the smuggler's band, as we again see Schillerian robbers remade as mere criminals, these being willing to collude even with England's enemies.

Where Bertram pursues adulterous love, William is the defender of marital fidelity even when it conflicts with his commitment to his uniform. William's captain has fallen in love with Susan and, drunk, assaults her. William rushes in at the critical moment, crying, "Susan! and attacked by the buccaneers! Die!" (II, iii). He strikes his captain—now recast as a pirate—without having recognized him.

The last act reveals William facing a court-martial for attempting to kill his captain, who has survived. The court martial itself demonstrates that William, like Melville's Billy Budd,[24] is the best of sailors. William pleads guilty, admitting that he struck the captain, but explaining that he did it to protect his wife and not knowing it was Captain Crosstree. The Admiral, reminding William that "you, as a good sailor, must know the course of justice cannot be evaded" (III, ii), sentences him to death; and William agrees that he must be condemned to uphold military law even though he did not act from malice. He faces death, like Schiller's Karl Moor or Kleist's Michael Kohlhass, accepting his sacrifice to the moral order. Luckily for him, Susan's evil uncle has drowned and on his body is found William's discharge: he was not in fact a sailor at the time he struck his captain and thus he can be freed as a properly enraged husband.

While this play may seem completely distant from *Bertram's* Gothic gloom, it actually reworks the elements that make up the tragedy of Maturin's play into the domestic romance of Jerrold's nautical melodrama. As we have already seen, the rebellious robber band is converted into the totally villainous pirate crew. The morally conflicted and troubling villain-hero is replaced by several, morally typed figures. Where Bertram is both the charismatic, strong hero who comes to reclaim his love and his place in society and the driven villain who seduces Imogine into adultery and kills his rival, *Black-Ey'∂ Susan* offers conventional villains—Doggrass, the oppressive landlord, and Hatchett, the evil smuggler—and thus can also feature a perfectly moral, upright hero in William. Bertram's attractiveness as a character—both to others and to the audience—is signaled within his play by his sex appeal, which is in marked contrast to the bland, boring quality of Imogine's husband, St. Aldobrand. It is important that in *Black-Ey'∂ Susan*, while the villain Hatchett retains Bertram's desires and while Captain Crosstree as an admired military man who sexually harasses Susan is a gesture towards a more complex figure, it is William who is granted the sexual attractiveness that has won him the beautiful Susan. His sexuality —revealed in his nautical descriptions of Susan ("There's my Susan! now pipe all hands for a royal salute; there she is, schooner-rigged" [II, i]; "my wife—as sweet a craft as was ever launched" [III, ii])—can be embraced because it is contained within matrimonial bonds.

In more general terms, William represents an attempt to "clean up" both the dramatic figure of the Gothic hero-villain—who troubled conservative critics such as Coleridge—and the public perception of the sailor. Given the reputation of sailors in their relations with women and given their actual behavior in theatres such as Sadler's Wells, where, for example, they were known to jump, filled with drink, into the tank during naval scenes, it is somewhat surprising that the stage tar is such a figure of sexual propriety, righteous action, and domestic virtue; given that actual sailors participated in mutinies, it is significant that a figure such as William is made to be a spokesperson for military order even as it oppresses him. What I want to suggest, extending and refiguring Booth's statement on the myth of the stage sailor, is that the British tar is an ideological construct, part of a process of reactionary myth-making.

As such, the figure of the tar is usefully placed together with the homey figures at the heart of domestic melodrama, figures we might summon up through an image as powerful as that of Jack Tar, namely John Bull. The figures of domestic drama, like John Bull, are tied to hearth and land; they are figures of stability, almost stationary. John Bull, with his beer and beef, is an emblem of all that is supposedly worth protecting in England, a point made in a particularly forceful way when he is compared to demonized Frenchmen, as in Gillray's ironic etching of "French Liberty. British Slavery" (1792). While within the domestic melodrama the peace and tranquility of hearth and home may be threatened, there is never any doubt of the victory of traditional family values. Where the protagonists of Gothic dramas quest beyond the bounds of social mores and sexual rules, the melodrama insists upon returning to them. The tar is a key figure in this assertion of homey virtues, for he, like the Gothic or romantic figure, has left behind the confines of his home and yet, unlike these troubling presences, desires only to return to his home and all it represents.

Where John Bull sits complacently at home, the tar has gone out into the world, confronted the enemy, perhaps been shipwrecked or captured or sold into slavery. He has lived in proximity to the Other, and yet all he wants is a return to the same, thus validating, in a way John Bull cannot, the British status quo. One is tempted to see in the somewhat strange figure of the British tar—who, after all, is portrayed in rather outlandish, showy dress, usually with long hair (see, for example, William West's print of Cooke as William [1829]), who talks of his long days at sea with only his mates and the songs they sing together, and who speaks a "cant" language, though one made up of fictional nautical slang—a figure who has in some ways "gone native," who has left behind the confines of normative British masculinity, who has virtually become John Bull in drag with his own language and subculture. We can imagine lying behind this motif a host of cultural concerns, from worries over whether sons, husbands, and lovers would be altered by years at war at sea (think of the body of films about returns from Viet Nam) to memories of the fear that arose when British sailors almost embraced another county—that is, when the fleet at the Nore considered setting sail for a French port to join the Revolution. But, of course, the stage sailor does not embrace some other version of self or society but instead fights to return to his wife and home. It is significant that what William longs for is to leave the navy, that the sympathetic Gnatbrain imagines William with "a little cot, with six feet square for the cultivation of potatoes" (II, iii), and that William is saved from execution by the fact he has been dismissed from service and can thus act as husband rather than sailor. We might imagine that the voyage abroad would change the sailor—witness Hamlet's transformation when he returns in the final act of his play after going to sea and suddenly finding himself in the romance world of nautical adventures and pirates, or the alterations in Bertram forced to wander the world—but the point is that Jack Tar is always the same, that all of his experiences have not fundamentally changed him. At some level, these nautical melodramas want to assert that all the dislocations of years of war, of internal political strife, of deep social and cultural questioning ultimately leave the order of the family, the military, the state, and providence in place.

Put simply, the Gothic drama enacted the revolts—both personal and collective, both erotic and political—of the age of democratic revolution, while the nautical melodrama works to discipline any rebellious tendencies, harnessing sexual energy within the institution of traditional marriage and staging the end of revolt in the ritual of a court martial in which the offender is a willing participant and upholder of the law. Turning to two other "classic" nautical melodramas, we find John Thomas Haines's *My Poll and My Partner Joe; A Nautical Drama in Three Acts* (Surrey, 31 August 1835) revealing how far these plays go in disciplining sexuality and Douglas Jerrold's *Mutiny at the Nore; or, British Sailors in 1797* (Royal Pavilion, 7 June 1830) most fully exemplifying the melodrama's conversion of history into myth.

Haines's *My Poll and My Partner Joe*[25] tells the story of Harry Halliyard, whose "Poll" is his beloved Mary and whose friend Joe, the "Byron of Battersea," is a fellow waterman who likes to compose songs. Harry makes the mistake of crossing the villainous Black Brandon, a slaver and loan shark, when Harry and Mary save the elderly Sam from debt by giving him all the money they have saved towards marriage. In retaliation, Brandon has a press gang come to seize Harry and Joe, but Joe is a fire officer and thus cannot be pressed into service. Harry is dragged off to the navy, leaving Mary with Joe, who confesses that he loves her as a friend.

We then meet Harry at sea, four years later, as he is being prosecuted for having lead an assault that, while victorious, had not been ordered. Like William in *Black-Ey'd Susan*, Harry is all too happy to be sacrificed to military rule, but the confused relationship between victory, honor, and military subordination is evident in Captain Oakheart's statement for the court: "To preserve the necessary discipline, we are compelled to reprimand a brave man for an act of honour that confers honour on the British flag; yet, while obliged to condemn, we shall applaud and honour in our hearts, — one of the best seaman that ever trod a plank . . . his very courage must be restricted with severity, or his example and extraordinary success will banish subordination from the fleet" (II, i). When we note that similar scenes — becoming almost a ritual of the nautical drama — are found in such plays as Fitzball's *Pilot* and Jerrold's *Mutiny at the Nore*, we get the sense that the sailor represents an energy that, while essential to British success, must be disciplined in order to maintain the British status quo. If marriage is often used to image the movement of potentially unsocial energy within a communal frame — we can think of the warriors turning into lovers in *Much Ado About Nothing* or of rakes becoming husbands in Restoration comedy — here it is the self-affirmed court martial that is the best model for bringing individual energy within social control.

Harry is saved when, in the midst of his trial, his ship encounters Brandon's slave vessel. While the play is vaguely set during the wars against France, true British values are better highlighted in defeating dastardly slavers. Still, in the melodrama, revolt and piracy are essentially the same thing: after taking Brandon's ship, the British sailors, led by Harry, attack a fort run by the slavers and some convenient pirates who fight under not the black flag but the revolutionary tricolor. In a scene that ends many nautical plays but here closes the second act, Harry hoists the British standard as the orchestra plays *Rule Britannia*.

Haines's *My Poll and My Partner Joe* contains the actual naval actions included in naval spectaculars but not *Black-Ey'd Susan*, but it has completed that aspect of the plot by the end of the second act. The third act is given over to the return home always invoked in these plays: Harry, now the heir of his superior officer whose life he once saved, returns to claim his beloved Mary and his old life in Battersea. However, he discovers that everyone believed he was dead and that his mother, dying in despair, has asked Joe and Mary to wed. They have done so, out of respect for her and out of a shared commitment to Harry. Before Harry discovers their reasons for marrying, he despairs: "I — I find her false — the friend I loved a villain" (III, i). It seems as if he will have his life and love taken from him by his best friend. However, Joe dies conveniently after an accident, but not before he can tell Harry the truth about the marriage. The play ends with this wonderful bit of stage business:

HARRY: He is dead! Mary!
MARY: Harry! Harry! [*they rush into each other's arms, recollect themselves and kneel in prayer by the side of* JOE —*the others take off their hats and surround him, and the curtain slowly descends.*]

Where in *Bertram* it was the villain-hero himself who plotted against domestic virtue and where the threat to domestic bliss in Jerrold's play came from the various, almost Gothic plots on Susan's virtue, here even the threat to domesticity is domesticated, is rendered into an action done to fulfill an old woman's dying requests. In a sense, Mary's and Harry's sexual feelings are even further disciplined than in other nautical plays, for here they must catch themselves in the middle of their joy at being together in order to mourn for Joe; Eros is no match for the social conventions devoted to Thanatos.

Or perhaps we should see the title and the play as meditating upon the tensions between heterosexual and homosocial desire. After all, the play opens with Watchful Waxend, a psalm-singing cobbler known as the bishop of Battersea, whose flight from a woman he has promised to love brings him to join the crew of a slaver. Harry himself sacrifices his money and thus his chance to wed Mary to help his friend, Sam; and when Mary still agrees to marry him, he is suddenly pulled back into the male world by the press gang. Joe does wed Mary, but he tells her that he loves her as a friend and his feelings for her are clearly mediated by his attachments to his partner Harry. This triangulation of Joe's desire for Mary through Harry and the movement of men from the company of women back to the society of other men are made clear in the play, but it is the final scene's regulation of heterosexual desire that is the most telling, for it points to a tension in these plays. These dramas wish to embrace marriage and the heterosexual desire it contains, but these romances contain a fear — as old as romance itself, from Odysseus with Calypso to Chrétien de Troyes's Erec with his Enid — that even the married male will be overwhelmed by sexuality, will become uxorious. There is a tension between the demands made by the marriage bed and those made by society, by one's Poll and by one's partners. In Schiller's *Robbers*, Karl Moor must sacrifice his beloved to prove his commitment to the group. In *Black-Ey'd Susan*, while William assaults his captain to save his wife, he must then concur in his own court martial, in his recognition of the demands of society over against those of his love. In Haines's play, such acts of control and self-denial are even further internalized, as Harry must recognize not the claims of a libidinous superior officer but of his closest friend: Mary and Harry court-martial their desire in the final scene, finding it — no matter how right—an affront to decorum, as if their hope of becoming a family is a violation of family values. One imagines them living out their love life together with a portrait of Joe staring down at them from their bedroom wall. Marriage and the court-martial are secret sharers in these plays, twin institutions needed to assert social control over an energy revealed in desire and in acts of bravery or self-assertion.

Such claims for independence do at times in this play seem to engage a spirit of protest—when the sailors threaten to resist the bailiff sent to arrest old Sam, when Harry, taken by the press gang, exclaims, "What! force a man from his happy home, to defend a country whose laws deprive him of his liberty?" (I, ii), and when in act III Harry lashes out in despair against a society that proffers false promises of marital bliss and male bonding. However, as we have seen, such threats are always contained, as Harry pledges allegiance—at the very moment of his court-martial—to the government he had criticized and as he and Mary are brought within the stockade of domestic proprieties. Even the protest against an economic system that allows people like Brandon to prey upon others and that drives people into bankruptcy is contained. In the scene that immediately follows the threat to Sam and the people's protest, we find Mary talking to another girl and saying, "London is a large place, and the industrious never need starve in it" (I, ii): there may be evil people, but the economic system is inherently fair. All protest is rewritten as a reaffirmation of the status quo.

It is worth noting that "D. G." in his introduction to the Cumberland edition of Haines's play worries about a loss of patriotism among the lower classes and argues that "truly English" plays such as *My Poll and My Partner Joe* are important in reviving it: "Let the public be won by patriotic spectacles, and we shall not have cause to lament that our national character among the humbler orders of society is degenerated into apathetic not to say brutal, indifference. Though *now* dwelling in peace, the trumpet of war may ere long startle us from our pleasant dream of security; and to whom shall we *then* turn for protection? . . . It is wise to diffuse *amor patrie* into popular amusements" (7). Evoking war in the midst of peace, D. G. suggests that nautical melodrama is to keep alive at all times a sense of the threats facing England—foreign threats, domestic threats, threats to domesticity itself. Nautical melodrama is the drama of England's post-Napoleonic "cold war" against revolution and reform.

Jerrold's *Mutiny at the Nore*[26] most directly confronts the historical events that might have troubled the domestic and patriotic myth embodied in nautical melodrama, but it does so only to replace history with that myth. The play, which actually treats both the mutiny within the Channel Fleet at

Spithead and that within the North Fleet at the Nore, not only makes important changes in the historical record but also works to render the mutiny into a domestic tale: Jerrold has rewritten the mutinies of 1797 in the image of his own *Black-Ey'd Susan.*

Jerrold includes the first mutiny at Spithead near Portsmouth in order to frame his account of the Nore mutiny, to present a "good" mutiny before taking on the more dangerous events at the Nore. The first act is given over to the Channel Fleet mutiny and to the fictitious figure of Jack Adams, the play's hero and its tar. This initial movement enacts the basic moments of the nautical melodrama, as Adams saves the day and marries his beloved Molly. Adams claims to be a leader of the mutiny, and his rival for Molly calls him the "principal rebel, and spokesman of the whole mutinous fleet" (I, iii). However, this mutineer wants nothing to do with the sailors' Court of Delegates convened on the *Queen* (the play's version of the mutineers committee which first met on the *Charlotte*), which he feels "isn't worth a bucket of spray" (I, ii). He urges the men to have faith in the Admiralty, earning the respect of their captain (despised by the other men) who says of Adams, "Had all my ship's company been such as you, I should have been proud of commanding them — as it is, I blush to have ever been their captain" (I, ii). Adams essentially embraces the position of William of *Black-Ey'd Susan* or Haines's Harry: even as he sees the injustice within the navy, he affirms the right of the powers that be to exercise power over him.

Adams is ultimately proven correct in a scene (I, iv) in which history is rewritten to alter the moral balance of power between the mutineers and the government. The mutiny of the Channel Fleet, which had been halted on 23 April 1797 after a royal pardon had been issued, recommenced on 7 May, with both the Plymouth and Portsmouth detachments concerned that Parliament would not pass the "Seamen's Bill" they had been promised. A group of delegates from the mutiny sought to board the still loyal *London,* but Admiral Colpoys tried to prevent them by having the marines fire on the crew; they killed one man and injured others, but then capitulated to the mutineers who almost killed Colpoys before imprisoning him. As a result of this action, the bill was approved and signed that day, the news of the parliamentary victory reaching Portsmouth on the ninth and Admiral Howe spending three days reassuring the crews, who celebrated their victory on the fifteenth before sailing off for blockade duty on the sixteenth.[27] In Jerrold's play, the delegates arrive at the *London* and are opposed by Colpoys, who claims that the leaders of the mutiny have misled naive sailors: "It is such knaves as you, you villain, famous alike for your turbulence and cowardice, that bring honest simple men into tumult and disgrace" (I, v).

When the mutineers insist upon entering the ship, it is one of their number who fires, hitting a lieutenant. The marines never fire, never kill anyone. The mutineers are successful, but when they strike the admiral's flag Adams appears, crying, "Hold! hold the day is ours — Lord Howe is arrived — the Admiralty consents to our claims — here is the paper!" The sailors rehoist the admiral's flag amidst cheers. There is literally no time here for violence or for the sailors' acts to have an effect. In Jerrold's version, government forces shed no blood, and a resolution is reached not in response to the violent revolt of the mutineers but out of the goodness of the Admiralty's heart. Calm having returned, Adams proclaims, "I always said that, when I managed to settle the mutiny at Spithead, I'd be married" (II, i) — the mutiny now reduced to a mere interlude in his pursuit of marital bliss.

This first movement within the play, then, enacts the standard plot of the nautical melodrama, with Adams playing the part of the tar who wins his girl by surrendering his will to his superiors even when they are in the wrong. The second act introduces the historical figure of Richard Parker, the leader of the mutiny within the North Fleet at the Nore. Parker, a "quota man" brought into the fleet under Pitt's Acts of 1795 and 1796 who found himself the leader of the mutiny only to be executed as a self-styled "Martyr in the cause of Humanity,"[28] is redefined by Jerrold, who places him within a thoroughly domestic plot. We first meet Parker in domestic scenes with his wife and son, where the value of the family is extolled and his wife tells him that, no matter what trials he must undergo, her love and female strength will see him through. We discover that Parker has gone to sea and experienced troubles there all because of his wife. A "genteel, high-spirited young man" (II, i), he sought his beloved Mary's hand only to be contested by a Captain Arlington and opposed by her father, who disinherited her upon their marriage. When she became pregnant, Parker had to join the navy, only to find himself under the command of Arlington, who then unjustly accused Parker of theft. Parker deserted to escape punishment; at the time of his recapture, the true thief had been apprehended, but Parker was tried anyway, his death sentence being commuted to a flogging throughout the fleet. Parker has been mistreated not by the naval system but by a sexually jealous superior; his mutiny is driven less by a sense of the injustice suffered by all seamen than by his personal desire for revenge against his rival.

The moment of mutiny is also converted into a scene from domestic melodrama. The officers side with their captain, and a lieutenant asks, "let every blue jacket who remains true to king and country, walk on this side of the deck" (II, ii). Only Adams joins the officers, telling the men they should write to the Admiralty about the injustices they experience. Parker moves to take the ship by seizing the forecastle guns and turning them on the officers. However, he does not realize that his son (mysteriously on board) has fallen asleep with his head resting against the mouth of the gun. He is about to fire, when Adams springs forward to save the child as *"Parker and the crew recoil with horror."* The Captain now seizes the child, proclaiming that he will kill him if the crew continues the mutiny. Not even the marines can stomach this gesture, and they join the mutiny; Parker closes the scene in triumph as Arlington surrenders. The mutiny has arisen from jealousy; its outcome has hinged upon the treatment of a child.

The actual mutiny at the Nore collapsed when the government, with the key support of Sheridan, decided to reverse the tactics used during the first mutiny and to oppose the mutineers. The ships were isolated and supplies cut off. Anyone going ashore was arrested, and Parliament passed three bills giving the government extraordinary powers against the mutineers, now depicted as the dupes of Jacobins or worse. When Parker and his committee threatened to take the fleet to France, the Admiralty removed the buoys necessary to navigate the Thames; plans were made to use East India ships against the fleet. The mutineers themselves were divided, and by June 14 the fleet had surrendered. Court-martial proceedings were ordered on 19 June, with Parker and at least 36 others out of 52 convicted being executed; an additional 350 men were punished outside the court-martial process, with sentences ranging from floggings to life servitude in the colonies.[29]

In Jerrold's play, the Admiralty meets the demands of the sailors, its only condition being that Parker be given over for trial. When the marines led by Arlington arrive to arrest the mutineer, the captain insults Parker's wife, and Parker, who has admitted to his wife that it was personal triumph over Arlington rather than concern over the sailors' plight that motivated him, kills the captain, just as William struck his captain to save Black-Ey'd Susan. Parker then allows himself to be arrested, agreeing—like all good melodramatic sailors—that the charges against him are just: "Though they might have saved the mutineer, they must not, cannot save the murderer" (III, iv).

Parker, acquiescing in his own conviction, is concerned only with his family, particularly his son. Convincing his wife to live so she can care for the boy, he also commends his child to the king and to Adams, who promptly tatoos the boy with the king's mark and proclaims he will grow up to be an admiral—the mutineer's son is a future Colpoys. While we do not witness the court-martial in this play, Jerrold does stage the execution, much to the pleasure of D. G., who comments in the Cumberland edition of the play that "Those who cannot conveniently attend a naval execution, may have their soft sympathies excited, and their curiosity gratified, by witnessing this drama" (8). Even the appeal of the execution scene, with (D. G. tells us) "a frantic wife, and a poor unconscious infant," is domestic — and nationalistic. Parker dies, not a martyr to humanity, but a true patriot: "My shipmates, hear the last toast of Richard Parker: — 'here's a health to my king, and God bless him! confusion to his enemies, and salvation to my soul!" (III, v). Thus ends *Mutiny at the Nore*, with even the mutineer proclaiming the value of hearth and home and saluting those who execute him. The mutiny that almost brought England to its knees in 1797 is in 1830 transformed into a matter of personal jealousies, the protection of one's children, respect for the family, reverence for the monarchy, and the belief in subordination.

Such a taming of force of the mutineers was still not enough for Cumberland's commentator D. G., who — remembering that the mutiny "hoisted its red flag, and waved it insultingly above the imperial standard of old England" (6) — worried about the fact that the play granted Parker any sympathy at all:

> Parker is elevated to a hero, and the admiral's lady draws largely upon our pity . . . these mitigating circumstances, when put forth in connection with history, and aided by scenic effect, are likely to produce a wrong impression — to inspire horror at the sword of justice, when justice is mercy (8).

D. G., unmoved by the historical inaccuracies that are used against the mutineers, is clearly concerned that, given the plot involving Parker's wife (and given the power of "illegitimate" spectacle), Parker is not made villainous enough, that he is too close to the morally mixed figures of the Gothic and romantic drama, that he is not thoroughly melodramatized. D. G. worries that the audience will sympathize with Parker's sufferings and thus will not come to judge him with the harshness D. G. believes the mutineer deserves. In D. G.'s comments, we see the ultimate goal of the nautical melodrama: to insure that the audience performs upon its own emotional responses the same kind of discipline that the plays perform upon the thoughts and feelings of their characters. Just as the hero of the nautical drama must endorse the very authority that punishes him, we are to suppress our sympathy and to embrace the "sword of justice" as if it were merciful in the very moment in which it is being used to execute someone we see as innocent. When we recall D. G.'s comments on Haines's play, with their evocation of the uneasy peace of a "cold war" ("Though *now* dwelling in peace, the trumpet of war may ere long startle us from our pleasant dream of security"), we can see the nautical melodrama as a form dedicated to reminding the audience of the dangers that always threaten the reactionary order (because there would not be a *reaction*ary order without a perceived threat) and of maintaining in the audience a kind of military discipline of the emotions even during peace. What is finally most surprising about the nautical melodrama is that it seems to have fulfilled its ideological function. Where audiences of the late eighteenth and early nineteenth centuries would rise up in riot, where theatre officials were concerned that, for example, a Jacobite song might stir the crowd to violence, where the examiner of plays would not allow any allusion to events in revolutionary France or in fact to contemporary events at all[30] — by the time of Jerrold's a play, despite D. G.'s worries, an inflammatory pamphlet, pointing out the gap between the pay for officers and that for sailors and closing with the call, "redress yourselves! — Rule Britannia! and three cheers for Richard Parker!" (I, i), can safely be read on stage. Of course, the audience, hearing this, did not turn to revolt in the streets but returned to the security of their homes: they had learned to court-martial themselves rather than rise to the challenge of such mutinous calls.

Notes

1. For defenses of the melodrama as "popular" and "radical" see, for example, Michael Booth, *Prefaces to English Nineteenth-Century Theatre* (Manchester: Manchester University Press, 1980), 27; Elaine Hadley, "The Old Price Wars: Melodramatizing the Public Sphere in Early-Nineteenth-Century England," *PMLA* 107 (May 1992): 532; and Frank Rahill, *World of Melodrama* (University Park: Pennsylvania State University Press, 1967), xvii.

2. *Hegel on Tragedy*, ed. Anne and Henry Paolucci (1962; reprint, New York: Harper and Row, 1975), esp. 92. See Michael R. Booth, "East End and West End: Class and Audience in Victorian London," *Theatre Research International* 2 (February 1977); or Clive Barker, "The Audience of the Britannia Theatre, Hoxton," *Theatre Quarterly* 9 (1979).

3. Samuel Taylor Coleridge, *Biographia Literaria*, ed. James Engell and W. Jackson Bate, vol. 2 (Princeton: Princeton University Press, 1983), 221.

4. Michael Booth, *English Melodrama* (London: Herbert Jenkins, 1965).

5. David Mayer, *Harlequin in His Element: The English Pantomime, 1806-1836* (Cambridge: Harvard University Press, 1969), 271.

6. The anonymous print is reproduced in the catalogue for *The Shadow of the Guillotine: Britain and the French Revolution,* David Bindman with Aileen Dawon and Mark Jones (London: British Museum Publications, 1989), p. 185, item 182. For the Canning song, see James Epstein, "Radical Dining, Toasting, and Symbolic Expression in Early Nineteenth-Century Lancashire: Rituals of Solidarity," *Albion* 20 (summer 1988): 277.

7. John Stevenson, *Popular Disturbances in England, 1700-1870* (London: Longman, 1979), 181-84.

8. Roger Wells, *Insurrection: The British Experience, 1795-1803* (Gloucester: Alan Sutton, 1983), 242.

9. Quoted in Clive Emsley, *British Society and the French Wars, 1793-1815* (Totowa, N.J.: Rowman and Littlefield, 1979), 64.

10. Quoted in Emsley, *British Society,* 61.

11. Epstein, in "Radical Dining," tells us that "At Hunt's trial, the prosecution had argued that the black flag which Saddleworth radicals carried to Peterloo was the ensign of piracy" which "carried a revolutionary message" (290 n).

12. Booth, *English Melodrama,* 93.

13. See Cox, "Ideology and Genre in the British Antirevolutionary Drama of the 1790s," *ELH* 58 (1991): 579-610.

14. From playbill, quoted in Dennis Arundell, *The Story of Sadler's Wells* (New York: Theatre Arts Books, 1965), 53.

15. Charles Beecher Hogan tells us the play made "the largest amount known for a single performance at either Drury Lane or Covent Garden at any time between 1700 and 1800: £1,526.11s"; *The London Stage, 1660-1800,* part 5, vol. 3 (Carbondale: Southern Illinois University Press, 1968), 1570.

16. *Professional and Literary Memoirs of Charles Dibdin the Younger,* ed. George Speaight (London: Society for Theatre Research, 1956), 60-62. See Derek Forbes, "Water Drama," in *Performance and Politics in Popular Drama,* ed. David Bradby, Louis James, and Bernard Sharratt (Cambridge: Cambridge University Press, 1980) 91-108; and Arundell, *Sadler's Wells,* 68-78.

17. Booth, *English Melodrama,* 104.

18. The text for *Bertram* is taken from *Seven Gothic Dramas, 1789-1825,* ed. Jeffrey N. Cox (Athens: Ohio University Press, 1992). Act and scene numbers will be given in the text.

19. The text for *The Purse; or the Benevolent Tar: A Musical Entertainment in One Act* is taken from Dick's edition (London, 1872) 11:27-32. Scene numbers will be given in the text.

20. John Genest, *Some Account of the English Stage from the Restoration in 1660 to 1830* (1832; reprint, New York: Burt Franklin, 1965), 7: 147.

21. Coleridge, *Biographia Literaria,* 222.

22. Edmund Burke, *Reflections on the Revolution in France,* in *The Works of Edmund Burke,* 3 vols. (New York: George Dearborn, 1836), esp. 1:488-89. Hannah More, *Village Politics,* in *Burke, Paine, Godwin, and The Revolution Controversy,* ed. Marilyn Butler (Cambridge University Press, 1984), 181. On George III as the "father" of his country, see Linda Colley, *Britons: Forging the Nation, 1707-1837* (New Haven: Yale University Press, 1992). Marilyn Butler places the reaction to the *Memoirs of the Author of a Vindication of the Rights of Woman* (1798) in the context of a turn to a domestic ideology in *Romantics, Rebels and Reactionaries* Oxford: Oxford University Press, 1982), 94.

23. The text for Jerrold's *Black-Ey'd Susan; or, All in the Downs: A Nautical Drama in Three Acts* is taken from *English Plays of the Nineteenth Century,* ed. Michael R.

Booth, vol. 1 (Oxford: Clarendon Press, 1969). Act and scene numbers will be given in the text.

24. For a reading of *Billy Budd* that compliments my argument, see Larry J. Reynolds, "*Billy Budd* and American Labor Unrest: The Case for Striking Back," in *New Essays on Billy Budd* (Cambridge: Cambridge University Press, forthcoming).

25. The text for Haines's *My Poll and My Partner Joe* is taken from Cumberland's *Minor Theatre*, vol. 9 (London, 1835). Act and scene numbers will be given in the text.

26. The text for Jerrold's *Mutiny at the Nore* is taken from Cumberland's edition (London, 1830). Act and scene numbers will be given in the text.

27. Wells, *Insurrection*, 87.

28. Quoted in E. P. Thompson, *The Making of the English Working Class* (1963; reprint, New York: Vintage, 1966), 168.

29. Wells, *Insurrection*, 89.

30. On theatrical riots, see Marc Baer, *Theatre and Disorder in Late Georgian London* (Oxford: Clarendon Press, 1992). The incident with the Jacobite song can be found in George Colman, letter to James Winston, from the Broadley Collection (Little Haymarket Theatre, fol. 93), Westminster Public Libraries, quoted in Sutcliffe, "Introduction," in *Plays by George Colman the Younger and Thomas Morton* (Cambridge: Cambridge University Press, 1983), 6. Colman, the examiner of plays after Larpent, testified before the 1832 Select Committee that he would ban "anything that may be so allusive to the times as to applied to the existing moment, and which is likely to be inflammatory"; *Report From the Select Committee Appointed to Inquire into the Laws Affecting Dramatic Literature,* Irish University Press Series of British Parliamentary Papers: Stage and Theatre, vol. 1 (Shannon: Irish University Press, 1968), 66.

10

RADICALISM IN THE MELODRAMA OF THE EARLY NINETEENTH CENTURY

HARTMUT ILSEMANN*

*T*HE DRAMATIC CORPUS GENERALLY REFERRED TO AS MELODRAMA assumed various guises in the early nineteenth century, one of which was the "domestic play," and a few of these are of particular interest because their content addresses contemporary social problems. Unlike most melodramatic works, these plays do not entertain the audience solely by creating illusions and by alienating the audience from reality.

Among the melodramas offering this new content are J. B. Buckstone's *Luke the Labourer* (1826), Jerrold's *The Rent Day* (1832),[1] and Walker's *The Factory Lad* (1832).[2] Timewise, these plays emerge in the period just prior to the Reform Bill of 1832, so their effect can best be understood in connection with the agitation and the arguments spurred by the Radical movement of the day. However, it would not do justice to the meaning and achievements of these melodramas if analysis were limited to material from such extratextual sources.

Equally important from an aesthetic point of view are the ways in which these plays stray from the usual melodramatic patterns. In terms of the audience, these variants not only carry with them an emancipatory potential, they also preempt the received modes of reception. One might even go so far as to say that this difference constitutes the beginning of a series of developments that, toward the end of the century, will lead to both realistic and naturalistic drama. Sean O'Casey and George Bernard Shaw, for example, were never able to completely deny their melodramatic heritage. In retrospect, this, too, seems to suggest a connection between the socially critical content of early-nineteenth-century melodrama and the new plays crafted from the remains of the melodrama in the early twentieth century.[3]

Michael Booth dealt in some detail with this question in an essay with the programmatic title, "A Defence of Nineteenth-Century English Drama." In it he emphasizes the correspondences between the raw materials that Ibsen fashioned into tragedy and those that emerge in the work of Boucicault and Tom Taylor in the form of characters who, when confronted with the tensions, conflicts, and disharmony of their domestic situation, try to free themselves from the shadow of the past.[4]

Other titles, such as Jerrold's *The Factory Girl* (1832), G.F. Taylor's *The Factory Strike; or, Want, Crime, and Retribution* (1838), Haines's *The Factory Boy* (1840), and Stirling's *Mary of Manchester; or, The Spirit of the Loom* (1847), point to the endurance and spread of social themes even after the collapse of the Radical movement. In the second half of the nineteenth century in particular, in works such as *The Labour Question* (1861), Boucicault's *The Long Strike* (1866), *Free Labour* (1870), and *The Miner's Strike* (1875), and George Fenn's *The Foreman of the Works* (1866) as well as *Work and Wages* (1890), a dramatic conception becomes visible that is increasingly defined by new content rather than inherited form.[5]

Traditional form still dominates in the three plays mentioned first. But while their aesthetic structures retain all the hallmarks of the prevailing melodramatic style, they suggest new ways of linking that style to current social problems. This is most evident in *The Factory Lad*, the work of an otherwise unknown author by the name of John Walker, which opened on 15 October, 1832 at the Surrey Theatre in Blackfriers Road. Blackfriers was a workers' quarter at the time, and close to the Surrey lay the Rotunda, where members of the labor movement met every Wednesday to debate. In the eyes of the authorities they also raised the specter of revolution. At the time, Radical demonstrations were the order of the day. In addition, the artisans' and workers' desire to educate themselves led to a series of cultural activities, one of which was the publication of an illegal weekly, the *Poor Man's Guardian*, which dealt in detail with the situation of the worker.

The *Factory Lad* was staged at the Surrey a few months after the Reform Law of 1832 was passed by the House of Lords and despite the fact that the theatre was only licensed to present burletta. Given these facts, one can surmise that the mode of reception calculated into the structure of the play was meant to produce a reaction to the Reform Bill among the spectators. Only a more detailed analysis of the work can demonstrate the validity of this assumption, but such an analysis will also require some additional investigation of the affective structures of texts that stem from a somewhat earlier period.

The scene of the action is Bury, a town near Manchester, and the time is 1832—an early and obvious indication of the play's claim to topicality. In addition, the bill announcing the play offers the following:

> This evening . . . will be produced an entirely new and original Domestic Drama, of deep interest, and founded on Passing Events, called *The Factory Lad: or, Saturday Night.* . . EXTERIOR OF LARGE FACTORY . . . The interior lighted with gas. Determination of the men to resist the introduction of Steam and Manufactory by Power Looms. Fatal Consequences of Combination, &c. Destruction of the Factory by Fire! Romantic View by Moonlight with Factory in the distance, still burning. The Imposition of the Soldiery to quell the rioters—their Capture—Examination—Commitment for Trial, &c. &c.[6]

This preparatory information would no doubt remind the spectators of certain events that had taken place prior to the passage of the Reform Bill of 1832, especially the Bristol Riots (1831) and the demonstrations by the radicals from the artisan and shopkeeper camp as well as from the working class. And since *The Factory Lad* takes up the question of machine breaking, the play also brings to life the Luddite movement from the years 1811-1812. Furthermore, the ruthless behavior of the factory owner and the representatives of public order could well embody a reference to the Peterloo massacre.

But, as the *Poor Man's Guardian* had recently reported, workers had been condemned to death in 1832 as well: "having unlawfully and maliciously destroyed a mill at Beeston . . . unfortunate fellow-creatures condemned to be sacrificed upon the bloody altar of property."[7] If one accepts Thompson's description of the situation, the possibility of a revolution had never been greater than at this time, given the militant Radicals' readiness for an armed confrontation.[8] Knowledge of the conflict that had arisen between the radicals of the middle and working classes after the passage of the Reform Bill—a conflict that had also split the radical workers movement—seems to be another important prerequisite for understanding the play.[9]

The action opens at eight o'clock on a Saturday evening in front of a factory building. After finishing work for the day, the workers—Allen, Hatfield, Wilson, Sims, and Smith—hurry to get their pay, the first they will receive from the new owner, who has taken over the factory in place of his father. The father had been highly respected by his workers and now, after his death, they expect a continuation of the old relationship, a relationship founded on reciprocal loyalty and responsibility towards the weak of society. To the observer, this shows that employer paternalism, though recently on the wane, was still the foundation for social usage as well as social structure as far as workers are concerned.

It seems, therefore, that socialism of an Owenist inspiration is at work here—a socialism that envisions cooperation and harmony as the basis for society rather than competition and exploitation. But it is precisely the latter combination that is conjured up by the dialogue between the factory owner, Westwood, and his workers. Their discussion provides a commentary on the factory system that a policy of laissez faire will produce. Here is a hierarchically arranged list of the areas of conflict that seem of particular concern: (1) the problem of the impoverishment and alienation of the proletariat, (2) the closely related discussion of economic theories, especially Adam Smith and David Ricardo's principle of supply and demand and idea of maximizing profit, (3) eighteenth- and nineteenth-century demands for human and civil rights, and (4) the "special" procedures undertaken regarding the reform bill (procedures that would be set aside by [3]). At this point, the laws had already been passed in the House of Lords and the radical workers movement felt betrayed by the radicals of the middle class.

> **WESTWOOD.** I've come to speak my mind. Times are now altered.
> **ALLEN.** They are indeed, sir. A poor man has now less wages for more work.
> **WESTWOOD.** The master having less money, resulting from there being less demand of the commodity manufactured. . . . If not less demand, a greater quantity is thrown into the markets at a cheaper rate. Therefore, to compete with my neighbours —that is, if I wish to prosper as they do —I have come to the resolution of having my looms propelled by steam. . . . Which will dispense with the necessity of manual labour, and save me some three thousand a year (44).

Westwood's stance, aimed as it is at pursuing his own interests, is in accord with the ideas found in the doctrine of natural rights espoused by the Calvinists and the Puritans and, furthermore, with Locke's expositions on the legitimacy of private property. According to the so-called founding, or social, contract, retaining one's property ("the preservation of their property") is the most fundamental human right, while the observance of this right is the highest duty of the individual and the state.[10] Thus, it is not difficult for Westwood to refute the claims of his workers by drawing their attention to the question of property relations.

WESTWOOD. Don't you buy where you please, at the cheapest
place? Would you have bought that jerkin of one man
more than another, if he had charged you twice the sum
for it, or even a sixpence more? Don't you, too, sow
your garden as you please, and dig it as you please?
HATFIELD. Why, it's my own.
WESTWOOD. There it is! Then have I not the same right to
do as I please with *my own*? (44-45).

With these words, the manufacturer broaches the themes of human and civil
rights. Equality, freedom, security, and property are addressed more or
less explicitly, and Westwood's example shows clearly that these requisites
are put forward by the bourgeoisie for its own benefit. They do not seem to
be indivisible and available to all. Thus, at the very beginning of *The Factory
Lad*, the collapse of the alliance between the middle class and the lower social
strata (which had already occurred by 1832) is acknowledged to be the
result of deep and unbridgeable class differences. This allows us to assume
that the creation of an independent class consciousness is an intended aspect
of the perspective offered by the play.

Westwood, who first uses the principle of equal opportunity to his own
advantage, dismisses his workers on economic grounds in the lines that follow. Machines and steam power will replace them. A rational response, one
that draws on current social concepts, is not only not to be found in any
explicit form in the text, it is absent from the overall political consciousness
of the play. In the lines that follow all that can be discovered are the misery
and sentimental laments typical of the melodramatic form. Allen, who must
provide for his wife and children, and who, because of this, has already been
put forward as a hero and an object of identification for the spectators, falls
to his knees begging for mercy but is rejected out of hand. As a result,
Hatfield swears bitter vengeance, thereby foreshadowing an extension of the
conflict, which, up to this point, has only been verbal.

The remaining material of the play corresponds to the level of awareness
and the expectations of the audience. The workers believe that the only way
they can defend themselves is by attacking the new machines. They succeed
in setting the factory on fire, but they are recognized by the guards stationed
around it. Later, the police search for the ringleaders. They are all arrested
and brought in to be questioned by a magistrate. No one has any illusions
about the judgment to come. Although Allen's wife, Jane, implores
Westwood in heartrending fashion, begging him to spare her husband, he
is ruthless in his accusations. He loudly announces his belief in the principle
that "Justice shall have its due," and says they are all equally guilty. These

are also his last remarks. Rushton, the outlaw hunter and poacher who had earlier taken all the onus on himself—claiming that he had urged and provoked the fire for personal reasons—shoots Westwood and instantly finds himself surrounded by soldiers with rifles at the ready.

This brief summary should make it clear that the repertoire of historical material selected and dramatized in the play specifically aims at an unvarnished representation of conditions much as we know them from the history of the Industrial Revolution. But the political radicalism of the spectator that has been calculated into the reception of this play is nourished far less by the analysis and intellectual investigation of these economically threatening transformations than by the personal disappointments and existential threats faced by the play's working-class figures. Changes that seem to be founded on the laws of nature as far as an employer is concerned would necessarily seem contemptuous and humiliating to the workers who are their helpless victims.

The degree to which this sort of audience perception might arise from an awareness of contemporary reality or from the melodramatic repertoire that the spectators had at their disposal can only be determined through an aesthetic analysis of the dramatic construct that takes into account the decoding mechanisms already in operation at the time. What is strikingly new in all this is the way in which the melodramatic elements of the play function within a field of tension, one extreme of which is provided by illusionistic, sensational, and alienating features that are in total accord with the traditional melodrama while the other is constituted by disillusioning effects, everyday objects, and circumstances from real life.

Were the dialogue cited above to be read today, it could be regarded as a reproduction of socio-historical reality. The arguments reconstitute the known positions espoused by factory owners and workers of the era. But contemporary, proletarian spectators would evaluate matters differently. They would immediately bring to bear criteria that, instead of testing the rationality and validity of the opposing arguments, would lay the blame for these socio-historical changes on the person who was the presumed cause. That is evident from the information available to the spectators prior to the play, not only in the title, which brings in extratextual material, but also from the specific expectations that accompany the genre and that, among other things, presuppose a villainous opponent, a role that the audience would project onto the factory owner, Westwood. It is up to this "scapegoat" to draw the immanent anxieties of society onto himself and thereby contain the chaotic element in the Manichean structure of the melodramatic world-view. On the other hand, the text itself first casts Westwood in a negative light at the end of the opening scene. As he leaves, the stage direction reads:

"Westwood into factory, sneeringly" (45). At this point, after a mere fifty lines of dialogue, the basic constellation of spectator allegiances is firmly established; they are for the discharged factory workers and against the factory owner thanks to the touching and sympathy-generating aspects of the scene and to the stock presentation of a villain with a diabolical laugh.

Another instance of socio-economic transformation and of material offered to the spectators for the sake of identification emerges in the next scene. Just before the newly discharged workers arrive, the poacher, Rushton, has a monologue in which he considers the justness of the current hunting laws:

> RUSHTON. That be sure for a good'un —ha, ha! The Game
> Laws, eh. As if a poor man hadn't as much right to the
> bird that flies and the hare that runs as the rich tyrants
> who want all, and gripe and grapple all too! I care not
> for their laws. While I have my liberty or power, or will
> live as well as the best of 'em (45).

For hundreds of years common lands had been available for everyone's use and were, therefore, an important source of food for a village community, but with the greater exploitation of agricultural spaces and the accompanying enclosures and restrictions on land ownership in the eighteenth and early nineteenth centuries, county folk experienced life-threatening changes in their situation. Not only did the mechanization of agriculture take work from them, legal measures were introduced that denied them rights that had helped keep them alive.

Laws passed in 1816 and 1831 had turned trapping rabbits and hunting pheasants, partridges, and the like into poaching, a crime punishable by transportation to the colonies. Even in 1832, if a landowner ultimately managed to convince the court that the poacher was actually a thief, the death penalty was also a real possibility. One of the justifiable fears among members of the organized work force was that a false charge of poaching might be made against "undesirables"—labor spokesmen and agitators—in order to get them out of the way and, at the same time, discipline the remaining workers. Rushton's extralegal behavior points toward this possibility and would suggest to the spectator the possible fate of workers who had been dismissed as part of the process of industrializing the country. This is a scenic display of events stemming from changes in the agricultural realm that in fact preceded such developments in the industrial sphere, so in this respect Rushton's situation introduces additional elements of tension from outside the play into the action.

For Sims, Smith, Wilson, and Hatfield the immediate question is how to respond to being dismissed. To rely on parish charity is simply out of the question given Rushton's experience with the workhouse:

> Ay, or a pauper, to go with your hat in your hand, and after begging and telling them what they know to be the truth—that you have a wife and five, six, or eight children; one, perhaps just born; another, mayhap, just dying—they'll give you eighteen pence to support them all for the week; and if you dare to complain—not a farthing, but place you in the stocks or scourge you through the town as a vagabond! This is parish charity! I have known what it is. My back is still scored with the marks of their power. The slave abroad, the poor black whom they affect to pity, is not so trampled on, hunted, and ill-used as the peasant or hard-working fellows like yourselves, if once you have no home nor bread to give your children (46).

They decide, therefore, to find Allen and go talk things over in The Harriers. For the audience, the chance meeting between Rushton and the workers symbolizes a normal and natural moment of solidarity, one that ought to be protected from the scrutiny of the authorities. At the same time, Rushton, who is made to speak primarily in monologues, is so conceived as to sharpen awareness of the actual threat to the individual that accompanies deracination.

Scene structure supplements character conception as a means of organizing the spectators' reception. After the accidental meeting between Rushton, the village outcast, and these workers who have been cast out of the industrial sphere (I,ii), their planned reunion does not take place until the fifth scene. In order to create tension, a view of domestic life (1,3) is set in between that provides a moment of contrast and also serves to justify the results of the later meeting. This scene revives the perspective organized by the opening of the play and visibly displays the virtues of an intact worker's family. At the same time it reveals the misery that comes with the impending destruction of this impoverished but idyllic life. Rushton's earlier history is clarified somewhat, too. After Allen's wife, Jane, expresses some thoughts about emigration, Allen replies:

> Ay, some foreign outlandish place, to be shipped off like convicts to die and starve! Look at Will Rushton, who was enticed or rather say ensnared there with his wife and four children. Were not the children slaughtered by the natives, who hate white men and live on human flesh? And was not his wife seized too, your own sister, and borne away and never returned—shared perhaps the same fate as her children, or perhaps worse? And has not poor Will,

since he returned, been crazed, heart-broken, a pauper, poacher, or anything? (49-50).

Allen's reply contributes to a second level of characterization here. Rushton, in addition to functioning as the deracinated but socio-historically comprehensible hero of the play, is also its melodramatic hero—in resolute conflict with the powers of fate, with nothing more to lose, and determined to fight to the bitter end.

Jane, who cannot cope with his dismissal, faints as Allen hurries out of the house to the meeting at The Harriers. This gesture marks her as a melodramatic heroine—a figure exposed in all innocence to the hard and execrable world outside the village. Unable to protect herself, she can only wait for the day that fate will atone for the injustices she has lived through and repay her for each of her injuries. Her state of collapse visually symbolizes her absolute need of protection, and no sympathetic spectator could fail to be affected or to wish her the help she deserves.

This scene takes place at eight thirty on a Saturday evening. In contrast, the one that follows (I,iv) depicts Westwood's home during the evening meal and the conversation with the servants indicates that it is eight o'clock. Clearly, then, the scenes do not unfold in chronological order; they are arranged in terms of their thematic and structural links to the preceding and following scenes. Westwood's monologues in the fourth scene demonstrate a hardhearted attitude toward his father's long-time servants: he dismisses them. Furthermore, his ruminations on business matters probably appeared to the contemporary spectator to be a detailed catalogue of current principles of exploitation. That Westwood has taken precautions for his safety and that he plans to take full advantage of the workings of the law further heightens the tension while also providing a counterpoint to the scene in The Harriers with the conspirators that unfolds next. Up to this point, then, the play is in complete accord with the black-white model provided by the melodramatic paradigm. The opposition that was first laid out in the exposition hardens here thanks to the unbending attitude of the manufacturer and—in conformity with the melodramatic prescription—the misfortune that looms the horizon for the Allens. At this point, then, the legitimacy of any action taken against the oppressor seems unquestionable.

Threatening events seem to have an unavoidable aspect on the syntagmatic level as well. The plot that Rushton organizes—the dimensions of which are hidden from the audience, since the plotters speak mostly in whispers—is put into action in the next scene and takes on the trappings of a campaign of vengeance. "Blow for blow, . . . and blood for blood" is its rallying cry (55), and as Rushton offers encouraging comments to the workers (I,vii), "Break, crack, and split into ten thousand pieces these engines of your disgrace, your poverty, and your ruin" (56), Westwood appears with the police. When the workers flee, Rushton prevents Westwood from pursuing them and sets fire to the factory. In his subsequent monologue (II,i), which is delivered at some distance from the burning factory, he enjoys his brief triumph to the hilt:

> RUSHTON. Ha, ha! This has been a glorious night—to see the
> palace of the tyrant leveled to the ground, to hear his
> engines of gain cracking, to hear him call for help, and
> see the red flame laugh in triumph! Ah, many a day
> have I lain upon the cold, damp ground, muttering
> curses; many a night have I called upon the moon, when
> she has frenzied my brain, to revenge my wrongs. For
> days and nights I have never slept—misery and want,
> and the smart of the lash, with visions of bygone days,
> have been like scorpions, rousing me to revenge; and the
> time has come. I have had partners, too, in the deed—
> men who, like myself, glory in the act (56).

At this point, there is nothing the manufacturer can do but to complain mournfully about his loss: "Is not all a heap of ashes—all burnt and destroyed? Villain, have you not deprived me of bread, and set fire to my dwelling, reckless who might perish in the flames?" (58-59). Knowledge of the traditions guiding the melodramatic repertoire would suggest that, at this point, the play should be over. The villain has been punished and unjust suffering has been avenged. But the pressure of the reality underlying the play's subject matter prevents it from lingering in a terminal stage of wish fulfillment. The well-known story of the Luddites must run its course. When Allen returns home in the following scene (II,ii), there is once again a move toward sentimental affect. This is manifest in the discrepancy between the information available to Allen and the spectators and that possessed by Allen's wife. She and her children are obviously helpless and innocent victims as far as the fire and its provocation are concerned.

> JANE. 'Tis too true, child. Oh, mercy—mercy! The flames have
> caught the farm next to it. I can no longer look. The worst
> of thoughts crowd upon my brain: my husband's absence
> —his wild and distracted look—the factory in flames! (57).

The shock she expresses at the thought of Allen's participation in the conspiracy witnesses to her gentle nature and pure conscience. Once again Jane confirms her status as melodramatic heroine par excellence: in complete accord with the pattern of behavior one expects of her, she selflessly offers to help Allen escape and, shortly thereafter, begs Westwood for mercy after he and a constable arrive to arrest Allen. In the larger system of communication within which the play is staged, the uselessness of her effort is obvious. That other forms of action beyond an appeal to Westwood's humanity are required is also confirmed by the new momentum provided by the play's internal system of communication when Rushton suddenly bursts in, threatens Westwood, and manages to free Allen. During his flight Allen becomes physically exhausted and falls into a state of utter confusion. Something similar happens to Jane when she faints. Even Rushton is not fully in control of his senses when the fate of his family is mentioned during the conversation with his friends. He is racked by painful memories, and from them emerges his need for revenge. This striking accumulation of exceptional pathological states involving feverish delusions draws on the subconscious in such a way that one can assume that partial loss of consciousness is a typical element of melodramatic characterization, and of the manipulation of sentimental affect.

That said, the heroic configuration (Jane, Allen, Rushton) and the way in which the action unfolds (struggle and defeat of the heroes) also initiate variations on the melodramatic mode that, in terms of their function, move away from prescribed and established structures. Of course, the initial impression is that this melodrama, too, has an inflexible basic structure — the principle feature of which is the predictability of the situations — in which only the already known can be actualized and then varied in unexpected ways. Thus, for example, Johann Schmidt's assessment of *The Factory Lad* is based on the assumption that it offers moments of renewal within the established conventions. "Other plays often deviate considerably from the prescribed mode of construction by dropping just one of the component characteristics I will enumerate here. It might be that they offer no real villain *(Masaniello)*, or next to no comic relief *(The Bells)*, or the final rescue with its obligatory 'poetic justice' fails to materialize in time *(Simon Lee)* or is deliberately left aside *(The Factory Lad)*".[11]

As I indicated in my introduction, such an evaluation could well result from an underestimation of the potential for innovation in the melodrama. Therefore, it might be best if my elaboration of a counterthesis began by taking up and examining what Schmidt and others propose as the central element in the developmental logic of the nineteenth-century English drama, that is, the way it responds to "collective desires, the socio-psychological depths of which remain to be plumbed."[12]

It has usually been assumed up to now that plot and characterization in the melodrama possessed a quality demanded by the audience—that of a corrective dream world—and that they also confirm the integrity of the spectator's moral feel and the self-esteem derived from wholeness of being. If this is the case, then it could be said that *The Factory Lad* as a whole has, at best, the qualities of a nightmare and presupposes ongoing changes in the way such plays are received. In order to describe these changes in socio-psychological terms it will first be necessary to return to the typical protagonist in the melodrama of the epoch, that is, to the figure who was without doubt the most important on stage in terms of audience identification. As already indicated, such heroes, through no fault of their own, find themselves in a position in which external threat combines with self-pity. A comparison of numerous plots shows, however, that the impetus for the action that follows does not derive from the hero or heroine. Instead, it comes from the antagonist or else from some external source. This leads Schmidt to remark that "In the anthropological model used to describe the manner in which melodramatic figures are conceived, the villain is the driving force. He is the being that truly acts and has an effect; he is, therefore, the *primum mobile* behind all the unfolding conflict."[13]

On the other hand, protagonists (and Jane, too, in *The Factory Lad*) just wait for a change in their situation and for recognition of their steadfastness in the face of all injustice. From the psychological point of view they are narcissistic creatures who expect to be cared for by others or by fate. They remain inactive themselves, or they react within a predefined network of dependencies. Erich Fromm considers this type of pronounced narcissism to be a fundamental survival mechanism. He explains that, "while from a standpoint of values the maximal reduction of narcissism is desired, from the standpoint of biological survival narcissism is a normal and desirable phenomenon."[14] In that sense, the repertoire of melodramatic texts from the early nineteenth century has a strong affinity with the situation of collective self-defense in which the social class to which the audience belonged actually found itself. In other words, the audience allowed its own narcissistic needs to be confirmed by the illusion of the play. This hypothesis about the collective needs of the public can be firmed up by looking at the abstract and generalized features that define the hero's opponent. Here, too, we come up against a clear-cut spectrum of behavior. Villains always take what they need without working for it. They share none of their possessions with others. They are thieving and exploitative by nature, or feel that isolation alone can assure their security. When not in the process of cheating someone, they see themselves as orderly, parsimonious, and obstinate. It is no accident that

Fromm characterized the middle class of the nineteenth century in precisely this way.[15]

It seems evident that the conflict between the hero and his environment proper to literature and the extratextual relationship between the oppressed lower strata of society and the propertied classes can be correlated in terms of their similar psychological structures. When it comes to the psychology of the individual, the two contrary character structures are separated by differing developmental processes. According to the Freudian schema, the oral-receptive character expects to be fed materially, emotionally, and intellectually and is unable to master the material world. This is the character type I would connect with the lower classes by way of the psychological structure of the melodramatic hero. After this come the oral-sadistic and the anal-sadistic types. The final character structure is the genital, which Freud says belongs to mature and fully developed individuals as opposed to those who are fixed in a prior stage of development. In Jane's case, as in that of all other melodramatic figures with whom the audience can identify, the oral-receptive structure clearly applies, while the characteristics I have ascribed to the antagonist point toward the oral-sadistic and the anal-sadistic. Among others, one conclusion that could be drawn from this is that the narcissistic behavior of the popular audience in the early nineteenth century is to be understood either as psychological regression in the face of the harsh external world or as retarded maturation.

With regard to the social function of the melodrama, the following seems to hold: when, in the course of the action, a hero is subject to robbery or extortion and nonetheless manages a triumphant victory at the end, the melodrama, unlike reality, fulfills a wish. It proffers an illusion that can only grant ersatz satisfaction, since it returns the public to reality at the end of the performance. So, in addition to granting the individual spectator narcissistic satisfaction, it seems that this literary mode has a surrogate function within the given social context.

The variant on the traditional melodramatic structure that emerges in *The Factory Lad* is clearly at odds with a model that offers no socio-critical content and uniform, narcissistic, affective structures. But the potential effect of this variant is relevant in relation to the literary tradition I have been discussing not because it lacks distinctive melodramatic features or because it changes the model in some other way, but precisely because it first sets in motion the spectator's narcissistic disposition and then frees it from its psychological rigidity.

Although Jane and Allen have melodramatic character traits that fit the typical description of the roles assigned to their inherited positions, Rushton and the other workers seem to function differently. They react instead of remaining inactive; they make an attempt to overcome their helplessness, even when, as in Rushton's case, a profoundly wounded narcissistic personality comes to the fore, and despite the fact that the workers' pursuit of a radical goal depends on their following precisely this leader. A new plot departure should arise of necessity out of character impulses that deviate from the norm, but not a hint of such a shift is to be found in the plays that immediately precede *The Factory Lad*. In both *Luke the Labourer* and *The Rent Day*, the heroes are already beaten down by fate and only the restorative power of poetic justice can ensure a happy end. The impetus necessary for this closing action comes either with the return of a lost son or, as in *The Rent Day*, the return of the squire himself—after he realizes where his true duty lies. In the latter play, Martin Heywood is in financial difficulty and unable to rely on the Squire's help. But at the very last moment—as his furniture is being carted off—he discovers a handsome legacy in a chair that had belonged to his grandfather, thus relieving himself and his family of all their cares.

The same sort of villain that was introduced into the English melodrama in *A Tale of Mystery* appears in these "domestic plays." Luke commits his crimes because he has been led astray by the Squire, and because of a need for revenge triggered by this single individual. This is also true of the steward, Crumbs, who enriches himself by vindictively turning on the tenants, making them pay for misdeeds of the old Squire. These scoundrels are injured creatures, and the injustices that they work on the hero or heroine have previously been inflicted on them. Finally, therefore, the source of all this melodramatic evil can be located in the human weaknesses of the person who first initiated the chain of transgressions.

Insofar as this strategy led to the spectators' increased emotional involvement and produced a frightening awareness of the entanglements of fate— thereby satisfying the didactic need to improve human nature—the function of the plays that immediately preceded *The Factory Lad* seems to be primarily reconciliatory. The happy end and the comparatively mild punishment dealt the villain are comfortably balanced, which indicates that the affective structure of *Luke the Labourer* and *The Rent Day* promotes submission and conformity with the system rather than social change.

On the other hand, Westwood's villainous deeds do not arise exclusively from a human causality that makes them forgivable, although greed certainly plays a role. Instead they are the upshot of an incomprehensible, ungodly, and lifeless system. From this point on, the melodramatic heroes in the paradigmatic group of plays dealt with here begin to react, to use force and to manifest a need for revenge that puts them in the position assigned to the antagonist in most previous discussions of role types. This slippage is so completely at odds with the melodramatic expectations heretofore attached to the role of the hero that it alters the inner logic of the new melo-dramatic structure. Where the earlier affective complex developed in such a way that the happy end combined a narcissistic triumph over personal suf-fering caused by someone else (plot) with insights about the weakness of human nature (the antagonist), the orientation of the spectator now shifts from an illusionistic mode of perception to one that is more realistic and analogous to the final stage of socio-psychological development, which, because of its genital orientation, possesses a high degree of equilibrium in regard to the external world.

In this process, variations in the ways in which characters are figured play an essential role. When the hero appropriates the character traits of his opponent and thereby overcomes an oral-receptive disposition he also takes on the fate normally assigned to the villain. This places him in the wrong and in conflict with the existing social system without costing him his status as hero and object of audience identification. Such a constellation is unthink-able within the rules governing the illusionistic melodrama, so its realization depends on the framework provided by concrete social tensions. At the same time, a change in the public is implied. Through an expanded conception of the hero's role, the audience, too, is pulled out of its oral-receptive mode of perception and led toward a stance that is anticipatory and projective. Thus, in this part of the early nineteenth century, the developmental ten-dency is for the English melodrama to move away from the narcissistic structures of illusionistic performance towards those reality-oriented psy-chological modes of understanding and dealing with experience that are set in motion by the new melodramatic variants in plot and character.

In a like manner, the way in which the text segments are structured assists in the process of liberating the spectator from dependence on the established melodramatic decoding processes. While the extratextual material has already indicated that the resolution of these conflicts will be painful, there is also a ten-sion between the (melodramatic) expectation of a happy end and the life-threatening apprehension that emerges in the action itself when the moment of satisfaction about burning the factory blends with the start of the chase. The contrast between Jane's lamentations and the actions taken by Westwood seems almost repetitive. Her helplessness is already apparent when Allen is first arrested at their house. It emerges once more in the moonlight of an open field when she again pleads in vain with Westwood, then falls in a faint and is left behind as the soldiers march off. The pointlessness of the sentimental ele-ments she introduces is also demonstrated by the juridical proceedings in the play. Thus, the audience, because it continuously experiences situations of unresolved wish fulfillment, is necessarily pushed toward acceptance of feelings it may be somewhat reluctant about. But the break with the old melodramatic norms is not abrupt and absolute. The play's rather remarkable conclusion can be understood as an indication of its position as mediator between two aesthetic forms and their normative powers. Westwood's death — his punishment as the villain — and Rushton's unmasking of the judge — appropriately named Bias — reveal the heroes to be the moral victors and confirm the old narcissistic disposition. At the same time, however, the victors are the vanquished; they are badly dealt with and obliged to accept their fate without being able to once again flee from reality into narcissistic desire.

This has also become impossible for the spectator. *The Factory Lad* opens with the received view that the Reform Laws are to be seen as a political trap and a betrayal of the Radical movement and then moves on to portray all the reform efforts of both middle-class and labor Radicals as mistakes. It does so by drawing on events from the preceding twenty years (thus, during the period of reform agitation, too) to show that middle-class interests had continually run counter to the interests of the lower classes. What is remarkable is that this reorientation of the mode of reception is achieved precisely through variations in the old melodramatic repertoire.

Of course, it must be noted that *The Factory Lad* closed after only six performances. This may have happened for legal reasons, or possibly because the people of London had little direct experience of the factory system. It could also be argued that the mass public of the epoch preferred more "entertaining" melodramas. But this "domestic drama" must have spoken directly to the souls of the politically active laborers, skilled workers, apprentices, and small shopkeepers in the vicinity of the Rotunda. In conjunction with the political content of other plays, it contributed to the emergence of public consciousness about reform, and it confirms Clive Barker's thesis about a close connection between the theatre and reform: "I have presented the case for a wider series of studies and a continuing examination of our theatre up to the 1843 Theatres Regulation Act. The Act represents simply a moment in time when the forces inhibiting reform became weaker than the pressures for reform."[16]

Notes

* Translated by Michael Hays.
1. Both are to be found in *British Plays of the Nineteenth Century: An Anthology to Illustrate the Evolution of the Drama,* ed. J. O. Bailey (New York: Odyssey, 1966).

2. *Victorian Melodramas*, ed. James L. Smith (London: Dent, 1976), 39-63, and *English Plays of the Nineteenth Century*, ed. Michael R. Booth, vol. 1 (Oxford: Clarendon, 1969), 201-233.

3. See, for example, Harry M. Ritchie, "The Influence of Melodrama on the Early Plays of Sean O'Casey," *Modern Drama* 5 (1962-63): 164-73, and Martin Meisel, *Shaw and the Nineteenth-Century Theatre* (Princeton: Princeton University Press, 1963).

4. Michael R. Booth, "A Defense of Nineteenth-Century English Drama," *Education Theatre Journal* 26 (1974): 11 ff.

5. See the foreword to *The Factory Lad* in *English Plays of the Nineteenth Century*, 203-206.

6. *The Factory Lad*, in *Victorian Melodramas*, 40. All further page references will appear in the text.

7. Robin Estill, "The Factory Lad: Melodrama as Propaganda," *Theatre Quarterly* 1 (1971): 23.

8. E. P. Thompson, *The Making of the English Working Class* (New York: Random House, 1963), 807-17.

9. Thompson identifies William Cobbett as the leader of the Radical faction that urged "acceptance of half a loaf." *Making of the Working Class*, 817.

10. See Manfred Buhr and George Klaus, *Wörterbuch der Philosophie*, vol. 2 (Reinbek: Rowholt, 1975), 779.

11. See Johann N. Schmidt, *Aesthetik des Melodramas: Studien zu einem Genre des populären Theatres im England des 19. Jahrhunderts* (Heidelberg: C. Winter, 1986), 53.

12. Schmidt, *Aesthetik*, 40.

13. Schmidt, *Aesthetik*, 170.

14. Erich Fromm, *Greatness and Limitations of Freud's Thought* (New York: Harper and Row, 1980), 45.

15. Fromm, *Freud's Thought*, 56, 62.

16. Clive Barker, "The Chartists, Theatre, Reform and Research," *Theatre Quarterly* 1, no. 4 (1971): 10

Part IV

Gender, Class, Culture

FIGURE 4. From *The Corsican Brothers.*
FROM THE COLLECTION OF THE AUTHOR.

11

PARLOUR AND PLATFORM MELODRAMA

DAVID MAYER

*A*MATEUR PERFORMANCES, I AM AFRAID, have done much to destroy the old mystery and romance of the Stage. I believe the lack of enthusiasm in our audiences is due to this. There is a deficiency of lively susceptibility and a want of interest in the grand works which constitute our national drama. Ah! this is the crying shame of the age.

So, in a public lecture to a London audience in 1871, explains the actor Henry Neville. Neville continues his lecture with an anecdote that recalls Hamlet's "mousetrap":

I once heard a lady say she had read "Enoch Arden" often without shedding a tear, but she was so overcome by a clever *recital,* that she was obliged to leave the room after those harrowing lines, where Enoch, having returned to his native village, found his wife married to another, and, heart broken, looking upon the happy home, "beheld. . . ."

To illustrate his point, Henry Neville goes on to recite, to perform for his audience, thirty-nine lines from Tennyson's narrative poem—the very passages that had so affected his female informant.[1]

Neville's lecture-performance draws upon a range of intertwined cultural developments of the later nineteenth century. These developments, understood and altogether unnecessary to state to his educated—or partly educated—middle-class audience, underlie my exploration of parlour and platform melodrama. Although these developments are inextricably interconnected and interrelated to the point of overlapping, of being described as concurrent, simultaneous, or complementary, I have, for the purpose of this essay, chosen to treat them as discrete phenomena, each subject to separate analysis and explication:

1. *The still uncertain status of the professional theatre.* The theatre, deserted by the new middle classes in the 1840s, is regaining its audiences in a still limited number of theatres with a stage repertoire that acknowledges this audience's values, requirements, and tastes. Although there is, necessarily, a link, or even a continuous thread, between the repertoire of the late-Georgian theatre and the resurgent theatre of the 1860s, there is also such a difference in emphasis, tone, and subject matter of melodrama as to provide observable differences.

2. *The growing emphasis on private domestic life and the middle-class family.* To this class, the home is not merely sacral and redemptive, but is also the increased focus of social entertainment. The family home and entertainment venues that offer the family and its respectable neighbors comfort, "improving" recreations, and well-mannered society may be perceived as preferable to more questionable public venues.

Because the two developments referred to above have been the subjects of earlier and more thorough studies, I shall discuss each only briefly.

3. *The growth of amateur performance both at the domestic hearth and in new venues: lecture halls, private and municipal "concert" halls, and church halls.* Such locales distinctly differ from commercial theatres, the usual place for Victorian audiences of all classes to encounter and enjoy melodrama. At these amateur recitals, penny readings, the performers are of the same social class, often from the same family or social circle, and share the same tastes and susceptibilities to dramatic and literary performance as those who are entertained. For rural folk and for the artisan and working classes there are such additional venues as the hired halls and fairground tents of itinerant showmen.

4. *The presence of the professional reciter.* Some, perhaps many, of the reciters are professional actors—Henry Irving is prominent among and, to some extent typical of, these—who develop a repertoire of recitation pieces, which they offer at various public benefits. Other performers make recitations the center of their careers, and some—missionaries, temperance workers, and, from the late 1870s, itinerant showmen—integrate their recitations with impressively ample displays of apposite "magic lantern" slides. The use of projected images is an indication that recitations, much as the professional theatre and the playhouse, were becoming industrialized, susceptible to scientific and technological innovation, new working practices, and change. Eventually, these short melodramatic texts illustrated on lantern slides were again before

the camera in the early years of the current century, chosen to furnish material for some of the earliest dramatic motion pictures. Unfortunately, because these pieces and their interpreters whom I describe stand at some distance from the public playhouse, their history is shadowy, their performances largely unrecorded. Early motion picture exhibitors and their brief ballad-inspired dramatic films are only marginally better documented.[2]

5. *The availability of a large repertoire of recitation materials readily accessible to the public in weekly or monthly journals, published anthologies, and printed sheet music.* A publishing industry, drawn from the extant music-publishing trade and from conventional publishing houses, both now freed from restrictive taxes and technically enhanced by modern "steam printing," develops to service this home and platform market. Manuals for the home and platform reciter also offer detailed instruction on elocution, deportment, and acting, and some of these manuals, addressed chiefly to the amateur reciter, but with the amateur actor also in mind, constitute an important source for the study of Victorian stage technique and early film acting.

6. *The existence and use of a recitation repertoire that closely resembles material performed upon the public stage.* Many of these performance materials legitimately may be described as abridged melodrama or abbreviated comedy. Although melodrama of far briefer duration than any stageplay, it is nonetheless melodrama that exhibits many, if not most, of the qualities and conventions that Victorian audiences and we have learned to expect from theatrical performance, and its existence and survival serve to demonstrate the extent to which a melodramatic perception of experience characterizes the thought and emotional rhetoric of the Victorian age. Such material, narrated or, more often, performed in role, offers the same experiences to spectators and demands from amateur performers the same performance skills—if scaled down—as stage plays.

Because parlour and platform narratives were often composed by dramatic authors who regularly supplied melodramas to the professional stage, such correspondences are not remarkable. Despite obvious differences between theatrical pieces and ballad narratives, it is possible to recognize in the work of some authors a continuity of thought, techniques of characterization and expression, emotional shadings, and moral and social outlook.

Such continuities are especially significant to the propagation and dissemination of melodramatic subgenres. By the second half of the nineteenth century, the theatre is largely supplied by authors whose living depends chiefly upon their writing. Some authors are exclusively dramatists, but some notable dramatists and melodramatists—Arthur Shirley, Cecil Raleigh, Robert Buchanan, and Henry Saville Clarke come readily to mind—ply other literary crafts and rework playhouse successes for the printed page. Others—nondramatists, but authors with a working knowledge of theatre who contribute to this body of recitation literature—are theatre critics (Clement Scott) and novelists (Marie Corelli).

Additionally, as middle-class and artisan-class entertainment becomes more private and centered on the parlour hearth, family theatricals become the locus of carnivalesque indulgence, festive inversion, and temporary liberty. As Neville demonstrates, the processes of becoming and remaining middle class involve education in class values and mores. It is not always enough to enjoy theatregoing: theatre must also be understood to be a serious art. However, in private the seriousness of professional theatricals and the activity of theatregoing as a respectable high-minded process is inverted even as it is celebrated. Because these parlour pieces are performed by middle-class persons who are also spectators at commercial theatres where they have learned to take stage performance seriously, even solemnly, a portion of the reciters' repertoire is made up of burlesques that ridicule popular stage pieces and fashionable operas.

It is also characteristic of these burlesques that their authors and, presumably, their home performers and audiences are somewhat uncomfortable with the conventions of melodrama and that if melodrama, whether novel, drama, or recitation-ballad, offers a view of contemporary experience, then that view is flawed. However, burlesques of melodrama tend to be critiques of specific plays or of melodramatic subgenres, such as the nautical melodramas of earlier decades, and it is consequently difficult to pursue the cause and extent of dissatisfaction. What such burlesques demonstrate is the persistence of an ironic querying of melodramatic interpretations of the Victorians' world, but it is an irony that rarely translates into resistance or rebellion.

Despite its ambitious title, Neville's sponsor and host, The Society for the Encouragement of Fine Arts, was not a learned society of the first-rate, but one of the many ephemeral ad hoc lycea formed by entrepreneurs and philanthropists—as well as by educated people genuinely concerned—to raise public taste and to assist in distinguishing "high" or "fine" art from the less-regarded genre painting and more readily obtainable manufactured decorative arts. The setting for this lecture, a commercial art gallery in Conduit Street bearing in its trading name the term "Fine Arts," testifies to the linking of commerce, class aspirations—which include acquiring the knowledge and good taste to recognize, to celebrate, and, ultimately, to possess (and be known to possess) "fine" art—the constant wish for self-betterment, and belief in "rational recreation." The presence of Henry Neville, a theatrical professional recognized as a respectable and rising actor since creating the role of Robert Brierly in the 1863 Olympic Theatre Production of *The Ticket-of-Leave Man,* is likewise significant. Neville, linking his modern theatrical trade to a historic past from which he recalls the names of Shakespeare, Aeschylus, Sophocles, and Euripides, argues for a commercial professional theatre and respectability. His solemn lecture and brief tear-evoking performance in this setting remind the gallery audience that theatrical art, no less than other arts, has educative and ennobling functions. It, too, can be "fine" art.

Critically for this essay, Neville has not mentioned melodrama. Although most of his roles between 1860 and 1871 had been in what we today would identify as melodramas or comedies, Neville appeared before his art gallery audience as an actor dedicated to performing and achieving success in pieces other than conventional popular fare. Therefore, if Henry Neville is making some kind of distinction between The *Ticket-of-Leave Man, Jean Valjean,* and *Henry Dunbar* and pieces *that are indisputable melodramas,* we need to enquire into his thinking and into that of his auditors who tacitly accept this distinction.

What we shall find is that by 1855 *melodrama* is on its way to becoming an obsolescent, even taboo, term amongst the middle-class and in theatres that cater to predominately middle class audiences. Although serious dramas continue to employ rhetorical structures, emotional palettes, theatrical and musical effects, situations, and solutions that we recognize as belonging to the well-established conventions of earlier melodrama, the pieces themselves, more often than not, are called *dramas.* Moreover, as many of the melodramas — now *dramas* — after 1855 are addressing topics of immediate concern, and as Neville prominently figured in a melodrama/drama of 1863 that seriously questioned the Home Office's policing practices and the necessity of a bill then before Parliament,[3] there are grounds for him to have argued that melodrama might have become, if not a "fine" art, then a socially useful art in keeping with the scientific spirit of the age, directly investigating, questioning, commenting. Thus, by appearing, performing, and citing illustrious precedents, Neville is negotiating a reappraisal of contemporary drama, which includes melodrama by practice, if not by name, and he is fortifying his argument with an extract from a piece of parlour-and-platform melodrama that he hopes his auditors are prepared to accept as fine art.

My intent is to address separately these closely intertwined concerns and to so indicate the shape and dimensions of this network in which scaled-down drama, melodrama in particular, so prominently figures. Inevitably, I must question ideas about and definitions of melodrama, especially those ideas and definitions that tend to view melodrama — a slippery, elusive, protean, and turbulent subject—as a stable and predictable genre. My response is not of a single or simple paradigm—that of reciter-auditor—but of a multitude of texts (in the full understanding of this term), performer-reciters, audiences, venues, and likely events.

1. *The still uncertain status of the professional theatre.* Historians of the Victorian stage are in agreement in describing a crisis in theatre attendance that begins in the late 1830s and continues for approximately two decades. Theatre audiences in London and, to a lesser degree, in provincial cities are ceasing to attend with their former frequency. A favored explanation for this alteration is the presence of actively soliciting prostitutes in public playhouses, which so offends respectable playgoers that they withdraw patronage. While it is arguable that prostitution increased in direct proportion to the growth of English cities and to concurrent dislocations in employment, altered demographic patterns, and ruptures in family life occasioned by industrialization, there may be two further explanations. One, the result of rapid urbanization, which outraces the supply of clean water and the provision of sanitary waste disposal in city centers, is the recurrence or fear of recurrence, from 1832, of pandemic cholera, typhus, and typhoid. A second explanation is the increase in the character and force of British evangelicalism in shaping the middle classes. In fact, it may be reasonable to assert that prostitutes had always frequented, or attempted to frequent, theatres, but it was not until the late 1830s, when the middle classes and, in particular, female spectators became an identifiable and influential social grouping, that the presence and conduct of prostitutes became cause for complaint and action. Historians such as F. M. L. Thompson underscore religious evangelicalism as a determining social factor in shaping the behavior of the English middle class.[4] These historians cite a general withdrawal from areas of public life that formerly offered pleasure with the attendant description of playgoing and other recreations as "frivolous," or "extravagant," or "sinful." It was a mindset that, in some quarters, was to last well into the next century. But it was not general or all-pervasive. The same historians who describe the middle-class flight from public theatres in the 1830s and 1840s note the importance of the Charles Kean management of the Princess's Theatre from 1850 and Kean's success in bringing the fugitives back into his well-furnished, comfortable auditorium to view a new repertoire of melodrama and comedy and well-appointed Shakespearean productions.[5] Other London theatres—the refurbished Olympic where Neville made his name is one of these—and provincial playhouses offering greater comforts begin to cater to class-specific audiences. The number of new theatres rises incre-

mentally in the 1860s and 1870s, but audiences have meanwhile discovered pleasures to be had elsewhere.

These developments both accompany and cause significant changes in the melodramatic repertoire. Michael Booth has pointed to the decline in nautical, gothic, and oriental-ized melodrama and the corresponding increase in domestic and urban melodramas that more closely reflect current preoccupations. He likewise indicates the extent to which the work of English novelists—-notably Mary Braddon, Charles Dickens, Ellen Wood, and Charles Reade—is adapted for the stage.[6] Such changes further confirm the ubiquity, whether in novel, play, or narrative ballad, of melodramatic genres and the requirement that the stage, employing melodrama as the means, speak to contemporary concerns and issues.

However, if melodrama gains in becoming more apposite to contemporary concerns, there is also something of a loss. Early conservative observers of melodrama are critical of the form's capacity to invert the social order and to reject intellectual argument and exposition for emotionally weighted issues, personages, and situations. Melodrama's first heroes are the dumb, tongue-tied, inarticulate, and partly educated. Those who can speak or fend for themselves are objects of suspicion or derision. Our readings of melodrama from the early 1800s through the 1830s acknowledge these tropes, but by the 1860s it has become harder to find stage melodrama that so regularly and thoroughly questions class, privilege, possessions, learning, middle-class occupations and trades, and money. These changes in the vectors of melodrama are the consequence of the new audiences and the new dramatists who speak in their name.

2. *The growing emphasis on private domestic life and the middle-class family.* In the enlargement of industrial and commercial cities, the evangelical movement recognized turmoil, disruption, and, everywhere, temptation to vice which was at once ungodly and a source of contagious disease. Clergy, their congregations, and writers of many descriptions, in response, extolled the home as a refuge, a sacred space—and perhaps a sanitary space—untouched and unspoiled by disorders and contagions so evident in public. However, the same urban expansion that troubled evangelicals and sanitary engineers meant that there was now a far greater stock of housing of all prices. Married couples no longer were obliged to lodge with parents or in-laws until the elders' deaths brought title to the dwelling, but could move to comfortable homes of their own furnished with creature comforts and decorative objects to their personal taste. Private space for most members of the family—and even servants—became an expected norm.[7] Domestic energy and expenditure as well as moral pressure focused upon the home.

As enfranchisement was extended first to the freeholder and in subsequent legislation to the leaseholder, the home became a political as well as domestic unit. A consequence of these several changes was that families, imbued with the aspirations of the new property-owning or property-leasing middle class, sought appropriately uplifting entertainment and the society of those who held corresponding values and tastes. One taste, widely shared across the middle class, was music.

Without question, the moral and social focal point of numerous families' drawing room diversions became the piano. The piano represented an investment in money and time and was therefore an indication both of wealth—necessary to purchase a piano and sheet music and to engage a piano teacher—and of sufficient leisure to pursue study. The French firm of Pleyel had introduced the upright piano in 1827, and British manufacturers were swift to copy and modify it. By the 1880s the cost of a "cottage piano" had fallen to twenty guineas.[8] Sheet music normally cost between one and four shillings, the price determined by the length and newness of the piece. On the piano or, in some families, the harmonium, musically accomplished members might play hymns for family prayers. Alternatively, the instruments might provide a variety of secular entertainments: instrumental music, parlour songs, or the sort of incidental music required for all melodrama, whether staged or merely recited. The significance and function of music in these performance will be discussed below.

3. *The growth of amateur performance both at the domestic hearth and in new venues: lecture halls, private and municipal "concert" halls, and church halls.* Ronald Pearsall has effectively described the development and range of parlour music, including the performance of the sung ballad.[9] J. P. Thompson, likewise, has indicated the function music served within middle-class society,[10] and Florence Smith and Brooks McNamara have more recently demonstrated that American home performances integrated songs and recitations and that the latter were conventionally dependent on musical accompaniment.[11] However, because recitations are only in part musical, only Smith and McNamara have discussed the nature of this material or the circumstances of these performances.[12] What British authors overlook is that much poetry was written to be read aloud and that by 1845 Robert Browning, not uniquely, had published and enjoyed critical praise for his dramatic monologues.

Sadly, the moment is unrecorded when the first—or even the thousandth—family member added recitation of poetry or the staging of charades—tableaux or brief dramatic scenes to set a puzzle where the viewers were required to deduce a word or phrase[13]—to an otherwise domestic musical evening, but there is little doubt that the practice had arisen by the mid-1840s and that poems and narrative ballads were being declaimed in the family drawing room or parlour. As families entertained their social circles with musical evenings, it became customary, even expected, for guests to bring with them music or recitation pieces. By the same date, evening and afternoon penny readings and matinees—in the original sense of the word, morning events—were being offered by amateur readers at church—or charity-related social events in church halls or other respectable venues hired or borrowed for the occasion. The amateur status of the event assured audiences that money taken at the door went to a designated worthy cause and, further, guaranteed that the reciters were of a respectable class. Nevertheless, both for auditors and reciters there were frissons of excitement when recitations required their performers to assume dramatic roles and sometimes to perform multiple parts within the narrative—an innocent witness and a murderer and a would-be adulterer who covets his brother's wife thereby breaking both the Seventh and Tenth Commandments; or a Corsican Brother, an imprisoned madman, a betrayed and troubled railway signalman, a frightened child—and then, with each drama's end, to become again a respectable family member and model citizen.

There was a further source for home and amateur readings: professional and amateur theatrical performance. Some, perhaps many, of the middle class did attend stageplays where they observed and learned to mimic favored performers. By the 1840s some middle-class males were attending "spouting academies"—evening acting classes—where, hoping to lose accents and manners that may have indicated their plebeian origins, they were instructed in elocution and deportment. Moreover, spouting academies indulged a taste for stage performance not otherwise sanctioned, and, in the company of professional actresses hired for the occasion, these tyros appeared in semirespectable theatricals to which their families and friends might be invited. That these amateur actors replayed their roles at evening "at homes" is known through the jokes and cartoons at their expense. Weedon Grosmith in his *Diary of a Nobody* describes Mr Burwin-Fosselton, who ordinarily acts with "the Holloway Comedians," but who, on one memorably miserable evening, disrupts a lower-middle-class parlour with his incessant and imprecise imitations of Henry Irving in *The Bells*.[14]

4. *The presence of the professional reciter.* With professional performances we are on more secure ground. Bills advertising actors' benefits, charitable events supported by the theatrical profession, and routine commercial endeavors provide a list of dates, venues, performers, and material on offer. Whereas many actors invited to appear at benefits volunteered scenes

favored by their patrons, other actors, principal among them Henry Irving, chose dramatic recitations that, in scaled-down melodrama, recapitulated themes and situations that in many instances formed the core of their theatrical careers.

Additionally, we have the mid-century examples of professional entertainers associated with the Howard Paul Company provincial tours of musical and recitation evenings and similar kinds of London performances at the Regent Street Polytechnic and the German-Reeds' Royal Gallery of Illustration. Ronald Pearsall, although inexact about the content of these performances, characterizes the musical element of these evenings as chiefly sentimental and comic,[15] and it is in such surroundings offered by the Howard Paul and Priscilla Horton managements, dedicated to the moral and social comfort of middle-class patrons, that burlesque material tested and safely mocked ascription to the new literary and theatrical values that so identified this class. Readers familiar with the theatrical burlesques and parodies of Mark Lemon, Henry J. Byron, and Frank Burnand will recognize how frequently these dramatists rely on puns for their humor. One reason lies in the importance the middle class placed upon the prescribed — in their view the proper—use, spelling, and pronunciation of English. But English, as the pun reminds, does not invariably behave according to prescription, rules, and logic: words with quite different meanings sound alike or almost alike. For the expected or "proper" word, substitute an altogether different word that is spelled, or which sounds, nearly alike the appropriate word, and one's faith and teaching in the propriety of proper English is pleasurably shaken. Thus a society that has been educated in the importance and infallibility of rules will experience delighted shock at the rules' inconsistencies. In a similar fashion, audiences educated to the new melodrama at the Princess's Theatre were able to enjoy a musical burlesque of Boucicault's *The Corsican Brothers*, "The Corsican Brothers; or, La Vendetta —An Entirely New Version of a Popular Ghost Story, Containing valuable Hints on the Subject of Spiritual Manifestations, Mental Psychology, Clairvoyance & Spirit Rappings as Seen Through a Comic Medium." This duet, sung by J. W. Sharp and T. Henry, was purported to come from the pen of the pseudonymous Scrutore Trappe, Esq.,[16] a reference to Charles Kean's stage machinery and the "ghost glide" effect. Significantly, not only does the duet's libretto remove all solemnity from the plot, but the accompanying vocal and piano music repeats and draws attention to the tremolo "ghost melody" from Kean's first and final acts. Even the lithographed sheet music cover, drawing on other illustrations of the Princess's melodrama, reduces *The Corsican Brothers* to an amusing strip cartoon. Such burlesque treatments did not altogether destroy one's enjoyment of melodrama but added an element of ironic distancing to the performance, in effect giving an audience permission required at any stage performance—melodrama especially—to accept the events staged before their eyes as actually and plausibly happening, but also to accept that, as spectators, they were willing participants in a contrived reality—"to believe and not believe."

Henry Irving, in 1849 still a day-school pupil seeking material for a speech-day event, worked up a performance of Henry Glassford Bell's "The Uncle." His biographer and grandson reports that Irving was dissuaded from performing this macabre piece and that "The Uncle" was replaced by another recitation.[17] However, Bell's dramatic depictions of a guilty man who, coveting his brother's wife, jealously murders and conceals the corpse of that brother, and of the innocent child who hears his confession, remained in Irving's benefit repertoire along with Thomas Hood's "The Dream of Eugene Aram." By the mid-1880s Irving had commissioned the composer Sir Julius Benedict, who had also provided the incidental music for the Lyceum production of *Romeo and Juliet*, to provide a piano score for "The Uncle".[18] Both pieces, "The Dream of Eugene Aram" and "The Uncle," together with Arthur Conan Doyle's 1895 monologue *A Tale of Waterloo*, were Irving's principal offerings at benefits.

An additional advantage to the actor lay in the choice of solo material. The actor was not obliged to find a performer who would support—but not overshadow—him and who would rehearse the piece with him. Such conveniences and economies of solo performance and the near certainty that the performer might offer someone else's newly minted material but not pay copyright royalties further encouraged many actors to resort to one-person recitations. An undated bill surviving for a lecture hall in Margate indicates how a Frederick Bolton, an aging and needy actor, has assembled a program of narrative ballads by the melodramatist, popular balladeer, columnist-journalist, and social reformer George R. Sims.

Sims (1847-1922) is a key figure in that his professional career indicates the extent to which the various elements of the parlour-and-platform-melodrama molecule interlock and bond. Sims, an aspirant novelist and poet, left a job in his family textile business to become, in 1877, a journalist–theatre critic for the *Referee*. Within two years he had established himself as a writer of narrative ballads, many of which were to appear in that journal, a novelist, and a dramatist. His investigative work for the *Referee* in the early 1880s, in particular a series titled "Horrible London," brought him to the attention of social reformers and crusaders, and Sims was invited to testify to committees of enquiry and to lead Parliamentary expeditions into the East End slums. He drew upon these forays when writing the socially orientated narrative ballads that continued to appear in the *Referee* and in other popular journals. Also by the early 1880s, Sims was established as one of the West End's more promising new dramatists, recognized by British and foreign critics alike. Most of Sims's theatrical output between 1881 and 1905 are melodramas, some written in collaboration with Henry Pettitt, but many written wholly by Sims himself for the Princess's and Adelphi theatres management. A popular and successful novelist who created a female detective, Dorcas Dene, Sims also turned his own plays back into novels, on one occasion tipping the plots and characters of two early melodramas, *The Lights o' London* (1881) and *The Romany Rye* (1882), into a single, if overintricate, work of fiction.[19] In the 1890s Sims switched his attention to musical comedy and collaborated with composers Henri Clay and Charles Corri in devising comic operas and burlesques. Throughout this period and until his death, Sims remained active in controlling the stage rights to his still popular melodramas and in republishing his ballads and negotiating to adapt dramas and poems into motion pictures.

Each of Sims's ballads is an actor's opportunity for melodramatic performance because the reciter usually assumes multiple roles: the narrator — almost invariably a character of a different social class and occupation from the reader/listener — and at least one character from the narrative itself. As the ballad, in its several voices, enacts within a ten-minute span a tale of contentment blighted by poverty, squalor, vice, deceit, and despair — sometimes lifted by self-sacrifice, bravery, altruism, and redemption — reaching a moral, if not conventionally "happy" conclusion, the performer and audience experience a rich range of situations, emotions, expectations, and satisfactions.

What also distinguishes Sims's ballads — and what separates narrative ballads from stage melodrama — is the ironic voice of the narrator. Heroism or virtue, as Sims depict them, are both invaluable behavior — distinguishing the exceptional individual and defining human life, as opposed to mere animal survival — and qualities that would be wholly unnecessary in less class- and money-ridden or more compassionate societies. In "The Road to Heaven" and "In the Work House, Christmas Day," two of Sims's ballads chosen for Frederick Bolton's performance, one of "two little homeless arabs, waifs of the London street" escapes drowning in the Thames to die in a paupers' hospital ward believing that this squalid sanctuary is heaven, and a pauper sneers at the virtuous sanctimony of the charity commissioners who, after his wife has died of starvation in this wealthy capital city, now have the effrontery to offer him Christmas dinner. Stage melodrama, even Sims's, because its conventions and formulae oblige — and even more because its audiences require—just or upbeat or even "happy" endings, and also because the dramatist must exercise care that the very genre of melodrama not be too closely questioned, has no place for such ironies. There is no way, unless actors deliberately play "against the text" and with inflection instruct the audience, for the seriousness of melodrama to be subverted or for the moral actions of its characters to be undermined. The ballad's reciter-narrator, standing apart from the characters she or he also enacts, places weary and overstretched moral maxims against bleak practicalities and juxtaposes easy sentiment against tearless reality. What evolves from these contrasts is a knowing, hardboiled ironic ethic that offers some insight into the social penalties of industrial and imperial progress and little comfort.

The controversy, moral outrage, and adulation surrounding another of Sims's recitation ballads, "Ostler Joe," confirms the impact of such performances. Introduced to American audiences by Mrs. James Brown-Potter in 1885 and to British audiences in the following year by Madge Robertson Kendal, the poem's ambiguous moral stance first provoked the charge that Algernon Swinburne was its author. Sims's narrative of a stableboy's stoic and faithful endurance of his wife's adulterous elopement with the local squire, the ensuing death of Joe's abandoned son, the wife's career as a society courtesan, and her eventual succumbing to (implied) venereal infection also brought newspaper editorials, sermons that observed Joe's steadfast goodness and faith in the teeth of such wickedness, and bumper audiences. Professional reciters on both sides of the Atlantic insisted that Sims had contrived "Ostler Joe" for their exclusive use, and a bemused and exasperated Sims, who had earned no royalties from the numerous American recitations, denied an intentional connection with any performer.[20]

The bill for the Margate performance—with Sims's name misspelled—is worth quoting in its entirety:

LECTURE HALL
BOTTOM OF DANE HILL, KING STREET, MARGATE
First appearance before a Margate Audience for the space of 32 Years

Mr Frederick Bolton,
(Formerly Prompter and General Actor with the late Mr
Richard Thorne, of the Theatre Royal, Margate,) [proposes] to
give an original and unique

RECITAL ENTERTAINMENT,
At the above Hall on the evening of
MONDAY, DECEMBER 16TH, AT 8 O'CLOCK,
ENTITLED
A Night with Mr. Geo. Simms

The friend of the Homeless outcast, and Arab Waif
of the London Streets

THE Program WILL EMBRACE
The LIFEBOAT, or the Lost Son. BILLY'S ROSE:
The ROAD TO HEAVEN. CHRISTMAS DAY IN THE
WORKHOUSE.
NELLY'S PRAYER, or the Power of Faith.
The BUNCH OF PRIMROSES, or Self-denial.
DUTY, or the Pointsman and his Child.
The MAGIC WAND, or the Pantomime Fairy.
The STREET TUMBLERS, or Poor and Content.
The TICKET OF LEAVE, or Self-Sacrifice.
The TWO WOMEN, or Vice in Velvet and Rags.

And writing of Mr SIMMS, let us here record our admiration of
that noble nature of the man, who, amid the whirl, excitement, and
adulation attendant on a brilliant career, can bestow thoughts, so
tenderly expressed, upon the houseless poor of the London Streets.

In the course of the evening there will be a brief synopsis of the
remarkable career of a wandering actor for the space of 32 years.
These incidents, which have been appropriately named
THE MARGATE MYSTERY,
will be recorded, not that he may be held up as the hero of a wild
romance, but rather cited as a living instance of the unceasing lov-
ing kindness and mercy of that Beneficent Being who has answered
his prayer, expressed in the psalm: —
"Cast me not away in my old age, forsake me not
when my strength faileth me."

TICKETS 1S AND 6D. EACH,
To be procured of MR BOLTON, Buchan Villa, Dane Road, Margate

OPEN AT 7.30. COMMENCE AT 8 0'CLOCK[21]

Technological developments assured that Sims's material and similar ballads — because Sims was by no means unique in producing such narrative
dramas — were further exploited by professional entertainers. From as early
as 1850 and the aggressive marketing of the oil-fueled portable "magic
lantern," missionaries, temperance lecturers, and showmen working church
halls, public lecture rooms, and fairs had interspersed "dissolving view"
gospel, homiletic, and travel narratives with recitation-performances of
popular ballads, the subject matter hand-painted or — by the 1870s — pho-
tographically imprinted on glass slides. By the latter date, James Bamford,
operating from his photographic studio in Holmfirth, Yorkshire, had found
that he could stage the subjects of these ballads before his studio camera.

Each ballad chosen became a sequential narrative in approximately fifteen photographic tableaux, and the completed slide set was then sold for home or commercial use.[22] At least three of the Sims ballads from Frederick Bolton's Margate program, "The Lifeboat," "Billy's Rose," and "Duty," and two additional Sims ballads, "Ostler Joe" and "The Level Crossing," became Bamford slide sets. Now, in pre-cinema conditions, the reciter and his musical accompaniment stood to one side of the projector and declaimed.

It is therefore no accident that ballad melodramas provided the subject matter for early silent motion pictures. Because the first dramatic films on serious subjects rarely exceeded a running time of ten minutes, their compressed plots adapted more easily to film than those of full-length stage melodramas. Such brief films readily lent themselves to projection in music halls and variety theatres, where the ballad-based films were accompanied by incidental orchestral or piano music and live declamation.[23] Bamford himself produced such films between 1908 and 1914, and, in America, Biograph produced an Ostler Joe[24]—with D. W. Griffith cast as the villainous squire who seduces the village maiden Annie from her marital home and, having introduced her to a world of luxury, vice, and disease, abandons her—all within a time span which comfortably fits the concurrent recitation of Sims's narrative poem.

5. *The availability of a large repertoire of recitation materials readily accessible to the public in weekly or monthly journals, published anthologies, and printed sheet music.* Although narrative ballads had been available to the reading public before the 1840s, an immediate stimulus to publication was the repeal, in 1841, of stamp duty on printed journals and the consequent fall in the price of magazines and newspapers. From that date the number of weekly and monthly periodical publications addressing a wide and varied readership burgeoned. Many of these periodicals addressed a household, rather than a literary, readership, and it was chiefly to these morally, domestically, and entertainment-orientated journals that balladeers submitted their dramatic narrative poems. In turn, enterprising publishers, meeting the authors' small fees, gathered these poems and, with the inclusion of appropriate short prose works, returned these collections to the public as elaborate anthologies introduced by a sequence of chapters which instructed the anthologies' users in techniques of public recitation.

The dominating, but by no means the only, recitation anthology is Alfred Miles's *The New Standard Elocutionist*,[25] its enduring popularity confirmed by the frequency of volumes that continue to be found with presentational bookplates or inscriptions attesting that the *Elocutionist* had been awarded for school, church, or Sunday school attendance, as a school literary prize, or as a valued birthday gift. Miles was a prolific compiler of recitation anthologies and had preceded his most successful text with *The A-1 Reader* (1882), *The A-1 Elocutionist* (1883), *The Aldine Reciter* (1888), and *The Sunday School Reciter* (1891). First published in 1894 for three shillings sixpence Miles's *Elocutionist* by 1915 had reached its twelfth edition. Miles, meanwhile, refused to rest, publishing in 1902 *The Royal Reciter, The Imperial Reciter,* and *The Temperance Reciter.*

Miles's *Elocutionist* openly assumes that each of its five hundred selections has been chosen to be memorized and performed, but Miles also assumes a usership of different interests and skills and therefore offers the selections under a range of headings, which include "Readings in blank verse," "Poetry for junior students: lyrical, narrative, reflective, and dramatic," "Poetry for senior students: lyrical, narrative, reflective and descriptive," "Poetry for advanced students . . . ," Dramatic studies . . . " "Indian poetry," "Ballads of cavaliers and roundheads," "of the sea . . . of war . . . of the American war," and "Humorous verse." The volume begins with Miles's exhortations to his readers to select examples within the range of their abilities and experience, then, typically, follows with a medical surgeon's chapter on "vocal hygiene," — care of the throat, lungs, and teeth, and advice on breathing, projection, and enunciation. Finally, and again typically, the *Elocutionist* offers instruction and advice, with appropriate examples, of recitation with incidental music.

Less typical of such anthologies, but stressing the point that recitations are melodramatic performances, is the compilation by Hugh Campbell, R. F. Brewer, Henry Neville, Clifford Harrison—who had contributed a similar segment on musical accompaniment to Miles's *Elocutionist*— Frederick Corder, and Robert Blackman, *Voice, Speech, and Gesture.*[26] Published in 1895, *Voice, Speech, and Gesture* is similar to Miles's and comparable anthologies in that it gathers and classifies material by subject matter and by the comparative skills of its users. It, too, has chapters on the voice and on the necessity and use of incidental music. Where this collection differs from other anthologies is in the inclusion of a lengthy and richly illustrated chapter on parlour and platform gesture by the actor Henry Neville, now a well-established and respected actor who has opened his own academy of dramatic art and who now, his opinion on the subject changed, professes sympathy with the amateur actor and reciter. Neville dismisses any question that the reader-declaimer merely stands behind a lectern and reads his or her text—for although his text uses neuter or masculine pronouns, Neville's illustrations now assume that females, as much as males, will perform. Neville, himself, is depicted in a range of active gestures, stances, and movements. Many additional illustrations display, albeit unnamed, other leading performers closely associated with productions of melodrama—Edward Willard, Ellen Terry, Jesse Millward, and William Terriss—in theatrically telling moments. Neville then draws upon the Victorian science of physiognomy: Millward is further illustrated displaying a range of facial expressions which are said to denote specific emotions and states of mind. In my view this chapter makes the entire volume an important source for the study of melodramatic performance and texts, but it is probably due to the volume's overall emphasis on amateur and platform performance that this text has been so marginalized or overlooked by scholars.

While many balladeers were content to have their works culled from periodicals by other hands and anthologized to others' profits, some popular poets found publishers and readers for their verse. Felicia Dorothea Hemans, perhaps best known for "Casabianca" and "The boy stood on the burning deck . . . ," and active chiefly between 1815 and 1830, enjoyed brief fame as a poet whose works were declaimed in drawing rooms before her death in 1835. With her demise and without the certain protection of copyright, her poems regularly found their way into reciters. Eliza Cook, like Mrs. Hemans a prolific poet who turned her hand to far more than narrative verse, found publishers to publish and prosper on their collected works.[27]

Prominent in this group is George Sims. Sims himself saw his ballads into print from the pages of the *Referee*, where he had signed his poems "Dagonet," the name of King Arthur's jester. His *Ballads of Babylon* was followed by *The Lifeboat and Other Poems*, *The Land of Gold and Other Poems*, and the full output was gathered in *The Dagonet Reciter* and *In the Harbour*.[28]

That music publishers offered composer-balladeers a somewhat similar route to publication is evidenced by the printed works of the singer-composer Henry Russell. Russell's musical career was on the concert stage, where he specialized in "musical scenas," dramatic scenes or narratives that were, by turns, sung, intoned, and spoken. Russell rarely composed lyrics, but took popular poems, including those by Eliza Cook, and composed his own musical settings. Today Russell, if recalled at all, is remembered through contemporary parodies of his pieces, most notably "The Maniac's Tear," Tom Taylor's burlesque in *The Ticket-of-Leave Man* of Russell's "The Maniac." Russell's musical scenas, "The Newfoundland Dog," "The Ship on Fire," "The Gambler's Wife," "The Gin Fiend," "The Maniac," "Man the Life-Boat," and "The Slave Ship," were first released through various London and provincial music publishers in the late 1850s and 1860s, then subsequently anthologized in one of the numerous *Musical Miracles* publications from Davidson.[29] Russell's skill lies in choosing, or in some instances writing, vivid dramatic poetry in which characters are placed in physical or moral peril or in which personal emotions are beyond, or nearly beyond, control. Musical accompaniment for these scenas therefore becomes the means of restraint. His music is informatively mood-inducing. The auditor is unconsciously aware of emotional and psychological undertones, but the music, in its tonalities and loudness, is limiting and only hints at excess.

A Russell scena is melodrama decorous enough for the parlour or for a middle-class evening concert, and its melodic accompaniment is another important form of melodramatic music. Therefore, when speaking of melodrama, the term "incidental music" may be misleading. In melodrama, music is far from incidental or accidental, but, whether composed and orchestrated for a specific drama or culled for the occasion from a *chef d' orchestre*'s collection of all-purpose "melos,"[30] music is essential to establishing and maintaining the emotional tone and overall tempo of melodramatic action. It is no less essential to scaled-down melodrama. When applied to dramatic verse by such craftsmen-musicians as Henry Russell, music—a third voice added to those of the author and performer—supports the narrative, backing the reciter's voice with tonal nuance, indicating pauses, stresses, moments of anguish, horror, triumph, joy, but it is also appropriately decorous. In this respect incidental music serves to enclose stage and recitation performances, separating them from everyday speech, encouraging performers to extend and hold gestures. It may also be argued that, away from the public stage and its range of visual effects, music becomes a kind of audible scenery in that it adds to the recitation descriptive color, atmospherics, and sense of place.

6. *The existence and use of a recitation repertoire that closely resembles material performed upon the public stage.* Like their full-size theatrical counterparts, recitation dramas enact or narrate a wide variety of experiences and to some degree recapitulate the generic classifications of melodrama that have been described by many writers on the subject. Thus one can discern parlour and platform pieces which in subject matter are "domestic," "military," "nautical," "urban," "industrial," and "imperial." As much to the point, these pieces, whatever their subject and preoccupation, are structured to provide similar emotional and moral experiences and to generate similar intellectual responses and understandings as the larger range of stage melodrama.[31]

Although parlour melodrama meets many, if not most, of the configurations of stage pieces, there are differences, and most of these lie in the poets' view of causality. Although from the 1860s there are signs of an increasing awareness of a complex and inherently contradictory and anomalous world and a corresponding readiness to describe that world in their

plays, stage melodramatists nonetheless regularly connect reversal of fortune to malign human behavior. Even those melodramatists of the 1880s and
1890s who begin to come under the influence of Darwin and naturalism are
reluctant to forsake deliberate viciousness—villainy—as the root cause to
a stage crisis. By contrast, some balladeers, taking advantage of the narrator's independent voice, describe wider and, sometimes, less malevolent
causes, on occasion linking their narratives and the crises that test character and resolve to such general conditions as "bad weather" or "hard times."

Again George Sims, described by contemporary critics as "a Cockney . . .
with a touch of Zolaism"[32] or "Zolaism . . . watered at Aldgate Pump,"[33]
offers examples, on the one hand, of adherence to stage formulae and, on
the other hand, of his readers' and interpreters' awareness of the economic
cruelties inflicted by industrial capitalism. In his *The Last Chance,* an Adelphi
melodrama of 1885, Sims places his action in the midst of an industrial
depression that is none of his characters' making, but he has nonetheless
peopled his drama with malign shop stewards, fellow workers, and employers to vex his put-upon heroes. However, Sims's verses, such as "Billy's
Rose" or "In the Work House, Christmas Day," depict victims who fail,
starve, and perish in cities where poverty is general and malefactors
unnamed. It is, however, true that these ballads indict an indifferent society, and, if there are nameable humans at fault, then the readers or listeners
themselves are not exonerated. Other ballads in this genre describe high-
minded altruism of the sort where one man offers his life for another, usually so that a favored young couple can be reunited or united in marriage.
Nevertheless, the circumstances of such self-sacrifice are natural calamities
such as storms at sea, or imminent large-scale human disasters such as near
train wrecks, where no blame attaches to Sims's characters. Sims does not
altogether omit villainy from his narrative ballads, but is more interested in
the singular character, male or female, who rises above the limitations of
class and environment to act with heroism or to endure life in sordid surroundings with modest dignity and reclaimed virtue.

From all available evidence, George Sims's ballads, like much recitation
material, were written without a specific theatrical interpreter in the author's
mind, and these narrative pieces therefore stand at some distance from his
theatrical writings, which were undertaken for established actors and known
theatrical managements. The ballads, available in print, were there to be
found and, if appropriate to the impressions the reciter hoped to make,
snatched up by a myriad of performers. No favoritism was shown.
Professional actors were no better catered for and were compelled to consult
their own interests. To this extent, Henry Irving may be said to be typical.

Irving, unsupported in his early career by house dramatists, instinctively chose recitation pieces entirely to his advantage. Irving's preferred choices, "The Uncle" and "The Dream of Eugene Aram," instigate melodramatic performances that directly extend his stage roles. On consideration, many of his successful stage parts—Mortimer in *The Iron Chest*, Mathias in *The Bells*, Dubosc/Lesurques in *The Lyons Mail*, Synorix in *The Cup*, Macbeth, Louis XI, Eugene Aram in W. G. Wills's adaptation of Hood's poem, even Mephistopheles —are identifiable as men who, repressing suppurating memories of evil acts, pretend to an innocence they cannot maintain and, in unaware moments, reveal streaks of cruelty, ruthlessness, and seasoned guile.

The plot of H. G. Bell's "The Uncle" shares unmistakable similarities with that of Colman's *The Iron Chest*. The first—the outside—voice speaking the poem's narration is an adult who recalls his orphaned childhood in the care of his guardian, the uncle. Then, now in the persona of the child he had been, the narrator describes the uncle's gloomy saturnine character and his excessive care of a locked iron chest. One day the child's gazing upon the picture of his deceased mother prompts the uncle to speak. The reciter now becomes the uncle speaking of his unrequited love for the boy's mother, his tormented jealousy of his brother—the boy's father—undermining reason and brotherly regard. The brother, the uncle tells the child, disappeared; the mother, mourning her missing husband, died of grief without ever returning the uncle's love. The uncle beckons the child to the old chest and, touching a spring, abruptly opens it to reveal the skeleton of the child's father. The shock of confessing his murderous act is too much for the uncle and, a sinner to the end, the narrator recalls, he dies blaspheming. In less than ten minutes, Irving—or his imitator—has performed three contrasting roles, the third and most dramatic the guilt-ridden criminal so admired and expected by Irving's Lyceum audiences. Thomas Hood's dramatic narrative "The Dream of Eugene Aram" is again similar to Irving's stage persona: a man who has murdered for greed—and Mathias again comes to mind—who has failed obliterate the memory of that act. Again, the guilty secret is exposed; again the murderer dies, a victim of his own criminal actions. We cannot condone covetousness and murder, but we can offer pity to all within the world of the drama because Providence has imposed a moral solution.

Such links between the professional stage, the recitation platform, and the nascent film industry are still visible as late—or as early—as 1907 in Herbert Booth's "The Entrancing Story of the Early Christians." Booth, the youngest son of the Salvation Army's founder William Booth, had left his father's organization to lead his own evangelical temperance drive, drawing audiences to his sermons with a melodramatic slide show misleadingly described as a "bioscope." Illustrations taken from Booth's slides reveal that his plot draws heavily upon, if not plagiarizes, Wilson Barrett's "toga" melodrama *The Sign of the Cross*, while the painted backcloths are derived from the same drama and from William Young's stage adaptation of *Ben-Hur*.[34]

Individually and in the aggregate, such recitations help to demonstrate that melodrama had become one of the established modes of thinking and expression that extended well beyond the theatre. Just as burlesque, travesty, and parody underlined and indirectly expressed middle-class anxieties about order, rules, form, and propriety, so theatrical and recitation melodrama expressed a rarely fulfilled desire—and need—to reconcile human behavior, a behavior legitimated by the ethos of Victorian capitalism and its scientific counterpart Darwinism, with Christian morality. Capitalism and Darwinism, separately and differently, justified aggression, assertion, individual achievement, and self-fulfillment—both Mortimer of *The Iron Chest* and the unnamed uncle of Bell's poem are unabashed and remorseless in exercising these traits and seeking these objectives. Christian morality celebrated passivity, compliance, spiritual peace, the triumph of the weak, and the ultimate fall—through the agency of Providence, not by overt human action—of the wicked. Again both stageplay and poem enact these doctrinal points.

Additionally, as the Victorian family and their private home were celebrated as a sanctuary set apart from a corrupting world, and as the domestic hearth became the principal locus for family activity, the family itself was brought within the scope of melodramatic conflict and subjected to scrutiny. Danger and harm, both verse and stage melodrama inform the Victorian audience, may come from within the family. Those close to us—siblings, uncles, but never parents and rarely spouses—might offer serious rivalries or wish us harm. The family, the very institution Victorians are being instructed to revere uncritically, may be no less a source of peril than the world without.

Drama and dramatic verse bring moral and compassionate interventions to these fictive worlds—metaphors for current actual worlds, where injustice, hostility, oppression, and catastrophe are normally inexorable and alarmingly close to hand. Each melodramatic recitation, each metaphor, explores these irreconcilables and a perilous environment that might offer random human or natural dangers. Each recitation provides a resolution that promised or—as with the ballads of Sims and other poet-reformers—ironically queried the existence of stability, sufficiency, mercy, and justice. However, few recitations, any more than few stage melodramas, provide effective answers, true enlightenment, or, to those seeking it in the performance, permanent gratification. Melodrama affords only temporary satisfaction, then bafflement and frustration because experience and reflection tell us that we have not been told the entire truth. But these fictions are nonetheless persuasive and satisfying enough to be addictive. So the quest for enlightenment and satisfaction—through another melodrama—is repeated ad infinitum.

If our lengthy repertoire of theatrical and recitation melodrama is the ultimate consequence of this quest, we have still only bestowed historical and critical attention on the fraction that relates to performances of full-scale stageplays. It is now time for historians to examine in detail not only the full recitation repertoire but also the practice of theatregoing and, where possible, the incorporation of theatrical and narrative materials into Victorian daily life. The brevity of this essay, which identifies some melodramatic material and practitioners but which altogether stints other genres, and my essay's location in a volume which otherwise treats stage melodrama should draw attention to work and study still undone. It is work for many hands and many critical minds.

N o t e s

1. Henry Neville, *The Stage: Its Past and Present in Relation to Fine Art* (London, 1875).
2. John Barnes, *The Rise of the Cinema in Great Britain*, vol.1, *The Beginnings of the Cinema in England, 1894-1901*, vol 2, *Jubilee Year, 1897* (London: Bishopsgate Press, 1983); Charles Musser (in collaboration with Carol Nelson), *High Class Moving Pictures: Lyman H. Howe and the Forgotten Era of the Traveling Exhibition, 1880-1920* (Princeton: Princeton University Press, 1991).
3. David Mayer, "The Ticket-of-Leave Man" in Context," *Essays in Theatre*, (November 1987): 31-40.
4. F. M. L. Thompson, *The Rise of Respectable Society*, (Cambridge, MA: Harvard University Press, 1989), 250-67.
5. George Rowell, *The Victorian Theatre* (Cambridge: Cambridge University Press, 1949); M. R. Booth, *English Plays of the Nineteenth Century*, vol 2, *Dramas, 1850-1900* (Oxford: Oxford University Press, 1969) and *Prefaces to English Nineteenth-Century Theatre* (Manchester: Manchester University Press, 1983).
6. Booth, *Dramas, 1850-1900*, 13-15.
7. Michel Perrot, "At Home," in *The Rise of Private Life from the Fires of Revolution to the Great War* (Cambridge, MA: Harvard University Press, 1990), 340-43.
8. Ronald Pearsall, *Victorian Popular Music* (London: David and Charles, 1973), 74.
9. Pearsall, *Victorian Popular Music*, 85-97.
10. Thompson, *Rise of Respectable Society*, 251-55.
11. Florence C. Smith, "Introducing Parlor Theatricals to the American Home," in *Performing Arts Resources* vol. 14 (New York: Theatre Library Association,

1989), 1-11, and Brooks McNamara, "'For laughing purposes only': The Literature of American Popular Entertainment," in *The American Stage: Social and Economic Issues from the Colonial Period to the Present*, ed. Ron Engle and Tice Miller (Cambridge: Cambridge University Press, 1993), 141-58.

12. A singular exception to this dearth is J. S. Bratton, *The Victorian Popular Ballad* (London: Macmillan, 1975). Prof. Bratton's detailed study concentrates on ballad content and the class contexts of these pieces rather than on the technique or sociology of performance.

13. Charles Harrison, *Theatricals and Tableaux Vivants for Amateurs, Giving full directions to stage arrangements, "making up," costumes, and acting, with ninety-two illustrations* (London, n.d. [ca. 1885-86]).

14. Weedon Grosmith, *The Diary of a Nobody* (London, 1892), ch. ii. See also David Mayer, *Henry Irving and The Bells* (Manchester: Manchester University Press, 1980), 57, 88nn. 11-13.

15. Pearsall, *Victorian Popular Music*, 48-55.

16. The song was published in London by John Shepard, n.d.

17. Laurence Irving, *Henry Irving: The Actor and His World* (London: Faber and Faber, 1951), 40-41.

18. The exact date of this commission is unclear. Benedict died in 1885, but the cover to the printed music, published by Goodwin and Tabb, refers to "Sir Henry Irving." Irving was not knighted until 1895.

19. George R. Sims, *Rogues and Vagabonds* (London, 1885).

20. George R. Sims, *My Life: Sixty Years' Recollections of Bohemian London* (London: Eveleigh Nash, 1917), 181-189.

21. The Sims material on offer, published in the *Referee* between 1879 and 1882, and Bolton's references to Sims's work on behalf of the Royal Commission enquiring into slum conditions, 1883-84, places this performance in the mid-1880s.

22. G. A. Household and L. M. H. Smith, eds., *To Catch a Sunbeam: Victorian Reality Through the Magic Lantern* (London: Michael Joseph, 1979), 7-10.

23. Between 1894, when motion pictures first appeared in commercial form, and 1910, few motion pictures exceeded a running time of twenty minutes. By 1905, most films ran for approximately ten to twelve minutes.

24. Library of Congress Paper Print Collection, FLA 5622, 1908.

25. Alfred H. Miles, ed., *The New Standard Elocutionist* (London, 1879).

26. Hugh Campbell et. al., *Voice, Speech, and Gesture: A Practical handbook to the Elocutionary Art*, ed. Robert D. Blackman (London, 1895), reprinted in 1897, 1904.

27. Felicia Dorothea (Browne) Hemans, *The Poetical Works of Mrs Hemans* (London: 1825 and 1839), and Eliza Cook, *The Poetical Works of Eliza Cook* (London, 1869).

28. George R. Sims [Dagonet, pseud.], *Ballads of Babylon* (London, 1880), *The Lifeboat and Other Poems*, (London, 1883), *The Land of Gold and Other Poems* (London, 1888), *The Dagonet Reciter* (London, 1888), *In the Harbour* (London, 1892).

29. Henry Russell, *100 Songs by Henry Russell/Songs and Scenas./Music and Words for a Shilling* (London, n.d).

30. David Mayer and Matthew Scott, *Four Bars of "Agit": Incidental Music for Victorian and Edwardian Melodrama* (London: Samuel French and the Theatre Museum, 1983).

31. David Mayer, *Playing Out the Empire: "Ben-Hur" and Other Toga Plays and Films* (Oxford: Oxford University Press, 1994), 5-7.

32. Augustin Filon, *The English Stage* (London, 1892), 301.

33. William Archer, *The English Dramatists of Today* (London, 1882), 298.

34. *Illustrated London News*, 31 August 1907, 305.

12

WHAT THE HEROINE TAUGHT, 1830-1870

LÉON METAYER*

*W*ORK, FAMILY, NATION. During the July Monarchy and the Second Empire the French melodrama only invested in reliable commodities. The Bourgeois order was in place, and its credo had spread in all directions. Order: the domination of the weak by the strong—workers obeyed their employers, children their fathers, wives their husbands, soldiers their commander. Better still, they not only obeyed, they were expected to do so voluntarily and, if possible, with gratitude. Indeed, it was normal for the worker to thank the employer who offered him work, the wife the husband who had chosen her, and the soldier the commander who gave him the opportunity to sacrifice himself. And all this could be found faithfully reproduced in the melodrama.

Caricature? Perhaps not. Limitations on space prevent me from dealing with all of them, so I have chosen to leave aside workers and soldiers and focus on *la femme* since, during a good part of the nineteenth century, "woman" was central to the preoccupations of moralists and politicians, despite her unassuming position in the social hierarchy. At the start of the romantic movement the purveyors of "*la littérature de prostitution*" had attacked the principles that sustained existing family structures. They criticized the laws that made a woman a minor for life, subject first to the authority of her father and then her husband, without rights to her property or herself. They demanded the reestablishment of divorce and supported a woman's right to keep her children if she left her husband. These were just a few of their demands. In response to these assaults the bourgeoisie lent its support to those authors who offered ideal images of woman: adorned with all possible virtues, she is portrayed as the figure through whom the world can and must be saved. If she allowed herself to be corrupted, nothing would remain

of the things that make a society strong—the continuity of the family, pro-
prietary rights, the stability of governments, religion—everything would be
menaced. And since everyone knows how fragile "woman" is (see, for example,
the *Discours sur les deux natures*), she can make no better choice than to submit to man's rule, since only it can keep her on the straight and narrow.[1]

What I am suggesting is that the real theme of melodrama lies barely hidden behind its extravagant peripeties. Most of the intrigues revolve around
a woman: a man desires her; a man has dishonored her; one wants to make
off with her fortune; someone has taken her children; her father wants her
to marry against her wishes—it is her emotions that give meaning to these
episodes. Indeed, a list of the melodramas that bear a woman's first name or
family name in their titles would undoubtedly be quite long, and even in
other cases (*Robert Surcouf, ou le Naufrage de La Pérouse,* for example) a woman
is not far away.

Taking up this theme, a good dramatic "carpenter" could easily construct
an action with enough suspense to hold the interest of the public, and their
counterparts among the scene designers excelled at constructing more and
more elaborate stage machines *(le Tremblement de terre de la Martinique)* and
painting exotic or picturesque scenes *(la Case de l'Oncle Tom, les Fugitifs, les
Mystères de Paris)*. And all this drew the multitude. The Ambigu, the Gaîté, and
the Porte-Saint-Martin were filled almost every evening with a public that discovered, if not always the essential, at least a good part of its values on their
stages. Despite the attacks of the moralists and the efforts of others who
wanted to encourage reading among the working classes, a large segment of
these ordinary people sought their pleasures in the theatre, and more especially
in the melodrama. Others sensed a danger there. The press was filled with
warnings about bad examples—those that could transform the working classes
into dangerous classes—and there were calls for government intervention.

However, nothing much was done, and censorship, frequently unrea-
sonable in other instances, had little impact on the melodrama. Moreover,
why should it? The melodrama's authors seldom balked at the instructions
they were given. With the exception of the writers belonging to the school
that "glorified [the working classes]" (Royer describes them as the
"Anabaptists of the boulevard" and says they preached "Mephistophelean
sermons"), who were few in number, everyone else was more or less of the
party in power and hardly bent on overthrowing a society that, in the final
reckoning, treated them fairly well.[2] Therefore, the lesson they repeated endlessly was precisely the one the governing order wished to have circulated:
anyone who fails to submit to the rule of the class in power deserves the
heaviest of punishments—and death is not the worst.

This was especially true for women. I believe the melodrama represented their status and roles in a manner that was not far from reality—as long as one takes into account what in the melodrama as elsewhere, is conveniently referred to as "dramatic necessity." How then does the heroine's career actually unfold? As the action begins, her position is generally one of weakness; she is dependent on her surroundings. If poor, she is an orphan, the daughter of a laborer, a peasant, or even a criminal; if rich she is surrounded by people who conspire against her—starting with her father, whose ambition, greed, or simple stupidity will lead to disastrous decisions concerning her. In the former case she will be tempted by wealth and in the latter by the snares of idleness. The greatest menace always comes from a man—the villain of the play. Regardless of whether he is attracted by her charms, her fortune, or both, he will use whatever means necessary to make her yield, including kidnapping, false marriage, or rape. Faced with these assaults, she has only her faith and a desperate confidence in Providence to protect her. It is probably best that she not count too much on assistance from the hero. His naiveté, stubbornness, awkwardness, and blindness often border on the pathological. There is no "triumphant adventurer" here, no "bad" woman who succeeds; she will first make her appearance at a later date.

Despite her diminished status, the public demanded that the heroine satisfactorily fill a certain number of roles, all of which were complicated and in some way tied to sexuality. If she is unmarried, she has to remain a virgin no matter what the temptations and regardless of the forces leagued against her. If she succumbs, she is lost. This obligation is paired with submission to the rule of the father, who, because he is God's representative, is not to be quibbled with. This is especially true when it comes to choosing a husband. The slightest hint of resistance brings with it the threat of malediction, brandished by a father whose motives are not always as pure as they might be. Of course, all this unfolds against the background of a "matrimonial market," the rules of which have very little to do with sentiment. The future husband must belong to an honorable caste, his fortune must be guaranteed. His past should be unblemished—at least in terms of bourgeois criteria—and he must be appreciably older than his bride to be.

Once married, the heroine finds herself caught in a network of obligations that result in her new position being as devalued as the old, and her new roles just as difficult to fill. In other words, at the same time that vaudeville played freely with the sacraments of marriage, melodrama enforced civil and religious codes in the strictest possible manner.

An essential: motherhood. Woman was meant to be a mother—of males as much as possible. Without this, difficulties would arise in passing on one's name and inheritance. In conformity with the reigning ideology, therefore, the melodrama inscribes the role of mother as the noblest, the richest, and most enviable, despite its suite of servitude. This is especially true when the villain endangers her children, which, of course, he will not fail to do. In addition to Marie Dorval, who triumphed in *Marie-Jeanne*, Marie Laurent and Mme Lacressonnière are among the actresses who became famous by playing the persecuted mother.

Another obligation was absolute fidelity, even at the level of mere appearances. Nothing should give rise to doubt, no matter what conjugal misery the heroine might experience. Of course, her difficulties are numerous, especially if her father gets involved. A husband dislikes his wife, or he is morbidly jealous; he leaves on a trip that lasts months, or goes to war and is away for years; he is unfaithful and appears in public with his mistresses; he abandons her for drink and/or gaming; finally—though there are worse possibilities—he may be exposed as a criminal. None of these events could justify rebellion, and still less abandonment, since a wife is supposed to be as submissive and attached to her husband as she was to her father. There is no room in the melodrama for "Vesuvians" (volcanic types) or *femmes saucialistes*.[3]

Despite all this, a woman occasionally succumbs to temptation and transgresses against the law by giving herself before marriage or by cheating on her husband. Given what she has done, death is the usual outcome. This punishment is unavoidable, since public opinion is on the lookout. Public opinion may not fill a generic role in the melodrama (though it does have one in the revue), but it has a significant place. In the name of society, it serves to reveal what has happened or could have happened, and it obliges men (father or husband) to act in consequence. Since there is a solidarity among men in terms of the fight against sexual dissipation in women, no man has the right to show any weakness or mildness in such instances.

The heroine never has a valid excuse, no matter whether her slip is voluntary or not: to expose herself to risk is already to transgress against the rules and, therefore, to be to some degree complicit. A woman caught is a woman who obviously let herself go, and, thus, a courtesan. She must pay. This is true even when nothing has happened. It is sufficient that appearances are against her. Abduction, rape, fake marriage, and false identity are not attenuating circumstances. Moreover, this concept is unknown in the rhetoric of the melodrama. Love, idleness, bad advice, the illusions of the city, nothing mitigates the fault. No matter whether it is a woman who allows herself to be kept due to hunger, a poor peasant woman, a working girl fascinated by the prestige of a nobleman, a mother who wants to save her children, or an adventurer who has decided to do whatever necessary to rise in the world, the transgression is the same, and the punishment must be equal to it in severity. A woman's punishment, that is. The question of male responsibility and punishment is seldom raised.

The penalties that await the sinner are as varied as the latent sadism of the spectators allows. At the very least, her father is going to suffer and, for his child, that is only the first sorrow. Often, even with the best of intentions, she is the source of the family's dishonor, which—needless to say—her father cannot endure. This turns her into a parricide. If he survives, he will curse her and she will be forsaken by God. One can well imagine the impatience of the audience as it awaits the grand and obligatory scene in which the curse falls, a scene that, in the hands of an experienced author, was always one of the high points of a work.

Already responsible for her father's despair, the heroine will also suffer because of her children. If married, she will be obliged to hand them over to her husband, no matter how odious he may be. Not only does she lose her exalted status as mother, she becomes the agent of all the misfortunes that inevitably befall her children. If they die (because of her misstep, naturally), the upshot is that she is both a parricide and a child murderer. Furthermore, she also runs the risk of bearing illegitimate offspring, and a bastard child would just be another aspect of her punishment. Condemned by the very nature of his birth, a bastard son is almost inevitably drawn toward crime, or, better still, he may be deprived of all the opportunities for happiness granted to others. And he owes this to his mother. Thus, the spectacle of the heroine's pain at the moment she learns of the judgment passed against this son is another of the high points in more than a few melodramas.

The husband scorned will also prove useful to the workings of divine vengeance. Obviously, he may kill his guilty spouse—as authorized by social mores and the law. But that happens only rarely, either because of the obvious dramatic disadvantages of such an event, or because most authors preferred to show the scorned husband's magnanimity through a grand scene of forgiveness, one that frequently takes place when the heroine is already in the throes of death. As is fitting, the demise of the heroine is usually the final step in a whole series of more or less brutal degradations that separate her from her highly desirable status as wife. One of the best examples of this scenario is found in Scribe's *Dix ans de la vie d'une femme*, which opened at the Porte-Saint-Martin in 1832. Once she is publicly rejected and reviled, her fate lies in the hands of the man for whom she went astray. But in the melodrama the seducer is seldom a reliable protector. Either he dies almost immediately, or he flees, or he is sent to prison for some crime or other; at best he reveals a pitiful emptiness of character. Thus, the wife finds herself alone with her guilt and her newly acquired status as kept woman. In fact, in the eyes of everyone she has become a courtesan. Even if she manages to secure a divorce, even if for some exceptional reason the courts find in her favor, in the public's mind she will still be a woman who did not know how to keep her husband. And if she contracts a new marriage, she will remain under the ban of the better classes. As for her lover, or her second husband, he will never be at peace. Once fallen. . . .

However, in certain cases—where the heroine has only been acting in self-defense—madness is sufficient punishment, and also a deliverance. For this reason a woman loses her sanity (sometimes only for a short while) when the accusation made against her is false. When the truth comes out, she regains her senses and, after asking pardon from her husband for the worries she has caused him, she is allowed to return to the security of her home and family. On the other hand, if nothing pleads in her favor, her fall is brutal. Sheltered from need in the beginning, she falls into misery that is more and more abject, with prostitution the final stop. Melodramas that specifically portray such situations are fairly rare, but allusions to this final degradation abound, since it is the inevitable end for an unprotected woman. At that point, death is little more than a release to be hoped for. But who knows, the torments of the other world might be worse.

Fortunately, the heroine can be pardoned after having undergone a punishment proportional to her fault. After all, a man who has the right and the means to chastise her also has the ability to pardon her. Thus, the father may withdraw his curse—another scene that normally leads to a "succès de mouchoirs" (a successful tear-jerker). Perhaps, because his daughter has repented before the fact, or because the man to whom she has given herself has atoned for her mistake, or because the crime was not actually committed, her father sometimes pardons the heroine. When the culprit fails to sufficiently demonstrate her repentance, a truly noble father will bend only when she is on her death bed, and then only at the urging of his entourage. Furthermore, he often dies at the same instant. In every case, it is the good will of a man that assures a woman's well-being.

The possibilities offered to a husband who has been betrayed (or who thinks he has been) are far more varied. His severity may soften somewhat if his unfaithful spouse is on the verge of death, but, like her father, he will be somewhat reticent, and it may be his new wife who urges him in the direction of clemency. Of course, clemency is easier if the heroine is innocent. But even if it is only appearances that are against her, she still must ask for forgiveness since she has given cause for suspicion. Things are more complicated when she has only had the will to sin, but has been held back in time by some good influence, by an incident that enhances her esteem for her husband, by a timely stop in a church, or simply by chance. In such cases, her pardon depends on the manner in which she expresses her regret and her willingness not to stray in the future. A heroine overwhelmed by shame, humiliating herself before a man ennobled by legitimate anger is a gratifying spectacle—at least for the masculine part of the audience. On the other hand, everything is much simpler if the heroine redeems herself by saving her husband's life. In this case he cannot be implacable, especially since he has revealed that in certain circumstances he needs his wife. Finally, though such instances are rare, a man can pardon a real fault "for no reason." He offers her unreserved forgiveness—out of love, or generosity; or because he feels neither superior nor safe from temptation; or out of Christian charity. It goes without saying that such behavior meets with disapproval in the newspapers of the day. It sets a bad example.

In other words, every transgression by a woman has to be sanctioned, since society insists on it. A man is not free in his actions. As the representative of society he must carry out its requirements. Otherwise, he too will be found guilty. Therefore, he (and others) must watch his spouse and make sure she is kept in her place. As for her, it is normal that she would willingly forgive if she is the one offended, first because it is understood that her failings are infinitely greater than those of a man, and, further, because society expects her to show proof of tenderness and mercy—like the Blessed Virgin.

This, in bold strokes, is the career of the heroine in the melodramas that were staged every evening for the edification of thousands of spectators in Paris and other major cities in France. And it seems to me that the unflagging repetition of this twofold lesson fidelity and submission to the male—more or less invites some further questions about the functions of the melodrama.

Some are evident. The most obvious is amusement. The search for a missing heroine, the adventures of a woman pursued by a villain or searching for the children who have been taken from her, these are just so many pretexts for leaping into a different epoch or milieu. The sense of foreignness or difference in certain scenes is reinforced by the efforts of the set designers. A certain eroticism ensues, tuned to the mores of the age. There are plenty of exotic themes that allow women to be represented in ways well suited to stimulate masculine fantasies: harems *(Constantinople)*, plantations *(la Case de l'Oncle Tom)*, etc. And if the action does not lend itself to this sort of thing, it can be interrupted in order to exhibit a "naked" horsewoman *(les Pirates de la Savane)*, for example. In addition, the authors of these pieces exploit every occasion that allows them to play with the ambiguous charm of cross dressing (e.g., Mlle Garait, Ida Février, Marie

Laurent and especially Déjazet). All of these elements of the play—linked as they are to the era's well-established belief that all actresses are prostitutes and, therefore, more or less available—can feed the fantasies of those males in the audience who do not have the wherewithal to indulge in the luxury of "tableaux vivants."

Another level on the scale of pleasure is reached when a woman is the victim of physical violence. Of course, violence is everywhere in the melodrama, but it is especially gratifying when it is directed against a woman. A heroine in disarray ("her clothes in disarray" is an omnipresent stage direction), terrorized by the gesture of a man who is on the verge of striking her—such scenes frequently appear on playbills. They are the nineteenth century's equivalent of the more daring scenes in today's cinema. That such publicity also depicts the indubitable superiority of the male is merely another indication of the type of satisfaction sought by one part of the public.

The sadism of this segment of the public is gratified all the more if the heroine belongs to the dominant classes. A battered working woman is a spectacle one can observe on the street. To gaze upon a bourgeois or aristocratic woman who has been degraded and has become a victim of terror is a different sort of pleasure, one in which a latent element of class struggle shows through. As for the audience's masochism, it too is abundantly gratified: quite a few observers, after noting the many drunkards in attendance at what the British then referred to as "delirium tremens dramas," have wondered what these individuals might have felt. As for women—and they made up a sizable portion of the audience—what confused pleasure might they experience watching so many heroines move toward a downfall that many among them already lived as their quotidian reality?

Clearly, amusement is an important aim of these plays, but I think the essential aim is to be found in their moralizing function. Though the romantic drama, along with the plays of Dumas *fils* and most vaudevilles, can be accused of failing to respect the morals of the day, and although the few authors then inclined toward socialism (Félix Pyat and his plays *le Brigand et le Philosophe* [1834], *Ango de Dieppe* [1835], or *le Chiffonnier de Paris* [1847] are always cited at this juncture—without paying much attention to the social ambiguities in the plays) use the melodrama as a vehicle for their propaganda, on the whole the form remains a veritable ideological apparatus of the state. This is especially true in regard to women, who are treated no more equitably by the authors of the left than they are by those on the right. Playhouses dedicated to the genre were hardly places where female spectators could take lessons in feminism.

The regulatory function of the melodrama seems to be twofold. Its first aspect is political. The melodrama constantly espouses a particular position in regard to responsibility. Its doctrine is quite straightforward: society is not responsible for what happens to individuals. If a woman falls, and if she is punished, it is because she chose not to follow the precepts of religion and the moral regimen of society. In general, when the rapport between men and women, employers and workers, the governing and the governed is not good, it is individuals that need to be reformed, not structures. In regard to social mobility, for example, the melodrama clearly sides with the reactionary ideology of the day: one should not try to raise oneself too quickly, no skipping rungs on the social ladder. A woman who hopes to break through class barriers by marrying too far above her station will have to pay the penalty. On the other hand, if she knows how to show moderation, her reward will be proportional to her origins. This is demonstrated again and again. For example, if a supposed working woman becomes a princess in the last act, it is because she is, in reality, the daughter of a duke who had been kidnapped at birth by Gypsies.

The other aspect of its regulatory role is psychological: by reminding the public that a woman is at once both fragile and dangerous, and, therefore, that it is important to exercise careful control over her, and by putting on stage heroines who experience extraordinary adventures while embodying roles and social statuses drawn from reality, the melodrama offers women in the audience the opportunity to identify with characters who serve as models to emulate, as warnings, and as means of releasing internal tension.

Finally, the melodrama, because it stands in defense of the legitimate family, regularly presents situations in which one man (husband or father) is in conflict with another over a woman. His adversary (real or imaginary) may be his rival in love, but can also be a son of whom he is jealous. A third possibility sets him in conflict with the man his daughter loves. This enacts either the oedipal situation, where father and son struggle for possession of the mother, or the image of a father whose passion for his daughter at best allows him to accept a son-in-law that resembles himself—and that he has chosen. The cathartic function of such representations thus seems to be of a pair with the exorcism practiced on women.

It goes without saying that this insistent return to the problems created by women will inevitably have perverse and undesired effects. By constructing situations in which women are devalued, exploited, colonized, trapped in roles and by rules that deny them any freedom of development, the melodrama's creators may have also, in the long run, helped stimulate an unintended sort of reflection on the part of both male and female spectators. This is certainly a question that needs to be asked, but it seems to me the lesson the heroine offered her public in the nineteenth century is still propagated by a good number of films and television series today. It also seems that male behavior is not so very different from that seen on the stages of the Gaîté and the Porte-Saint-Martin.[4]

Notes

* Translated by Michael Hays.
1. *Romantisme* (1976), 13-14.
2. Alphonse Royer, *Histoire du théâtre contemporain* (Paris: Paul Ollandorf, 1878) 385, 394, 396.
3. The expression plays on "saucée" (scolding) and "socialist(e)," and gives an interesting and very real political dimension to what might otherwise seem to be a uniform and rather abstract set of attitudes concerning woman's place [translator's note].
4. Different aspects of the "lesson of the heroine" surface in a great many melodramas. The titles of some typical examples: Albert, *Juliette* (1834); Ancelot, *Léontine* (1831); Anicet-Bourgeois, *Marianne* (1850); le *Médecin des enfants* (1855); *l'Aveugle* (1857); *les Pirates de la savane* (1859); Antier, *l'Incendiaire* (1831); Arnault, *Constantinople* (1854); Dennery, *les Bohémiens de Paris* (1843); *Marie-Jeanne, ou la femme du peuple* (1845); Desnoyer, *la Folle* (1836); Ducange, *Trente Ans, ou la vie d'un joueur* (1827); Dumanoir, *la Case de l'Oncle Tom* (1853); Dumas, *le Marbrier* (1854); Fournier, *le Pardon de Bretagne* (1849); Scribe, *Dix ans de la vie d'une femme* (1832); Soulié, *la Closerie des genêts* (1846); Valory, *Vierge et martyre* (1846).
Some aspects of my argument have been more fully developed in Léon Metayer, "la Représentation des statuts et des rôles de la femme dans le mélodrame en France et en Angleterre de 1830 à 1870" (Ph.D. diss., University of Reims, 1981).

13

REPRESENTING A "GREAT DISTRESS": MELODRAMA, GENDER, AND THE IRISH FAMINE

JULIA WILLIAMS & STEPHEN WATT

> *If you will only look back to the years gone by, you
> cannot but be convinced that all our trials and troubles
> can be traced to the great distress during the Famine.*
> — HUBERT O'GRADY, *The Famine,* 1886

> *Barren, never to know the load
> of his child in you, what is your body
> now if not a famine road?*
> — EAVAN BOLAND, "Famine Road," 1975

*I*N HIS ACCOUNT OF IRELAND IN THE 1840S, Thomas Gallagher greatly
understates the case when asserting that the Great Famine was "to
shape the attitudes of Irish all over the world on into the twentieth century,"
for the Famine remains prominent in Irish thought even as this century
comes to an end.[1] Eavan Boland's poem "Famine Road" was preceded by,
among others, William Carleton and Liam O'Flaherty's novels *The Black
Prophet* (1847) and *Famine* (1937), Gerald Healy's play *The Black Stranger*
(1945), Patrick Kavanagh's "The Great Hunger" (1942), and Tom Murphy's
political drama *Famine* (1968).[2] To be fair, Gallagher was not referring to
texts treating the Famine, but rather to a larger cultural unconscious still
inflective of Anglo-Irish relationships. At times, its sway might appear
slight: the exchange over causes of the Famine between a British and Irish
hostage in Frank McGuinness's *Someone Who'll Watch Over Me* (1992), for

example. Other times, the evidence is more striking, such as the republica-
tion of Gerald Keegan's *Famine Diary: Journey to a New World* (1991), which,
only months after its release and ascent of bestseller lists in Ireland, was
revealed to be not an eyewitness account but a fiction.[3] This last scandal in
particular raises several questions we hope to explore in this essay: how are
histories of the Famine "emplotted"?[4] What relationship obtains between
melodrama and historical representation in the nineteenth century? If any
distinct line between fiction and history can be drawn, then the case of
Famine Diary demonstrates that even literate consumers are often incapable
of identifying it.

For students of nineteenth-century drama, the problematic of history
and fiction — or history *as* fiction (or melodrama) — acquires an added
resonance when one considers the often "complex and qualified ways"
in which the Victorian theatre added to the "web of meaning generated
and maintained by official documents, news reportage, romantic adventure
stories . . . whereby the Empire was naturalised."[5] Ireland, of course, was
part of this Empire, and one way of naturalizing imperial expansionism
was through an "archetype of the True Briton, naturally superior to
and fit to rule over subject races [like the Irish]."[6] The complement to such
a figure on the Victorian stage and emblem of a "naturally" *inferior* race
is the all-too-familiar stage Irishman: a character of "dishevelled appearance . . . and the shambling gait; the perpetual idiotic grin and the pose
evocative at best of naive innocence, at worst of stupidity."[7] And although,
as Richard Allen Cave explains, references to potatoes in connection
with this depiction fell into disuse after the Famine, he is surely right in
underscoring the "relentless" quality of the stereotype. Hence, it is hardly
surprising that plays and novels based on the Famine revise such stereotypes, both that of the stage Irishman and of the equally well-known
"colleen bawn."

This is as much to say that in "Famine texts," as we shall refer to them,
the gendered body is almost always *the* most prominent site of historical representation. And if, as Michel Foucault suggests, the task of a genealogy or
"effective history" is to "expose a body totally imprinted by history" and contained within "certain regulatory grids of intelligibility," then the Great
Famine ought to provide a fecund example for their exposition.[8] And it does,
insofar as journalistic and novelistic representations are concerned. The
drama, however, is a different matter. Given both the copious reporting from
Ireland in the 1840s and 1850s in such vehicles as the London *Times* and,
especially in the 1860s and 1870s, the success of Irish dramas on both West
and East End stages, one might have predicted a formidable canon of plays

UNION IS STRENGTH.

John Bull.—"HERE ARE A FEW THINGS TO GO ON WITH, BROTHER, AND I'LL SOON PUT YOU IN A
WAY TO EARN YOUR OWN LIVING."

FIGURE 5. An illustration for "Union is Strength." *Punch* 11
(July–December 1846).

based on this historical tragedy. Such is not the case. Is such an absence attributable to the nature of the material, making it ill-suited for the theatre? Or is it more likely attributable to the topic's potential undermining of the imperial project? As productions of Dion Boucicault's *The Colleen Bawn* (1860), *Arrah-na-Pogue* (1865), and *The Shaughraun* (1874), Edmond Falconer's *Peep o' Day* (1861) and *Eileen Oge* (1871), and Colin Henry Hazlewood's career at the Britannia Theatre, Hoxton, indicate, sensational Irish dramas were well supported by West End and popular audiences alike, even after the Fenian bombings of the later 1860s and even if British audiences might have found unsettling these plays' counterrepresentations of attractive and articulate Irish nationalists.

Not surprisingly, more Irish plays appeared on the later nineteenth-century Dublin stage, where revivals of Boucicault and Falconer competed successfully for audiences with more modern attractions, especially at the working-class Queen's Royal Theatre.[9] Yet few plays were based on the events of the Famine with the exception of actor-dramatist Hubert O'Grady's *The Eviction* (1879), *Emigration* (1880), and *The Famine* (1886).[10] How O'Grady's melodrama depicted painful episodes of national history is one subject of what follows. Still, even in plays so promisingly entitled for our purposes as *Emigration* or *The Famine,* a process of indirect historical depiction obtains. That is to say, on the one hand much of the dramatic action of O'Grady's plays resembles the characteristics of East End melodrama outlined by Michael Booth: the "powerful expression of powerful emotions," a "dramatic climax involving vigorous action," and the "placing of the heroine in a situation of the most desperate peril from which she is snatched at the very last moment."[11] But, on the other hand, given the devastating realities of the Famine, such an energetic plot formula can hardly be sustained: while the powerful emotions are present, the vigor required for dramatic rescues and, indeed, liberal-humanist conceptions of subjectivity that subtend notions of the melodramatic heroine are challenged by Famine. Peter Brooks's privileging of the heroine's centrality to melodrama, therefore, his thesis that melodrama *is* a drama of "virtue persecuted," in which the heroine's innocence and goodness are finally "made visible and acknowledged," is rendered problematic by the Famine, which alters its conventions and transposes its values into a different ideological register.[12] Why we believe this to be so and how both dramatists and novelists adapted melodrama to represent the Famine are the subjects of what follows.

I.

The Union [between England and Ireland in 1800] was . . . described . . . not as a marriage but as a 'brutal rape', and Ireland was compared to an heiress whose chambermaid and trustees have been bribed, while she herself is dragged, protesting, to the altar.

—CECIL WOODHAM-SMITH, *The Great Hunger*

The relief proposed will be afforded by the distribution of food, clothing, and fuel, but in no case [our emphasis] shall money be given to the parties relieved. . . . Should it be in any case practicable, some return in work . . . will be required from the individuals relieved.

—BRITISH ASSOCIATION FOR THE RELIEF OF
EXTREME DISTRESS IN THE REMOTE PARISHES
OF IRELAND AND SCOTLAND, 1847

Discourse concerning the Famine often made use of and, depending upon its ideological valence, relied upon one of two representations: Ireland as a victim of a British rapine facilitated by her own greedy sons and brothers; or Ireland as the home of indolent recipients of British clemency, which is precisely why relief advertisements in the 1840s advised donors not to offer cash to victims and to exact a "return" of work when "practicable" to do so.[13] And articles in the *Times* echoed the notices' imputations against Irish men in particular. Reporting on an 1847 speech in which Daniel O'Connell urged the Irish Party to "force the government to give food to the Irish people," the *Times* asked "What next?" and then gave its own cynical answer:

> The corn, of course, must be ground; the meal, of course, must be converted into bread or pudding; and then, with something to give it relish, and something else to wash it down, *must be inserted leisurely and abundantly into each individual's mouth,* just when it suits *his* own private arrangements.[14] [emphasis added]

Such is the thrust of reports from Ireland in the *Times* and cartoons in *Punch* throughout the 1840s: the Irish formed a greedy collective mouth with little ambition and plenty of latent animosity. In several illustrations in *Punch,* the imperial largesse exaggerated by the *Times* is realized in the image of a well-fed John Bull extending a helping hand to a distraught neighbor (see figure 5).[15] Irish drama often supplemented these images by foregrounding the generosity of noble British soldiers or of wealthy Anglo-Irish toward their less fortunate countrymen: Anne Chute in Boucicault's *The Colleen Bawn* and Captain Molineaux in *The Shaughraun,* for instance. The representation of starvation and disease on stage, however, was often a different matter.

So, too, given this nightmarish context, was the creation of a "colleen bawn," as the portrayal of Ireland as a rape victim at the *beginning* of Woodham-Smith's *The Great Hunger* implies.[16] What sort of virtue is the rape victim supposed to manifest? What variety of melodrama can be derived from a history in which the violation of virtue occurs before the plot even begins? Recent photographic and journalistic representations of famine in Somalia and the Sudan—and accounts of the Famine in modern fiction and on the twentieth-century stage—might prove useful here. For whether exemplifying the tragedy of nineteenth-century Ireland or contemporary Africa, helpless, passive, and emaciated women (and children) nearly always predominate the historical scene. What sort of narrative can these bodies be made to tell? In short, who is the subject of Famine, and how might she be theorized?

Quite differently, we believe, from both melodramatic heroines and the "hunger artists"—bulemics, suffragettes, and hunger-strikers—whom Maud Ellmann has recently discussed. Although acknowledging that the "practice of the hunger strike in Catholic Ireland has a very different history from the cult of dieting in Puritan America," Ellmann nonetheless examines a purposeful, self-induced hunger: "Self-starvation is above all a performance," she insists, "staged to trick the conscience of its viewers, forcing them to recognize that they are implicated in the spectacle that they behold."[17] Restated in the familiar terms of self-presence underlying her conception of these political "artists," Ellmann for the most part relies upon a liberal-humanist subject marked by her presence or "identity" to self, by her "ego, consciousness, will, intentionality, freedom, [and] humanity," however diminished or inflected by social injustice or the regime of a ruthless code of beauty.[18] What happens to a narrative when most of these attributes are absent? And, more to the topic of this volume, around what sort of heroine might a drama representing famine be structured?

A number of Famine texts confront these issues directly. So, for example, the narrator of Carleton's *The Black Prophet* interrupts the novel's action periodically to remind his reader of the Famine's erosion of agency and consequent undermining of orthodox definitions of virtue:

> Every one acquainted with such awful visitations must know that
> their terrific realities cause [victims] . . . to forget all the decencies
> and restraints of ordinary life, until fear and shame, and the
> becoming respect for order . . . are thrown aside or resolved into
> the great tyrannical instinct of self preservation.[19]

And, although Mave Sullivan's later selflessness refutes this supposition —
she sells her hair to purchase food for the starving Dalton family — Famine
texts typically contain moments in which the concepts of womanly virtue
undergo profound reformulation. Such is the case with Bridie Corcoran in
Gerald Healy's *The Black Stranger*, first performed in 1945, who prostitutes
herself so that Mag, her pregnant sister-in-law, and her unborn child might
eat. While the Corcoran family is quick to condemn Bridie, Mag is equally
quick to defend her: "What's a little thing like that, or the sins of the whole
world, compared to the life of my baby?"[20] Frequently, as in the inaugural
scene of Tom Murphy's *Famine*, a potential heroine dies before the action
begins; in this instance, John Connor's "angelic" daughter starves so that
seed might be retained to plant next year's potato crop. Yet, for her wake
custom demands that mourners be supplied with food and drink, an irony
which causes one mourner to wonder, "What kind of plan is that?"[21]

Such scenes as these in which prostitution is defended or the exacerba-
tion of suffering is linked to Irish patriarchy were rare, however, in Irish
plays on the nineteenth-century stage. More common, especially in working-class theatres, were potent reformulations of Irish masculinity, as melodrama's typical focus on female sexuality and the body were replaced by
more local concerns. C. H. Hazlewood's Irish plays, among others, thus tend
to be structured rather differently from the longstanding Britannia "formula" of the plot following "the fortunes of some domestic heroine . . . and
the thwarting of [the villain's] schemes," culminating in the "ultimate triumph of persecuted beauty and innocence."[22] Of course, spectacular rescues
and lavish pictorial effects, as in Boucicault's plays, contributed to the popularity of Hazlewood's; handbills for *Poul a Dhoil; or, The Fairy Man* (1865),
for instance, promised viewers the "timely help and rescue" of a victim
"hurled" into a lake, and an exciting descent into a lead mine.[23]

One such play, a relatively mysterious one at that, is *The Emerald Heart;
or, a Poor Man's Honour* (1860s), the authorship of which is usually attributed
to Hazlewood, a prolific dramatist credited with the writing of some 120
plays between 1855 and the time of his death in 1875.[24] Hazlewood wrote
nautical dramas like *Ashore and Afloat* (1864), successfully adapted *Lady
Audley's Secret* (1863), and composed a series of Irish plays, most of which

were produced at the Britannia: *Poul a Dhoil, The Ballinasloe Boy; or, The Fortunes of an Irish Peasant* (1867), *Erin-go-Brach; or, The Wren Boys of Kerry* (1870), *Aileen Asthore; or, Irish Fidelity* (1871), and *For Honour's Sake* (1873). While much is known about these dramas—Frederick Wilton, stage manager of the Britannia during these years, refers to the productions of several of these in his *Britannia Diaries*, for instance—*The Emerald Heart* exists, to our knowledge, only in incomplete form, and is not referred to in discussions of Hazlewood's plays. Yet its very uniqueness suggests elements of East End drama that too seldom receive critical attention, the representation of gender as inflected by class concerns, for instance.

The Britannia-Hoxton was located in Shoreditch in northeast London, a district in which small manufacturers engaged in boot- and shoemaking, rugmaking, cabinetmaking, and the production of machine-made clothing.[25] From numerous eyewitness accounts, Clive Barker speculates that the large audiences supporting the Britannia at this time—the theatre could accommodate nearly 4,000 people in the mid-1860s—were composed largely of younger working men or the entire families of married laborers who had moved to the Shoreditch district in huge numbers during the middle decades of the century.[26] Between 1811 and 1871 the population of Shoreditch nearly tripled: from 43,930 residents in 1811 to 127,164 in 1871 (and then a decline in the closing decades of the century).[27] Part of this growth in mid-century was attributable to Irish immigration to the district, heavy enough to necessitate the building of a Roman Catholic Church on Hoxton Square.[28] But what else might account for the huge success of Irish dramas at the Britannia, and how are they related to melodramatic renderings of the Famine?

One answer to the latter question resides in the class and gender affiliations plays like Hazlewood's *For Honour's Sake* and *The Emerald Heart* developed between Irish peasants and working-class *men* in particular. In *For Honour's Sake*, subtitled a "Romantic Irish Drama," the gender dynamics typical of rescue scenes in sensational melodramas are reversed. Heroines are not saved from disaster, as in Boucicault's *The Colleen Bawn*; rather, at the end of act 1, Michael O'Neil, wrongly accused of the murder of the rapacious Lord Rankley, is rescued by the working man Crotty and his female counterpart Katty Moriarty (played by Sara Lane, actress and wife of the theatre manager, Samuel Lane). Similarly, at the end of act 2, Katty and Honour O'Neil throw themselves between soldiers and a trapped Michael and Crotty. It is Honour, in fact, who has killed Rankley, described as the kind of man who "wouldn't take no for an answer," to save her brother, who had come to her defense and was being overpowered by her assailant.[29]

Amid the exciting resolution of these complications, Hazlewood provides Crotty, the exemplary working man, with lines comic Irishmen in other plays seldom get. One speech in particular is a homily about hard work:

> It's industry that's the fine thing, and by reason of that I'm able to do what I'm doing. It's the poor boy I was at first, sir. . . . [But] I was the prudent boy, and wid the first money I scraped together I bought a donkey, then a pony, and then a horse with a car. And the beast and myself are now Crotty and Co., carriers in general (18).

Hazlewood incorporates more than ambition into Crotty, as he reveals later in a conversation with a grateful Michael O'Neil: "Ah, sir, poor as the Irish peasantry are, they're always ready to give first, no matter how they may be inconvenienced by it afterwards. . . ." (34).

Such a representation of the inherently noble working man with under-standable aspirations—opposed by an avaricious and brutal Irish bour-geoisie—centers Hazlewood's *The Emerald Heart*, alternatively titled *The Irishman's Home; or, The Stolen Sheep*. A note preceding the text hints at this intention: "The *faults* of the lower orders of the Irish are sufficiently well known; perhaps their *virtues* have not been proportionately observed or recorded. . . . In this view the drama is written, founded *on facts well remem-bered in Ireland.*"[30] Hazlewood's rhetoric clarifies both his historical and coun-terrepresentational intentions, his commitment to employ the well-known historical event to redact negative stereotypes of the Irish. The cultural work performed by *The Emerald Heart* hence parallels both that performed by Crotty in *For Honour's Sake* and, by way of negative example, the elitism of Brian O'Lancey's opening speech in *Poul a Dhoil*. Pointing to peasants danc-ing at the fair with which the play begins, O'Lancey remarks, "Bah, I've no patience wid them entirely, why don't they join us to raise up ould Ireland from under the heel of the Saxon, so that the Green Isle may flourish as it did of ould" (5). The variety of nationalism he endorses—one, as another character remarks later, tending toward the "dishonour" of Ireland—is strongly inflected by cowardice and class prejudice; as such, it would have been quickly discountenanced by a largely working-class, predominantly male Britannia audience.

The Emerald Heart begins in front of the Shamrock Inn in Wicklow with the Irish bourgeosie as Dennis Doran, in town to conduct business, entrusts some of his money to the Shamrock's unscrupulous innkeeper, Andy Harrigan. Doran does so because he is afraid the desperation he has seen might induce a peasant to rob him: "The typhus fever is raging in all its terrors, and in the country there's a corpse in every third house, and in every one there is what has made the corpse — hunger" (4). One living corpse then wanders onto the scene, Michael Carrol, "pale and emaciated leaning on his spade," who announces his dire predicament: "No work, no food, and no strength" and a family starving at home (4-5). Traveling to the Wicklow marketplace in hopes of being hired by a farmer, Michael is greeted rudely by the Irish steward of an absentee landlord. He then spies a British barrister, Mr. Sebright, in need of a porter. Offering to carry the gentleman's bags, Michael is rebuffed, for Sebright assumes the worst of Michael from his appearance: "Ah, I see, the old story, too much whiskey, I suppose" (6). Moments later, Sebright softens and searches for Michael, vowing to help "the poor fellow," but he is too late; distraught, Michael leaves Wicklow resolved to make certain his family will eat even if he must hang for it. Meanwhile, the real thief is Harrigan, who denies having received money from Doran upon his return to the Shamrock to reclaim it. Sebright comes to the rescue, devising a plan whereby Dennis can regain his money, and the double ideological charge of the play is ignited: British law as represented by Sebright is resourceful and humane in addressing what seem to be insoluble problems; Irishmen like Michael Carrol, honorable though they may be, will break the law to save their families, which is precisely what Michael does. He steals a sheep and in the climactic end of the first act is apprehended by Gerald Harding, the ruthless steward who rebuffed him earlier. Indifferent to the "misery" of the Carrols' situation and threatening to "pull down" the family cabin, Harding insists that "an example must be set" for other peasants, and Hazlewood's stage directions intimate the scene's intent: this last bit should be "worked up to a good climax" (39).

Played at the Britannia, *The Emerald Heart, Poul a Dhoil,* and *For Honour's Sake* could elicit strong sympathy for the Irish without threatening the imperialist project or alleging British complicity in the Famine. At the same time, *The Emerald Heart* transposes the notion of heroism from the register of romance to the more workaday reality of feeding one's family. *The Emerald Heart,* much like Hubert O'Grady's plays to which we shall turn very briefly, does not so much revolve around misrecognitions of the heroine's virtue but around the dilemmas of the working father desperate to save his family. Such plays finally have little to do with *sexuality,* with the lust of the heroine's pursuer or the chastity of his pursued, and much more to do with the presentation of an exemplary masculinity marked by class affiliation and conducive to the creation of a community. That is, although by the 1880s and 1890s annual pantomimes at the Britannia drew their audiences from all classes, the audiences in the 1860s were clearly not so variegated.[31] Going to the theatre then (and in 1898 as well) was a five-hour activity in which working-class men and families were not only entertained but also dined together (seemingly, quite sumptuously, at least from H. G. Hibbert's account).[32] Contrasting sharply with the poverty represented in *The Emerald Heart*, this culinary opulence might suggest yet one more component of the social consolidation facilitated by the ideology of such plays in East End theatres.

Although quite different, a play like Hubert O'Grady's *The Famine* resembles Hazlewood's dramas in its representation of Irish masculinity. Produced at the Queen's Royal Theatre in Dublin and popularly supported at provincial theatres as well,[33] *The Famine*, which takes place during the later "Bad Times" of 1879-1881, begins with a lengthy prologue reminiscent of the early moments of *The Emerald Heart*. Set in the village of Swords, a desperate Vincent O'Connor pleads with Lumley Sackvill, an overseer of the Relief Works, for employment. Before this, we learn that O'Connor had sided with the Land League (cofounded by Charles Stewart Parnell in 1879) and supported its "No-Rent manifesto," which asked tenants to "pay no rents . . . to their landlords until the government relinquishes the existing system of terrorism."[34] One such landlord was Sackvill's father, who was emotionally and financially destroyed by the manifesto, and his son seizes this moment to exact his revenge against O'Connor; after refusing him the work necessary to feed his dying family, Sackvill advises an associate to watch him carefully. Like Michael Carrol in *The Emerald Heart*, O'Connor cannot allow his family to starve, so he steals a loaf of bread. Returning to his cottage with the bread just as the police arrive, O'Connor realizes that while his hungry children might survive the night, his wife has not; the prologue ends with his cries of grief over his wife's body as he is arrested.

The play proper begins fifteen years later with Sackvill preparing to marry the Lady Alice Raymond, a social advancement that will be ruined if Nelly O'Connor, one of Vincent's two surviving children, should reveal her former intimacy with him. Nelly, once a serving girl in Sackvill's house, in a "weak moment and under the promise of marriage" to him "compromised" herself (34). She refuses his bribe to immigrate to America, divulges her past at a party celebrating the impending marriage, and, through various devices, is imprisoned in a "Lunatic Asylum" until rescued by her brother John, who has just returned from military service in India. By the end of the play, Nelly is rescued, Sackvill is shot and his greedy accomplices arrested, brother and sister are reunited. Yet it is neither Nelly's virtue nor a sensational rescue around which O'Grady's plot revolves but the revelations of Vincent and John O'Conner's nobility, bravery, and loyalty to their family. Analogous to the portrayal of a humane British lawyer in *The Emerald*

Heart, in O'Grady's play Sir Richard and Lady Alice Raymond, whom Nelly serves after leaving Sackvill, treat her with great generosity in John's absence. The final curtain of *The Famine,* therefore, falls on much the same depiction of the Irish peasantry that Hazlewood advances: peasants are industrious, courageous, and generous to a fault; and it is rather a corrupt bourgeois class, not British rule, that is largely responsible for the Famine. On stages in Dublin and the provinces, as on East End stages like the Britannia, this counterdiscourse to the denigrating portrayals of the Irish so prevalent in Victorian media seemed to take precedence over more conventional emplotments and concerns, transforming melodrama in the process.

II.

Alas! the famine progresses; here it is in frightful reality to be seen in every face. Idle, improvident, reckless, meanly dependent on the upper classes whom they so abuse, call the bulk of the Irish what we will, & no name is too hard almost for them, here they are starving round us, cold, naked, hungry, well nigh houseless. To rouse them from their natural apathy may be the work of future years. To feed them must be our business this.

　　　　　　　　　　　　—ELIZABETH SMITH, *The Irish Journals,* 1847

I told you before to love this Irish earth as your mother. How? Ask the people. They know. It's in their veins. It's only when we deny our instincts, through greed or cowardice, that we sin. So humble yourself. . . . The future is still holy. Let the people cast stones if they wish. The people are always right in the mass. For the moment they may be wrong or for a generation. A generation is only a moment in history.

　　　　　　　　　　　　—LIAM O'FLAHERTY, *Famine,* 1937

Our study of Famine texts from the mid- to the later nineteenth century has focused primarily on melodramatic representations. As we move into the twentieth century and the focus shifts to fictional Famine texts, one might be tempted to believe that melodrama has been abandoned. Rather than deny a connection between nineteenth-century melodrama and twentieth-century fiction, however, we wish to demonstrate how dependent Famine fictions like O'Flaherty's *Famine* are upon these earlier texts. In particular, the connection is fixed in the feminine figure of the melodramatic heroine, the Colleen Bawn. Even as we sketch the manly Irish peasant as he emerges from within late nineteenth-century melodrama, we are tracing a representation of the male gender wholly at odds with its female counterpart. For while melodrama's treatment of the Great Famine provides dramatists with the opportunity to revise the stage Irishman stereotype, the same opportunity to revise female stereotypes is not, in general, detectable. We considered further how impossible it might be to represent women victimized by Famine on the stage, if, that is, they were to be portrayed according to eyewitness descriptions, as nearly naked, emaciated, and screaming (see figure 6). Pretensions to this degree of realism might also have had the opposite effect that revisions of stereotypes were intended to produce, to demonstrate the dignity and even superiority of the Irish peasant. Our study of Famine texts, therefore, clarifies one important dimension of the representation of women in these works of melodrama. Since the demands of realism cannot be accommodated, female characters are pushed to, or even beyond, the limits of mimesis, significant in their absence from these texts. The reappearance of women in Famine texts of the twentieth century, in Liam O'Flaherty's novel *Famine* in particular, signals for us an important transformation in the telling of the Famine story. The mimetic representation of Famine women can occur within the pages of a fictional text, and even gain the approval of censors, if that representation serves a nationalistic agenda by portraying some aspect of the Irish national identity. The fact that the author of the text, which attracts the admiration of Irish nationalists, may envision his work as a critique of Irish nationalism only reinforces our sense that the Famine over time becomes a highly contingent, fluid event.

Early in Liam O'Flaherty's novel *Famine,* Father Tom Geelan, curate to the parish of Clogher, urges Dr. Hynes, the local physician, to "[l]earn to love this Irish earth, as your real mother. . . . Then it will speak to you and tell you deep, deep things and beautiful things that are stronger than any misfortune."[35] Here Geelan invokes Ireland in a metaphoric, nationalistic representation, as the "real mother" who will, if one attends to her carefully, reveal deep, beautiful "things." But paradoxically this same mother — Ireland in the midst of the Famine — withholds deep, essential things from her children. She is, after all, the biologically determined provider of sustenance that comes from her own body, but she is also the land that cannot feed her children. She has, therefore, failed to fulfill her function and has contributed to the suffering and deaths of millions. Blame for the Great Famine has been, in the intervening years, assigned variously to the British colonial administration, the Catholic Church, God, even the Irish peasants themselves.[36] But the implied inadequacy of a mother to provide for her children is, we would argue, imbedded in this notion of Ireland as mother/land.

Among Famine texts, O'Flaherty's fictional representation of the "Great Distress" marks an important intensification of its many significations. O'Flaherty's text offers a particular invocation of history that throws our analysis of both melodramatic and fictional representations of the Famine into stark relief. *Famine* received positive literary notices at the time of its publication, and even contemporary critics consider it one of his best works.[37] More precisely, the achievement of *Famine,* for Paul Doyle, lies in the way two elements are handled. In contrast to other treatments of the famine theme, O'Flaherty does not rely on a melodramatic portrayal of his main characters, although Chadwick, the land agent, seems like a "stereotyped villain out of melodrama."[38] O'Flaherty's narrative approach—direct and almost documentary in style—avoids overstatement, managing to "convey the degradation and horror [of the Famine] without either sentimentality or a note of falseness. Such a subject as the famine could easily be melodramatically overpainted and lack authenticity."[39]

Clearly, in Doyle's formulation, melodrama represents flawed technique; history, on the other hand, is valorized in the way O'Flaherty "presents a historically accurate picture of the most dismal event in Irish history."[40] We anticipated that somehow the representations of Famine victims would change over time, and by the twentieth century that the depiction of women we noted in nineteenth-century first-hand accounts would eventually be supplanted by different depictions as information about the Famine—economic, agricultural, epidemiological, and historical knowledge—increased. But, at first, quite the opposite seemed to be true. Rather than altering representations, O'Flaherty's fiction appears to perpetuate the dehumanizing representations of the previous century. Kitty Hernon, for example, who is one of the first female characters to exhibit the physical symptoms of famine, begs food from her neighbors, the Kilmartins, who are only marginally better off than she. Mary Kilmartin, the moral center of the Kilmartin family and of the novel as a whole, has not yet suffered the deprivation Kitty has, but she sees the transformative power hunger has over the other woman: "[Kitty's] face was emaciated and over-wrought. She seemed to have contracted . . . [a] nervous twitching of the eyes and lips. The veins stood out clear under her skin" (148-49). The irony of the scene emerges as Kitty begins to eat the food offered her as though she were an animal—"She now fell on her food ravenously"—although she knows that she is not hungry: "Indeed, she had just had supper before leaving her house and she had eaten a far better meal than what the Kilmartins had" (148). Her natural Fig appetite—normally regulated by sensations of hunger and satiation—has been disturbed by the influence of famine.

Later in the novel, Kitty's animal appearance serves as a measure of the effects of famine in Mary Kilmartin's own face, suggesting that starvation has also reduced her to a brutish state. Mary's transformation is, however, more significant, since she fulfills an important symbolic function in the text. A member of the Kilmartin family by virtue of her marriage to Martin Kilmartin, she represents—until the onset of the potato blight and famine— an improving, almost bourgeois, influence on the family. Furthermore, her appearance alone, with its "gracious dignity of a queen," suggests a connection between her character and the familiar representation of Ireland in the figures of Kathleen ni Houlihan and the Countess Cathleen (122). Unfortunately, famine puts an end to Mary's improving influence, altering her character as profoundly as it alters her appearance. Although Mary remains beautiful, she behaves more and more like an animal; her eyes are "fierce" and "suspicious," her hands are never still, and she attacks her food "greedily," guarding it from others (337).[41]

Mary Kilmartin has been called the author's "most admiring portrait" of the "survival instinct"; it seems, however, that women pay a high price for their survival.[42] The hard choices women must make, choices never demanded of men, are overdetermined by their gender roles, as mothers must decide how their children will avoid suffering the effects of the Famine. O'Flaherty indicates that emigration to America and Canada, an option many followed, is not without its own risks, as historical records of deaths during the Atlantic passage attest. Kitty Hernon even risks her children's souls when she begs Mr. and Mrs. Coburn, the Protestant minister and his wife, to take them in: "I can't ask you for the love of God to take them, sir, and I knowing it will damn their souls. All the same, take them, put them in a home, even if they are brought up as Protestants" (212). Most desperate, however, is the act of Sally Hernon, who invites Mary in to make the sign of the Cross over her "sleeping" children. As Mary leans over the bed and discovers that the children are dead, Sally describes how she smothered her children after first feeding them boiled dog:

> All they needed was a bit of meat. At first it sickened them. The little one was the first to get sick, but she soon quietened. Then the other two started. I didn't want them to wake the little one, so I made them lie down beside her and I put the cloth over their heads. They soon stopped crying after that. Now they are as quiet as lambs (412-13).

As a mother who has also had difficulty feeding her child, Mary is understandably hysterical, but Sally's explanation offers a glimpse into a particular logic that the Famine inspires: "I had a right to put them out of their suffering . . . and I'll bury them, too, when I have done my share of looking at their faces. God gave them to me. I couldn't let them lie there screeching with the pain and nobody to help them" (414).

Sally's act of murder, however, poses an important dilemma: as her behavior seems to demonstrate, mothers are socially and biologically determined to feed and protect their children. If children suffer because mothers cannot provide for them, these mothers who commit murder are, Sally argues persuasively, protecting their children from additional harm. On the one hand, the Famine has rendered her logic perverse. On the other hand, however, O'Flaherty demonstrates the manner by which Sally's act is normalized, so that a mother's act of murder may appear logical within the dimensions of the Great Famine. A dilemma arises when we attempt to reckon a justification for infanticide against both legal and religious codes of behavior that would have been formulated according to Catholic doctrine.[43] Obviously there is a code at work in O'Flaherty's novel that has the power to supersede both the legal and religious codes we identified: the code of Irish nationalism. While O'Flaherty's animal imagery at first appeared to us as the continuation of nineteenth-century stereotypes, the debased justification of infanticide in the text points toward an important revision of the representation of the Famine in O'Flaherty's text.

We began this section with the image of the motherland, Ireland, who, in the time of Famine, cannot provide for her children. The representation of Ireland as mother at first suggests that O'Flaherty is engaged nonideologically with nationalistic representations like Kathleen ni Houlihan. Less obvious is the author's cunning critique of these representations and his equally subtle revision of stereotypes of Famine women. We would argue that O'Flaherty admits the conventional portrayal of women in order to shed light on the way they function within a nationalist mythology that in effect draws power from its apparent powerlessness. The Famine, we have suggested, is the crucial watermark within Irish nationalism, the nodal point of the trouble, oppression, and suffering of all the Irish through time, endowed with a potency to focus the attention and passion of a nation. But this same potency can justify almost any behavior that appears to serve the nation's ends. Thus the images of starving women and children may be invoked over and over again to highlight the injustices suffered under colonialism and to argue for national independence, while ignoring the effects of deprivation upon the individual. In the case of *Famine*, O'Flaherty finds the appropriation of the suffering of women and children by nationalistic interests itself perverse and immoral. Consequently, in unraveling the logic that Sally Hanlon employs to justify her act, the author can show how diabolical such logic can be. It can, in effect, transform the murder of children into an important implement for a nationalist movement by heightening nationalistic feeling within the Irish community, both at home and abroad.[44]

III.

In *The Field Day Anthology of Irish Writing*, the most exhaustive compendium of Irish texts assembled since the 1920s, general editor Seamus Deane states that the "Irish Famine was the last disaster of its kind in Western Europe, although it was by no means the first in Ireland."[45] Among its numerous long-term effects, Deane suggests, is the conviction of many Irish that the Famine originated in or was exacerbated by England's policy of genocide in its handling of the Irish crisis. As part of a centenary memorial of the Famine, the Irish Folklore Commission sent out a questionnaire, "to discover what memories of and beliefs about it survived"; a "high percentage" of the respondents indicated a "belief in the conspiracy between the Irish landlords and the British government to break the spirit of the Irish people and, if possible, to exterminate them."[46] The popular view represents, however, a stark contrast to the academic. The Famine does not now appear "quite so apocalyptic," Deane contends, because of the revisions of historians, economists, and folklorists, to name only a few, who have studied the event and its aftermath.

Clearly, an important difference of opinion persists. The process of a Famine reassessment has begun, an attempt perhaps to properly fix the value of this moment of Ireland's past for the nation's future generations. But belief in the genocide theory—as well as other Famine facts and fictions—continues, despite the work of revisionists, more research and study, and, it seems, Deane's own assurances to the contrary. This phenomenon—the proliferation of meanings produced in the very act of delimitation—is, we would argue, the substance of the Famine. We have scrutinized only two aspects of the Famine as a signifying event, but these two alone starkly illuminate its contingent nature. In London in the nineteenth century, the Famine is a call for English and Irish working-class men to recognize their solidarity in labor. In Ireland in the early twentieth century, the Famine is a call to Irish Republicans to raze their colonial history and begin building their nation.

Finally, no matter how the Famine is read, gender plays a crucial role in its most powerful representations. In many respects, the gendered body is yet another Famine text, a tablet upon which multifarious desires—imperial, colonial, racist, patriarchal, national—are inscribed. The process of revising Famine stereotypes, therefore, means merely writing over, but never obscuring completely, those marks made earlier by various hands.

" RINT " *v.* POTATOES.—THE IRISH JEREMY DIDDLER.

" You haven't got such a thing as Twelve-pence about you ?—A Farthing a week—a Penny a month—a Shilling a year ? "

FIGURE 6. An illustration for " 'Rent' v. Potatoes.— The Irish Jeremy Diddler." *Punch* 9 (July–December 1845).

Notes
....

1. Thomas Gallagher, *Paddy's Lament: Ireland 1846-1847*, (New York: Harcourt, 1982), xiv.
2. The authors are indebted to Patrick Burke for making a copy of Gerald Healy's play available to them.
3. For a discussion of the history of *Famine Diary: Journey to a New World*, see Jacqueline Kornblum, "Mixing History and Fiction," *Irish Literary Supplement* 11 (spring 1992): 10.
4. See Hayden White, *Metahistory: The Historical Imagination in Nineteenth-Century Europe* (Baltimore: Johns Hopkins University, 1973), esp. 1-42.
5. J. S. Bratton et al, *Acts of Supremacy: The British Empire and the Stage, 1790-1930* (Manchester: Manchester University Press, 1991), 3.
6. Bratton, *Acts of Supremacy*, 18.
7. Richard Allen Cave, "Staging the Irishman," in Bratton, *Acts of Supremacy*, 63.
8. Michel Foucault, "Nietzsche, Genealogy, History," in *Language, Counter-Memory, Practice*, ed. Donald F. Bouchard (Ithaca: Cornell University Press, 1977), 148; Judith Butler, *Gender Trouble: Feminism and the Subversion of Identity* (New York: Routledge, 1990) 130-31.
9. For a discussion of the Queen's Theatre, see Stephen Watt, *Joyce, O'Casey, and the Irish Popular Theatre* (Syracuse: Syracuse University Press, 1991), 48-66. See also, Séamus de Búrca, *The Queen's Royal Theatre, Dublin, 1829-1969* (Dublin: de Búrca, 1983).
10. For texts of O'Grady's *Emigration* and *The Famine*, see *Journal of Irish Literature* 19 (January 1985): 14-49. Further references to O'Grady's plays are included parenthetically in the text.
11. Michael R. Booth, "East End Melodrama," *Theatre Survey* 17 (May 1976): 61.
12. Peter Brooks, *The Melodramatic Imagination: Balzac, Henry James, Melodrama, and the Mode of Excess* (New York: Columbia University Press, 1985), 27.
13. As Terry Eagleton discusses in *Heathcliff and the Great Hunger: Studies in Irish Culture* (London: Verso, 1995), a third representation of Irish children as "starving scarecrows with a few rags on them" appeared often in such periodicals as the *Illustrated London News* (3).
14. *Times* (London), 18 January 1847, p. 4, col. 2 (emphasis added). Several passages in Gerald Keegan's *Famine Diary*, passages that contributed to its aura of authenticity, advert to hostile editorials and news items, particularly those in the *Times*.
15. "Union Is Strength," *Punch* 11 (July-December 1846): 6.
16. Cecil Woodham-Smith, *The Great Hunger* (New York: Harper and Row, 1962), 16.
17. Maud Ellmann, *The Hunger Artists: Starving, Writing, and Imprisonment* (Cambridge: Harvard University Press, 1993), 13-14,
18. Maud Ellmann, "'Eating Well,' or the Calculation of the Subject: An Interview with Jacques Derrida," in *Who Comes After the Subject?*, ed. Eduardo Cadava, Peter Connor, and Jean-Luc Nancy (New York: Routledge, 1991), 109.

19. William Carleton, *The Black Prophet* (1847; reprint, Shannon: Irish University Press, 1972), 222.

20. Gerald Healy, *The Black Stranger* (Dublin: Duffy, 1950), 37.

21. Tom Murphy, *Famine* (London: Routledge, 1968), 14.

22. Jim Davis, "Introduction," in *The Britannia Diaries of Frederick Wilton, 1863-1875*, ed. Jim Davis (London: Society for Theatre Research, 1992), 8.

23. Colin Henry Hazlewood, *Poul a Dhoil; or, The Fairy Man* (London: T.H. Lacy, 1866). Further references to this play are included parenthetically in the text. Hazlewood, of course, knew Boucicault's work well. In his introduction to the *Britannia Diaries*, Jim Davis alludes to Hazlewood's writing of *Eily O'Connor* in 1860, a play that took both its title and much of its action from Boucicault's hit of the same year, *The Colleen Bawn* (Davis, "Introduction," 19).

24. In *East End Entertainment* (London: Arthur Barker, 1954), not always the most reliable source, A. E. Wilson claims that Hazlewood's contract at the Britannia called for him to "furnish a new drama every fortnight or so" (169). See also Barker's "The Audiences of the Britannia Theatre, Hoxton," *Theatre Quarterly* 9, no. 34 (1979): 27-41.

25. For further discussion of the Britannia audience, see Jim Davis and Tracy C. Davis, "The People of the 'People's Theatre': The Social Demography of the Britannia Theatre (Hoxton)," *Theatre Survey* 32 (November 1991): 137-72. The authors wish to express their gratitude to Jim Davis and Tracy C. Davis for their generous counsel.

26. Wilson claims that after being rebuilt in 1858 the Britannia could seat 3,200 people with standing room for "as many as 4,790" (174); Barker places the seating capacity in 1858 at "nearly 4,000" (28).

27. Allan Stuart Jackson, *The Standard Theatre of Victorian England* (Rutherford, NJ: Fairleigh Dickinson University Press, 1993), 23.

28. Davis and Davis, "People's Theatre," 159. In their essay Davis and Davis cite Shoreditch as the "fasting growing parish" in mid-Victorian London (159).

29. C. H. Hazlewood, *For Honour's Sake: An Original Romantic Irish Drama* (London: Samuel French, n.d.), 7. *For Honour's Sake* was first produced at the Britannia Theatre on 13 October 1873. Further references to the play are included parenthetically in the text.

30. All quotations from *The Emerald Heart* come from the manuscript copy located in the Theatre Collection of the New York Public Library, catalogue number 42X601. Further references to the play are included parenthetically in the text.

31. See Bernard Shaw, "The Drama in Hoxton," in Shaw, *The Drama Observed*, vol. 3, *1897-1911*, ed. Bernard Dukore (University Park: Pennsylvania State University Press, 1993), 1032-37.

32. In *Fifty Years of a Londoner's Life* (New York: Dodd, Mead, 1916), Hibbert describes "trays groaning beneath the weight of pies" and a large assortment of breads and cheeses passing through the audience (64).

33. O'Grady, in fact, died in Liverpool on a tour of mostly British industrial towns on 19 December 1899.

34. See Norman Dunbar, *The Irish Land League Crisis* (New Haven: Yale University Press, 1940), 297.
35. Liam O'Flaherty, *Famine* (Boston: David R. Godine, 1982), 123-24. Further references to the novel are included parenthetically in the text.
36. For recent economic analysis of the causes of the Irish Famine, see Joel Mokyr, *Why Ireland Starved: A Quantitative and Analytical History of the Irish Economy, 1800-1850* (London and Boston: Allen and Unwin, 1983), Mary Daly, *The Famine in Ireland* (Dundalk: Dundalgan Press, 1986), and Cormac O Grada, *The Great Irish Famine* (London: Macmillan, 1989). See also the recent reprinting of Austin Bourke's agricultural analysis, *"The Visitation of God?": The Potato and the Great Irish Famine*, ed. Cormac O Grada and Jacqueline Hill (Dublin: Lilliput, 1994).
37. Paul Doyle, *Liam O'Flaherty* (New York: Twayne, 1971), 108, 11 passim.
38. Doyle, *Liam O'Flaherty*, 98.
39. Doyle, *Liam O'Flaherty*, 99.
40. Doyle, *Liam O'Flaherty*, 106.
41. As John Hildebidle observes, "the Famine makes an utter hash of . . . humanizing and shows how pointless civilization is when confronted with the elemental fact of hunger." *Five Irish Writers: The Errand of Keeping Alive* (Cambridge, MA: Harvard University Press, 1989), 22.
42. Hildebidle, *Five Irish Writers*, 21-22.
43. See Terence Brown, *Ireland: A Social and Cultural History 1922-79* (Glasgow: Fontana, 1981), 28-29.
44. It is widely agreed that the memory of the Famine inspired the Fenian uprisings of the 1860s, as well as guaranteed financial support for Irish anticolonial military efforts into the twentieth century.
45. Seamus Deane, ed., *The Field Day Anthology of Irish Writing*, vol. 2 (Derry: Field Day Publications, 1991), 115.
46. Deane, *Field Day*, 120.

A·P·P·E·N·D·I·X*

ꟼHE ꟴNCLE

Poem by

H. G. Bell

as recited by

Sir Henry Irving

With musical accompaniments

composed expressly

by

Sir Julius Benedict

---

*The text and music for "The Uncle" printed here come from the private collection of David Mayer. We wish to express our gratitude for his generosity in making them available to us.

The Accompaniments throughout must be played with the utmost discretion
so as never to interfere with the recitation. J.B.

"THE UNCLE"

The Poem by
H. G. Bell

The Music by
Sir Julius Benedict

Andantino con moto

I had an uncle once — a man, Of three score years and three, —

And when my reason's dawn began, He'd take me on his knee;
And often talk, whole winter nights, Things that seemed strange to me.

He was a man of gloomy mood, And few his converse sought;
But, it was said, in solitude His conscience with him wrought;
And there before his mental eye, Some hideous vision brought.

There was not one in all the house Who did not fear his frown,
Save I, a little careless child, Who gambolled up and down,
And often peeped into his room, And plucked him by the gown.

I was an orphan and alone, — My father was his brother,
And all their lives I knew that they Had fondly loved each other;
And in my uncle's room there hung The picture of my mother.

There was a curtain over it, —   'Twas in a darkened place,

And few or none had ever looked,   Upon my mother's face;

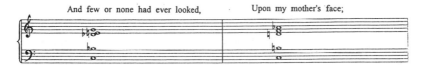

Or   seen   her   pale expressive smile Of melancholy grace.

One night — I do remember well, The wind was howling high,
And through the ancient corridors It sounded drearily; —
I sat and read in that old hall; My uncle sat close by.

I read — but little understood The words upon the book;

For   with   a   sidelong   glance I marked My uncle's fearful look,

And saw how all his quivering   frame In strong convulsions shook.

"Come hither, boy!" my uncle said, — I started at the sound;
'Twas choked and stifled, in his throat, And hardly utterance found; —
"Come hither, boy!" then fearfully He cast his eyes around.

"He was my brother, but his form Was fairer far than mine;
I grudged not that; — he was the prop Of our ancestral line,
And manly beauty was of him A token and a sign.

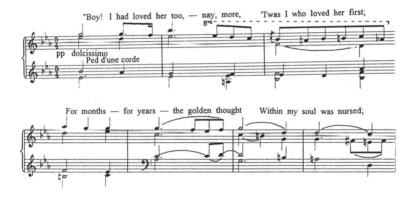

He came — He conquered — they were wed; — My air-blown bubble burst!

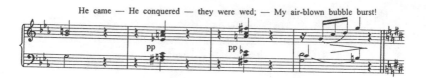

"Then on my mind a shadow fell, And evil hopes grew rife;
The damning thought stuck in my heart, And cut me like a knife,
That she, whom all my days I loved, Should be another's wife!

"I left my home — I left the land — I crossed the raging sea; —
In vain — in vain — where'er I turned, My memory went with me; —
My whole existenece, night and day, In memory seemed to be.

"I came again — I found them here —

Andantino   Thou'rt like thy Father, boy, —

He doted on that pale face there, I've seen them kiss and toy, — I've seen him look

in   her   fond   arms,   Wrapped in   delirious   joy!

"By heaven! it was a fearful thing To see my brother now,
And mark the placid calm that sat For ever on his brow,
That seemed in bitter scorn to say, I am more loved than thou!

"He disappeared — draw nearer, child! — He died — no one knew how;
The murdered body ne'er was found, The tale is hushed up now;
But there was one who rightly guessed The hand that struck the blow.

"It drove her mad — yet not his death, — No — not his death alone;
For she had clung to hope, when all Knew well that there was none; —
No, boy! it was a sight she saw That froze her into stone!

"I am thy uncle, child, — why stare So frightfully aghast? —

"I'll show thee what thy mother saw, — I feel 'twill ease my breast,
And this wild tempest-laden night Suits with the purpose best. —
Come hither — thou hast often sought To open this old chest.

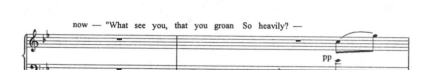

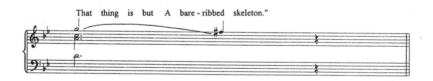

A sudden crash — the lid fell down — Three strides he backwards gave, —

"Oh God! it is my brother's self Returning from the grave! His grasp of

lead is on my throat — Will no one help or save?"

That night they laid him on his bed, In raving madness tossed;

He gnashed his teeth, and with wild oaths Blasphemed the Holy Ghost;

And, ere the light of morning broke, A sinner's soul was lost.

rallentando e mo - ren - do

L·I·S·T   O·F   C·O·N·T·R·I·B·U·T·O·R·S

MICHAEL BOOTH teaches Theatre History at the University of Victoria, British Columbia. He has previously taught at the University of British Columbia, the Royal Military College of Canada, the University of Guelph, and the University of Warwick, serving as Chair of Theatre at Guelph and Warwick, as well as Victoria. He is the author or editor of, among other works, *English Melodrama* (1965), *English Plays of the 19th Century,* five volumes (1969-76), *Victorian Spectacular Theatre* (1981), *Theatre in the Victorian Age* (1991), and *The Lights o' London and Other Victorian Plays* (1995).

MARVIN CARLSON is the Sidney E. Cohn Professor of Theatre and Comparative Literature at the CUNY Graduate Center and editor of *Western European Stages.* He has received the George Jean Nathan Award for Dramatic Criticism and the ATHE Career Achievement Award and has been a Walker Ames Professor at the University of Washington and a Fellow at the Institute for Advanced Study at the University of Indiana. He is the author of many articles and books, most recently *Performance: A Critical Introduction* (Routledge, 1996).

BARBARA T. COOPER is Professor of French at the University of New Hampshire and is a specialist in early nineteenth-century French drama. She is the editor of a forthcoming volume of the *Dictionary of Literary Biography* devoted to *French Dramatists from 1789 to 1914,* co-editor of *Modernity and Revolution in Late Nineteenth-Century France,* and author of more than 30 articles on French drama. She is also on the editorial board of NCFS.

JEFFREY N. COX is Professor of English at Texas A&M University where he is also a member of the Interdisciplinary Group for Historical Literary Study. His work on Romantic drama includes *In The Shadows of Romance: Romantic Tragic Drama in Germany, England, and France* and an edition of *Seven Gothic Dramas, 1789-1823.* He is currently completing a book on poetry and politics in Leigh Hunt's "Cockney School".

JIM DAVIS is currently Head of the School of Theatre and Film Studies at the University of New South Wales in Sydney, Australia. His publications include a study of the nineteenth century actor John Liston, an edition of the plays of H. J. Byron, and an edition of the diaries of the stage manager of the Britannia Theatre. He has also published a number of articles on nineteenth century British theatre and is currently engaged in a study of London theatre audiences in the nineteenth century.

LOTHAR FIETZ holds the Chair of Modern English Literature at the Eberhard-Karls-Universitaet at Tuebingen. His publications on English, German, and American Literature (Fulke Greville, Shakespeare, Tourneur, Sheridan, Pinter, Shaffer, Swift, Dickens, Wilde, Lawrence, Huxley, Durrell, Kafka, Mann, Hesse, Broch, Hemingway, etc.) are mainly concerned with structural and functional aspects of literature. A forthcoming book of which he is the editor offers a comparative analysis of ridiculous and ludicrous objects in the history of German, English, French, Italian, Spanish, and American Literature.

MICHAEL HAYS is currently affiliated with the Center for 21st Century Studies in Cambridge, MA. He has published widely in the areas of nineteenth and twentieth-century European theatre history and theory. He is also an editor of *boundary 2*, an international journal of literature and culture. In a forthcoming book he will explore the cultural and ideological factors at play in the critical reception and evolution of the early modern drama.

HARTMUT ILSEMANN studied philosophy, pedagogies, English, and geography at the universities of Bristol and Hannover (Dr. phil. 1974). He teaches English literature in the Department of English at the University of Hannover and has published a number of articles on various aspects of drama research, particularly in the field of nineteenth-century melodrama. His current research focuses on computerized drama analysis and includes the compilation of comprehensive Shakespeare statistics.

DAVID MAYER, a U.S. citizen, has lived and worked in Britain since 1966. He is now Professor of Drama at the University of Manchester. He researches, writes, and publishes extensively on British and American popular entertainment of the nineteenth and early twentieth centuries. His recent writings explore the interstices between the late-Victorian stage and early motion pictures. His most recent book, *Playing Out the Empire: Ben Hur and Other Toga Plays and Films*, is published by Oxford University Press. He is currently preparing a study on theatrical and filmic responses to the perceived crisis in western immigration, 1890-1910 and another study of theatrical photography.

LÉON METAYER is senior lecturer in the Department of Information and Communication at the University of Bretagne Occidentale, Brest, France. He holds doctorates in sociology and comparative literature and has written several articles on nineteenth-century melodrama and social psychiatry. He is the author of *La Representation des statuts et des rôles de la femme dans le mélodrame en France et en Angleterre de 1830 à 1870.*

ANASTASIA NIKOLOPOULOU teaches in the Department of English at the National Central University in Taiwan. She has contributed articles and reviews on melodrama and nineteenth-century theatre in *Essays in Theatre, Poetica,* and *European Romantic Review.* She is currently working on a book on the English historical melodrama and its audiences.

THOMAS POSTLEWAIT, Professor in the Department of Theatre at Ohio State University, is the author of *Prophet of the New Drama: William Archer and the Ibsen Campaign* (Greenwood) and the forthcoming *Introduction to Theatre Historiography* (Cambridge University Press). He edited Archer's essays on Ibsen and co-edited (with Bruce McConachie) *Interpreting the Theatrical Past.* He serves as editor of a series on theatre history and culture (University of Iowa Press), and is currently President of the American Society for Theatre Research.

KORNELIA TANCHEVA recently defended her doctoral dissertation at Cornell University. She has published on French and English nineteenth-century melodrama, American dramatic and theatrical modernism, Sophie Treadwell, and Marsha Norman. She is currently researching American and British women dramatists.

STEPHEN WATT is an Associate Professor of English at Indiana University. His publications include *American Drama: Colonial to Contemporary* (1995), cowritten with Garry A. Richardson; *Joyce, O'Casey, and the Irish Popular Theatre* (1991); and *When They Weren't Doing Shakespeare* (1989), edited with Judith L. Fisher. His works in progress include *Marketing Modernisms,* edited with Kevin J.H. Dettman; *Arthur Kopit: A Casebook* (1997), a book length study of postmodern theatre; and a study of theatrical representations of Ireland in the nineteenth century.

JULIA WILLIAMS is Assistant Professor of English and Coordinator of Communication at the Rose-Hulman Institute of Technology in Terre Haute, Indiana. She is the author of "'Fiction with the Texture of History': Elizabeth Bowen's *The Last September,*" published in *Modern Fiction Studies,* and "This is (Not) A Canon: Staking Out the Tradition in Recent Anthologies of Irish Writing," which appeared in *The Journal of Women's History.* She is presently at work on a book entitled "The Nation Articulate: The Discourse of Nationalism and the Protestant Ascendancy Novel."

I·N·D·E·X